# YOUNG CONSERVATIVES

# Young Conservatives

J. O. HOLROYD-DOVETON

WITH A FOREWORD BY
BARON FINSBERG OF HAMPSTEAD, MBE

The Pentland Press
Edinburgh – Cambridge – Durham – USA

First published in 1996 by
The Pentland Press Ltd
1 Hutton Close
South Church
Bishop Auckland
Durham

ISBN 1-85821-360-6

Typeset by Carnegie Publishing, 18 Maynard St, Preston
Printed and bound by Antony Rowe Ltd, Chippenham

# Contents

# Foreword

In its heyday the YC movement was the largest voluntary political youth movement in the free world. Its history commenced in 1945 when it took over the Junior Imperial League which had flourished before the war.

The YCs were a growing influence within the Party and had seats and votes right up to the highest levels including its National Executive. It was the training ground for vast numbers of local Councillors as well as MPs, some of whom went on to become Ministers in the Conservative Governments.

It may have had a reputation of being a marriage bureau (the evidence is still with us), but it performed sterling service for the Party. Canvassers, deliverers, constituency officers, candidates for Councils and Parliament, speakers and debators were forthcoming and did much to sustain the Government between 1951 and 1964.

Competition was fierce not from our political rivals but, in the country from the young farmers' organisation and in towns where there was a growing variety of other things to do at night. We had a great advantage over our rivals who were disbanded more than once by their party organisation – a fate which we avoided by hard work and by proving our usefulness.

What was the secret which gave us the success we undoubtedly enjoyed. It was, I think, the ability both to mix politics with fun and to play an important role in the policy machinery and organisation of the party.

I enjoyed my time in the YC as Constituency and Area Chairman as well as being Deputy Chairman of my local Association. This was excellent training for when I finally had the privilege of being National Chairman from 1954–1957, a period covering the 1955 General Election as well as the Suez Crisis. Loyalty was the movement's hallmark because we realised that disunity in public only helped the enemy – the socialists. I only wish that many in the parliamentary party today would remember that.

Finsberg of Hampstead

# Acknowledgements

I wish to acknowledge with thanks assistance with the preparation of this book from Dr Sarah Street and Dr Martin Maw, the Conservative party archivists at the Bodleian Library. Mr Alistair Cook, director of CPC at Conservative Central Office for giving me permission to see various records both at Central Office and the Bodleian Library without which my task would have been more difficult and the Liberal party for allowing me to see their closed records.

Mr Bird and his staff of the Museum of Labour History at Manchester and the archivists of the former Communist Party archives at Hackney and also assistance received from both the Labour and Liberal Party Youth Offices.

Dr B.S. Benedikz of Birmingham University in connection with the papers of Lord Avon graciously permitted by Lady Avon; the librarian of Trinity College Cambridge in respect of Lord Butler's papers.

The Conservative Area offices of Yorkshire, Midlands and Wales and the Constituency offices of Kensington, Cambridge, Torquay, Hornsey and Macclesfield for allowing me to inspect the substantial records they have in their offices and other constituency officers for allowing me to see the closed records at various Record offices and finally Sir Edward Heath and all the former chairmen and officers in giving of their valuable time in assisting me.

I am grateful also to the staff of Exeter Reference Library for invaluable help.

# Introduction

Fifty years of the Young Conservative movement – a rapid rise and decline. Why is it now so small? Why is it no longer the nursery for Conservative MPs as it was for forty years? Is it due to changes in the social climate or is the party in any way responsible? Does the Conservative party need a youth movement? In what way would the post-war history of the Conservative Party vary if, in 1943, the committee constituted to consider the desirability of establishing a youth movement decided against it?

The Youth Conservatives were set up as a result of the Palmer report in 1943, at a time when the Conservative party was contemplating victory, not defeat, in any post-war election.[1] If the Conservative party was to recover from the defeat of 1945 it was urgent for the Young Conservatives to be turned into an effective youth movement and in this Anthony Eden, its first president, Lord Woolton, the Party chairman, and his able assistant Sam Oliver, the Young Conservative organiser, succeeded because of their enthusiasm.

The Party regarded the success of the Young Conservatives as an essential piece of its strategy for recovery and this is shown by the fact that, at each of the conferences, 1946, 1947 and 1948, there were debates relating to the Young Conservatives. The Party was rewarded for its efforts. In the late 1940s the political views of undergraduates showed a marked shift to the right and this trend was followed by four elections in which, on each occasion, the Conservative party improved its position.[2] During virtually the whole of this period the Conservatives were in government. The change in the attitude of the young to the Conservative Party was also remarked upon by Labour MP, Dick Crossman (Ch. 6).[3]

In the fruitful days of the Conservative party of the 1950s that sense of urgency in the development of the Young Conservative movement evaporated, indicated by the cancellation of the Scarborough Week and the failure to hold any national event in 1954 and 1957. Northern Area had no topline speakers for thirteen years but such neglect may be indicative of a wider neglect of the North at the expense of other areas of Great Britain.[4]

In spite of the Party propaganda of the continued success of the Young Conservatives it will be seen that by 1959, YC membership was only 50% of that in 1950. By 1960 the Party could no longer obscure this decline. Optimistically, the Party thought the decline could be reversed by making the movement more political but it was to be proved wrong. As Beatlemania swept the country and young people increasingly owned cars the Young Conservatives failed to compete with the alternative forms of youth entertainment and the

numerical decline of the Young Conservative membership continued until
1975. During the ten years of Edward Heath's leadership he gave every
encouragement possible to the YCs and they continued to embody the one
nation politics that had dominated the Conservative Party since 1945. The
emergence of Margaret Thatcher as leader in 1975 resulted in a far more
dynamic right wing policy thereafter. Against a background of general dissatisfaction with the Callaghan Government the YCs had a remarkable revival.

By 1979 as the Unions had procured the defeat of both a Labour and a
Conservative administration the Prime Minister, Margaret Thatcher made
certain that she was not going to be a third victim and as by then there was
much public support for the view that Parliament, not the Unions, should run
the country and she was able to fulfil the policy of controlling the Unions
which she did with vigour, skill and courage. The move of the Party away
from the policy of one nation politics expounded by Disraeli and followed by
Eden, Macmillan and Heath brought much enthusiasm through sections of the
Party but would it have won the 1970 election? If Harold Wilson had won
another decisive mandate he would indeed have been in a very strong position.

Margaret Thatcher's most severe critics must acknowledge that more people
voted for her over a longer period than any other modern British politician.
There was a tremendous decline in the YCs of the 1980s for which both the
Party and YCs must bear responsibility. Previously, following a general election,
the Conservative party reconsidered its policy towards youth and the YCs. In
1960 it instituted a year long recruiting drive and policy groups (Chapter 8)
and in 1965 the Macleod Report (Chapter 9) and after the 1970 election victory
of Edward Heath, Jimmy Gordon, Youth Development officer was appointed
(Chapter 11).

After the 1979 election the Party considered other matters were more
important than any new initiative concerning its youth movement. In 1981 it
made the fatal mistake of reducing the YC budget by 70% and withdrawing
the regional organisers. Unlike the situation following the 1959 election
(Chapter 8) the party missed a golden opportunity, with the Labour party in
turmoil after its crushing 1983 election defeat, not to have instituted a major
new YC initiative. Another reason for decline in youth politics which has also
affected the membership of the main political parties is the tremendous increase
of interest in one issue politics. I believe this can be undesirable as governments
and local authorities in making decisions have to balance a number of competing
issues and those who participate in youth party politics hopefully learn this.
Although the destruction of beautiful countryside in building the Newbury
by-pass may be deprecated the decision makers have to weigh up the loss of
the countryside against the creation of employment in the area following the
construction of the road. Those who find employement because of improved
communications would favour the road.

Political leaders' control over the country's destiny is limited by external
forces such as the high rise in the price of oil following the 1973 Arab–Israeli

War. This book seeks to answer the question how different the political life of this country would have been since 1945 had not the Young Conservative movement existed.

To what extent is the prosperity of the country the result of government action and to what extent is it influenced by world events? If Churchill had won the 1945 election in what way would a Conservative government have improved on the performance of the Attlee government? In spite of the Labour party's claim during the time of the Attlee government that it was responsible for low unemployment and that unemployment would rise under the Conservatives, in the period 1945 to 1960 unemployment was low. Between 1929 and 1935 it was high whether there was a Labour or Conservative government.

What would have been the position if the Conservative party had won the 1945 election and the Labour party the 1950 election? I believe that the difference for the average person would not have been as great as the politicians allege. Nevertheless, the country would have made a greater recovery during the period between 1945 and 1950 as the country would have been spared the more extreme bureaucratic measures such as a payment of a development charge for those who wished to develop their own land. This hampered house and the commercial development. Another example was a system whereby it was illegal for a company to transport its goods from its own factory except within a stated radius.

A Labour government in the 1950s would have hampered industrial recovery by a lack of enthusiasm for removal of controls such as the government having the sole right to import certain commodities.

As in other aspects of public life politicians need to have luck on their side to succeed but the politicians who succeed are those who are able to benefit from such fortune. If Gaitskell had lived, Harold Wilson would probably never have been Prime Minister.

There are two factors in the British political system differing from those of other countries. Because our system of 'first past the post' a party also needs luck. Not only must the successful party poll sufficient votes it must also receive them in the right area. Twice, in 1951 and 1974, the party obtaining the most votes did not win the election so if the same total number of votes had been cast for each of the parties but in different constituencies, Attlee would have won the 1951 election and Heath the 1974 election. The British system is also subject to the political skill of the Prime Minister in selecting the right day to call a general election, unlike the situation in the USA where they have fixed presidential terms. If James Callaghan had gone to the Country in 1978 he might have won and bearing in mind how ruthlessly the Conservative MPs deal with defeated leaders there might have been no Thatcher government and the strong leadership under Margaret Thatcher, even if her critics say it was misguided, might never have taken place.

My assessment is that the YCs' greatest impact was in the constituencies. Those like Abram & Little and the *Independent* trivialising the YCs because they were seen to be enjoying themselves were wrong.[5] The *Daily Herald*, the Twickenham Young Socialists and the Young Communists rightly regarded the fact that YCs were enjoying themselves as an asset not a liability.[6] This need not detract from political work and although most commentators also trivialise YC political work as insignificant, this is not true, as was acknowledged by the two political commentators on the Young Conservatives whom I found to be wholly accurate, Dr David Butler and Dr Zig Layton Henry and the two studies of the election campaigns of the 1950s in Bristol and Greenwich.[7] It was certainly not true of YC John Major who worked very hard in the 1959 election.[8] Even if a Young Conservative branch had just one political meeting a month they had more political meetings than their senior association.

The YCs gave young people in their late teens and early twenties a chance to assume responsibility by becoming officers. In the words of Gerry Wade, a national vice-chairman of the late '60s and now a successful business man 'it was the best training I ever had'.[9] Many young people were given the opportunity of addressing over 1,000 people at the YC conferences. The majority of people who were the Young Conservatives of the 1950s are still alive and have regularly voted Conservative at least at general elections. The evidence of this is that the Conservatives have generally done better than their rating in the opinion polls.

It is an important function of the voluntary party to win elections. The number of young people sufficiently interested in politics is small. If the Party extracts work from people who are not interested in politics it is a matter of skill not censure and if they politicise the few who would not otherwise be interested in politics it is a matter for congratulation not scorn. Former national officers, Nicholas Scott and Michael Jack both said apart from other benefits it was enjoyable being a Young Conservative.[10] Sydney Chapman and David Hunt each stated they owed their political career to the Young Conservatives.[11] After the fourth term victory of the Conservatives in 1992, an article in the *Guardian* expressed the view that Britain was a very conservative country; the activities of Young Conservatives were a contributing factor.[12]

The most significant influence of the Young Conservatives at national level is seen in the number of Conservative MPs who have learned their politics in the movement. In the 1970 election out of the Conservative intake of 330 Conservative MPs, 108 had been Young Conservatives: prominent YCs Lynda Chalker, David Hunt, John Gummer and John Macgregor are or have recently been government ministers as well as one rank and file member, John Major.

At national level, I believe but for the Young Conservative intake to the House of Commons the Conservative party would have been more right wing. Virtually all the prominent Young Conservatives have been on the moderate wing of the party. Peter Walker, the last 'wet' to survive the Thatcher years, although an Englishman, became the best Secretary of State for Wales and careful intervention in the economy in accordance with the principles of the Industrial Charter as contemplated by Rab Butler did much to make Wales the spearhead rather than the lame duck of the British economy.

David Hunt suffered humiliation at his adoption meeting at Plymouth Drake as he was too left wing for some of the constituents (Chapter 11).

Have the YCs in any way influenced policy? I think their greatest influence was between 1968 and 1975 by support given to the pro European lobby at the critical party conferences of the late 1960s and early 1970s and their support for direct elections to the European Parliament. Another outstanding area was race relations because of their liberal views on immigration advocated by David Hunt and Robert Hughes, the latter's speech received boos at the party conference.

The YCs also claim to have defeated the Night Assembly Bill but this was disputed by Jerry Wiggin, the proposer of the Bill.[13] It does not seem that Margaret Thatcher was influenced by the YCs' view because she allowed the Youth & Community Bill enthusiastically supported by YCs to fall without any apparent regrets.

YCs' moderate political outlook had an influence on those YCs who were successful in being elected as MPs: Robin Squire was opposed to the Poll Tax on the grounds that it was basically unfair and criticised both in a speech in the Commons and in private conversations with Mrs Thatcher[14] as did the interest in the deprived areas of the Third World shown by Lynda Chalker as Minister of Overseas Development.

The YCs have produced a number of policy statements such as the key statements during Michael Jack's chairmanship but none was more radical or received as much publicity as the Greater London Young Conservative report in 1969 'Set the Party Free'. Although few of the reforms have been implemented, Eric Chalker helped to establish the Charter Movement to campaign for greater democracy in the Conservative party.

Another influence of the YCs was at the Party conferences. Every constituency which had a YC group was entitled to send seven representatives. As two were required to be Young Conservatives, the impact of the young was considerable.

Outstanding YC performances were Frances Vale's eloquence in persuading the Conference to reject a report prepared by the Party on the Women's Charter (Chapter 29) and David Hunt's amendment which was instrumental in the decisive rejection of Enoch Powell's motion criticising the Government for allowing the Ugandan Asians into the country (Chaper 29). However, I believe that the greatest achievement of any single YC was that of Chris Gent. After Lord Thorneycroft, chairman of the Party, had rashly announced before a NU meeting that the Party would not become a corporate member of the Joint Action against Racialism Chris Gent persuaded the National Union executive to join.[15]

During the time Edward Heath was leader of the Conservatives and Prime Minister, YCs were often selected to propose a motion, such as Hugh Holland's in 1969 on Northern Ireland, and John Watson's on population control in 1971 and Peter Price's in 1971 on the European Community.

Another achievement of the NAC was the variety of the fact-finding missions, to places such as, Northern Ireland in 1969 and 1970 and the important people they were able to see. The same applied to their historic visit to China in 1976 arranged by Edward Heath.

It was Eric Chalker who first publicly drew attention to the fact that the YCs did not have as much power and influence as they were told they had by their seniors. Eric Chalker said 'By 1965 I started to realise the way the Young Conservatives were treated and we started actively to try to influence the Party with the power we were led to believe we had. We were concerned at our lack of influence at the Party conferences.'[16] From conversations with Zig Layton Henry and his article in *Contemporary History*, Eric Chalker stated that the attitude of party leaders to the YCs was patronising and the publicity given to its influence on the Party was exaggerated.[17] Surprisingly, the Young Conservatives' opponents envied the supposed greater influence wielded by the YCs. Nicholas Scott, chairman 1964/1967 thought the Young Conservatives had little influence in the party and rightly so.[18] His predecessor in office, Terence Wray stated that in the one matter in which they did have influence it was they had representatives on all committees of the party. Terence Wray claims YCs did have power and used it to obtain the election of candidates of their choice although no other chairman claims the YCs used such power. Another instance of joint action by YCs of considerable significance was the joint decision of YCs on the Enfield selection committee to support the parliamentary candidature of Iain Macleod which enabled him to enter Parliament at the 1950 election.[19]

During the time of Edward Heath's leadership he gave to the officers of the Young Conservatives access to ministers that few political youth movements enjoyed. All the parties at some time or other experienced rebellion from their youth wing which they had not anticipated. On occasions the Young Conservatives have been in conflict with the senior movement.

The Party has been so much more successful controlling its youth wing when it desired to do, as it was aptly described in *The Times*, by a combination of tolerance, flattery and absorption, than its opponents.[20] If the test of who is fit to govern is determined how the party controls its youth movement there is no doubt the Conservative party should win. The leadership allowed the Young Conservatives considerable scope to develop as they wished, nevertheless the Party kept the power vested in it by control of the Young Conservative budget. The Young Conservatives never had any control over their own budget unlike the Federation of Conservative Students who received a grant from Central Office. Surprisingly, the plans for the National Committee to find an alternative source of finance was opposed by them. (Chapter 13) On other occasions apparently the NAC accepted Central Office control.

However, if the organising secretary of the YCs, an employee of Central Office supported the NAC, then of course it was easier to resist the pressure.

When Central Office tried to prevent the circulation of a daily newspaper at the Party Conference the organising secretary[21] vigorously opposed such interference. On two occasions during the 1980s the NAC were informed of matters they were not competent to debate. First, Tim Mitchell's appointment as organising secretary[22] and, more oddly, membership figures supplied by Central Office.[23] It seems that in the late 1980s as the factions fought for control of the YCs Central Office felt they had increased justification for interfering with YCs, for example preventing a debate at the 1988 YC Conference on the merits of charging for dental and eye examinations.

Richard Cuming, Western Area chairman stated that during the later part of the 1980s unless one supported either the moderate or the Thatcherite faction it was impossible to attain high office.[24] During the mid-1980s there is evidence that the struggle between the factions increased attendance at the YC conferences. But it was at high cost to the YCs as the media played havoc with these divisions. The saddest aspect is that YCs of that generation regarded these divisions as normal and this amused the media who conveniently forgot the unity of the YCs that had existed from 1945 to 1979.

I disagree with the suggestion that I am looking at pre-1979 YCs with rose coloured spectacles. I base my judgement not only on my own observations as a YC, but also on a study of the many YC records I have researched and Richard Kelly supports my views (Chapter 28). Unity was its strength as it was also with the Parliamentary Conservative Party compared with its Labour opponents, a message which the present Conservative Parliamentary Party and YCs would do well to remember.

# Chapter 1

# Politics for the under-15s

As far as schoolchildren were concerned it was the Left which first realised the potential of indoctrinating the young.

Socialist Sunday Schools appear to have first been opened by Mary Gray in Battersea, London in 1892 and the first National Council of British Socialists' Sunday Schools was formed in 1908. The aim was to help the schools in every possible way in their work to teach socialism. Teaching was to be strictly humanitarian, non-theological in character, paying exclusive attention to the present life and one's duty to lead a moral life. Therefore, the only similarity with traditional Sunday schools was that they took place on Sunday. The declaration that was asked of children was noble enough: 'we desire to be just and loving to all our fellow men and women, to work together as brothers and sisters, to be kind to every living creature and so help to form a new society with justice as its foundation and love as its law'.[1] The Socialist precepts were as follows:

1. Love your schoolfellows who will be your fellow workmen in life.

2. Love learning which is the food of the mind. Be as grateful to your teachers as to your parents.

3. Make every day holy by good and useful deeds and kindly actions.

4. Honour the good, be courteous to all, bow down to none.

5. Do not hate or speak evil of anybody. Do not be revengeful but stand up for your rights and resist oppression.

6. Do not be cowardly, be a friend to the weak and love justice.

7. Remember that all good things of the earth are produced by labour. Whoever enjoys them without working for them is stealing the bread of the workers.

8. Observe and think in order to discover the truth. Do not believe what is contrary to reason and never deceive yourself or others.

9. Do not think that those who love their own country must hate and despise other nations or wish for war which is a remnant of barbarism.

10. Work for the day when all men and women will be free citizens of one fatherland and live together as brothers and sisters in peace and righteousness.[2]

There is little to which a Christian could object.

A pamphlet on the ownership of land would not find favour with parties of the right. It stated that ownership of land had evolved as follows: In hunting times land belonged to no one; in tribal times the pastures may have belonged to the tribes. In feudal times the king was supposed to hold the land in God's name. In recent times the king gave grants of land to his favourites and the latter added to their estates by enclosing a part of the commons. In modern times in most parts the land belongs to the descendants of the above. The pamphlet then criticised the modern landlord for living on rents paid by the labour of others and then stated that the socialists' principle of common ownership of land was just.[3]

Noble as such teaching might sound this century has shown in the USSR that such ideals have not helped the workers in practice who had remained considerably poorer than their colleagues under capitalism as, for example, in East and West Germany before reunification.

There has been a tremendous desire until at least the present decade for British people to own their own homes. As far as land owned for commercial purposes is concerned, a company which has no interest in land will find it far more difficult to raise money for its development and expansion. However grandiose the collective farms might have been in the USSR it is not generally known that Russia, despite all the ills of the Tsars, became in 1915, ahead of the USA, the biggest exporter of grain in the world. However, after years of collective farms, the USSR has experienced chronic food shortages in contrast to the situation in post-war Western Europe. The surplus of food produced has become an embarrassment as under the Common Agricultural Policy the surplus food is bought up in order to maintain the farmers' price. Such a system where half the world is starving and the other half is producing food and then destroying it must at best be crazy, and at worst immoral.

The Communists in the UK had their own organisation for children called the Pioneers. The Pioneers appeared, according to the knowledgeable thesis of Mike Waite, some time in the 1920s and adopted the name 'pioneers' to bring it in line with its counterpart in the USSR.

The programme of activities for the early Pioneers may be neatly summarised: they wished to have free meals in schools for working class children, provision of boots and clothing, abolition of caning and the use of the strap, the establishment of an anti-Empire Day and an annual International Children's week. It published a monthly paper and campaigned against poor social conditions and caning. On the lighter side it had a programme of rambles, picnics, singing, games and children's camps. Letters to young comrades abroad was another activity.

Mary Docherty, a young Communist League member in Fife in the 1920s was in charge of the local children's section and recorded some recollections of the children's meetings and activities. At the beginning of each meeting the children were asked about the use of the strap. How many at one time to each child and parents were requested to complain.

The children's parents were mainly members of the Communist or Labour parties or the ILP. Although children approaching the Pioneers directly or through school friends would certainly not have been turned away there is little evidence that there was any aggressive recruiting campaign attempting to capture the children for the Communist cause.[4] The Pioneers apparently continued in existence until the 1930s. However, one of the main differences between them and the Socialist Sunday Schools was that the Communist party attacked the methods of the other youth organisations in particular the Boys' Brigade and the Scout movement, which most people regarded as highly respectable. The Communist party considered the Boys' Brigade had an un-desirable political dimension, besides being a form of recreation of the upper working class/lower middle class.

They produced a pamphlet stating that the Scout movement was a mere tool of the Conservative party under the mask of being non-political. It was a cunning hypocritical pose which deceived many workers, even members of the Labour movement. Thinking only of the physical welfare of their boys and girls they forgot that once inside their children would fall victim to poisonous Tory propaganda.

Scouts were banned in Communist USSR. The Chief Scout was attacked over his attitude to the General Strike of 1926. He apparently said that it was a silly thing with the workers cutting their own throats. The Chief Scout added that the Scouts participated in a volunteer service organised by the government, as the Scouts supported anyone in distress. Heated correspondence passed between the Young Communist League and Robert Baden-Powell. A letter written by William Rust of the Young Communist League said:

> I received your evasive letter of the 16th instant and note that you do not answer any of the charges made in my letter. It appears to me that further correspondence will be useless and the controversy can only be settled by means of a public debate. I therefore repeat my offer to publicly debate the question of whether the Scout movement should be supported by young workers. If you are unable to accept I should be pleased to debate with any other representative Scout leader, preferably the London Scout Commissioner.
>
> Yours truly
> (signed) WILLIAM RUST

Robert Baden-Powell replied saying:

> In reply to your letter of the 18th instant, since you are not to help the working class boys but merely to promote the political views of Moscow I do not think further correspondence is called for. My own aim being

as I have told you before, is not to argue but to try and help the poorer boy to get his fair chance in life.

(*signed*) ROBERT BADEN-POWELL

A pamphlet produced by the Young Communists stresses the anti-working class character of the Scout movement and the Young Communist League calls on young workers to firmly boycott the Scout and Guide movements. 'We appeal to young workers in the Scouts to leave it right now and come into the ranks of the Young Communist League where a hearty welcome awaits.'[5]

There is evidence of the Scouts doing philanthropic work in the 1930s. There was a special branch which was formed to give help and develop Scouting among boys with physical and mental handicaps. Great strides were made at this time under the enthusiastic leadership of Montagu Burrows, the first headquarters commissioner and his successor Dr C. W. Durward.[6]

To counter the left wing organisations which were established for school children the Conservative party formed the Young Britons in 1925.

The object of the Young Britons was stated in 1933 to be to teach good citizenship, love of Empire and the realisation of simple Conservative principles. By 1952 the objects had been changed: love of Country had been changed to patriotism; and good citizenship and the realisation of simple Conservative principles had been replaced by the basic principles of the Conservative way of life and to instil into Young Britons the need to set a good example on matters of discipline and behaviour.

Although the figure of half a million members had been mentioned, bearing in mind the exaggeration of the numbers in the membership of the Young Conservatives, it is highly unlikely that such a figure was attained.

In the final report of the Young Britons it was stated that party politics were not taught, although literature of the time indicated it was as political as its socialist counterpart.[7]

Rowena Harrison remembers how, as a Young Briton, she used to assist in addressing envelopes and conveying the poll cards between polling stations and committee rooms although, like many other Conservative organisations in connection with electioneering it carried this out rather more subtly and competently than its opponents.[8] However, the minutes of Ealing Conservatives Grosvenor Ward would indicate the branch was non political.[9]

In a pamphlet the aims of the Young Britons were stated to be:

The Conservatives are rather like a sensible person with good car which for some reason is not running well, suppose instead of opening up the bonnet and looking inside to find out what is wrong you seized a huge hammer and started smashing the car into scrap iron. Let's scrap it and try another one. I am sure you would carefully examine how to put right the defect in the car which you know from experience is a very good one, instead of scrapping it in favour of another one which no one knows anything about.

The Conservatives know there are times when our laws do not seem to be working quite well but unlike the Socialists they say there must be a great deal of good in the way we are governed for our ways have made us a very great country.

We now all wish to see the world as a better and happier place to live in but it is useless to make plans for a better and happier country and have ideals unless we have common sense as well and make our plans in a way which it is possible to carry out. Experience teaches us what is possible and what is not possible. Conservatives will not promise what is impossible to perform.

We all know the good old nursery rhyme: 'If wishes were horses then beggers would ride'. The trouble with the Socialists is that they so often make promises which they cannot fulfil. They will not be guided by experience like the Conservatives and so they often bring bitter disappointment and hardship to many people who have put their trust in them.[10]

In 1948 it was decided to revive the Young Britons but following the Second World War it never regained the success it achieved before the War. Young Britons had thrived among the more patriotic working class but social habits were changing. More and more families acquired a motor car and were becoming more mobile. Taking the family to the sea and countryside at the weekends became popular. Many schools arranged ambitious out of school activities for school children.

Similarly the Socialist Sunday Schools after the Second World War failed to regain the popularity of pre-war years.

Few Conservative agents were prepared to give the Young Britons much support and by 1964 there were only twenty-four Young Britons organisations remaining. The Socialist Sunday Schools had similarly declined and there were but twelve left.

The working party set up by the Conservatives in 1964 decided the Socialist Sunday Schools no longer constituted any threat. Accordingly, it was resolved to close down the Young Britons organisation.[11]

Henceforth none of the political parties had youth organisations for children under the age of 16. In the sense that the Young Britons had seen off the Socialist Sunday Schools they had served their purpose. From this time the Party's efforts were devoted to capturing the support of young people over 16 and the votes of those over 18. Although some, particularly those former members of Socialist Sunday Schools and Young Britons, may regret the passing of these organisations I do not believe they should do so as 16 is an early enough age to introduce children to party politics.

*Chapter 2*

# Junior Imperial League and pre-war Labour and Liberal Youth movements

The Junior Imperial League (the Imps) was formed in July 1906. The need for the formation of a youth wing was as a result of a crushing defeat by the Liberals in the general election of that year. Its objects were stated to be to create a practical interest in political work among the youth of this country by organising a junior association in every parliamentary division and throughout the Empire to co-operate with existing Conservative and Unionist associations in advancing the cause of Imperial unity, upholding constitutional principles and actively furthering the Conservative and Unionist cause.

Membership was confined to boys and young men between the ages of 14 and 25. In its first year the League established six branches and by 1914 the number had risen to 300 with a membership approaching 100,000. Among its objectives were 'To promote respect for law and order, without which freedom is impossible' and 'to promote the true comradeship of all classes by more effective co-operation between employers and employed in the interests of both, and of the nation as a whole'. At the outbreak of war in 1914 the League almost disappeared and by 1918 only six active branches remained.

In 1918 after the First World War progress in the League was assisted by the Representation of the People Act 1918 conferring the franchise on women and thereafter the League was open to both sexes. By 1930 it was claimed there were more than 1,900 branches with over 150,000 members.

The League formed an important part of the Conservative party organisation, not only by providing recruits for the senior association but, also, a large number of Constituency agents and organisers. Young men and women were given an opportunity to develop their interest in politics, and possibly progress through to local government or as Members of Parliament, and provide practical help to the Conservative cause. Apart from the political side, sporting activities were encouraged and a national sports gathering was held at Crystal Palace in 1930. In the field of social service, substantial financial aid was given to many charitable institutions. Well known personalities who held office in the JIL were Lord Burghley, the famous athlete, and the future Prime Minister, Sir Alec Douglas Home.[1]

The Junior Imps ceased its activities at the outbreak of the Second World War but the success of the movement was obviously an influence when the decision was taken to set up the Young Conservative & Unionist Organisation in 1945. However, it was decided it would be more advantageous if the new youth movement were an integral part of the constituency organisation rather than a separate body.

Similar to the position after the war the political usefulness of the pre-war Labour League of Youth compared with the Junior Imperial League was very much impaired because the relationship between the senior and junior party was far from comfortable. Until 1918 one could not be a individual member of the Labour party it was a purely Trade Union organisation. However, individual members could join the Independent Labour party which, until 1932, was affiliated to the Labour party. The Labour party had seen the importance of attracting the young by fixing their lowest age for full membership at 16.

The Conservative party having successfully formed the Junior Imperial League the Labour party established a youth movement in 1924 whose aim was mainly educational and recreational.[2] The Conservative and Liberal parties accepted that their youth wings would wish, and in most cases were encouraged, to discuss policy although to what extent the parties listened to their advice varied according to the leader at the time. Many in the Labour hierarchy believed that young people should be instructed in Labour policy, undertake election work and also enjoy themselves. Among the League's stated aims was to provide non political activities such as sports, music and dramatics but that they should leave the question of policy to those older and wiser. This caused a strong reaction from the young people.

In 1925 the name the Labour Party League of Youth was adopted and it was agreed that people between the ages of 21 and 25 might remain members providing they also became members of the Labour party.[3] In 1926 the ILP, concerned that its own membership would suffer if large numbers of young people were recruited into the League, established its own Guild of Youth which achieved considerable initial success as after the first year of the ILP's Guild of Youth there were 182 branches and 9,000 members.[4] In 1929 an annual conference of the Labour Party League of Youth took place and a National Advisory Committee, consisting of members of the League was established.[5] It was agreed in 1934 that the League should be represented at the annual conference of the Labour Party and its chairman should be a member of the National Executive.[6] These changes did not satisfy the League of Youth which asked that its advisory committee be given executive power. (Incidentally, in spite of its influence, the National Advisory Committee of the Young Conservatives has never requested executive power.) The League also campaigned for the annual conference to be empowered to debate and criticise party policy. Many intellectuals of the 1930s were left-wing, and were horrified by the rising tide of national socialism.

Branches tended to be small supporting a policy that there should be a united front between the Labour party and the Communist party (a policy advocated by Sir Stafford Cripps and for which he would be later expelled by the Labour Party). The progress of the League of Youth had been going well and there were 526 branches in 1935. Of these 110 had been formed in the previous year.[7] A Socialist Youth Day was arranged with demonstrations all over the country and the League began to publish its own magazine *New Nation* and a successful youth conference was held in London. The Labour party's executive stated it was not established to make policy but to recruit and educate young people for the Party.

At the Brighton Conference of 1936 a resolution was moved referring back the decision to suspend the conference and prevent the youth movement from passing policy resolutions although they were free to discuss policy.[8] At the Edinburgh Conference in 1937 the report presented by the Executive strongly attacked the conduct of the Labour League of Youth. After advocating the right to discuss and adopt resolutions dealing with party policy the Executive proposed taking the drastic step of disbanding the National Advisory Committee of the League suspending publication of its journal *New Nation* and not convening the League's annual conference in 1937.

The Executive asked the Party Conference to give it full authority to re-organise the League as a youth section of the Party based upon loyalty to the Party and its conference decisions to restrict membership to those under 21 instead of 25 and to ensure that the new organisation would not meddle with policy and would confine itself to recreational, educational and election work. There was to be an annual conference and discussions on policy were permitted provided there would be no resolution on Party policy.

Although at the Conference various delegates challenged this decision the decision of the Executive was overwhelmingly endorsed. In 1938 there was an attempted revival of the National Advisory Committee of the League which was allowed to function and a League Conference was allowed.

In March 1939 the NEC swooped again cancelling the appointment of both national and local advisory committees of the League and refusing the convening of its annual conference. The Executive's action was challenged at the 1939 Southport Conference but attempts to secure the reference back were lost.[9] Although the pre-war League of Youth has often been criticised as being revolutionary, this is too simplistic as a letter from a former chairman of the Hornsey branch to Morgan Phillips the chairman of the Labour party in 1960 on the occasion of the formation of the Young Socialists recalls 'the League of Youth worked very hard and conscientiously in the 1931 General Election. They had many forms of recreation such as hiking and social events such as dancing and debates.'[10]

Zig Layton Henry has written an interesting article on both the pre-war and post-war Labour party youth movements.[11]

Meanwhile two Young Liberal organisations were formed in 1903, one in London and one in the Midlands and, like the other two parties' youth organisations, were established in times of adversity.

The Liberal party had not been in government since 1895. Almost immediately in 1905 under Asquith's leadership a landslide Liberal victory was achieved and they won 397 seats. His government was re-elected in 1910 but nobody envisaged this would be the final Liberal electoral victory. In 1923 they won 159 seats and then, after a split in the Party during the 1931 slump, those Liberals who had not supported the national (coalition) government were limited to 20 in 1935.

In 1908 the fifty-six branches of the Midland and London organisations amalgamated. At a lunch to mark the occasion the guest of honour was the Liberal MP, Winston Churchill who criticised the Conservative government for saying that India, not unemployment, was the biggest problem facing Britain. The Young Liberals, soon after their formation, adopted a radical stance by advocating votes for women and the abolition of the hereditary principle in the House of Lords.[12] They admitted women as members before women received the vote. The Junior Imperial league did not have any women members until women received the vote after the First World War. Although the annual reports during the inter war years did not admit there was a decline, in 1911 the membership was stated to be 125,000 and in 1932 30,000.[13]

One activity of the Young Liberals started in the 1930s was flying squads in order to supply assistance. This operated in London and members were asked either to undertake canvassing or delivering literature or they were used as speakers or demonstrators.[14] However, all three youth movements ceased operation upon the outbreak of war in 1939.

## Chapter 3

# Post-war Labour and Liberal Youth Movements

The Labour Party has had four different forms of Youth movement. First there was the Labour League of Youth which survived until 1955. The Party then decided that instead of having a separate organisation it would have a youth section and in 1959, it was decided to form the Young Socialists. The repeated allegations of the Young Conservatives that the Young Socialists were being penetrated by Trotskyists is surprisingly supported by the Labour party's own records. The fact that this was not a transient problem is indicated by reference to it in the 1950 Labour party report mentioned below and ten years later in *New Advance* an editorial appeared 'Is there a Trotskyist at the bottom of your garden?'

> The term Trostskyist is a term increasingly well-known to Young Socialists who are told that they are trying to break up their organisation. How true is this and what exactly is a Trotskyist's views? They have nothing but contempt for the Soviet Union which they state practises State Capitalism. They are not fussy about the methods to bring about revolution. Interference in industrial disputes is one of their favourite weapons.

It therefore seems that the editor of *New Advance* in 1960 was better apprised of the problems of the Trade Unions of the 1960s, 1970s and 1980s and the need to address them. The article continues:

> They have turned their attention to the Young Socialist movement because they are dismayed at the existence of such a large brilliant organ of democratic socialism which they wish to smash at an early stage and take away many of its members. Beware of Young Socialists frequently turning up at your branch, uninvited, distributing literature and inviting your members to attend meetings preaching democratic socialism. Believe in nothing of the sort! They worm their way into constituency and ward parties and attempt with their own superficial attractive doctrine to take people away into their own organisation. Even if they achieve their dream of world dictatorship their government would quickly fall apart as Trotskyists can never agree among themselves for very long . . .'[1]

In 1946 the Labour League of Youth was re-established but in view of its pre-war experience the NEC was reluctant to allow it a national committee (which it gained in 1948) or to hold a national conference which the NEC finally permitted in 1951. Until that time it was to enjoy reasonable success with a membership of 30,000. However the Labour party and its youth movement appeared to have no illusions that the movement lagged a long way behind the success of the Young Conservatives. In the Wembley Labour Youth magazine of 1950 it stated 'The increasing membership of the Young Conservatives is proof alone that there is something seriously lacking in the Labour League of Youth.'[2]

A memorandum in the name of Maureen Windsor of North Kensington Constituency Labour Party and Fred Jarvis of Wallasey, Peter Morris of Barnsley and W. Bonney Rust of North Paddington CLP formerly President of the National Union of Students, together prepared a report in 1950. This said 'We feel that the Labour Party is failing to attract the younger generation at a time when it is of critical importance to recruit new ideas and enthusiastic workers.' It acknowledges that the success of the League had been moderate compared with that of the Young Conservatives. 'There is no doubt that the Young Conservatives had greatly increased its strength during the last year and we cannot allow the social nature of some of their activities to blind our eyes to the fact that a membership of 200,000 represents a considerable political force at election time.'

It blamed the NEC for trying to stifle the League.

The NEC's attitude to the League was described as if it 'was forcing it to grow as if it was a stick of rhubarb'. The understanding was that in view of the Labour party's experience with the League of Youth between the wars the NEC's attitude was that if the members of the League wished to contribute towards Party policy they could do so through the constituency association. The report states that by setting up the League as a separate organisation the Party itself acknowledged that it was necessary to cater for the particular interests and needs of Party members aged between 16 and 25 and, therefore, it complained of the failure of the NEC to agree to allow them to have a national platform by agreeing to the League holding an annual conference at which obviously the policy of the Labour party could be discussed.

It proposed there should be a national committee with advisory powers but its resolutions, as with the Young Conservatives, would be purely advisory and any resolution would go forward as a recommendation for the National Executive of the Labour party or the Party Conference. The League should also have the power to elect its own National Executive Committee and a representative of the NEC should sit on this League of Youth Executive committee and member of the League's National Committee should sit on the National Executive Committee.

Views were expressed that young people at the Labour League of Youth Conference were likely to pass resolutions of a more radical nature than the Party could accept. 'We recognise this as a probability but would suggest that the constitutional framework would provide a platform for ideas, a channel for grievances, and would increase the responsibility of young members.' It is right that young people are less conservative than their seniors and are usually attracted towards the left or the right. (For many years the Young Conservatives were further to the left of the mainstream party and then moved to the right.) The report then proceeded to acknowledge that the majority of young people leaving school are both unpolitical and have a bias towards the existing order. It more correctly anticipated the tremendous swing of young people to the right whereby during four general elections the Conservative vote increased by saying, 'it is becoming the cult for youth to be Conservative.' Even more depressing for Labour was the remark that if you were radical it was no longer exciting and progressive to be a member of the Labour party. Many intelligent Young Socialist joined the Communist party because it promised radical action and the stimulus of opposition.

The impetus given by the 1945 election had slowed down as a result of the attainment of many of the early aims: nationalisation, the health service and social security scheme, and it was hard to become excited about improved administration. It was a fact that the radical reforms of the 1945 Labour government were carried out in the first two or three years and for the rest of the administration a more pragmatic approach was taken. The youthful Harold Wilson's act of scrapping controls received less enthusiasm than the passing of the nationalisation legislation.

The financial restraints imposed by Stafford Cripps who had the unenviable task of working out how Labour's expensive programme could be financed and stimulus provided for the export trade were matters which received little enthusiasm from young and old Labour party members. Also, the compilers were ahead of many party workers who were still embedded in the class struggle of previous eras. They failed to realise that the 1950s would be electrifying times when there would be a tremendous leap in prosperity for the average working man. Facilities for foreign travel and modern labour saving equipment, together with the opportunity to buy one's own home, previously attainable only by the more affluent, were now to become universal. It acknowledged that many working class young people were becoming more ambitious by stressing the importance of increasing its appeal to young people with the development of travel and holiday schemes at home and overseas. It also referred to the fact that there was a sports and holiday centre for the Swedish Labour Youth League: could not a similar scheme be developed in the UK with voluntary construction work carried out by our own young people? An element of group competition could be introduced by giving different branches separate sections of the building to complete.[3]

What the report did not indicate was that the country was deeply divided on nationalisation. Many to the left of British politics thought nationalisation was the answer to all our ills which would be remedied if the country owned all the great industries: coal, railways and power. In practice, management was very remote from the workforce. Ultimately, the Labour government acknowledged there was a need for skilled managers to run the nationalised industries in the same way that the private sector was managed and it was necessary to offer good salaries to attract good personnel from private industry.

As has been seen in Communist countries, it is disastrous for Civil Servants, and even more so for party workers, to be responsible for the management of these nationalised industries. There would be no need for strikes in nationalised industries, yet the strikes continued and possibly were as great as in the private sector. The breakdown of class barriers and improvement in the standard of living of the working man would not be through the nationalisation of the 1940s but through the private enterprise of the 1950s.

Another problem of the Labour party was that except for the few it was difficult to motivate young working-class people to take an interest in politics. This was acknowledged in an article in *New Advance* in the 1960s when it was recommended a Young Socialist branch should be started in a middle-class area rather than a working-class area in order to find members with education, imagination and drive who would become officers or committee members with little initial training. The failure of the Labour party to obtain more youthful support from the working-class population was the greatest factor in ensuring that the second half of the twentieth century politics was mainly Conservative.[4]

In a book published by the Labour party on advice to constituencies concerning establishing and running Labour League of Youth branches stress was given to the variety of social events to be run by the League. For the indoor enthusiast: table tennis, billiards, chess, visits to the theatre, concerts and cinemas, musical and dramatic groups, choirs, concert parties and dances. For those more inclined to the outdoors: rambling, cycling, camping, swimming, physical culture, football, cricket, netball, tennis and rugby. It also mentioned that dances, whist drives and concerts were important fund raising events. Indeed, if the writer of the pamphlet had been able to instil into party workers enthusiasm for these events perhaps the Labour League of Youth would have rivalled the Young Conservatives.

It also stressed the importance of young people being able to work out how to run their branches in their own way. It said:

> Once it has been established, the aim should be to encourage the members of the branch to feel a sense of responsibility for the welfare of their own organisation. The senior party while always being ready with help and guidance should avoid the mistake of imposing supervision, allowing young people to develop their branches in their own way and use their own ideas in securing the branches' growth, subject to the necessity of avoiding contravention of the Party's constitution.[5]

When the youth sections were formed the need for branches to have an attractive social programme was stressed by Alan Williams (national youth officer) who stated that although politics must be the main aim and dominate the programme in order to become a useful unit to the party organisation it must not become too top heavy. Its members will want to rock 'n' roll and in order to give all members a chance to show their talents the programme should include: folk dancing, play reading, acting and even handicraft work.[6] One wonders how many young people of the 1950s would want to spend their time on handicrafts!

A publicity pamphlet of the Young Socialists in 1961 stated that most people joined the Young Socialists because they wished to meet others of their own age and take part in activities which especially appealed to them. At first only a few would be strongly political so there should be a broad programme including dances, jazz sessions, visits to the theatre and cinema; sports, debates, discussions, dramatics, organised outings, camping and holiday groups. It is quite clear that the party organisers of the Labour youth movement (in whichever of the forms it took) intended branches to match the social appeal of the Young Conservatives. In most cases branches failed.[7]

Although the Young Conservatives and the media have often derived amusement from the Young Socialists, branding them all alike, there is no question that Young Socialist branches varied in the usefulness of their work and their relationships with their constituency parties. It seems that, at least in the hierarchy, there was less opposition to Young Socialists having opposition speakers, which the Conservative Central Office decried. Indeed, even the Conservative party would have approved of West Lewisham Young Socialists who invited their prospective Conservative candidate, John Gummer, to attend. But in case it was thought John Gummer might convert the Young Socialists they invited a member of the Lewisham Anarchist party to speak immediately before him. Besides John Gummer they also invited speakers from the Communist party, the ILP and Socialist party of Great Britain as well as having a debate with North Lewisham Young Conservatives.[8]

The problem with the Labour party's youth section, as with the Young Conservatives, is always that young people seldom stay in one area and branches of the League of Youth formed, dissolved and re-formed as was stated in a history written of the Chichester Labour party. The author also referred to the useful work carried out by the branches such as a survey of entertainment centres in Bognor Regis in 1963, an activity which the Young Conservatives might just as easily have undertaken.

It appears that, at least in Sussex, as the constituency party had a better understanding of young people, compared with other sections of the Labour party, a good relationship was enjoyed between them. As well as appreciating that the conditions in the 1960s, with the upsurge of youthful identity, were very different from the 1940s, it recognised that the emphasis between the League and the Young Socialists was different.

The League of Youth represented members of the Labour party at a time when people's politics were more staid. They adopted their family's Labour view from childhood and took it for granted. They later learned socialism by attending summer schools and Labour youth conferences. The feeling of continuity in the Labour movement from children's Christmas parties to the election of official delegates to one or other of the sections was total. The Young Socialists of the 1960s coincided with an upsurge of youthful identity which wished to re-examine socialism and the feeling that the leadership of the Labour Party was compromising socialist ideals by failing to apply them to transforming capitalist society.

The Chichester Labour party accepted a resolution in 1965 from Bognor Regis Young Socialists for submission to the NEC and the Parliamentary Labour Party that the Labour government should take a moral course in all its undertakings and pay no heed to vested interests. They contended it is too facile to say that young people in the Labour movement are inevitably left wing.

Most young people with political interests start out as radicals in every generation but the present leftward trend of the Young Socialists at local level at least shows a radical return to socialist principles and impatience with those Labour leaders seeming to them unprepared for any transformation of social structures. It is a kind of fundamentalism which, in the view of many experts, exerts a healthy pressure on the Party. The Young Socialists see themselves as fulfilling their constitutional objective to secure the support of young people for the principles and policy of the Labour party. The argument arises from the different meaning placed on the words principles and policy.

The dilemma for Labour is whether the party intends to be a socialist or Labour party. The report very aptly states the difference between the Young Socialists at local and national level. At local level at the Chichester branch, the Young Socalists hotly debated issues whereas at national level the debates were only too frequently personalised and trivialised by the media. It, therefore, appears that because the Party in Sussex appreciated their young people a better understanding existed.[9]

None of the problems arising at so many other branches occurred at Chichester. Another good branch was Twickenham. It always enjoyed a friendly relationship with the constituency party. Membership had fluctuated over the years although the going had sometimes been hard in an overwhelmingly Conservative area. In 1967 the branch had a membership of about 30 with an average attendance of about 10 to 25. Like the Young Conservatives, their problem was a continuous loss of active members to university and college outside the area.

They compiled an extremely good report answering a number of questions raised by the Labour party. They stated that the Labour party needs a youth movement in order to recruit young people into the Party when the older members wear out. It was also stated that young people should fully partake in the political life of the Party and the day to day running of it. It should be a two-way channel of communication between the young people and the Party which, at the same time, provides political education by conducting political campaigns on issues of concern to young people either in favour of or against Party policy. As to the question of whether ties should be loose with the Party or fully integrated, it stated they should play a full part in the life of the Party, but should not be integrated. They further advocated mass rather than a selected membership,[10] but, in the political climate of the 1960s, increase would be slow and they were more realistic than Iain Macleod.[11]

There was a considerable argument over the years about whether the age limit for the Labour party's Young Socialists should be restricted to the age of 25 or whether it should be 30. They favoured it should remain at 25 otherwise it would be under the domain of the older members of the Party.

A suggestion that there was no need for a national structure or to hold an annual conference was strongly disputed in the report. They maintained the function of the National Committee should be to carry out policy as laid down at the National Conference to organise national campaigns and be responsible to Conference for the day to day running of the organisations. They also stated that the organisation should be responsible for its own budget,[12] echoing the words of Eric Chalker. It was a thoughtful document and this pamphlet could just as easily have been written by the Young Conservatives of the 1960s.

Almost from the beginning of the 1960s during the rapid increase of Young Socialist branches problems, not faced by the Young Conservatives, engulfed the Young Socialists. One of the matters to dominate the Young Socialists and Young Liberals was support for CND which indicated that their hearts ruled their heads. As early as 1961 the North Hammersmith Young Socialists submitted a resolution to their CLP urging de-selection of the sitting MP Frank Tomney who was not a unilateralist and requesting the selection of a unilateralist candidate for the next election.[13]

The nearby North Kensington Young Socialist branch was disbanded in 1961 because of complaints by local police and clergy of a rowdy dance. At the time of its closure there were only six or seven members. It was stated that the dance was held without the consent of the CLP and one wonders why the consent of the CLP was necessary to run a dance. Only three years later three of the leaders of the Young Socialist Party were expelled by the main party.[14] In 1964 Streatham Young Socialist branch continued to meet after it had been suspended. They stated, 'The suspension of our Young Socialist branch is part of a national network of the right wing against the Young Socialist movement.' They appealed for all Young Socialists to attend a meeting to defend Streatham.

After six of the eleven members of the national committee elected at the 1964 Young Socialist conference were expelled during the subsequent twelve months, in 1965 the NEC attempted to ban the National Conference. However, in defiance of the Party, the conference was held. At that conference it was resolved to establish a Young Socialist organisation without the approval of the Labour party. The Labour party resolved to change the name of its Youth organisation to the Labour Party Young Socialists but by 1970 the left wing pressure group of notoriety, 'Militant', was controlling the LPYS.[15]

Militant's action towards the LPYS was not only condemned by the Conservative Party but by at least one LPYS branch. Windsor LPYS in the magazine
*Progress* in 1985 stated that the LPYS national chairman treated non militant
branches with contempt in not informing the branch or the constituency Labour
party he was speaking at Windsor's boys' school and they similarly treated their
representative with 'a verbal blunt instrument'[16] when he attended the National
Conference. However rather than reimposing Draconian measures the NEC
determined instead to give its youth movement increased power. In 1972 they
gave it a seat on the NEC. Except for 1974 Militant continued to control the
Labour party's Young Socialists National Committee. The only occasion it did
not control it was in 1974 when the Militant chairman, Peter Doyle was
disqualified when it was discovered that he was 27 and too old to be a Young
Socialist. The chairmanship therefore passed to the defeated candidate a non
Militant Rose Degiorgio.[17]

In the post-war 1945 election the Liberal party was ill-prepared and only
able to field 309 candidates and even in some Liberal held seats such as Bristol
North a candidate could not be found. The Liberal party strength at Westminster
fell from eighteen to twelve. The Party leader, Archibald Sinclair, was defeated
as well as the most prominent Liberal at that time William Beveridge responsible
for the wartime report on social security. Until Rochdale in 1958 when the
Conservatives were pushed into third place and at Torrington when the Liberals
won a by-election, the period 1945–58 was one of extreme depression for the
Liberals. It seemed that this party of such historic traditions would finally
collapse.

An ill-considered election plan of 1950 to fight on the broadest possible
front and field 475 candidates, ended in disaster with 309 of them forfeiting
their deposits. Although few records survive the Young Liberals were re-formed
after the war. The records of the London Young Liberals show that in
1947 there were 350 members in 18 branches.[18] During the whole of this
period there is evidence of Young Liberal activity in London. A Young Liberal
branch was formed in November 1948 in South Kensington which held a
rally in Trafalgar Square in September 1949 and in 1950 at an open air meeting
in Stratford. Winston Churchill, once a Liberal MP, was enthusiastic that
there should be an anti-socialist front and the Liberals and the Conservatives
should combine to defeat the Labour party. This policy was backed by Lord
Woolton who made overtures to the Liberal party to combine with the
Conservatives.

When Winston Churchill became Prime Minister in 1951 and the Liberals
had a mere six seats in Parliament, their leader, Clement Davies was offered a
seat in the cabinet in a key position as Minister for Education. Clement Davies
refused the offer and his decision was wholeheartedly endorsed by the Peckham
Liberal Association; their spokesman said that Liberalism is above purchase by
expediency.[19] There is little doubt that this decision would have received the
full support of the Young Liberals, who appeared undeterred by the tremendous

set-back received by the Party at this time, in maintaining that the Party must not enter into electoral pacts.

Throughout the 1950s Liberals were elected in Bolton and Huddersfield because of electoral pacts. In each town in one seat the Conservatives stood down and allowed the Liberals to fight Labour and vice versa in the other seat. Although this agreement provided the Liberal party in 1950 with two out of a total of nine seats the Young Liberals were unimpressed.

In 1950 the Young Liberals asserted that the Liberal party must continue to fight as an independent force, having connections with no other political party, and should either official or unofficial arrangement be concluded the National Executive would not consider it binding on the National League of Young Liberals and would constantly work to secure the adoption of Young Liberal candidates if necessary in order to sabotage such pacts. Finally the committee considered it undesirable for any person acting under such arrangement to remain a member of the Liberal Party.[20]

The Young Liberals continued to adopt this stance and they opposed the Liberal party forming any coalition with either the Conservatives or Labour. When there was talk inspired by Edward Heath between June and the October 1974 election for a Government of National Unity, the Young Liberals made it clear that they were against any such pact[21] and also at their conference in 1977 at Weston Super Mare they indicated they were less than enthusiastic for the Liberal/Labour pact which was agreed during the Callaghan minority administration. A motion, passed by a large majority, called on the Liberal MPs to pursue Liberal policies and to attack the Labour party for its conservatism.[22]

There is certain evidence that a Liberal revival following the disastrous General Elections of 1950 and 1951 was spearheaded by the Young Liberals. The Manchester Young Liberal Association emerged as an extremely powerful political force in the North-west. The militant body led by Dennis Wrigley set out on an ambitious systematic long-term programme of expansion in forty constituencies around Manchester and the number of branches increased from a mere six to over forty. A central speakers' panel of over 100 was in action. Hundreds of enthusiastic new members joined.[23] In London there is a note in 1953 that four new branches were formed. This was against a depressing picture for the Party at senior level. Activists withdrew at an alarming rate. Two-thirds of the Party's experienced candidates in the 1951 election never stood again neither did 70% of those who stood for the first time in 1951.

Affiliated Liberal branches which had risen to 235 at the 1945 election to 367 in 1951 declined to 231 by 1958 and then dramatically rose to 436 by 1963.

This decline affected the Party's finances and in February 1957 the Liberal Party Headquarters informed the constituencies that the Party had only enough money to carry on until the end of March. This apparently had some effect because there was an improvement in financial support from the constituencies.

Following the election successes at Rochdale and Torrington, in the 1959 General Election the Liberals fielded twice as many candidates as in the elections of 1951 and 1955 and their share of the votes increased to 5.9%. It appeared after all that the Party would survive.

In December 1959 the London Liberal party reported that the National League of London Young Liberals had approximately 330 members, roughly the same figure as in 1947.[24] In January 1959 nationwide the Young Liberals had 243 branches, one-sixth of the YC branches. In March 1963 the branches dramatically increased to 493 when it was calculated the national membership was about 15,000.[25]

The Liberal revival continued so that at the 1964 election the number of Liberal MPs increased to nine seats and they doubled their popular vote to 11.2%, although the number of candidates who stood had increased by 50%. The Young Liberals became increasingly radical. In 1968 the National League organised a Vietnam week. They distributed leaflets in Winchester city centre calling on the US to halt the bombing and enter into peace negotiations and they carried out a survey showing that 69% thought that the bombing should stop and 31% thought it should continue.[26] Peter Hain, who subsequently left the Young Liberals and became a Labour MP, emerged as the most outstanding of the Young Liberals. The Young Liberals in 1970 were prominent participants in the successful 'Stop the South African Cricket Tour'. They made it clear that it was a non-violent campaign as, they did in another campaign against a Greater London Motorway scheme.[27]

Peter Hain's radical views were not always accepted. He proposed that abortion should be available on demand. 'I am concerned for the mother of an unwanted child. She is solely responsible and should take the decision whether or not the baby should be born.' The Conference agreed with the views of David Mumford, the Young Liberals vice-chairman, complaining that abortion might become the alternative to contraception.[28] Peter Hain did not impress Winchester branch who, although supporting a national campaign investigating certain aspects of juggernauts, unanimously condemned Peter Hain's proposal to use illegal tactics to combat the menace as inappropriate.[29]

At this time the Young Liberals intensified the uneasy relationship with the senior party by inviting Aba Omar, a member of Al Fatah, the Palestinian guerilla organisation to attend their conference. Also, they were critical of British troops' involvement in Northern Ireland.[30] The more bizarre behaviour of the Young Liberals reduced their standing as a serious political group. In 1972 they resolved that at the Conference social function every delegate would dance with another person of the same sex for some of the time.[31]

However, the Liberals made a dramatic advance during the Heath government, first winning a crop of by-elections and then gaining 6 million votes in the February 1974 General Election. The youth vote particularly increased. The Liberals failed to maintain their momentum during the Callaghan government, similar to the position during the 1964–1970 (Harold Wilson's government) and the 1979 election was almost as disappointing a result as in 1970.

In 1977 their standing was further damaged at the Conference, fighting with stewards after they tried to persuade the Conference to hear an emergency debate on unemployment.[32] The Young Liberals became increasingly left-wing, advocating such measures as withdrawal from NATO. Their impact on the Liberal revival after the establishment of the Social Democratic party in the early 1980s was far less significant than in the period of Liberal revival in the early 1960s and the 1970s. The belligerent attitude of Young Liberals at national level was not always shared by the rank and file at branch level. In 1975 when a Young Liberal branch was established at Fulham the officers stated their main object was to help the senior association and they were not in complete agreement with the Young Liberal hierarchy on the radical approach to politics that Peter Hain and other Young Liberals advocated.[33]

In 1977 the Chairman of Wanstead & Woodford Young Liberals was more outspoken describing the Young Liberal leadership as rather an immature group of middle-class trendies who are completely irrelevant to politics as the mass of people see it.[34] Some senior party workers also severely criticised the behaviour of the National Young Liberal leaders. In East Surrey they were described as 'people who espouse violence, bigotry and hatred rather than tolerance and fairmindedness' but the East Surrey Young Liberals were described 'as fine men and women and although the men's hair is not too short and the girls' skirts overlong they are a splendid example of a civilised and radical younger generation. They are intelligent too. Their chairman, John Watton is a brilliant mathematician and a worthy successor to liberalism'.[35]

A significant role the Young Liberals played was in pursuit of community politics to encourage people to use their political power at a local level to achieve their desires rather than lobby MPs to effect change or leave it to the executive. Due to the energy of the Young Liberals the 1970 Liberal Assembly formally approved such tactics.[36] An amendment by the Young Liberals for a primarily strategic emphasis on community politics was passed 'and that our role as political activists is to help organise people in communities to take and use power to use our political skills to redress grievances and to represent people in all levels of the political structure.'

The Liberals first advocated this policy in the Ladywood Division of Birmingham in 1969 where whole areas were threatened with redevelopment. The result was petitions, advice centres and community newsletters. The Liberals supporting such policies had a spectacular success in Liverpool where by 1973 from a non existent base they managed, in about two years, to become the largest political grouping in the council and had won a parliamentary by-election. The most important gain from these policies was in housing. Before the Liberal influence large areas had been bulldozed for slum clearance. This policy was reversed and no dwelling was demolished if it was structurally sound during 1978 and 1979. Of the 30,000 houses in various action areas 85% have been modernised.

In my view although community politics, such as the housing programme in Liverpool, has much merit there are occasions when national interests must override local interests. The Victorians succeeded in building a national railway network within twenty years. Had they not been ruthless in the pursuit the system with all its benefits would have taken much longer to construct. Another disadvantage of community politics is that it is often more expensive and resources may not be so well used if a housing authority divides its territory for administrative purposes into small areas. There may be a dearth of a particular type of accommodation in one area and a surplus in another area. Community politics by the ruling Liberal party was established in Tower Hamlets. This brought notoriety when Liberal councillors, who were censured by the national party, campaigned on a racist platform but, in the opinion of a local resident, small units can also encourage racism reflecting the feelings of persons living in a particular area.[37]

Young Liberals were more serious than their YC counterparts. A five months' weekly programme of the City of London & Westminster Young Liberals showed they, too, had time to enjoy themselves. Like the YCs at that time in Kensington the programme advertised a local pub where Young Liberals could drink together on Sundays. However, that they were more serious than the YCs is indicated by the fact that in the programme only St Valentine's Day persuaded them to abandon their weekly political programme for the dance floor.

Finally, how far did the policy of one youth movement affect the other youth movements. In view of the bad name the Young Socialists earned in many cases, not always justified, neither the Young Liberals nor the Young Conservatives wished to model their organisation on the Young Socialists; but the reverse was not true.

It seems clear that when the Young Socialists were formed in 1960 Morgan Phillips the secretary of the Labour party hoped that as far as providing electoral help, social activities and loyalty, its youth movement would be similar to the YCs. Writing to a friend he said, 'The Young Tories are certainly very active'[38] and he hoped his youth movement would compete on equal terms as it could learn much from the Young Conservatives. This counters the argument that in latter years the media often tried to convey that the YCs of the 1950s were not a tremendous asset to the Conservative Party. In view of the uneasy relationship between the Young Liberals and the senior party from 1960 doubtless the senior party often wished its youth movement acted in a more responsible way as the Young Conservatives usually did.

The strength of the Young Liberals was in their belief that their radical approach was the correct one and was one which the senior party should follow. On the other hand there is evidence that both the Young Socialists and the Young Conservatives thought they could learn from the Young Liberals' campaigning methods. The Twickenham Young Socialists thought its party could learn from the Liberal Party which allowed its Young Liberals much greater freedom than the Labour Party allowed them. It stated that the Young Socialists should be free to adopt its own policy as did the Young Liberals.[39] Praise was given by Clive Landa, chairman of the Young Conservatives, for the way the Young Liberals campaigned although not necessarily for the subject of their campaign. He said, 'If the Young Liberals can achieve success with five members then we ought to do better with fifty.'[40]

# Chapter 4

# Politics in the Second World War

Most political activity was suspended during the Second World War apart from a handful of Junior Imperial League branches and perhaps one or two Young Briton branches.

However, Labour and Conservative constituency offices appear to have remained open, some manned by agents who were too old for call up. Political activity by all the parties was at a low level.

People unaware of conditions in pre-war Britain find it difficult to envisage the poverty that existed. A retired clergyman, Archdeacon Arthur Ward recollects that when he was a curate in Newcastle, he called at the home of a family on Christmas Eve and finding they had no food for Christmas in the house except a loaf of bread and condensed milk, he had to rustle up food for them from his own household.

At that time if a person needed State help a Civil Servant would visit the applicant and before granting help, applied a strict means test which could result in the sale of any furniture beyond the bare necessities, such as a bed, table and chairs.[1]

Many of those who fought in the First World War returned home in 1919 expecting to find a land flowing with milk and honey but instead found high unemployment. The Second World War, like the First, had brought together people of many classes, particularly amongst the young and, even in the South where the depression had been less severe, the young servicemen and women thought it was time for a fundamental change.

The politicians' favourite phrase when proposing a policy such as nursery education is, 'when the country can afford it'. This did not appeal to the electorate of 1944 and 1945. Between the wars Conservative politicians had told the country it could not afford the expenditure that would substantially lessen the divide between rich and poor. Those who were both poor and sick were particularly disadvantaged. Yet the government had been seen to finance the war at record levels.

The wartime cabinet realising the mood of the nation, in spite of the demands of prosecuting the war, still found time to deal with social legislation. Under the enthusiastic leadership of Rab Butler who was Education Secretary in 1944, the Education Act 1944 was passed which provided the framework for three types of schools: Secondary Modern, Technical and Grammar schools and raised the school leaving age to 15. The main provisions of the Act was to remain on the Statute book until the 1980s. The Beveridge Report in 1943 which described how a universal benefit system could be implemented was also initiated by the Coalition government. Therefore, the Labour party's very expensive programme of wholesale nationalisation did not frighten the electorate.

The nation was already heavily taxed and the voters were looking not for reduction in taxation but for the government to implement the Beveridge Report giving universal retirement pensions, unemployment pay and sickness and accidents at work benefits. Also, there was to be a benefit called Family Allowance now called Child Benefit, whereby a weekly payment was to be made to mothers of children up to the age of 16, or until completion of education (for many years the first child of a family was excluded) and there was to be a free health service.

The Conservatives were also promising a free health service. The Labour party favoured one organised at national level with the doctors being employees of the National Health Service. The Conservatives were in favour of the doctors retaining their independence and the hospitals, many of which were already managed by the local authority, to continue to be managed by the local authority.

During the war there was a political truce between the coalition parties which meant that neither party was allowed to criticise its opponent and when there was a by-election, (the General Election due in 1940 being postponed until the termination of hostilities against Germany) the party holding the seat nominated the new candidate and the other parties of the Coalition did not oppose him or, in those days very occasionally, her.

This brought forth criticism of party workers from both the Labour and Conservative parties as is shown in correspondence. A Conservative constituency officer wrote to Conservative Central office informing it:

I am frequently meeting people who will follow the slander press and blame Baldwin and Chamberlain for the war because neither addressed the nation of the coming danger, at the same time knowing of vast quantities of war material going to Germany. Can you tell us how Central Office is dealing with the slander and whether there is any published reply?

Central Office replied:

The issue of a publication to rebut the pre-war preparation would however provide the kind of controversy that has been forcibly deprecated by the Prime Minister and under present circumstances we must abide by that advice.[2]

However, this generosity of Winston Churchill put the Conservative party at a tremendous disadvantage. They were unable to repel attacks alleging that the Baldwin and Chamberlain governments were to blame for our lack of adequate armaments at the beginning of the war because the Labour party had shamefully tried to arouse public opposition to the pre-war rearmament programme as they had been even more lukewarm about the need to rearm than the Conservatives. The Labour party consistently voted against the Service Estimates. Their spokesman George Hall said, 'In our opinion bigger and better armaments have never saved a Nation from war nor have they given security to either strong or weak nations against attack.'[3] Indeed, it was fortunate that Labour was not then in power because if ever superior arms were to save Britain in its hour of greatest peril in 1940 it was because the Spitfire was superior to the German fighters. Labour opposed the enlargement of the RAF in 1936 and, in 1939, opposed conscription.[4] Most Liberals supported Labour, their leader, Sir Archibald Sinclair saying 'Armaments by themselves can never give us security, that security can only be obtained by a wise policy directed at the achievement of enduring peace based upon a collective system of general disarmament.' Even more bizarre, the Liberal party in 1936 accused Stanley Baldwin of rearming when he was pretending he was not doing so.[5]

During the war years the prominent Labour politician and future Foreign Secretary, Ernest Bevin generously acknowledged:

> After Dunkirk we found ourselves in a very grave situation with a short supply of various vital and essential materials. I do not think there are any grounds for blaming anybody. For instance if anybody asks me who was responsible for British policy leading up to the War I will as a Labour man myself make a confession and say all of us. We refused absolutely to face the facts when the issue of arming or re-arming arose. People who have an inherent love of peace refused to face the real issue at a critical time but what is the point of blaming everybody. We cannot act retro-spectively. Whatever we do we have to start from new and do the best we can.[6]

It seems the Conservative party kept the spirit of such truce more enthusiastically than its Labour counterparts. The minutes of the Reigate Conservative party (appendix 1) show the numerous ways in which that constituency assisted the war effort.[7]

Many Labour constituency workers however did not like the attitude of the Labour leadership. A branch resolution was passed complaining of,

> the comparative small amount of opposition of the Parliamentary Labour Party and the failure of the Labour Ministers to appreciably influence national policy and as a direct result of the aforementioned the inevitable identification is growing and strengthening in the minds of the Labour movement of a period of muddle and incompetence of national affairs.[8]

In 1943 Sir Richard Acland, a landowner of considerable wealth, who owned a country estate at Killerton, near Exeter in Devon established  a Christian Socialist party calling itself the Commonwealth party, which was not bound by the political truce. Upon the cessation of hostilities he gave his whole estate in accordance with his principles to the National Trust. It was then the largest gift they had ever received. Commonwealth candidates and other independent candidates started to defeat Conservative candidates at by-elections when the existing members died or retired. The Commonwealth party fielded candidates at the 1945 election but none, including Sir Richard Acland, was successful. Shortly afterwards the Commonwealth party ceased to exist, showing there is no room in English politics for a fourth party, like Oswald Mosley's New Party earlier, and David Owen's Social Democrats of the recent past. Richard Acland joined the Labour party and in 1947 was elected an MP. The by-election losses, and as early as 1943 a Gallup poll result, showed that even with Churchill as their leader, the Conservatives were already 7% behind Labour. This should have been a warning to the Conservative party that they had a mammoth task to win an election on the termination of hostilities. This encouraged the Labour National Executive in 1944 to state they would fight the next election alone rather than continue in any coalition. From the time of the twin triumphs of El Alamein in October 1942 and Stalingrad in February 1943 it became clear that Germany would lose the war. In the opinion of Robert Blake it did not matter when the election was held after 1942 as the Conservatives would have lost.

The other difficulty facing the Conservatives was that the two most prominent people in their party, Winston Churchill and Anthony Eden had both been party rebels. Not only did Winston Churchill and Anthony Eden both disagree on the alleged policy of appeasement with Germany, Eden resigning in 1938, but also disagreed with much of the pre-war Conservative domestic policy advocating the concept of 'One Nation Tory', first proposed by Disraeli: that the Conservative party should be a party representing all classes. Sir Anthony Eden is noted in history, as the wartime Foreign Secretary and for his involvement in the Suez débâcle, but he was very much a 'One Nation Tory' anxious for social cohesion and with a lively concern for domestic affairs.

Harold Macmillan, too, had been extremely critical of the pre-war policy of the government and R. A. Butler stood firmly for discarding the *laissez-faire* attitude and supported the Industrial Charter. Nevertheless, Churchill wanted to do all he could to prolong the coalition at least until the end of the war against Japan. He argued privately that it was necessary not only for there to be a united front against the Japanese but also against the Russians as there was the fear that having defeated Germany, the Russians might then attack Western Europe. There were even tentative plans to rearm the Germans.

The Labour leadership were still not convinced that Labour would win. Attlee and Bevin were prepared to agree to prolong the coalition, believing the Conservatives would win a general election on the strength of Churchill's reputation; but the rank and file of the Labour party wanted an election, many of their supporters feeling the time was ripe for the final electoral victory of the working class.

It was astonishing, in view of the adverse Gallup poll and the performance of Commonwealth candidates during the war, that there was so much complacency among Conservatives who thought, from Churchill with his fine war record downwards, the electorate of 1945 would want to allow him 'to finish the job'. The Conservative press were of the same opinion. It was surprising that even Beaverbrook thought that the Conservatives would win. His efforts to frighten the electorate against voting Labour might well have had the opposite effect. Of a Labour government in 1945 the *Express* said, 'Will you go down in history as the man who smashed human tyranny in Europe when too tired or bewildered or too dazed by your own glory to save yourself from tyranny at home. After ripping the Gestapo out of Germany will you stand for the Gestapo under another name at home?[9] However, when the results of the election were known and Beaverbrook realised that the majority of his readers had voted Labour he said, 'There will be no captious criticism of the new government . . . no attempt to turn the nation's discontents into Party capital.'[10]

Churchill's message was:

> On 3rd September 1939 we began a heroic crusade for right and freedom. Our job is not yet finished. We still have to beat the Japanese. We still have to work within our wills to ensure that victory leads to a durable peace to put the land on its feet again. I invited the leaders of the Labour party and the Liberal Party in opposition to help finish the job. They refused. Men of goodwill of no party or other parties have accepted the invitation. Together we shall tackle the problems that lie ahead. When these policies are solved and Britain is a going concern again there will be plenty of time to argue about whether we want to discard our whole system of society in favour of some form of strange ideas which are quite out of favour with our hard won individual freedom.[11]

In using the word 'strange' Churchill appears to have misread the mood of the nation. The people desired not only freedom from the external forces that Churchill had gained for them but freedom from hunger and unemployment.

As the election approached Gallup was showing a 13% Labour lead but, as often happens, there was a swing back in favour of the government and by 4th July this had been reduced to 8.9%. Gallup had been surprisingly accurate. When the result of the election was finally known Labour's lead was was 8.4% and Labour had won 393 seats to the Conservatives 213 giving them a huge majority. It was a Labour victory throughout the land. Two million middle–class voters had voted Labour to give it its most decisive victory in its history.

By 1955 the Conservative party had regained their position and the Young Conservatives were to play a significant part in a remarkably quick revival which few could have envisaged in August 1945.

## Chapter 5

# Rise of Young Conservatives during Attlee governments 1945 to 1951

The Conservative party was shell shocked by its serious defeat. It was a bitter experience for Winston Churchill that many of his former Cabinet colleagues were defeated at the polls. Eden, Macmillan, Butler and Maxwell-Fyfe, who were all to play an important part in the politics of the next fifteen years had survived, although in the early years Maxwell-Fyfe was heavily engaged in the Nuremburg War Crimes Trials. In a contemporary memorandum Rab Butler analyses the cause of the massive defeat:

1. Women disgruntled by queues and other wartime measures

2. Servicemen had grievances with regard to pay and leave.

3. Totalitarian instincts had been implanted in many young people by almost universal factory life.

4. Electors wanted change.

5. Electors were swayed by exaggerated Labour promises.

6. Years of left-wing propaganda accompanied by virtual cessation of right-wing propaganda had created an anti-Conservative atmosphere.

7. Cessation of political work in the constituencies, although Trade Unions throughout the war were operating mainly assisting the Labour party.[1]

The decisive role played by the USSR in defeating Germany also boosted left-wing ideology. A most surprising pamphlet on Russia issued by the Liberal party during the election campaign states, 'Liberals see much to criticise though much to admire in the work of the Russian Government especially since Stalin took over!'[2] It is now known that over 20 million Russians were killed under the Stalinist regime.

The Labour party proceeded to introduce legislation at a pace which has rarely been experienced in British history. Between the autumn of 1945 and the summer of 1947 six substantial measures of public ownership were carried out: the Bank of England, Cable & Wireless, civil aviation, coal, gas, electricity and rail and road transport. These measures received very little opposition. Generous compensation was paid to the shareholders. It must seem strange to the Thatcherites of the 1980s that bi-partisan initiatives such as the McGowan Report on Electricity and the Hayward Committee's report on Gas in late

1945 had already urged the cause of public ownership on the grounds of technical efficiency. Again the principle of municipal ownership of houses to rent had long been established. However, the nationalisation of iron and steel gave the Labour government more problems than all the previous measures.

Labour's honeymoon continued in the local elections. The early performance of the Labour government received popular acclaim. In the November 1945 Local elections Labour gained 1,000 seats throughout Great Britain. In January 1946 Labour were 19 points ahead of the Conservatives in the Gallup poll, 52½% to 33%. In the local elections of March 1946 Labour continued to make extensive gains, including the London County Council where the Labour party won 90 seats to the Conservatives' 30 seats. Even as late as the local elections of November 1946 Labour showed a further advance of 257 gains as against 98 losses. Indeed there was a feeling that Labour might virtually rule forever.

Conservative supporters regarded the Attlee government as near Marxist although in some respects it was quite right wing. Particularly, much to the horror of CND and the Young Socialist and Young Liberal sympathizers, the Attlee government thought it was wrong for us to depend on the USA. Consequently, they secretly authorised the manufacture of the atomic bomb when President Truman, reneging on a wartime promise of his predecessor, refused to share the US atomic secrets with Britain.

During the war a record number of regulations had been introduced to ensure that maximum resources would be channelled into the war effort and that the limited supplies available to the general public would as far as possible be shared fairly. During the early years of the Attlee government there was little desire to lift such controls because it was easier to plan centrally with extensive controls in place. However, one of the most youthful of the ministers was Harold Wilson then aged 33 in 1949. He changed the policy and managed to lift many controls. This policy brought criticism from certain members of the parliamentary Labour party who saw controls as the means to retain the socialist hold on the economy as well as the more laudable object of ensuring equal distribution in times of shortage.

Churchill's reputation as a wartime leader remained undiminished but many failed, unjustly, to give him any credit as a peacetime leader. One of the most important functions of any leader is to pick the right team and the selection of Lord Woolton as party chairman was a touch of brilliance.

Woolton had been a Fabian in his youth, went on to be managing director of Lewis's, and then a most successful Minister of Food in the wartime government. He had not become a member of the Conservative party until the day the 1945 election result was announced. He was so shocked by the huge Labour win, which he knew would mean wholesale nationalisation to which he was utterly opposed. Of nationalisation, he said those who wanted nationalisation did not trouble their minds with the practical issues of how it was to be fulfilled. In fact they did not know so they had to leave it to the Civil Servants who lacked the necessary expertise.[3] He was able to instill a sense of enthusiasm into the Party, dramatically increase membership, steer through reforms whereby candidates were prohibited from subscribing more than £25 per annum and in the case of a sitting MP £50, to the Local Associations.[4] He persuaded the local associations to raise money for central funds by organising social and other fund-raising events rather than from the pocket of the candidate or MPs to improve the finances of the Conservative party so it was not in any financial crisis. Since his retirement in 1955 the Party has had continuing financial problems.

He immediately recognised how important it was that the Party concentrated on winning the support of the young and this policy was to be richly rewarded. Within ten years it was not the Labour Party who was the dominant party but the Conservatives. The Conservatives' climb back can be traced to the first post-war Blackpool Conference in 1946 and such was the personality of Lord Woolton that those who gathered in considerable gloom left optimistic that the future would be theirs rather than the Labour party's.

Lord Woolton, in his autobiography, said that it was the young undergraduate (not the business community who were already Conservative) that he would first target. He relates how he went to Oxford and Cambridge Universities where he realised the future leaders would be found. He sold to them the Conservative policy of the Industrial Charter. Within two years the Conservative party had become the dominant party in both universities. To him nothing was more rewarding than attending crowded meetings at both universities. He said, no doubt reflecting on his days as a Fabian, 'we put to young people the policy which was in harmony with the idealism which forever is associated with the young. This is the reason why the Independent Labour Party, the Fabian Society and Social Democratic party during the early years of this century appealed to young people to express their hatred of a society where so many people lived in poverty.'[5]

The regaining of confidence by the Party was much assisted by the rapid rise of Young Conservative members. Fergus Montgomery said that one of the advantages the YCs had at this time was a pool of ex-officers who had been demobbed and found it strange that in civilian life they no longer had battalions to direct so if they could not run a battalion a Young Conservative branch was the next best organisation to manage.[6] Not only the increasing numbers of Young Conservatives but their participation in the affairs of the Party is born out by a letter from Rab Butler to Anthony Nutting reporting on a successful Conservative conference in February 1947: 'nearly all the people were young people and I think it is difficult for Young Conservatives to realise how little there was in the cupboard and how much there is now.'[7] The report of the Conservative Central Council indicates that by 31st December 1947 there were 1,546 branches and 104,000 members. A later report shows that during a period of twelve months membership had risen by approximately another 50,000 to 151,987. If such momentum was to be maintained one would have expected in the next nine months to September 1949 another 37,500 members to have been enrolled, but in the following nine months only 5,308 people joined.[8] The highest figure for membership at that time was quoted as 170,000 by Frances Vale, national chairman when she spoke at Wolverhampton on 12th November 1949.[9] It appeared the peak year of Young Conservative membership was 1951 and thereafter the membership declined so statements by certain sections of the media that there were a quarter of a million members seem false.

The rise of the Young Conservative movement was also helped by the fact the middle class did not prosper under the Labour government, no longer able to afford servants, taxed at nine shillings and sixpence in the pound and with labour-saving devices not yet arrived in quantity. No doubt many thought that not only would they be better off, and also their future prospects would be better, under a Conservative government. This situation created fertile ground for recruiting YCs.

However, as had often happened certain sections of the Labour Party behaved as if they were disinterested in obtaining re-election. In this case it was a cabinet minister, Aneurin Bevan who referred to the middle class as 'vermin', many of whom had voted Labour in 1945 to give Labour its massive majority.

Alfred Edwards a former Labour MP in addressing the City of London Forum said, 'how sorry I and the vast majority of people in my Party are that such a vulgar statement should be made by one of our ministers.'[10]

A further reason for the rapid growth of the YC movement was that young people had few social attractions other than the cinema (which was then in its heyday), football, cricket and tennis clubs so the Young Conservatives provided a congenial, economic place for young people to meet others of their own age. This was still the pre-television age as far as the majority of the population was concerned. When the City Forum of Young Conservatives was addressed in 1948 by Mr Orr Ewing of BBC Outside Broadcasts, only six of those present had seen television and Mr Orr Ewing remarked that the BBC could not give better programmes to the public without a bigger audience. The film industry would not sell even 10-year-old Mickey Mouse films and variety artistes were permitted by their Union to appear only if they refrained from appearing on the stage for thirty-two weeks following their television appearance.[11]

There was a keen interest in politics among the young when a debate on 7th October 1946 at the Albert Hall, Leeds between the Young Conservatives and the Young Communists attracted 1,000 people with 200 people unable to gain admission.[12] Beryl Goldsmith, a YC of the 1940s and later to become Norman Tebbit's researcher, tells how the movement grew not only among the young middle class but also among the working class. Some young people had a sense of patriotism and were indignant that the British electors had rejected Winston Churchill after all his wartime achievements.[13] Beryl Goldsmith's view that a section of working-class young people were attracted to the Young Conservatives is supported by Dr David Butler who stated, 'by the 1960s the YCs were in decline, no longer providing a gateway into the

Conservative party for hundreds and thousands of young people many from non-Conservative backgrounds as in their heyday in the late 1940s.'[14]

By 1951 weekly meetings of Young Conservatives became a regular feature of life throughout the towns and villages of England and Wales for the next twenty years. The programme was divided between political activities and social events. Even if most people joined for social reasons the advantage to the Party was tremendous. Politicians, before the days of television, had a channel through which they would address YCs and the YCs provided canvassers and their money was contributed to Party funds. Whereas in the 1930s it had been fashionable for the young to be to the left in politics, it then became popular for young people to be Conservatives, and this situation continued throughout the 1950s until the early 1960s when the Tory government ran out of ideas, and by defective government allowed Labour to regain their customary predominance among the young.

The inaugural meeting of the National YC Committee was held on the 6th July 1946 when Anthony Nutting was elected chairman.[15] Anthony Nutting was unique in that he was the only YC to be elected chairman when he was already an MP and, unlike any of his successors, he had to buy his own seat. He made rapid progress in the Party so that by 1950 he was chairman of the National Union of Conservative Associations and made a similar rapid rise in the House of Commons becoming Minister of State at the Foreign Office. However, he was one of the few Conservative MPs to disagree with the Suez operation and resigned from the government. He had written a number of books concerning the Arab world including, in 1967, his own appraisal of the Suez operation called *No end of a Lesson*.

In October 1947 he was succeeded by John Hay, a Brighton solicitor, who in 1950 became MP for Henley and during his parliamentary career held various ministerial posts as well as appointments with the European movement and the Council of Europe.

Frances Vale, an East Ham schoolteacher and the only woman national chairman of YCs, succeeded John Hay in 1949. This was the era of austerity and she had to carry out her duties entirely relying on public transport. Already as vice-chairman she had made her mark, speaking at both the Brighton Party Conference – making a strong speech concerning the lack of women candidates and at the Llandudno Conference successfully persuading it to reject the women's charter.

Following her retirement from teaching and upon the steel industry being privatised she worked in administration in the industry and was responsible for its fight against the re-nationalisation of steel under the Wilson government. She was then appointed to take charge of public affairs at RTZ, a job for which she was well suited in view of her contacts and she now lives in retirement.

She was a parliamentary candidate in the 1955 General Election for Ashton. The *Birmingham Post* noted

Frances Vale is the first woman candidate Ashton has ever had. Instead of burdening her programme with numerous indoor meetings she concentrates on loudspeaking street tours, factory gate meetings and has an eye on the vital housewives' vote, mingling with shopping crowds. For one thing she comes from London. She wants to make the most of every meeting to become acquainted with the electorate. She enjoys a hard scrap!

As National Chairman of the Young Conservatives she fulfilled a weighty schedule all over the country with meetings at the last two general elections. Before that she twice fought municipal elections in one of the strongholds of the East End, Little Hammond, reducing the socialist majority. Her main campaign was in support of peace through strength, living standards, improvement in housing, education, and benefits.[16]

Illness prevented her from seeking a seat at the 1959 election and thus the House of Commons was deprived of someone who would have made a considerable contribution to the House.

One of the problems that faced the Conservative party was that the Party was blamed for the economic failure of Britain during the period when Baldwin and Chamberlain were Prime Ministers of a Conservative or National Coalition government. Many of the electorate had not considered that high unemployment had affected most industrial nations during the 1930s. Further, although many blamed Neville Chamberlain's policy of appeasement, Labour, even as late as the spring of 1939, had opposed conscription.[17] This policy, referred to, in the National Advisory Committee minutes, also in a speech to a City of London YC Forum pointed out that between 1931 and 1939 steel production doubled.[18] Three million houses were built without subsidy and unemployment was falling by 100,000 a year. It is claimed that social security reforms between the wars was soundly based because it was followed by expanding production. The difficulty was that because social security was very limited many lived in poverty that was unknown after the Second World War.

The most important legacy of the Attlee government was the establishment of the National Health Service. From research of contemporary records little comment or discussion of the National Health Service appears to have taken place, either in the branches or at the meetings at area or national level although Dr O'Donovan gave a speech to South Kensington YCs (Appendix 2), hardly a vote catcher! One of the remarkable features of the Attlee government, compared with other post-war governments was that the Labour party did not lose a single by-election, indicating its popular appeal. Praise was not limited to Labour supporters but Clement Attlee also gained recruits.

Sir Geoffrey Manders a former Liberal wrote to Clement Attlee:

May I venture as a life long Liberal who had just joined the Labour party to put the position as I see it. The two party system is now fairly fixed such as some will regret so we have to choose right or left. Labour is now heir to that radical tradition as the Government has been doing thoroughly liberal things for the past six years.

In foreign affairs Labour has made the United Nations the fundamental base for its efforts to bring peace to the world. What a contrast with pre war Tory Governments which betrayed the League of Nations. Nobody wants war but peace is safe in the hands of Labour. It is through that party that Liberals can now achieve the ideals as I see it.[19]

A further tribute came from Kenneth Lindsay an Independent sitting for the Universities (which seats the Labour party legislated to abolish):

Now that Parliament is about to be dissolved and I cease to represent the Combined Universities as an Independent member may I write to express my decision concerning the forthcoming election. It is my belief of which I have made no secret especially in the recent debate on devaluation that the Labour Government has served the country well in five difficult years. In common with many of my supporters I have admired your strength and patience not only in the successful solving of the Indian Problem but also your courageous and balanced appraisal of the gigantic economic and social problems at home and your experience in Europe and the United States. I have formed the conclusion that many people are looking to Britain and the British Labour party for a strong and progressive govern-ment not only to consolidate our social services and thus demonstrate our effective answer to Communism but also to release the new energies of the British people with regard to the increase of national wealth thus showing the 20th century democracy means not only political liberty but wide extension of economic opportunity. I believe that the defeat of the Government led by you a disaster not only for this Country but for the world. I offer you full support in the forthcoming election and hope that many others will come to the same conclusion.[20]

Whereas in all other Labour governments performance had fallen short of what it promised this one had delivered full employment, nationalisation, free health service and universal benefits on the basis of the Beveridge Report.

However one matter in particular they did not deliver. There was a desperate need for housing, so many houses having been destroyed in the war; because of planning restrictions and the Labour government's policy of favouring local authority building rather than private builders, they could build cheaper and quicker than the local authority direct labour force. Labour failed to implement policies that would enable the houses that the nation required to be built. A resolution passed at the 1950 Conservative Party Conference that under the Conservative government 300,000 houses per year would be built met with Labour scorn. None the less 300,000 houses a year could be built and in the lifetime of the first Conservative administration the target was achieved. The Labour party stated that if the Conservatives removed controls unemployment would return. However unemployment did not return. Labour's scurrilous remark that Churchill was a warmonger proved entirely unfounded and they deserved to lose the election.

If a party accuses its opponents of matters later shown to be unfounded, the party making the allegation loses credibility and this happened. The Labour party retained power in 1950 by six seats but in October 1951 was narrowly defeated. Although the result was close it was a bad result for Labour as it was to take them fifteen years and four General Elections to obtain a working majority for only the second time in their history. Lord Woolton was of the opinion that the Labour party assisted in its own defeat 'While the Conservatives had fought a clean election the Labour Party by preying on the electorate's fears of war instead of appealing to their reason considerably narrowed the gap. Twenty-five YCs stood as candidates in the 1951 election. The confidence and high profile of the Young Conservatives caused by the movements's rapid growth must have made considerable impact on the younger voter.[21]

# Chapter 6

# Young Conservatives from the Defeat of the Attlee Government to the Suez Crisis

The main objective of the Young Conservatives – the defeat of the Labour government had been achieved in October 1951 although the Labour party had polled 13,717,538 votes, more votes than the Conservatives.

Perhaps the major difference between the elections of 1950 and 1951 was that the Liberals had fielded less than a quarter of the candidates in 1951 then they had in 1950. A major factor for the Conservative success in the 1951 General Election was that more former Liberal voters switched to the Conservatives rather than to Labour, either because there was no Liberal candidate or, if there was, the voter decided a vote for the Liberal candidate was a wasted vote. This was in contrast to the 1955 and 1959 General Elections when there was a marked shift of voters from Labour to Conservative. Oddly enough, membership of both the Conservative and Labour parties continued to rise. The Conservatives reached their peak in 1953 with 2,805,032 members.[1] The Labour party's individual party membership (excluding the Trade Union block votes) reached its peak in 1952 with 1,004,544 members.[2]

This increase was not matched by a rise in Young Conservative membership. It is clear that membership was on the decline although care was taken not to publicise this. The minutes of Yorkshire Area of September 1953 show a decrease in the membership and number of branches.[3] National membership figures for January 1953 are available and show the membership standing at 124,500 a considerable decrease of approximately 20% from the peak membership figure mentioned earlier.[4] Records of both Wessex and Eastern areas are available and show the downward trend.[5]

| | Wessex | | Eastern | |
|---|---|---|---|---|
| | Members | Branches | Members | Branches |
| 1949 | 12,983 | 212 | 10,515 | 172 |
| 1950 | 14,750 | 248 | 11,299 | 181 |
| 1951 | – | – | 11,405 | 215 |
| 1952 | 11,756 | 216 | 9,745 | 199 |
| 1953 | 10,230 | 204 | 9,376 | 184 |
| 1954 | 9,432 | 194 | | |
| 1955 | 8,487 | 182 | | |

The Conservative government was not initially popular. The Labour party policy, unlike that of the governments of Wilson and Callaghan did not believe in regulating the economy by variation of the Bank Rate and kept it at 2½% throughout its term. One of the first steps taken by the Conservatives on coming to power was to raise Bank Rate to 4½% with a corresponding increase in mortgage rates. The unpopularity was shown in the Gallup poll which indicated a Labour lead during 1952 ranging from 3½% to 10%. However, from 1953 onwards the Conservative party's fortunes improved and in May a by-election seat was won from Labour in South Sunderland, the first time a party in power had won a seat at a by-election since 1924. After poor local election results in 1952 the Conservative showing continued to improve.

A national YC Rally was held in Birmingham on the 14 June 1952 and a holiday week in North Wales in 1953. Following the holiday week a statement was read by Mr Ridgewell, the national YC organiser who had succeeded Col. Oliver to the NAC, that a similar event would not take place in 1954. The last event had cost Central Office some £900 and had entailed considerable time and effort by area organisers and concern was felt that all energies should be concentrated on arresting the decline in the movement and rebuilding branches.[6] This may well have been a short-sighted view because the staging of a high profile event was good publicity for the YCs and the more interesting activities the YC organised the easier it would be to attract members. As young people became more prosperous they would seek more sophisticated pursuits.

The Young Conservative movement had never held its own budget and a number of decisions were taken by Central Office. The first occasion the NAC passed a resolution criticising Central Office was for ceasing publication in 1953 of the magazine *Advance* without consultation, although a new magazine was published in 1954, *Rightway*, which continued through the 1950s.[7]

It has been alleged on occasions that the YC movement of the 1950s was docile. It was to be many years before the NAC would openly disagree with the Government or shadow Cabinet when in opposition. It is wrong to assume that no criticism was levelled against the Government. Until the 1980s there is no evidence that the Party ever tried to prevent its youth movement from discussing controversial matters.

In 1954 the Young Conservative Council for London and the Nottingham Young Conservatives criticised the government for agreeing to an increase of 50% in MPs' salaries. Geoffrey Finsberg (national chairman 1954/1957) and Fergus Montgomery (national chairman 1957/1958) proceeded to propose a substituted motion welcoming the statement on MPs' remuneration and pledging its full support for the Government in this matter.[8] The motion was carried showing YCs at this time had differing views.

In talking to many MPs who have been past YC officers, all relate the success and failure of the YCs to factors other than the government's performance. The Conservative government of 1951 to 1955 promised full employment, increased prosperity and peace and they achieved all these objectives.

A remarkable increase in the standard of living was occurring, partly due to the upturn in the economies of the developed nations. No apparent concern was shown that other European countries, particularly Germany, were capturing our markets. Between 1951 and 1955 the number of cars licensed rose from 2,288,000 to 3,309,000 and television licenses rose from 1,031,005 to 4,580,720. For this reason few YCs saw any reason to criticise the performance of the Government.

The three chairmen during the period covered by this chapter were William van Straubenzee, Peter Bailey and Geoffrey Finsberg. William van Straubenzee was the only national chairman who, when requested, felt unable to make any contribution to this book. Peter Bailey, a YC national chairman from 1953 to 1954 has died and I have been unable to find out much about him. Geoffrey Finsberg who, between 1970 and 1992 was the well liked member for Hampstead and a loyal MP received a peerage in 1992. He was elected chairman on 23 October 1954. Indeed he told a YC committee that the sole purpose of the Party was to win elections, a statement with which other YC chairmen have disagreed.[9] Andrew Tinney said, 'if I were to win elections and implement Labour party policy I would rather the Labour party implemented it.'[10]

As in 1956 the annual meeting at which the national chairman was elected was changed from autumn to spring, Geoffrey Finsberg was the longest serving national chairman as he held office until 1957. West Wickham magazine described Geoffrey Finsberg as an inspiration and driving force for the movement and also complimented him for his hard work in travelling 21,000 miles in his chairmanship to meet YCs.[11]

Young people in particular were benefiting from increased prosperity. A Labour party report called 'The Younger Generation' commissioned in 1959 stated that first and foremost the most striking fact about youth is its comparative prosperity. It reflected:

> twenty years of full employment and with increased economic wealth all wages have substantially increased but the under-21s have not only shared in the general advance but have done considerable better. Spending power among young people under 21 may amount to £5m per annum. For the first time in British history the likes and dislikes of the teenagers are expressed through purchasing power.

Teenagers were larger, heavier and healthier than their predecessors through better standards of nutrition and medical care. Prosperity was assisted by the fact that 'between 1950 and 1955 employment in the UK rose by one million and the number of vacancies far exceeded the number of young people seeking work.' Alan Williams the Labour party youth officer agreed that teenagers earned more than their predecessors and a large proportion came from working-class homes because many teenagers of middle-class homes were still at school or in higher education.[12]

Perhaps the greatest achievement of the 1951 to 1955 Conservative administration was in housing. At the Blackpool Conference in 1950 a resolution was passed that if the Conservative party was returned to power 300,000 homes a year would be built. Under the able leadership of Harold Macmillan, Housing Minister, the target was reached during the lifetime of the 1951–1955 parliament.

One of the failures of the Attlee government was the disappointing record for the building of new homes. The Girwood report in 1949 had drawn attention to the fact that houses were taking 26% longer to build than in 1939. In 1951, Attlee's best year, 198,171 dwellings were built. Under free enterprise in pre-war Britain and with inferior building techniques 344,000 homes had been built in a year. This difference was partly caused by the tighter planning control following the Town & Country Planning Act 1948 coming on the statute book. In pre-war Britain one did not normally require planning permission before building except in specific cases. From 1935 onwards one could not, without the consent of the Minister, build on land adjoining a trunk road. Planning permission before building was to become a permanent feature of post-war Britain. Building was also hampered by the requirement to pay the Government a 'development charge', a sum equal to the increased value of the land when planning permission was obtained. The unintended effect of this was to discourage development and it was abolished by the Conservatives.

Labour were to make a number of serious miscalculations during this time. The Labour MP, Woodrow Wyatt, to the right of centre, argued in the *Daily Herald* in 1950 that 'after the Conservatives had gained control of Birmingham City Council they encouraged the tenants to buy their own council houses and only 3,296 out of 60,000 responded to an enquiry from the Council about purchasing their own house.' He, therefore, came to the conclusion that there was little demand for tenants to be able to purchase their council houses.[13] However, a young Labour supporter better understood the desires of young people as he wrote in the *Socialist Commentary*:

> Young people today believe rightly or wrongly that the economic evils of the 1930s will never return. My generation do not know economic fear but is living well and looking to the future that is where the Tories are looking. Indeed my working class friends: engineers, clerks and the like expect when they are older and married they will afford such a consistently high standard of living as to be able to own a house and car. No pipe dreams but the real beliefs of young people in the future.[14]

The Labour left wanted to perpetuate the class divisions and treat the middle class as an underclass, hence the use of the word 'vermin' (Chapter 5) but that was not what the working class wanted. They wanted the benefits of the middle class and for the first time they could enjoy labour-saving devices in the home, continental holidays and home ownership. I believe that the architects of the Attlee government's policy thought that the working classes would be quite happy to live in rented council accommodation and would not aspire to own their own properties.

It took until 1987 for the Labour party finally to realise that the majority of people wished to own their own home and made a complete U-turn on their policy on the sale of council houses following their 1983 election defeat. Ironically, Labour's change of heart may be too late as the 1990s have shown a tremendous change in people's attitude to house purchase because of the collapse of the housing market and, with the ending of much of the rent control legislation, there has been a significant rise in both the desire to rent and properties to rent. Only time will tell whether this is a temporary or permanent change.

The Labour party also failed to read the mood of the nation on their policy concerning commercial television. Although some Conservatives opposed commercial television Labour fought a vigorous campaign against the Bill establishing commercial television which resulted in the loss of the BBC monopoly. After the bill had passed through the Commons Labour made a valiant attempt to block it in the Lords. However, commercial television was to become so popular among its supporters that any opposition by the Labour party quickly evaporated.

The impact of commercial television appeared to pass almost unnoticed by most YC branches and the National Committee. However, the writer of an article in the West Wickham YC magazine was one of the exceptions. Commercial television was supported on the grounds that television programmes would be vastly improved. 'It has long been the axiom of newspaper life that nothing so improves an established newspaper as much as competition. So it will be with TV.[15]

Many of the members of the Labour party hierarchy were out of touch with reality as is shown by a speech given by Aneurin Bevan in 1953.

I regard modern advertising as one of the most evil consequences of modern society, which in itself is intrinsically evil and everywhere one goes one sees the consequences of this development. In a competitive society the consumer is passive, besieged, assaulted battered and robbed. Some of the worst features of competitive advertising must be controlled in the interests of the public as a whole so that we shall not need competitive advertising in order that the agents of publicity shall be restored to their pristine function to make mankind aware of what is available and not artificially to appeal to its worst instincts. You are harnessed to an evil machine which is doing very great damage to modern society.[16]

Another remarkable political development of post-war politics was how tenants in council estates in traditional Labour areas were re-located to the new towns. It was envisaged that they would maintain their loyalty to the Labour party but considerable numbers, upon changing their environment, changed their allegiance and voted Conservative. They moved to the new towns as either owner-occupiers or tenants and the change of allegiance was particularly evidenced among the young.

An article in *Crossbow* analysed the results in Hertfordshire of the 1955 and 1959 elections. A belt of new towns such as Hemel Hempstead, Stevenage and Hatfield had been created after the Second World war. The Conservative vote increased by 11,000 between 1951 and 1955 and 20,000 between 1955 and 1959. Between 1951 and 1955 the Labour vote, in spite of the influx, only increased by 6,000 votes, just over half the Conservative vote. Between 1955 and 1959, as against the increase of the Conservative vote of 20,000, the Labour vote decreased by 2,000.[17]

The painstaking work of Lord Woolton and others in targeting the universities and regarding the success of the Young Conservatives as a matter of priority was now reaping rich dividends for the Conservative party and there is no doubt that the more youthful image of the Conservative party and the Young Conservatives assisted this change of allegiance. This was the view expressed by Childs in *The History of Post War Britain* that the YCs probably did help to orientate young people towards the Conservatives in the 1950s. The swing to the Conservatives was nationwide, unlike the situation in the 1980s. In 1959 the Conservatives won four of the nine seats in Manchester. An analysis of the results of a Labour town, Rotherham, shows the shift in votes between 1945 and 1959. In both occasions there were straight fights.

| | Labour | | Conservative | | Electorate |
|---|---|---|---|---|---|
| 1945 | 35,654 | 1945 | 12,796 | 1945 | 62,635 |
| 1959 | 28,298 | 1959 | 16,420 | 1959 | 57,080 |
| | Decrease | | Increase | | Decrease |
| | 7,455 | | 4,376 | | 5,555 |

It will be seen that at least one in four of the votes which had been cast for Labour in 1945 was now being cast for the Conservatives. Many of the voters of 1945 and 1959 were not the same as a number of people had died and a younger generation had come on the Register. It is clear that an appreciable number of the younger voters were voting Conservative whereas their elders had voted Labour and, in spite of a reduction of 10% in the electorate, the Conservatives had been able to increase their vote by 25%.

One of the many people at this time who converted from Labour to the Conservatives was a Mr W. E. H. Dutton of Bradford. Writing in West Wickham YC magazine in 1959 he stated why, in his early twenties, he voted Labour in 1945.

Coming to power in 1945, their policy of Nationalisation appealed to the people, including myself, and as the result of our votes, we saw millions of pounds paid out in compensation, which I don't think will be recovered over the next fifty years.

On top of this the master planners of Transport House launched the African Groundnuts scheme and lost another £36m. It amazes me now, when I think back on those days, how gullible the British people were.

We certainly fell for a red herring, and any attempt by the Tories to pull them up sharp was met with abuse and catcalls. The House of Commons had become the laughing stock of the world.[18]

Churchill has often been criticised as a peacetime politician. In many ways the Conservative administration of 1951–5 with its meagre majority of seventeen was as successful as perhaps any of the other administrations which served this country since the Second World War. Basically, they were united by the thought that if there was disunity they would be assisting the return of the Labour government. As in each of the three General Elections, 1945, 1950 and 1951, the Labour vote had increased some pessimists in the Party thought that this country would virtually always be ruled by a left-wing government as has been the case in Sweden.

As always there was a vociferous element calling for fewer controls. The unity among MPs at Westminster assisted in keeping the Conservative party united in the constituencies including the Young Conservatives. This is in sharp contrast to the performance of MPs under John Major's leadership following the 1992 General Election with a slightly larger majority. When Winston Churchill resigned in 1955 the Conservatives faced the electorate with confidence and the Young Conservatives played their full part in many areas of the country by canvassing and delivering literature.

Dick Crossman writing of the 1955 election in the *Sunday Pictorial* said:

compared with Sir Anthony's team Labour looked too much like an old man's Party with its eyes not fixed on the future but on its past achievements. I should not be surprised if the statistics show that more young men and women voted Tory than at any time since before the First World war. The Tories have been streamlining their organisation so attracting the rising generation into it.[19]

Although their membership was probably 25% less than in 1950 the variety of activities undertaken by Young Conservatives besides electioneering did much to attract the young to the Conservatives rather than the Labour party.

It was reported to the Labour Party Conference at Margate in 1955 that there had been a phenomenal decrease in Labour League of Youth branches in recent years and the League was to be dissolved and a youth section in each constituency was to be formed.[20] Likewise, we have seen that this was not a success and after only four years it would be replaced by the Young Socialists (Chapter 3).

*The Times* leader during the 1954 Conservative Party Conference stated 'at no important point does it seem that the Conservative government's record is going to be assailable unless some unforseen economic developments intervene.' In the same leader it refers to 'the Conservative record of good husbandry'.[21] It was therefore no surprise that the Conservatives won the 1955 Election. A low key election, the proportion of people voting declined from 82.5% to 76.8% showing the contentment of the nation and the falling votes was in real terms greater because the election was held on a Register which was four months newer than that of 1951.

A party in power had for the first time in 100 years been returned with an increased majority.

Fortunately for Labour, Hugh Gaitskell was about to become leader of the Party and he would focus his attention on the future not on the past. Nevertheless, by the time Hugh Gaitskell had inherited the leadership of the Labour party it had thrown away the advantage it had gained by the crushing defeat of the Conservative party in 1945. Henceforth, millions of blue-collared workers and trade unionists, in spite of the protestations of their leaders, would vote Conservative as without their support the Conservative party would never have been able to obtain the support they enjoyed for the next forty years, except for the 1966 election.

The tenth anniversary of the YC movement was in 1955 and it was planned to celebrate it nationally with a holiday week at Scarborough. However, it was the decision of Central Office to cancel it on the grounds that as the General Election had already taken place it was of little use as a morale booster.

Many people having already arranged time off for their holidays were disappointed. In particular, Yorkshire Area committee passed a resolution deploring the cancellation. One might have thought that the Party would have been reluctant to alienate its younger members by taking this course and indeed what was to have been a pre-election event would have been one celebrating the election victory.

Such was the spirit among Young Conservatives, despite the U-turn of the Party, that 200 YCs, no doubt those who had already booked their holiday, arrived in Scarborough.

> The week started with a reception organised by Scarborough YCs and they met daily. A dance was held on the Monday at Olympia Ballroom and other events followed: a mystery tour and a sea cruise. Discussions were held for the more politically enthusiastic on leadership in the YC movement and the place of young Trade Unionists in our movement.

The report also stated that 100 YCs were the guests of the Scarborough Amateur Operatic Society, that a planned midnight swim was not well supported and the week ended with a final dance. The report closed with mention that 'Miss Wiseman and others went to the station to bid farewell to the visitors and as train after train steamed out an air of gloom descended. We were left with only memories, snapshots and the cries of seagulls ringing in our ears.'[22]

Many branches mounted a celebration of ten years of YCs with special events.

There were signs that an air of complacency was now influencing the senior ranks of the Conservative party which became as great a danger as the Labour opposition to post-war Conservatism. No longer was there that sense of urgency which had so assisted the rise of the Young Conservatives in the 1940s, a view which is supported by other evidence. The NAC complained that the only minister prepared to attend the dance following the 1956 YC Rally was Lord Mancroft (Chapter 26).[23]

All Areas were asked, before the 1955 election, to state how they saw the future of the movement. Among the replies the West Midlands acknowledged, in the event of a close election result it would not be so difficult to keep the Young Conservatives alive particularly if the election results went against the Conservatives. But should the Conservatives be returned with a working majority (which they were), it would be more difficult to extend the organisation. Indicating that many of the Young Conservative officers were realists.[24]

It appears that in 1956 the Young Conservatives had their most successful recruiting campaign, terminating with a rally at the Royal Festival Hall addressed by the Prime Minister, Anthony Eden. Of the 547 constituencies in England and Wales only 15 did not participate. Of those who did not, some wished to run their own campaigns while others had no effective constituency organisation. Over 200 members were enrolled by 11 constituencies and 4 members recruited more than 50 members each. The number of new members enrolled was 27,751.

In spite of this recruiting campaign the numbers of Young Conservatives fell from 125,400 in 1952 to 92,756 in 1957. The fall from 1952 until about 1956 would have been greater but for the recruiting campaign. Further evidence that the movement was again on the rise is a minute of the National Committee of 17 March 1956: 142 new branches had been formed against 51 that had collapsed which indicates the high turnover of branches as well as members.[25]

Three constituencies: Skipton, Newcastle and Newark won prizes for the success of their recruiting campaign; two members of each of the three winning branches to be entertained in London with two nights' accommodation at the Regent Palace Hotel, commencing with a tour of Conservative Central Office to be greeted by the chairman Oliver Poole, followed by a visit to Downing Street. The party were entertained to lunch at the House of Commons with dinner at Veeraswany's Restaurant and finally to the Coliseum to see the American musical *Pyjama Game*.[26]

After the election victory of 1955 Anthony Eden's position looked unassailable as did Margaret Thatcher's in 1987 but unexpected problems can defeat the most experienced of politicians. In under two years from 1955 Suez would blow the Government off course and Anthony Eden would resign.

Suez was to Anthony Eden what the Poll Tax was to be to Margaret Thatcher.

Comedians poked fun at the Young Conservatives of the 1950s as being a marriage bureau; that is how comedians earned their living. However, the way the broadsheet press now trivialise the Young Conservatives of the 1950s, as with so many other institutions, is quite unjustified. There is evidence that their opponents acknowledged them to be superior to their rival youth groups in many respects. In 1955 the Young Communist magazine *Challenge* reported of the Young Conservatives:

> The Labour movement should not scorn to learn from the modern forms of organisation and colourful and attractive methods of the Young Conservatives which have helped to attract 150,000 young people to their ranks.'[27]

# Chapter 7

# Suez and Hungary

In 1956 a major international crisis arose when President Nasser of Egypt decided to nationalise the Suez Canal. This was seen by many as a prelude to military action in support of the Arab World's threat to liquidate by force the State of Israel, a member of the United Nations.

It is lawful for a member country of the UN to aid another member state which is being attacked. Britain, together with France, invaded the Suez Canal zone to try to prevent this nationalisation but, due to condemnation from abroad and a UK financial crisis caused by the conflict, a ceasefire was agreed. The crisis arose on 30 October and the ceasefire took place on 8 November. Hugh Gaitskell, Labour leader severely criticised the whole operation.

Labour misread public opinion. After initial doubt, support for Eden rose from 40% on 2 November to 53% on 15 November and there is contemporary evidence that many working class people supported Anthony Eden on patriotic grounds. In this case there was no bi-partisan agreement, unlike the other three occasions since the Second World War when British troops were used in a combative role rather than a peacekeeping or anti-terrorist role – Korea, the Falklands and the Gulf war.

In the other cases of international conflict, such as the Berlin airlift, Vietnam and Bosnia, despite some disagreement on tactics, Britain and the USA basically agreed on their common aim. In other crises there was a united front by all the Western nations including the USA but, on this occasion, France and Great Britain acted independently and received the official disapproval of the United States although Anthony Eden received many letters of support from individual Americans who admired his stand against their President.

The YC National Advisory Committee passed a resolution with one dissension stating that it represented members throughout the United Kingdom and wished to place on record its wholehearted support for the policy pursued by HM Government in the Middle East. It was further convinced that the courageous leadership of Anthony Eden had been responsible for the prevention of widespread war in the area, and also for the decision of the UN to create an international police force.[1]

YCs have been criticised for being passive but some of the credit for this support must be due to the leadership of Anthony Eden. He, with Churchill, in the inter-war years had warned the country against Nazism and his remarks passed unheeded. He served the country with much distinction in the wartime Coalition government, as he did in the same position in the Churchill government between 1951 and 1955. It is not correct to say that there were no

dissenters but the majority recognised the Prime Minister's tremendous knowledge of foreign affairs and they had confidence in the Prime Minister's
judgement.

Pamela Pardey vividly recollects a meeting of Southampton Test Young
Conservatives addressed by Bill van Straubenzee on Suez. Even if the audience
had not supported the government at the beginning of the evening they certainly
did by the end.[2] The YCs gained their reputation for meekness partly because
no branches either opposed the operation or argued that we should not have
halted the operation when we did. From reading Branch minutes and YC
magazines I can find no occasion of a branch criticising the operation or
advocating we should not have halted the military operation when we did.

Most of the YC magazines were devoid of any serious discussion on the
courses open but, as usual, Ealing magazine led the field with an article written
before the military action. In view of the tone of the article there is no doubt
that 'Politico' (the writer) would have approved the government's action in
mounting the operation although perhaps would have been less enthusiastic
about the ceasefire. 'The fact that we know now Israel and Turkey are among
our true friends in the Middle East. Let us hope the Government appreciates
their value and the folly of placating our common enemies at their expense.'[3]

However, some individual members and officers did oppose our action over
Suez. Fergus Montgomery, who at the time was national YC vice-chairman,
recollects the decision to support the government was not unanimous. The
NAC minutes confirm that there was one vote against the resolution enthusiastically supporting the government and one Northern Area woman representative was violently opposed to the whole operation.[4] A report in the Petts
Wood magazine of a weekend school shortly after the Suez crisis reads, 'It was
not surprising that after a discussion it was agreed by an overwhelming majority
to send a resolution of confidence to the Prime Minister. I might add that the
points finally put forward have finally converted me from a waverer to an
outright supporter.'[5]

The views of YC branches were similar to their senior associations, who
supported Anthony Eden and did not support the limited number of MPs who
opposed the operation. One such dissenter was Anthony Nutting the YCs'
first chairman, who opposed the government policy. As a result he received
much criticism from his constituency party and he subsequently resigned his
seat. The Bournemouth East Conservative Association passed an overwhelming
vote of no confidence in another Conservative MP, Nigel Nicolson, also
opposed to Government policy.

As Sir Anthony Eden's biographer stated:

Those Conservative MPs who were opposed to, or highly critical of, the
Government's action did not lack courage. All indications were that Eden
now enjoyed unparalleled support in the Conservative Party and a great

deal outside it. The letters and telegrams of support deluged Downing Street and also MPs' resolutions of complete support were passed with acclamation by Conservative Associations. To stand against all this was brave indeed.[6]

Why should the Young Conservatives be singled out for criticism while the main constituency associations were regarded as loyal? The one person who received no criticism was Edward Heath who, as chief whip, obtained the support the government needed among MPs without fuss. Many in the Party had every reason to be grateful to Edward Heath. When Harold Macmillan became Prime Minister, Edward Heath was the one person on whom Macmillan thought he could rely to the extent that Rab Butler said in a letter to a friend 'the PM was treating Edward Heath like God!'[7]

At the time the Suez operation was being undertaken the people of Hungary had mounted a serious challenge to the Communist regime, until the USSR put down the insurrection. The following motion was proposed by the National Committee:

> the Committee strongly condemns the action of the Soviet force in Hungary and extends its deepest sympathy to the people of Hungary and is in complete accord with the decision of HM Government to receive Hungarian refugees in this country. It further urges Area Committees to provide practical help for these people of Hungary by sending financial assistance to the British Red Cross for the purchase of medical supplies.[8]

Strangely the sentence urging Area Committees to help was deleted from the resolution. The rather timid behaviour of the national committee was in stark contrast to the Young Conservatives' attitude to the events which occurred twelve years later. During a similar show of strength by the people of Czechoslovakia, Rodney Gent organised a demonstration outside the Russian exhibition at Olympia London which was evidence of how much less passive the YCs had become. It seems wrong that the YCs should have paid such scant attention to the plight of the Hungarian people particularly as the revolution was inspired by the actions of the young, mainly students. Five hundred Hungarians were executed. However, the Young Liberals sent money and clothing to selected Hungarian relief agencies.[9]

It is strange that the YCs commemorated the tenth anniversary of the Czechoslovakian uprising in 1978, the fourteenth anniversary in 1982, and the twentieth anniversary in 1988 but the Hungarian revolution was never commemorated by the YCs.

Future historians may well regard 1956 as the high noon of Communism. Apart from Italy, Communist parties in Western Europe were decimated. The Danish Communist party, not insignificant before the Hungarian revolution, ceased to exist when the entire leadership including the secretary general formed a new party – the Socialist Peoples' party. In France votes for the French

Communist party at the next election after the Hungarian revolution were reduced by about a third. Any possibility of Communism gaining control of another country of Western Europe by subversion had evaporated. Although the official British Communist party, unlike in Czechoslovakia, twelve years later, supported the Soviet government this was by no means the view of all of the members of the Young Communist League as is illustrated by this letter written by a Young Communist which was published in a Young Communist Journal at the time:

> Under no circumstances could I justify the intervention of Soviet troops in Hungary. As Communists we must realise that one of the greatest forces in history is the struggle for national independence – and such a force is to be encouraged according to our principles of Marxism. The Hungarians wish to free themselves from Soviet influence and have their own way ahead, which of course, may now be in doubt. If so we can only blame those who were responsible for the use of Soviet troops in Hungary – and those who condoned their action. We in Britain have been implicated by our leaders in this mistaken policy. We have been blinded more than once by the 'bogey' of counter-revolution in Eastern Europe – and have favoured a policy which has surely gained us the suspicion and even hatred of the entire British working class.
>
> Their 'doubts' are not ill-founded. Surely talk of expanding our membership is utterly farcical in these circumstances. How can we expect the British working class to have confidence in a 'Russia is always right?' policy?
>
> The Russians would greatly benefit from the constructive criticism from fellow Communists, for they have perhaps a greater number of disadvantages facing them than have any of the people's democracies.
>
> Today Communists are standing the test. Although we remain united over the broad principles for which we are fighting, there is wide dissension on questions of interpretation and application.
>
> I speak for those who demand a radical change in policy and outlook.
>
> R. E. Swingler, London[10]

It is a matter of debate how far the Soviet Union was encouraged by the Suez operation to crush by military means the Hungarian revolution because the international community's attention was being diverted by the Suez crisis.

Geoffrey Finsberg the national chairman at the time of Suez rejects the criticism that because no YC branches opposed the operation the movement was docile and speaks in retrospect with pride of the enthusiastic way in which the YCs supported the government.[11]

Anthony Nutting wrote a book giving his reasons for opposing the operation. 'All the twists and turns of the Suez crisis there can be none that effected me more deeply than the casting of the two vetoes in the Security Council.' In commenting on whether the USSR was encouraged to intervene in Hungary following the uprising by the military action in Suez, Anthony Nutting said, Russia had invoked the veto 78 times since the UN started and again 'four days later when the Security Council voted to surpress the brutal suppression of the Hungarian rebellion but unlike Russia we are not going to get away with it as we are not ruthless enough or strong enough to carry the plan to the bitter end.'[12]

Shortly after the end of the conflict Anthony Eden, who received an enthusiastic reception, justified the decision to halt the military action. Speaking at a rally previously organised at the Royal Festival Hall he said that Britain, France and Israel had done what the United Nations had failed to do. No records have been found of any opposition from YCs to the abrupt end of the military campaign.

## Chapter 8

# Young Conservatives
# During the Rise and Fall of Harold
# Macmillan and Alec Douglas Home

Following the Suez misadventure Harold Macmillan took over a demoralised party but in a manner similar to that following the situation after the 1945 election defeat and the Westland affair in 1986, it made another remarkable recovery.

Peter Walker was elected national chairman in 1958 and became one of the most prominent of the Young Conservatives. He was one of many whose support for the Conservative party was fanned by Churchill's 1945 election defeat.[1] He became MP for Worcester in 1960 and gained high office in Edward Heath's government and his political outlook was very similar to that of Edward Heath. He was the last 'wet' survivor of Mrs Thatcher's government. Like so many other leading Young Conservatives his belief was that the Conservatives should be a centre party rather than a right-wing party which indicates the important influence of the Young Conservatives. By the time he was elected national chairman he had already established a well known unit trust.

In 1958 the Liberals made a remarkable revival in two by-elections. In Rochdale where Ludovic Kennedy stood for the Liberals, although he did not win, the Liberal vote dramatically increased and the Conservative share of the vote slumped from 51.6% to a poor third at 18% and at Torrington from 65.1% of votes cast to 37.4%. This was the Liberal Party's first success at a by-election for thirty years.

In that year the biggest defection discovered at a YC branch occurred when twenty-five members of the Exeter YCs joined the Young Liberals stating that they thought the Liberal policy was the right one but they failed to elaborate on how the Liberal policy was superior. One of their complaints appeared to be against the system of the whips. Their spokesman said optimistically, when the Liberals formed a future government he was sure they would govern with humanity and sympathy and would restore the individuals right to vote according to conscience.[2]

This was the age of affluence. Young people were remarkably better off than they had ever been and Iain Macleod aptly summed up the advantages of this prosperity. 'I love to see the result of this prosperity. Cars outside small houses, television aerials nestling in the roofs, labour-saving devices in the kitchen. Holidays for the family at home and abroad.'[3]

The YCs of this period have been accused of being docile but with full employment and rising prosperity they had little to complain of. It was against this background that Harold Macmillan won the election on the slogan of 'you have never had it so good'.

Harold Macmillan had made a tremendous contribution to the victory. As his party chairman Lord Hailsham stated, 'He had hardly put a foot wrong. He had restored relations with the United States reunified the Commonwealth, dominated the House of Commons and showed himself a moderate and progressive leader.'

The NAC paid a fitting tribute to Lord Hailsham's contribution as Chairman of the Party to the election victory. They passed a motion recording:

24 October 1959 – the NAC has pleasure in recording its deep gratitude to the Rt Hon Lord Hailsham for outstanding leadership as chairman of the Party and especially the remarkable way in which he inspired the Party when its fortunes were at a low ebb.[4]

Following the decisive election victory of 1959 it was decided to have a long YC recruiting campaign from October 1960 to June 1961, optimistically to double the membership by the next general election but its only achievement was to prevent a significant loss of membership. Nevertheless, the participation of 532 constituencies in the campaign, the same number as the previous recruiting campaign in 1956, is proof that the YC organisation was still nationwide.[5] Credit should be paid to the Party chairman, Rab Butler that the euphoria of a Conservative victory did not detract from the need for recruitment. Had his successors in 1971 and 1980 given the same attention to recruitment at that time the massive drop in membership during those periods could have been avoided.

Andrew Bowden became chairman in 1960. Like one of his predecessors in the chair, John Hay, he was a Brighton YC. He became the MP for Brighton Kemptown in 1970 and still remains. Two schemes to make the YCs more political were initiated during Andrew Bowden's chairmanship. The first was the YC annual conference. One wonders why it had been delayed for sixteen years. Very little discussion seems to have taken place in the Young Conservatives as to the desirability of a national conference and, if desirable, what it hoped to achieve. In the 1940s the NAC took the view that as the YCs had representatives on all committees it was unnecessary.[6] An element in the establishment considered that a conference might, like the pre-war conferences of Labour's League of Youth, become a focus of discontent. However, as the *Daily Mirror* aptly said in 1979 if the Conservatives ran their country as well as they ran their conferences then the country would be in for a good thing.[7]

Conservative Central Office, indeed, has considerable expertise in stage-managing conferences. The same article referred to the fact that the Tories love a winner and, unlike Young Socialists or Young Liberals, YCs at that time realised that a bad or rebellious YC Conference would do the Party's electoral chances no good. Until 1987 the conference had a remarkably good press, sometimes receiving front page headlines and speeches referred to in the leader.[8]

One is left to consider the Twickenham Young Socialists' report which in answer to the question is a national conference necessary, had no doubt it was. The advantage is that the formation of resolutions provides a focus within the branch to consider the challenge of national issues and it was a central part of the branch's calender and (unless the branch acts outrageously) it was the only way it could be heard at national level. However, on these points the Conservatives and Labour would probably be of the same mind. But they *did* differ, as Twickenham Young Socialists proceeded to show, particularly in the mandating of delegates.

It has always been considered that those attending Conservative conferences are representatives and are free to decided which way to vote rather than be instructed by the branch and, further, many rank and file Labour members, unlike their Conservative counterparts, feel that the conference should decide policy. The Conservative Party Conference only rarely determines policy. In 1950 it committed the Party to building 300,000 houses a year and in 1987 it committed them to introduce the Community Charge at once rather than in stages.[9] The policy of the national YCs was determined by the NAC, not the conference, hence until at least 1989, the rank and file decisions at the conference were normally more right wing than that of the NAC.

The first two conferences in 1961 and 1962 were rather tame but the third conference which took place on 16 February 1963 against the background of the highest unemployment since 1947 caused by severe weather. The debate on unemployment particularly was more lively and critical than debates at the first two conferences (Chapter 28).

The second initiative was the policy group. The NAC appointed an editorial board who compiled the report based on discussions held by those branches taking part, submitting their report to the Area who combined the reports to send to the editorial board. The subject was decided nationally. Two former officers interviewed had differing views on the extent to which the final statement reflected the editorial board's views or the majority of the Area reports. There was no provision for minority views and, therefore, any interesting radical views were unlikely to appear in the final report.

The first policy report called the 'Young Idea' among many topics dealt with the age group of 15 to 18 and advocated that youth facilities should be better advertised—one of the provisions of the ill-fated Youth and Community Bills (Chapter 11).[10] It proposed the abolition of the means test for students' grants. It would have approved of the decision of the YC conference in 1969 to reject the policy of student loans[11] and deplored the decision of the 1985 conference not to oppose student loans.[12] The second policy statement on the Commonwealth called 'Changing Partners' was released at the second YC conference which took place on 24 February 1962. Taking part were 2,627

YCs which represented less than 5% of the total membership.[13] On 22 January 1963 the third policy report, 'Taxation in the twentieth century', 150 groups participated proposing a sliding scale for taxation, ie two shillings in the pound for wages of between £1,000 and £1,500 and rising in stages to a maximum of ten shillings in the pound (50%). (Not so far off Lawson's top rate of tax of 40%.) There should also be a Social Service tax of a percentage of each person's earned income, subsequently implemented. Although the rates of 7% for employer and 5% for employee were initially charged at 9% for each.

It was also recommended there should be a selective pay-roll tax to influence employers to expand in areas other than the South East and the Midlands. This was a novel suggestion, never implemented, that might have helped to arrest the decline of the North as opposed to the South and neither the Wilson nor Callaghan administrations were able to arrest this decline. A corporation tax should be implemented on companies to replace the then present income and profit tax. Later, Corporation Tax was introduced. They also opposed the transfer of the educational budget to the Exchequer except for teacher training and salaries. They could see no alternative to the situation of local Rates.[14]

In 1962 the Young Conservatives produced their fourth Policy Group pamphlet on Law, Liberty and Licence (104 groups). Among the recommendations was the creation of an office of ombudsman not supported by the then government but subsequently instituted by the Wilson government. Televising of Parliament was also suggested and that traffic duties should be transferred from the Police to a special corps, which again was implemented. Payment of compensation for victims of crime was also suggested and later implemented.[15]

Two further policy reports were produced but there were fewer groups discussing each subject. In 1964, ninety groups participated in 'Reconstruction of Britain'.[16] Figures are not available for the final report on the Welfare State.[17]

Zig Layton Henry submitted as the reason that the NAC ran out of subjects and there was a desire for YC branches to discuss local issues.[18] Declining support must have been a factor in its discontinuance and indeed these statistics appear to prove that those who advocated the way to arrest the decline by making the branches more political were wrong.

A significant article appeared in *Crossbow* written by Richard Bing in January 1962, 'The YC decline'. He was the first person to ask openly the question whether the Young Conservatives movement was on the decline. In the article he estimated a membership of 150,000 (double the actual membership). His contention that the YC movement was in decline brought forth angry response from readers of *Crossbow*, including two YCs, John MacGregor and Keith Speed, who subsequently rose to ministerial rank, wrongly stating membership was rising. Cllr Reginald Watts the YC area vice-president of Essex and Middlesex was also wrongly convinced that membership was increasing. Cllr Watts mentioned that many branches were thriving referring to Thurrock which had weekly attendances of seventy, East Ham which had two branches and the Socialist areas Dagenham and Barking also had branches.

Nevertheless, his appraisal that branches were now better run, that the officers knew their duties better, the programmes were livelier, and politically the members were better informed, was probably correct.[19] The weekend schools and leadership courses, which it was claimed 3,000 attended each year were bearing fruit. By 1960 the YC movement was barely half the strength of the 1950s but the figures were camouflaged.

Peter Walker in his autobiography states that the YCs were at their peak during his chairmanship but this is not so. By 1957 they had lost 60,000 members from their peak in 1950. Apparently, he was not aware that there had been a rapid reduction in membership. A W Symes had a better understanding when he agreed with Richard Bing that there was a decline and made the pertinent point, as did others, that more emphasis should be placed on retaining members rather than recruiting new members. He also criticised the attitude in the Party which discouraged self criticism with appeals for loyalty. What the article and correspondence did not mention was that the new decade heralded the arrival of the Beatles and with them youth culture.

David Butler stated that by 1964 the Beatles had become so famous hardened politicians felt compelled to mention them in their speeches.[20] The position in Deptford as recorded in the Conservative Association magazine was becoming more and more common. It recorded the eventual closing of the YC branch after its membership had been dwindling for some time to the point when there were insufficient members to form a committee and nobody who joined had the gift of enrolling new members who were prepared to serve on the committee.[21] Discotheques and other places of entertainment were targeted towards the young. The YCs thereafter had to compete as a social club with many rival forms of entertainment. Another factor was that, after a decade when many people had confidence in the Conservative government (like the position after the withdrawal from the ERM in 1992), the Government was becoming increasingly unpopular.

There is mentioned in the minutes of the senior association of Barkston Ash in 1964 that the committee hoped that at a meeting with Selwyn Lloyd his attention would be drawn to the dissatisfaction with government policy among many supporters.[22] Further, a survey in March 1963 carried out by David Butler stated that, of the 21 to 34 age group, 25% supported the Conservatives, 49% Labour and 26% Liberal and that nearly half who had claimed to vote Tory in 1959 had switched to Labour or Liberal. The Government had tried to slow down the rapid increase in wages by means of a pay pause, then Harold Macmillan sacked half his cabinet in the 'night of the long knives' in order to try to restore his popularity.

The Government's first attempt to enter the Common Market met with a humiliating rebuff and, finally, they were beset with the scandal of the Profumo affair. The optimism of the 1950s sagged. A Gallup poll carried out in December of each year showed that, whereas between December 1957 and December 1959 the number of those polled who thought they would be worse off in the following year did not exceed 7%, in 1960 it had risen to 14% and in December 1961 to 18% and in December 1962 to 30%.[23]

Rises in earnings continued to outpace increases in the cost of living. Although there was criticism of inflation at the time, inflation was normally under 5% except for the year 1951–2. It first rose above 5% under the Wilson government then climbed to 12% in 1974 after Edward Heath, faced with the prospect of high unemployment, endeavoured to inflate the economy. It was worse under the Labour government of 1974 to 1979 when inflation never fell below 9.3%.

From 1961 to 1963 Terence Wray was national chairman replacing Andrew Bowden. The unpopularity of the Conservative party resulted in Terence Wray being beaten by both his Labour and Liberal opponent when he stood at a by-election at Derby in spite of the massive support from the YCs for their national chairman. This supports the view that electioneering has little effect on the outcome of an election. He was unique among YC chairmen in that he was the only chairman subsequently to support the Labour party and one of the few people who, in retrospect, praised Harold Wilson's premiership.

However, the Liberals were to experience another revival which culminated in the famous Liberal victory at Orpington. Whereas the Torrington victory in 1958 had been achieved in the Liberal party's darkest hours in a part of the country with a Liberal tradition the Liberal's success at Orpington was a gain in the Conservative heartland where there was no tradition of Liberalism. It is interesting to note that privately the Liberal party were far more cautious as to whether Orpington would lead to a revival as they acknowledged that many of the people who voted Liberal did so because they thought the Conservative party was not sufficiently right wing.[24] However, Orpington was the start of a remarkable feature in post-war British politics of spectacular Liberal successes in by-elections such as Sutton & Cheam in 1971 and Christchurch in 1993 often followed by general election disappointments. In 1962 the annual report of the Liberal party disclosed a dramatic increase in support for the Young Liberals and the Union of Liberal Students[25] and 1963 a steady growth.[26]

The minutes of the London Liberal Association shows further proof of the revival of Young Liberals in the early 1960s. The 1960 annual report records considerable progress during the year.[27] The 1962 annual report showed twenty new branches and affiliated membership had risen from 442 to 800 but, as usually happened, the drift back to the Government as a general election approached adversely effected the Liberal party.[28] The 1963 report showed that there was only a small increase of the Young Liberal membership.[29]

The Young Socialists, formed in 1960, achieved its greatest growth between 1959 and 1964. The number of branches had risen from 261 to 722.[30] This compares with a similar rise to 30,000 members when the Labour League of Youth was reformed after the war under the premiership of Clement Attlee.

Unlike the Young Conservatives their relationship with the senior party was fraught with difficulty (see Chapter 3). However, Harold Wilson deserved praise in rescuing the Party from the internal wrangling of the early 1960s and seemed to have a forward looking policy with the emphasis on modernisation. I have been surprised that politicians never felt their government's policies and performance has any effect on its youth movement. The contemporary reports of Merton and Morden Young Socialists clearly mirrored Harold Wilson's achievements as their records show:

It has not been a good year for the Young Socialists and although things which we have done deserve merit if we weigh up our position we are in a worse state than at the end of 1960. The reasons for our failure are internal and external, the external problems are those which have troubled the Party as a whole but the internal problems have to be dealt with if we are to have a Young Socialist branch at all. We must recruit new members.

In 1962 there was talk of the branch going out of existence but by 1963 they had doubled their membership. They described a comprehensive programme: thirteen talks including a visit from a USSR Embassy official, talks on Africa and comprehensive schools. The social side was not neglected with a bonfire night and bowling team.

It could easily have been a YC programme but the more serious nature of a Young Socialist branch was shown by the fact that representatives apparently attended every Council meeting and passed resolutions at meetings, something which Conservatives branches, as opposed to the Area committee, rarely do. By 1964 the national swing to Labour had resulted in increased membership of Merton and Mordon Young Socialists.[31]

In 1963 Alec Douglas Home became leader of the Party after the resignation of Harold Macmillan. He was a peer but a recent Act of Parliament enabled him to renounce his peerage.

Nicholas Scott was elected national chairman in 1963 and held various ministerial appointments without reaching high ministerial rank. Like Peter Walker, who preceded him, and David Hunt who followed him, he used his office to stress that the Conservative party was a caring party. He led the movement at the time of Harold Macmillan's departure and the surprise appointment of Sir Alec Douglas Home as Prime Minister. Iain Macleod and Enoch Powell refused to serve in the new administration. Nick Scott recalls the general disappointment of YCs that after there had been a Conservative government for the past ten years the hierarchy felt there was nobody in the House of Commons suitable to be Prime Minister. He has been the MP for Chelsea since 1974.

Nick Scott vividly remembers the night of the assassination of President Kennedy. Young people identified themselves with the optimism generated by the election of John Kennedy and therefore his death was a particularly tragic loss.[32]

In 1964 a new glossy magazine *Impact* was published which continued to be published at various intervals until 1969. It was a vast improvement on the previous magazine *Rightway*. Unlike *Rightway* it contained some provocative articles as well as others of general interest. In the first edition of *Impact* Nicholas Scott wrote:

The Tory Party must strive to create a more just society, nationally and internationally. In the 'Middle Way' Harold Macmillan condemned the 'casino economy' of the 'thirties. We have progressed far since then and we certainly do not want a society where a striving for equality hamstrings opportunity, but we must ever seek to see that initiative, enterprise and hard work and not 'Rachmanism' and spivery, attract the rewards of the system. We must also see that in a society in which education is increasingly important there is fair educational opportunity for all.

Overseas our major role, outside our short term strategy for survival, must be the lessening of the gap between the 'haves' and the 'have nots' who inhabit this globe. Each year that goes by the gap grows wider. We must act immediately to halt and reverse the trend.[33]

The 1959 Parliament was to be the only full term parliament lasting for the full five years since the Second World War.

Sir Alec Douglas Home narrowly lost the election and no group is more ruthless that the Conservative MPs with a leader who loses or is likely to lose an election. No account is taken by the Party of the state of the Party when the leader assumes power or as in John Major's case, the longer a party is in power the more difficult it is to win elections. If matters go sour the government has only itself to blame and the younger generation is unimpressed with constant harping back to what happened when the opposition was last in power. The average voter under 30 can hardly appreciate the effect of a Labour government and will point out that nobody now in the shadow cabinet held office in 1979.

Following the 1964 election defeat discontent spread throughout the back-benches and in characteristic unselfish fashion, which he displayed throughout his political career, Alec Douglas Home assured his successors that they would be elected democratically. Edward Heath emerged the winner.

Not everybody in the Conservative party, among them Anthony Eden, thought changing the leader was a wise choice. In a letter written to Sir Alec Douglas Home, Anthony Eden said: 'As you know I thought you had done a wonderful job to rescue the party from the efforts of Harold's last phase and Profumo. I could not have expected you to have run Labour so close. I am certain it was due to your personal leadership that did it.'[34]

The national chairman during both the 1964 and the 1966 elections was Sydney Chapman. His chairmanship marked a watershed in the Young

Conservatives. He rightly stressed the importance of using the office to project the YC movement to his own generation rather than use it to promote his own interests, ie conservation. He told me that he had always been enthusiastic about protecting the green belt but he was careful not to let such an interest play a major part in his duties as chairman.[35] Those chairmen of later years who failed to keep the Young Conservatives united could have learned from Sydney Chapman's behaviour. He was elected an MP in 1970.

## Chapter 9

# Young Conservatives in Decline During the Wilson Government

The Macleod Report, the one major report commissioned by the Party devoted to the Young Conservatives since the movement commenced was published following the election of Edward Heath. Alec Douglas Home asked Lord Blakenham to remain as chairman of the Party following the election defeat and to appoint a committee under Iain Macleod to consider the future of the Young Conservatives. The membership of the Young Conservatives had, except for the successful recruiting drive in 1956 when 27,000 new members were reportedly enrolled, dropped from about 170,000 in 1951 to 58,000 in 1964.[1]

Iain Macleod appeared to be an ideal person to act as chairman in view of the good relationship he had with the Young Conservatives and he held a number of YC presidencies, including that of Manchester and Greater London. His biographer, Nigel Fisher stated:

> his influence on the Young Conservatives was especially strong. When he was Colonial Secretary, he expressed their views at the highest level and he never lost their support and loyalty, listening to them with tolerance and respect. His humanity and idealism was an inspiration to them and he gave them generous encouragement.[2]

As Robert Carr at the Macleod Memorial Service at Enfield said: 'his influence on a whole generation of younger politicians will be his greatest legacy and it is in them that his talents will live and be amplified.'

The purpose of the Macleod Report recommendations published in September 1965 was to arrest the decline of the Young Conservatives and engineer a revival.

During the two other post-war periods when the Conservative party was in opposition the Young Conservative membership increased. Between 1964 and 1970 this did not happen. As the purpose of the report was to revitalise the Young Conservatives it can only be regarded as a failure, perhaps the biggest failure of Iain Macleod's distinguished career.

The main recommendations of the Macleod Report were to establish certain groups in every constituency where a YC branch existed and also that there would be various specialised groups. There would be in every constituency: a local group which in effect would be the present Young Conservative branch having the same mixed programme between social, general interest and political meetings. In addition, there would be a research group, to concentrate on political research choosing its own subjects, submitting reports to the Area research groups and also asked by national Area groups to comment on particular policy and to complete questionnaires.

The third group would be a local activity group concentrating on local government and community affairs. It might follow council business, discuss local government issues and attempt to channel the concern of the younger generation for better roads, schools and consumer services.

The Report proceeded to recommend to the YCs the need to offer a greater range of activities to attract new members by having numerous specialised groups. The normal and specialised groups in each constituency would be co-ordinated by the activity committee which was equivalent to the Divisional YC committee. A new officer would be appointed, a development officer whose job it was to organise new groups and to promote joint activities with the Federation of University students. Suggestions for specialist groups included: young business men's clubs or a group attached to a technical college.[3]

One of the special interest groups suggested was a supper club to try to attract back young married couples. This was not a particularly new idea because in the early 1960s a number of supper clubs had already sprung up, particularly in the North-west area. In February 1965 in the North-west there were no less than twenty-eight supper clubs, the majority directed at people aged between 25 and 45.[4] By 1992 this figure had been reduced to two. When the question of supper clubs was first mooted by a Blue Link Scheme in Kettering it was unenthusiastically received by the YC organiser, Tony Durant. The Blue Link Scheme was set up in 1961 and by July 1962 it had a membership of 150 and less than 10 were single. The average age was approximately 30. Some of the members were former Young Conservatives who had severed their link with the Party.[5]

Many of the members had young children and the programme of activities reflected this. The initial recruiting letter stated the accent would be to provide social activities for young married couples. The programme included monthly meetings of a social nature and of general interest. The male members also met monthly at a pub on a social basis. The female members met on another evening, which avoided the need for baby-sitters.

The group ran a number of fund raising activities and within nine months of the formation of the group £100 had been raised and about twenty members of the group helped with election work for the municipal election. The reservations of Tony Durant were not shared by the National Advisory Committee which in December 1962 carried by 18 votes to 12 a resolution supporting the formation of supper clubs.

It was also recommended that in each constituency there should be a finance officer to prepare a budget for approval by the activity committee in order that the YC organisation played its full part in the fund-raising activities of the constituency.

On 18 September 1965 the Macleod Report was placed before the NAC. Iain Macleod personally attended the meeting when it was expected that the meeting would enthusiastically accept the Report. The proposal presented to the NAC was that the Young Conservatives accepted the Macleod Report and agreed to implement the Report. Instead, immediate reservations about the usefulness of the report were indicated by the alternative resolution carried that the NAC accepts the challenge and spirit of the Macleod Report as the basis of a comprehensive overhaul of the YC organisation and will proceed to examine the proposals contained in Iain Macleod's letter of 15 September 1965 as a matter of urgency.

At the next meeting on 11 December 1965 the NAC's continued reservations were indicated by comments and criticism by various members. Mr Nigel Fiddes, of Greater London felt that the target of 500,000 members by Iain Macleod was unrealistic 'and in selling the Report we should not stress this as our immediate aim'. Eric Chalker showed his usual realism by stating that 'it must include a good social programme'. This was approved by the committee.[6]

Alan Haselhurst, in an article before the publication of the Macleod Report, said branches should concentrate on few but more ambitious events such as ski-ing holidays. He said there is no point having branch programmes of no interest to the members. Bigger and better balls, even if fewer, were what was needed. The desire of both the party and YCs was to multiply branches but the proliferation of small and ailing branches needed to be checked.[7]

Concern was expressed over the name 'activity committee'. The NAC decided not to take a vote on whether the report would be adopted perhaps because they did not wish to embarrass Iain Macleod and the other members of the committee. When the minutes were considered by the NAC meeting in April 1966, although the secretary had noted the remarks stated at the December meeting, these remarks were erased from the minutes and instead it was minuted that a full discussion took place.[8] Eric Chalker stated that there was vigorous opposition to the proposals in the Report by many YCs. The declared premise leading to the Macleod Report was that membership numbers would dramatically increase.[9] One suggestion in the Report to achieve this was to extend the upper age limit to 35. Like Eric Chalker, Torbay YCs were one of the branches unenthusiastic about raising the age limit to 35. They thought the difference in age between 15 and 35 was too great.[10] A recommendation in the Report was that no one over 30 could be elected to office at constituency level. However, people of the highest calibre were unlikely to want to become or remain members if they were unable to obtain office. Eric Chalker's opinion of the Macleod report was that in a bid to increase membership dramatically many of the activities suggested were considered to be completely diversionary and have an adverse effect on what the Young Conservatives believed.

The irrelevance of the Macleod Report was that the strong branches were already providing the activities recommended in the Report and the weaker branches would not have the personnel to establish or keep going the ambitious plans outlined in the Report. This is highlighted by two different constituencies.

In South Kensington after a discussion on the Report it was pointed out that in many respects the branch was already functioning on the basis of the Macleod Report's recommendations. Summing up, the chairman said 'our committee is basically the same as the activity committee and the sub-committees are not unlike the interest groups.' Being a large branch of some 600 member they already had a variety of sporting and social activities and the chairman questioned whether so many groups were desirable and whether they would find support.[11] This was the view already stated of Alan Haselhurst.

By contrast West Wiltshire decided that they were not strong enough to implement the Macleod Report and, indeed, it was obvious that the Macleod proposals would hardly be practical for the smaller YC branches without massive outside help or assistance from the senior association and even then there was no guarantee of success.[12] Other branches such as Torbay gave it scant discussion and decided that the only action that was needed was to call their committee the 'activity committee'. Obviously they had not entered into the spirit of the Report.[13]

The three factors which might have helped arrest the decline were not scrutinised. In Conservative-held constituencies MPs could do much to assist their YC branch such as encouraging visits to the House of Commons. Rear-Admiral Morgan Giles MP allowed the YCs to use the cellar of his house for social functions.[14] Also, the attitude of senior constituency members and the constituency agent was crucial in encouraging young people to undertake election work. The Report should have warned the Party that nothing deterred young people more than agents and/or party workers who are arrogant to their Young Conservative helpers.

I met both of these attitudes as a YC in the marginal constituency of Southampton Test.

The Report failed to consider whether extra resources should have been channelled to marginal constituencies as more realistic YCs of later generations were to do. The fact remained that for many years the number of Young Conservatives had been on the decline and the Macleod Report should have primarily directed itself to arresting the decline before talk of expansion.

Alan Haselhurst was elected chairman in 1966. Whereas virtually every chairman who served before him spoke confidently during their chairmanship to advertise the strength of the YCs, he took a most critical look at the movement and came to very different conclusions than those mentioned in the Macleod Report.

Another way to broaden the appeal of YC branches was to stress the importance of charitable work in promoting a branch. A wider range of young people might be attracted if, of the money raised, some be paid to the Party and some to a charity of their choice. The absence of suggestions about charitable work and Nick Scott's comments support my views. He stated that when the NAC had started to take an interest in charitable matters in 1963 it organised a collection in aid of the 'Freedom from Hunger' campaign and raised, £2,799 but there was some opposition from the Party.[15]

Perhaps if the Macleod committee had studied the various branches to discover why some were much more successful than others this would have given them better data. A local survey might have revealed that in some areas in 1966 Young Conservative membership was still satisfactory. In Amersham with a population of 14,000 there were 200 YCs well over 1% of the population[16] and East Surrey had 667 members.[17] By 1983 the average attendance in East Surrey was five which indicates the long term effect of the Macleod Report. Alan Haselhurst proposed more experiments with pilot schemes.

The Macleod Report had its supporters, among them David Atkinson who said the trouble was that branches failed to reform themselves on Macleod lines.[18] Some branches, such as Chelsea, were stated to be organised on Macleod lines. However, there is no record of any branch still run on Macleod lines following the dramatic drop in membership during the Heath premiership. Therefore the reforms proposed by Macleod were dead within ten years. It is surprising that neither of Iain Macleod's biographers consider whether it was a success or failure.[19]

Following on from the Macleod Report it was decided to mount a massive recruiting drive, called 'Action 67'. The recruiting drive had limited success. In a nostalgic look back to the happier times of the 1950s when two successful rallies were held at the Royal Festival Hall it was decided to hold another rally at the commencement of the campaign at the Royal Festival Hall at which Edward Heath gave the address. The general verdict was that it was only a moderate success.[20]

Dr Butler has given the Young Conservative membership figures in 1966 as 54,000. By the end of 1967 there had been a boost of 8,000 making a total of 62,000.[21] The YC national committee's verdict on the recruiting campaign: whereas some branches reported an increase of 30% the weaker branches continued to decline as they were too weak to mount an effective recruiting campaign.[22]

The Annual Report of the Portsmouth South Young Conservatives revealed in November 1966 the YCs set up a recruiting stall in Palmerston Road, Southsea, at which several new members were recruited. In October there were 71 members on 6 December there were 105 members and on 31 December membership had risen to 108.[23]

I consider that in many ways in this climate of youth unrest the additional members recruited in Action 67 was more laudable than the threefold numbers recruited in the peak campaign of 1956 when conditions for recruitment were so much more favourable.

This was the period of student revolt focused oddly enough throughout the world on the United States' involvement in Vietnam but overlooking that of the Soviet Union. In 1968 student protests took place at a number of universities including Cambridge and, among other places where there were protests were Poland (March), Japan(April), Colombia, Frankfurt and New York, but the most spectacular protests took place in France leading to the burning of the Bourse. However, the strongest evidence that the students' behaviour was irrational and out of step with the silent majority was shown when in view of the unrest General de Gaulle dissolved the National Assembly and called fresh elections which showed a dramatic swing to the right. The seats won by the right-wing Gaullist party increased from 97 seats to 197 seats and the Communists' seats decreased from 73 to 34. This took place before the USSR invasion of Czechoslovakia in August 1968 which was a further blow to Western Communist parties having been denuded of support following the crushing of the Hungarian revolution twelve years earlier. In spite of the pessimism which swept many Young Conservatives, their feeling at this time and their attitude of support for the establishment and law and order was probably closer to the thoughts of young people than the minority of students endeavouring to disrupt the rule of law.

In May 1968 the NAC expressed concern that the campaign gave an initial boost to membership, but in the latter half of the previous year membership had fallen off. The figures indicated that membership was probably at its lowest since the early years following its formation.[24] In the South Kensington minutes of December 1968 disappointment was expressed that the membership was down to 609 members but it was only marginally down from 643 the previous year against the background of generally falling figures throughout the country.[25].

The Young Liberals meanwhile had made remarkable progress in this period. Their more militant campaigning had gained them considerable support among young people. In 1965 the National League submitted an ambitious plan for recruitment and weekend schools in regional areas. The principal problem of communication between the Young Liberals and their senior associations remained.[26] The following year a report stated that the membership of 20,000 was larger than the Labour party's Young Socialists and the number of branches had risen to 500.[27] By 1969 national events affected the Young Liberals when it was stated that the National League were having difficulty maintaining their strength in the face of a strong swing against party politics.[28]

In 1966 Labour, having gained a majority of 100, the supporters throughout the country were in buoyant mood. They thought that the government would act decisively as the Attlee government had done in 1945 but they were to be bitterly disappointed. Within eighteen months the *Mirror*, summing up the political situation, described it 'as gloom all round', with industrial action from the railwaymen and dockers.[29] Harold Wilson was unable to inspire the electorate as Clement Attlee had done as champion of social justice. The Merton and Morden Labour party was typical in that in its Annual Report, 1966 was described as a historic year. Only three years later the Annual Report stated that those Labour supporters who were canvassed were disappointed by some aspects of the government's policy and, in two years, membership had fallen from 1763 to 1249.[30] By 1969 this Young Socialist branch had ceased to exist. Nationally, branches declined from 722 in 1963 to 457 in 1970.[31] Young Socialists were even more critical of Harold Wilson's premiership as is shown by their brochure for the 1967 conference. At home they bitterly complained of the Government's income policy, the betrayal of the old age pensioners, and they referred to the failure of the Labour government to repeal the legislation imposed by the last Conservative government restricting Common- wealth citizens residing in Britain. In foreign affairs they referred to Britain's support for the US policy in Vietnam as squalid. In 1974 when Labour were again in government their leader, Harold Wilson, was publicly criticised for having five homes.[32]

In 1968 the YCs assisted in a campaign against the Transport Bill. The Labour government had introduced a bill with the main purpose of transferring transport from road to rail. It was proposed to scrap the A B and C licences and free from control vehicles of less than 13 cwts. In spite of thirteen years of Conservative government freight transport was still substantially controlled. The Bill contained a provision that British Rail would be entitled to object to such licences on the grounds that it could provide adequate services.

There was bureaucratic provision in the Bill that for journeys of over 100 miles special authorisation would have to be obtained with details of the goods to be carried, the points of departure and delivery, the persons for whom they were to be carried and, where applicable, the occasion or circumstances in which they were to be carried. Obviously the delay and additional cost of making these applications would increase industrial costs.

Edward Heath gave an undertaking that any Conservative government would drastically amend the Bill. Peter Walker the shadow Transport Secretary was able to obtain a number of valuable amendments to the Bill.

The procedure of obtaining commercial licences was too far removed from everyday life and there appears no evidence that the numerous demonstrations mounted by the Road Hauliers Association up and down the country had any effect. This was not a subject to capture the emotions of the young, like Vietnam or anti-South African cricket tour campaigns which gained the Young Liberals considerable support. The highest profile event of the campaign was the Greater London YC Rally which occurred on 7 April 1968.[33]

Another issue of interest to the young was votes at 18. The Labour party decided to reduce the age of majority to 18 but this had little support from the Young Conservatives, which is surprising because as a youth political movement one would have thought they would wish as many YCs as possible to vote. As often happened, Eric Chalker, not following the pack, said: 'I initially opposed it, showing my ultra-Conservative background, but having thought the matter through I thought that as a youth movement it was essential that the YCs should actively campaign for it.' This was a minority view.[34] The rank and file did not support the reduction of the age of voting to 18 as was shown in the policy report published in 1961[35] and in the 1966 and 1968 YC Conferences they rejected any suggestion of the reduction of age for the vote.[36] In 1969 when the reduction of the voting age to 18 became law it was estimated that there was 7,000 voters in each constituency between 18 and 24. At that time it was seen that the capture of the youth vote was vital if the Conservative party was to be successful at the polls. Oddly, it was successful with an abysmally small youth vote of only 18%.

Hugh Holland became chairman in 1968 and was re-elected in 1969 for a second term. It had been the custom for a chairman who wished to stand for a second term to be elected unopposed but Eric Chalker was the first candidate to campaign vigorously visiting each elector. Although he fought several by-elections Hugh Holland, unlike the two previous national chairmen and the three to follow, did not succeed in being elected to Parliament. Nevertheless, the other officers at the time all spoke well of his quiet and efficient leadership and he saw the movement safely through a period when in Hugh Holland's own words 'youth was disenchanted with the establishment', but also stated that the vast majority were irritated by the over publicised minority demonstrating in a period of widespread demonstrations throughout non-Communist Europe and USA.[37]

In 1967 and 1968 the opinion polls were heavily against Harold Wilson and, as often happened in later years of a full term administration, there was a swing towards the government when nearing the end of their five-year term. By April 1970 the lead was only 3.5%. In May 1970 the Labour party did remarkably well in the local elections. They gained several hundred seats which had been lost in 1967. Harold Wilson could not resist the temptation to go to the Polls with every thought he would win.

Unlike the widespread defeatism in his own Party and the belief of the Press that Edward Heath would lose the election he confounded the opinion polls and won. A swing of 4.8% had been remarkably uniform throughout the country. As only 18% of the first time voters supported the Conservatives older voters had decisively rejected Harold Wilson and his policies. The Young Conservatives fully supported Edward Heath though he was never a politician to attract the masses. More important for a Prime Minister than popularity he was honest and efficient. These two qualities Iain Macleod admired although he never enjoyed a close personal relationship with Edward Heath.[38]

The *Ealing Chronicle*'s Chris Coolen reported: 'Ted Heath is popular among YCs because he obviously cares about their role in the Party.'[39] Nothing deterred him from attending the YC Conferences of which there were nine during his leadership, all of which he attended. In 1973 he flew straight back from Washington for the Conference and in 1974 interrupted his General Election campaign to attend the YC Conference at Southport. His question and answer sessions, which he initiated at the YC Conferences, were particularly popular and, unlike Margaret Thatcher, he did not stop these sessions when he became Prime Minister or, like his successor, complain about any of the questions. Again to quote Chris Coolen 'He does not hesitate in answering controversial ones.' Edward Heath's regard for the Young Conservatives is shown by a message sent to the 1975 Conference after his defeat in the leadership contest, made more effective by the fact he had nothing to gain.

All my political life I have owed a special debt to the Young Conservatives. Together we have attempted great things. Some of them we have achieved. Others still remain to be accomplished. Before us we have always had the vision of a Britain where barriers of class and privilege have been shattered; the vision of a society that was just, with a justice that does not drive out freedom. The vision of a Europe, united and strong, building for the future of our children and our children's children; the vision of a Conservative Party open to all the talents, standing for all our people. The trust I always gave to you was not misplaced, but there is still much to be done. The future and the vision is yours. To lift up your eyes to that future to make a reality of that vision, that is the trust I leave in your keeping now. I know you will not betray it. Good luck to you all.[40]

# Chapter 10

# Set the Party Free

The Greater London Young Conservatives' pamphlet, 'Set the Party Free', was the most significant written material the Young Conservatives produced and it was released on the first day of the 1969 Party Conference. The most eminent of the report's co-authors was Robin Squire, the Minister for Education. Other leading Young Conservatives on the editorial board were Eric Chalker and Clive Landa. It contained suggestions for major constitutional changes as well as a number of radical proposals to democratise the Conservative party.

By the British Constitution tremendous power is vested in the Prime Minister, unlike in many other constitutions, such as the USA's; he has the power to advise the Queen to dissolve Parliament. In addition to the Prime Minister's constitutional power the Conservative party has vested in its leader enormous power unrivalled by other parties. Therefore, the Conservative party, however undemocratic, has enjoyed electoral success unrivalled by its opponents.

I believe that a significant factor for the compilation of the report was that Britain had a Labour Prime Minister, Harold Wilson, and I wonder whether had the report been prepared by the GLYC when Margaret Thatcher was Prime Minister it would have proposed such radical reform.

What was not considered in the report was whether if the leader's powers were reduced Conservative success might be impaired. The Crown used to appoint a new Prime Minister after consultation with senior statesmen when a Conservative Prime Minister died or resigned as happened when Anthony Eden and Harold Macmillan resigned. Rules for electing a leader by the Parliamentary party were devised and they were first implemented when Edward Heath was elected leader and then revised for the elections of Margaret Thatcher and John Major.

At the election of Margaret Thatcher in 1975 the leadership election procedure was severely criticised. At the YC Conference it was considered quite wrong that candidates for the leadership did not have to declare themselves on the first ballot and if the first ballot was inconclusive the candidates could enter the contest at a later stage. Iain Macleod wrote a foreword to 'Set the Party Free' and ended with the words: 'We can meet their case either by agreement or argument and they are formidable. We dare not refuse to listen.'[1]

A response of the Labour regional organiser Bill Jones to action taken by Hendon and Wembley Young Socialists in distributing a pamphlet without the Labour party's consent was: 'no section, no constituency Labour party, no women's section, no ward, no Young Socialist branch may issue for national distribution any paper or journal, without the Party's consent.'[2]

Upon the publication of 'Set the Party Free' the *Daily Mirror* stated, 'Young Daggers are planted in Mr Heath's heart.' The reporter then stated that Edward Heath 'would need to keep an eye on Enoch Powell. Now he has to keep another eye on the Young Tories who are behaving like Young Socialists', but the reporter was wrong. Both Iain Macleod and Edward Heath received enthusiastic loyalty from their YCs by encouraging their Young Conservatives instead of trying to gag them as Bill Jones was trying to achieve with his Young Socialists.[3]

The document first made suggestions for constitutional change to make the executive more democratic which could only be implemented by legislation. It also contained proposals for change in the internal organisation of the Conservative party and if there was a desire for change it could be implemented by the Party.

Among changes that would require legislation the report proposed fixed term parliaments as a way of increasing the power of back bench MPs and, to ensure continuity, one-third of the MPs to retire every two years. It did not consider the extra expense. It advocated proportional representation with a single transferable vote at both local and general elections. 'Set the Party Free' implied that it was the Party hierarchy and Central Office rather than the rank and file members who opposed change to proportional representation.

However, this does not appear to be so. In 1975 a motion declaring opposition to any modification of the electoral system that would make voting more complicated for the elector, or increase the likelihood of ineffective minority governments was overwhelmingly carried.[4] Again, in 1978 a motion that the Party should examine the various forms of proportional representation and introduce the most appropriate was rejected by a large majority.[5]

I think it is doubtful whether the proposer was right in his assertion that if committed to some form of proportional representation the Conservatives would have won a landslide victory in 1979. Robin Squire would not have endeared himself to Margaret Thatcher, a vehement opponent of proportional representation, when he told the Kensington YCs in 1985 that the change to proportional representation was inevitable and that the first past the post system is unfair and said that Britain was the only country in Europe that does not have proportional representation.[6]

Clive Landa writing for CAER, Conservative Action for Electoral Reform stated that most Tory MPs oppose PR for self preservation reasons, although it is difficult to see why they should be less likely to be elected by PR. Central Office also opposed it, reflecting Margaret Thatcher's views but also that the opposition to PR indicates their opposition to any extension of democracy within the Conservative party.[7] However, I could envisage that a Conservative party would be undemocratic even if there was PR.

Robin Squire still favours proportional representation and fixed term parliaments. In his opinion both Harold Wilson in 1970 and Edward Heath in 1974 selected the wrong date to call an election.[8] Other reforms suggested were a Bill of Rights and reform of the House of Lords so that its sole function would be to act as a Supreme Court to ensure that legislation does not infringe the basic liberties of the individual and to make the implementation of election promises mandatory. The report did not consider the flood of litigation that would result from such reforms. YCs at the 1977 YC Conference rejected a motion supporting a Bill of Rights by a large majority.[9]

Proposals for local government reforms that required legislation were that (similar to parish meetings) every council would hold a quarterly meeting at which the electors could question councillors, committee meetings would generally be open to public and press, a reform subsequently enacted in the Local Government Act 1972.[10]

With reference to the internal workings of the Conservative party the most important change advocated was that the Party Chairman, who among his other duties, is in charge of Conservative Central Office, should be elected and not be an appointment of the leader. The first reason for the change was that paid employees of Central Office are currently not subject to scrutiny. When it is desired to censure Central Office redress can only be obtained by criticising paid officials, jeopardising their livelihood. The second reason for electing the Party officers is to achieve greater involvement in the voluntary side of the Party. Thirdly, electing Party officers would ensure to a far greater degree that the Party leadership is kept in touch with grass roots.

The change in the Young Conservative constitution for electing national chairmen supports this view (Chapter 16). If the Party chairman was elected it would increase the influence of the National Union of Conservative and Unionist Associations and, finally, for the first time the Conservative party organisation would be seen to be democratic.

The Labour and Liberal parties have both adopted a much wider franchise in the selection of their leaders although the report did not concern itself with the election of the leader. Nevertheless, in 1975 at the YC Conference suggestions were made that the leader should be appointed by an electoral college, the Conservative MPs would have two-thirds of the vote and the voluntary party one-third.[11]

Sir Edward Heath said he had no objection to the Party chairman being elected, his only reservation was whether the Party would select the best man or woman for the job.[12] There has never been a woman chairman of the Conservative party. During a full Parliament normally two chairmen are elected, the first to be a good organiser and fundraiser to replenish the Party funds after an election campaign and then, approximately two years prior to an election, a high profile candidate is selected.

The report also recommended that the chief whip should be elected by all Conservative MPs and also members of the standing committee on candidates should be elected. It favoured the retention of the approved list and considered whether the list should be open to public scrutiny. However, they came to the conclusion that persons should have the right to remain anonymous.

As far as the selection of candidates is concerned the report advocated that training in personnel selection by the constituency should be given to ensure the choice of a higher calibre of candidate.

As for choosing a parliamentary candidate from the approved list they argued that all members of the association had to be either registered on the previous 31 December or before the vacancy was announced in order to prevent the packing of constituencies with friends of a prospective candidate after the vacancy had been announced. A more radical solution would be similar to that governing primary elections in the USA. The selection committee would prepare a short list of persons considered to be the most able candidates. Upon registering with a political party one would be able to vote from 'a short list of candidates to select the strongest.[13]

Again, however, there appears no evidence of grass root support for any change as at the 1968 Party conference a resolution advocating primary elections was heavily defeated.[14] By the 1970s all the main parties were concerned at the quality of political activity in the constituency party.

The Conservatives tried to increase political involvement at branch level by the political contact system. Central Office circulates a written brief on a given subject with questions which it is hoped the political group in each constituency will answer although how far this is effective is questionable.

The report recommended that at both national level and constituency level there should be three committees. Finance – responsible for fund raising including social events, an organisation committee responsible for mounting 'winning' election campaigns. Thirdly, there should be a political committee with the purpose of communicating policy to the constituency members and the electorate, to question the conventional wisdom behind such policies, to provide research back up for Conservative councillors and especially between elections to persuade more people to vote Tory. Whereas they were advocating a uniform system at constituency level, is it not democracy to allow Conservative constituencies, within reason, to decide how they will organise their association?

Immediately after the Conference at a meeting of the Central Council, Hugh Holland the YC national chairman moved a resolution that the National Union executive committee should prepare a report on the extent to which the Conservative Party outside Parliament might be made more democratic. As a result of that resolution a committee under Lord Chelmer was set up. The committee first prepared an interim report. It made a number of detailed recommendations concerning the approved candidates list and also resolved that a selection committee should be appointed each year. It also forbade that spouses of candidates should be required to make a formal speech.

As far as the sitting MPs were concerned it required them to make a formal request to the Committee for re-adoption, confirming the right of constituency associations to consider other candidates approved by Central Office. There was vigorous opposition from existing MPs who felt that the report would encourage de-selection of existing MPs. Angus Maude led an attack on the new scheme describing it as disgraceful and utterly unacceptable. Accordingly the proposals were watered down. The selection committee was instead to be selected for each parliament and could have other duties.[15]

After publication of the report there was an acrimonious debate before the Central Council. A resolution was carried approving the report but postponing implementation until after the General Election. It was never implemented.

As the GLYC believed in democracy in the Party they should of necessity agree that if the constituency workers do not wish to become more democratic, that is their right. It appears that there is no great desire for radical reform. When radical proposals for change have been put to the Party conferences they have been rejected. Party workers have very much opted for the continuation of the *status quo*. However, when I put it to Eric Chalker that if people do not wish to be democratic that is their right. His answer was that, although the present membership may have no desire to make the Party more democratic there should be some procedure to enable future generations to be able to make the Conservative party more democratic if they so choose.[16]

# Chapter 11

# The Heath Premiership

The *Ealing Chronicle*, summing up the victory, said

I have the honour as editor of the *Chronicle* to congratulate the Rt Hon
Edward Heath, Prime Minister of Great Britain, Leader of the Conservative
and Unionist Party on a great victory. To him shall all the honours go.
There are pessimists in our ranks even in the high echelons of the Party
hierarchy that doubted Heath's leadership and the unselfish hard work of
the rank and file have ensured that the next government will be a Tory
one. Perhaps the most important job facing the government is the economy. I hope that Mr Macleod will follow President Nixon's courageous
decision in allowing the economy to expand without price and salary
restraint and allowing increased production to overcome inflation.[1]

Little was the editor to know that within five weeks Iain Macleod would be
dead. He had been a true supporter of the Young Conservatives. The report
of 1965 was named after him. The need for Edward Heath to find a new
Chancellor at short notice was one of the many problems which beset the
Heath government.

The government was to be dominated by two issues the first of which was
the successful negotiations of Britain's entry into the EEC and the bill's passage
through Parliament. Edward Heath is one of the few politicians who, since his
maiden speech in 1950, has never wavered from his opinion that Britain's
destiny is in Europe.[2] Harold Wilson, having failed to gain entry into Europe
because of de Gaulle's veto proceeded to oppose the Conservative government's
successful application. A sizeable number of Labour MPs opposed Harold
Wilson's policy so when the vote came on 28 October 1971 no less than
sixty-nine Labour MPs voted with the Government.

The second issue was the unsuccessful attempt to solve the economic
problems of Trade Union power, inflation and poor productivity. The government policy was to introduce an Industrial Relations Act providing legislation
for strikes and negotiations to be conducted under a new legal framework.
This was bitterly opposed by the Trade Union leaders although not necessarily
by the rank and file.

Several commentators have stated that both Harold Wilson and Edward
Heath were disappointments to their parties but whereas Harold Wilson in
1970 had lost the election with a swing of 4.8% the swing against Edward
Heath was only 0.8%.[3] In spite of much inconvenience caused to the public
by the power workers' strike and two miners' strikes causing electricity cuts it

was the Conservative MPs not the Party workers, who were calling for a change following the two defeats in 1974. During the course of Edward Heath's government he received much praise for his leadership. Major Graesser addressing the Welsh Conservative Party in 1971 said 'The Common Market has seen our leadership firm and resolute. In June 1970 the Conservative Government was given a tough assignment. It has measured up to the task and the confidence and loyalty shown by our organisation and supporters could now be seen to be fully justified.'[4]

Another problem to afflict the Heath government was the trouble in Northern Ireland. Increasing violence led to internment being authorised in 1970 and Stormont, the Northern Ireland Parliament, was suspended in 1972.

Housing was another major problem. An explosion of house prices occurred in 1972 and this was a matter of great concern to the Young Conservatives. In 1972 the prices of houses increased at a greater rate than at any time during British history so that they were out of reach for many first time buyers.

John Watson, who became national YC chairman in 1971 regarded his greatest achievement during his year of office was to have pressure for environmental matters to be regarded as a more important subject than had hitherto been the case. Clive Landa who was shortly to follow as chairman was another who, although an enthusiastic supporter of the Heath government policies, thought more emphasis should be placed on the environment. John Watson became MP for Skipton but was one of the few MPs to quit Parliament at the young age of 43 in 1987 when not defeated or in danger of defeat. Thereafter, he became the director of City Challenge for Bradford, a Department of the Environment initiative, for which, in view of his long interest in the environment, he was admirably suited.

John Watson did not seek re-election as chairman in 1972 and David Hunt was elected as national YC chairman. He had already made his mark in 1966 by being chosen to speak at the rally at the Royal Festival Hall and he won the Observer National Varsity debating competition in 1966, against Donald Dewar.

An interesting article on David Hunt appeared in the Law Society's Gazette.[5] David Hunt stood as the Conservative candidate in the Bristol South constituency in 1970. His political outlook was that the Conservatives must encourage a caring society. One of his interests as national chairman was in community industry which was one of the government funded training measures targeted at young people aged 16–18 who were low academic achievers and who experienced difficulty in finding and keeping employment. Frequently, their disadvantage included other personal and social problems, including drug and alcohol dependency and many showed criminal tendencies and lived in poor circumstances.

While he was national chairman, David Hunt led a deputation to Keith Speed, whose then Parliamentary under-secretary of State Dudley Smith, said he was extremely articulate and spoke with passion. As a direct result funding was secured.[6]

Speaking to the Torbay Conservative Women's Conference at Paignton in October 1972, David Hunt argued that higher paid workers should back-pedal on wage demands until the lower paid were given a chance to earn a decent living.[7] However he was to suffer considerable indignity upon presenting himself at the adoption meeting having been selected for Plymouth Drake. Adoption is normally a formality.

Having been proposed and seconded as the Conservative candidate an amendment was moved that the matter be referred back and 101 members voted for its referral and only 86 for David Hunt's candidature. Before the vote was taken he was questioned from the floor. He denied that he had lobbied and as a West Countryman he wished to represent a West Country constituency. After the vote went against him, David Hunt, indicated that he was not prepared for his name to go forward saying, 'if they wanted me they could have had me tonight.'

The following day the president of the constituency association of Plymouth Drake, Leslie Poole said, 'it has been a disgraceful operation and I would do anything to persuade Mr Hunt to submit himself again as I am quite convinced he was the best candidate. His performance at the meeting last night was first class both in his speech and answering questions afterwards.'[8]

Another achievement of David Hunt was to become chairman of the British Youth Council, which traditionally was a left-wing organisation. As the only chairman who had been a YC this was a considerable achievement.

Two major YC campaigns were launched during the Heath government by the Young Conservatives. The first was the CURE campaign appropriately launched by John Watson in 1972 in view of his interest in improving the environment by highlighting major problems such as disposal of industrial waste and local matters such as the provision of parks and play areas on former bomb sites which, according to *Tomorrow*, still incredibly exist twenty-seven years after the end of the Second World War.[9]

At the YC Conference in Bournemouth in February 1973 the second campaign CARE was to encourage YC branches to care for the whole community in their area as David Hunt described in the foreword to the 1973 conference brochure, 'We can show by political action that YCs are prepared to campaign for those who are less well off in our society and that we can give active support to the many organisations and societies working with the underprivileged.'

As *Tomorrow* pointed out, 'the national YC chairman, David Hunt, has shown that he is a politician who cares about young people and the issues that effect them.'[10]

David Hunt subsequently became MP for the Wirral and attained high political office as Secretary of State for Employment. He was the first Conservative minister to be invited to address the TUC.

In March 1973, Clive Landa became national YC chairman and he was the first chairman in many years to be elected unopposed and remained in office for two years. He subsequently married Lynda Chalker. Like his predecessors he showed a caring attitude. He had a particular interest in housing. Speaking at Bowness-in-Windermere at the Northern Area YC Conference in April 1973 he said

> young people are seeking from this government an even more dramatic improvement in housing conditions in the country than is forecast in the White Paper. We will not be content with the judgement that this administration does much better than the last . . . we must remove the blight where so many people exist rather than live in bad housing but an even more tragic group are the homeless people.'

He criticised the White Paper for giving too little attention to the lack of rented accommodation, the provision in many mortgages preventing home-owners with mortgages from sub-letting their surplus rooms.[11] The post-1979 Conservative Governments were to address the problem of the lack of rented accommodation by making it easier for landlords to obtain possession of their properties by successive amendments of the Rent Acts and encouragement for persons to let rooms in the house in which they are residing by exempting income not in excess of £3,250 from liability for income tax but the building societies do not possess the social conscience of Clive Landa and continue to discourage the letting of part of residential property by their borrowers.

*Tomorrow*'s headlines in July 1973 read 'Pop's Magna Carta'. The sweetest sound of all for the YCs who fought to put down 'NAB' ie the Night Assembly Bill which the reporter believed was the final triumph in a campaign against the Bill. This Bill was introduced by Jerry Wiggin, a Conservative MP in December 1971 in spite of opposition from all the national newspapers and Sarah Morrison the vice-chairman of the Party because the effect of the bill would be to stop pop festivals. She likewise thought such a complete ban was wrong. A YC lobby wrote to Peter Walker, the Secretary of State for the Environment, and said, 'if in the end this Bill cannot be satisfactorily amended at the standing committee or report stage then the Bill should be withdrawn.'

On 20 March 1972 David Hunt, Clive Landa and Roger Boaden (the YC organiser) met with Peter Walker who refused to withdraw the government's support of the Bill but asked the YCs to draft a charter to be distributed with the Act when the Bill became law. Peter Walker announced, on 5 May, the formation of a Pop Festival Advisory Committee and showed initiative by selecting a young chairman, Dennis Stevenson aged 27. David Hunt also sat on the committee. Meanwhile, when the report stage was reached on 7 May, the Young Conservatives had persuaded several of the younger members of the committee, some of whom themselves had been Young Conservatives, to prevent the Bill proceeding further. Among those was John Selwyn Gummer. He, by filibustering, was able to talk out the Bill. The Bill was dead.

The Pop Festival Advisory Committee report which took a year to publish eventually delivered its verdict to Geoffrey Rippon, the minister who had now replaced Peter Walker as Minister of the Environment. The report confirmed the views of the Young Conservatives that a pop festival was a perfectly reasonable and acceptable form of recreation. Rampant promiscuity and violence were not a feature of pop festivals although the report's findings that public parks and beaches are dens of iniquity by comparison with pop festivals was surprising. Participants in pop festivals were compared favourably with football crowds and rock music fans.

The committee thought that environmental damage, could be avoided by a series of rules, by which the promoters must abide, to ensure proper compliance with health and sanitation standards and local police should be called in to assist with security, the promoters to pay the cost. A joint working party for each festival consisting of the promoter and representatives of the local authority, Church and voluntary services should be established. Perhaps the YCs' idealism was exposed when there was no indication of what happened to those who broke the rules.[12]

*Tomorrow* may have exaggerated the YC influence in defeating the Bill but the YCs' close contact with the young MPs such as John Selwyn Gummer obviously increased their influence, unlike the Young Socialists national committee whose relationship was generally fraught with difficulty. No doubt a campaign by the Young Socialists against a Labour government's bill would have been treated by the Party with horror. The YC attitude in connection with this Bill was in sharp contrast to the lack of action of later YCs concerning the equally ill fated Football Spectators Bill, supported by the Thatcher government. This brought much ill feeling among young people but it was not the YCs action that killed the Bill. It was never implemented because of the recommendations of Lord Justice Taylor in his report following the Hillsborough disaster.

One matter of concern to the Conservative Party and particularly the Young Conservatives following the 1970 election victory was the abysmally low vote of 18% of the first time voters who voted Conservative compared with 34% for Labour.[13] During the 1950s there had been a tremendous increase among the young in support for the Conservatives but an equally rapid decline in the youth vote in the early 1960s at a time when Harold Wilson emerged as Labour leader. The Conservatives had surrendered to Labour its predominant position among the young which, following its decisive defeat in 1945, Lord Woolton's inspired chairmanship of the Party had done so much to increase.

The climate of youth rebellion in the late 1960s against the establishment was hardly a helpful environment in which to increase youthful support for a centre right party. The lack of enthusiasm of both the Conservative opposition and the Young Conservatives to an Act passed by the Wilson government to extend the franchise to those between the age of 18 and 21 was a hindrance in influencing those electors. However, the more aggressive policy and campaigning methods of the Young Liberals, particularly over their successful support of the banning of the South African Cricket Tour in 1970, gained for their Party much support from the more idealistic of the young between the 1970 and 1974 elections. The statistics indicate that the increase of support amongst first time voters for the Liberal party from 8% to 28% is as follows:

12% from those who failed to vote in 1970
7% from Labour
1% from Conservatives

There was also a tremendous increase in the Liberal vote between 1970 and 1974 first manifesting itself in successful by-elections and then in the February 1974 election the Liberal share of the votes increased by 11.8% which was responsible for the five years of Labour government notwithstanding that the Conservatives polled 0.7% more of the votes cast than Labour. The share of the votes cast for the two main parties compared with 1970 General Election fell:

Conservative          8.6%
Labour                5.9%[14]

This indicates that the rise of over 300% in the Liberal Youth vote between 1970 and 1974 was far greater than that of their seniors. Among young voters the damage caused by the Liberal party was greater, the reverse was the situation among the other voters.

As always, there was a conflict between the Young Liberals and their seniors as with the other main parties. The Liberal party was a coalition of those who saw the Party as a moderate party between the extremes of Labour and the Conservatives and those who advocated that the Liberal party should be a radical party of the left which was the opinion of the Young Liberals. They were propounding policies more radical than those of the Labour party, which had very much swung to the right in the late 1960s under Harold Wilson, in spite of protestation from the Conservatives to the contrary. At this time the Liberal party dithered. However, the above figures prove that had the Liberal party followed the lead of the Young Liberals it might have made dramatic inroads into the Labour vote. This could have provided the breakthrough it had strived for since the First World War but which had constantly eluded it. The Liberal party was assisted by the performance of the previously discredited administration of Harold Wilson.

The Conservative party, in spite of its 1970 election victory, rightly paid considerable attention to the youth vote. At the YC Victory Conference in 1971 Peter Thomas, vice-chairman of the party struck a sombre note when he said, 'If the party shall continue to obtain only a minority of the votes among young people then the long term prospects are very bleak.'[15] He was absolutely right. The failure of the Party to capture sufficient votes of the young between 1964 and 1974 resulted in the loss of three out of the four elections (a record for the Party worse than at any time since the First World War). If the Party had obtained the proportion of support among the young that it received in 1959 and 1979 three of those elections would probably have been won. It was decided that a long-term remedy was the appointment of a director at Central Office and twelve youth development officers one to each of the Area offices to work alongside the staff of the YCs and the Federation of Conservative Students.

The basic purpose of the director of youth was to encourage young people to form an allegiance with the Conservative party and the job description was:

i) to reduce the alienation of young people to the Conservative Party and to improve communication in both directions.

ii) direct as a link between youth groups and voluntary agencies in the Party at all levels

iii) to have a catalyst and stimulus role in relation to the established youth wings of the Party

iv) to develop opportunity for young people to participate in decision making processes.[16]

Jimmy Gordon who was formerly director of the Youth Rehabilitation of Offenders Agency, was a moderate Conservative and subsequently became an officer of the Tory Reform Group. Edward Heath gave enthusiastic backing to this project which was short-lived. However I have no doubt that Jimmy Gordon's achievement was one of the factors which helped the dramatic increase in the youth vote between 1975 and 1979.

After Margaret Thatcher became leader of the Party she showed little enthusiasm for this work. Jimmy Gordon left his office to go into commerce and thereafter no successor was appointed and the Party proceeded to appoint just a YC and FCS organiser thus reverting to the previous situation.[17]

Among activities Jimmy Gordon arranged was a seminar involving four senior Conservative spokesmen and the heads of over 100 major voluntary organisations. He claimed that a rapport of mutual trust had been built up which had not been matched by other Party organisations although Parliamentarians, in the Labour party in particular, still have an individual credibility with many voluntary agencies and have made great publicity out of those contacts. He also said that the performance of his department varied from area to area but it was a healthy sign that they were now being approached by a number of agencies to help in a furtherance of specific activities before they are launched on the world, a contemporary 'Shelter' report being an example.[18] In a radical change of Party policy Jimmy Gordon was happy to share platforms at youth meetings with Peter Mandelson who was employed in a similar role by the Labour Party. However, if the department was to be a success it was important that enthusiasm was instilled into the Areas to follow the same policy and it was claimed his department has achieved some success. The Annual Report of the 1973 Wales Youth Department revealed a youth survey organised by Welsh YCs which prospective candidates might find useful for organising election strategy.[19]

Contacts were made with outside groups to gather opinions for the ill fated Youth and Community Bill which Alan Haselhurst was intending to sponsor through Parliament. This bill proposed measures aimed at assisting young people under the age of 21 in developing personal and social relationships and instruction in participation in the community and had wholehearted YC support. Greater London YCs in the previous year had highlighted the problem by mounting a demonstration protesting at the lack of youth facilities with YCs wearing T-shirts with the slogan 'Youth is a wasting asset'. Clive Landa the GLYC chairman received notoriety by being called to speak at the Party Conference while wearing one.

The Bill encouraged greater use of the facilities by requiring the recreational and sporting opportunities available in the locality to be publicised. Further provisions in the Bill were the appointment of youth and community workers, the formulation of projects directed to assist young people who were not members of any club or similar organisation. Advice on careers and occupations and information and advice on welfare services for young people would be provided. Citizens Advice Bureaux already provided much information but young people might be more encouraged to seek advice from a body especially established for their needs, particularly if staffed by young people. It would also be the duty of the Local Authority to have regard for the special needs of young people suffering from mental or physical disabilities, those belonging to ethnic minorities and those appearing to be most susceptible to criminal and anti-social influences.

Another provision would be the establishment of a youth council in each area. A similar body, the British Youth Council, exists at national level. The purpose of the Council (with membership restricted to those under 26) would be to discuss the services available for young people and those services which were needed. The bill would place a duty on the local authority to provide suitable accommodation for those under 21 who no longer reside with their parents or guardians and have no permanent residence. In view of the considerable number of teenagers in our cities sleeping rough this seems to be even more relevant today than in 1974.[20]

Obviously, the implementation of the Bill would increase expenditure at national and local level but if young people were encouraged to use their time constructively instead of committing acts of vandalism and crime, as Alan Haselhurst stressed in the Second Reading debate, in the long term the Bill could result in a saving to the community if criminal activities reduced.[21]

The efforts for the Bill to be passed were frustrated by the February 1974 election. It was then included in the October 1974 Conservative election manifesto. One would have thought that this was a Bill for all-party support, but the 1974 Labour government showed no interest in the bill despite many Labour MPs, including Joan Lestor, giving the Bill their unqualified support at the second reading. The bill was re-introduced after Margaret Thatcher's government took office in 1979 but it was allowed to be talked out and the Government's lack of enthusiasm lends support to critics who maintain that since 1979 the Government has channelled too many resources into assisting bright young people at the expense of the less able. The YC minutes of 1979 and 1980 indicate that the YC leaders in the early days of Margaret Thatcher's premiership had no doubt about the desirability of the Bill.

Perhaps it was appropriate that Eric Pickles was the national chairman when the Bill fell. He was to become leader of Bradford City Council in 1989 and pursue Thatcherite policies (Chapter 13). In retrospect he had no doubt about the desirability of the Bill. He rejects any suggestion this was a socialist Bill. The treatment of the Bill in spite of the rhetoric at the end of the day, indicates that since 1979 the principles for which the YCs stood had no influence on the Cabinet.[22]

Between 1970 and 1974 the Young Conservative achievements were well documented in the YC newspaper *Tomorrow*. This publication was far more political than its predecessor *Impact* which was a glossy magazine. Although *Impact* had provocative political articles it also had articles of general interest. What *Tomorrow* failed to reveal was the rapid decline of membership at branch level. This indicated that the more political nature of the YC meetings hindered rather than aided recruitment in spite of advice constantly offered by the Party that the way to revive the movement was to make it more political.

Yorkshire Area minutes indicate that between 1969 and 1973 membership fell 35% from 1,350 to 900.[23]

The Secretary's report to the AGM of the West Wiltshire Conservative Association of February 1967 indicates that there were 60 YC members at Melksham, Trowbridge had 85 members and Warminster 60 members.

By 1970 the annual report showed that the organisation was basically still in good heart. By 1971 the report stated that there had been a marked decline in YC membership. Various reasons were advanced, that the movement thrived best in opposition and reported that there were no active branches. The Young Conservatives were limited to suppers at divisional level. The reality is that Young Conservatives now had to compete with other youth organisations and there was frequently a lack of suitable premises for meetings, coupled with a far greater mobility among the young, making the establishing and maintaining of a group much more difficult.

In 1973 the Young Conservative story was not a happy one. There had been a saga of struggle and reward in no way commensurate with the efforts, not unhappily confined to West Wiltshire. In 1974 it was a fact of life nationally that the Young Conservative movement was not what it was. It was also a fact that the Party needed the support of young people. The problem was how to remedy it.[24]

In Chippenham in 1967 there were 239 members, in 1968 157 members, in 1973 29 members, and by 1974 just 1. In common with YCs nationally, in 1972, Chippenham was struggling for survival and in 1973 the report said Chippenham must not be allowed to disappear.[25] Torbay YCs 1974 AGM held just after the fall of the Heath government stated, 'the YCs have not been too successful throughout the country during the Conservative government as membership fell but we hope it will pick up now.'[26] Their optimism was to be justified in the short term but not in the long term.

## Chapter 12

# YC Revival During Callaghan Government and Lib/Lab Pact

Having lost the October 1974 election the Conservative party were in a very pessimistic mood. They had lost nearly 1.5 million votes since February 1974 and were the main moral losers: almost 2 million less people voted in October 1974 than in February 1974.

One of the reasons why a lower percentage of the electorate voted was that the election was held on an older Register but it also showed that a vital percentage of the electorate who might have voted Conservative were disenchanted with the Party. The vast number of the people who voted in the February election but failed to register their votes in October appeared to have been Conservatives who were unenthusiastic about the return of another Conservative government. The only party to gain was the Nationalists, they gained 18 seats and the Conservatives lost 20 seats. However with a majority of only 3 it was not a victory for Labour as in 1966.

Considerable praise must be given to the political skill of Wilson and Callaghan who were able to survive for 4½ years with such a slender majority.

Evidence would indicate that the Conservative youth vote was as poor in October 1974 as it had been in February 1974.[1] Over eight years the Conservative party had lost three out of the last four elections and no parliamentary party is more severe on its leader, feeling he might lose the next election, than the Conservative MPs.

Edward Heath lost the first ballot and withdrew from the campaign before the start of the Young Conservative Conference, and, therefore, did not attend but sent the YCs a message but it is quite clear from the reports of the Conference that the YCs were still very favourably disposed towards Edward Heath, as were most of the constituency parties. Chris Gent said we wanted the grocer not the grocer's daughter alluding to the name given to Edward Heath by *Private Eye* because he was responsible for negotiating how a whole range of products would be treated under EEC legislation if our 1961 application to join the Common Market had been successful.[2]

With a slow start to Margaret Thatcher's leadership, as often happens when a new party leader takes over, the rank and file of the Young Conservatives were dismayed by the lack of attack. Supporters failed to realise that during the course of Parliament so much happens to make policies out of date and an opposition leader needs time to survey the situation and decide upon the tactics to employ and the people to take over the key positions in order to win the next General Election. John Smith and Tony Blair received similar criticism.

At the 1976 Conference, Roy Galley, Yorkshire Area chairman, said the leadership in the Parliamentary Party was working hard but however worthy its efforts the fact remained that in the eyes of the general public, it was a damp squib of an opposition. He said, 'Everywhere I go I find increasing frustration about the sound of silence on the front bench.' He went on to say with a feeling of nostalgia, 'Ever since the end of the Macmillan leadership the public perception of the Tory party has been abysmal.'

However many did not support that view because I believe it would be a strong argument to maintain that, of eight post-war Conservative administrations, the government between 1959 and 1964 was the least effective. Jennie Yarwood of Bristol went on to complain that the Tory party was dying on its feet, due to its inactivity in formulating policies; 'where are the policies?'

Phillip Taylor's remark that we needed leadership was somewhat premature, because Margaret Thatcher was to become a most dynamic leader of the Conservative Party. Some would criticise her policies but it would be difficult to criticise her leadership because of the way she dominated both the Party and the Cabinet. On occasion she even acted without the consent of the Cabinet, as when she gave the USA consent to use our air bases to bomb Libya.

At the 1976 YC Conference Margaret Thatcher said that Britain needed less bureaucracy, lower taxes, fewer controls and the difference between success and failure needed to be more marked. The *Yorkshire Post* commented 'had not the Tories always stood for these principles' and Edward Heath would have emphasised economic growth and more order in industry whereas Margaret Thatcher put more emphasis on freedom with economic efficiency an attractive by-product. Edward Heath's ambition was for a Britain noted for its efficiency whereas Margaret Thatcher's ambition was a Britain noted for its freedom.[3]

Under the influence of Rab Butler in 1946 the Conservative party moved to the centre and there it remained under the successive leaderships of Churchill, Eden, Macmillan, Home and Heath. Nevertheless, there had always been free market influences wishing to move the Conservative party much more to the right. Beaverbrook attacked the Industrial Charter and Enoch Powell persistently advocated a free market economy.

During this long period the membership of the Party was more to the right than its leaders and likewise there had also been numerous instances of Young Conservative membership being also more to the right. At the 1976 Conference the *Guardian* commented on the officers stating that, in tune with the change of leadership the YCs have moved to the right this year.[4]

For many years YC leaders' views continued to be nearer those of Edward Heath than Margaret Thatcher.

Keith Joseph, one of the great intellectuals of the Conservative party was almost unique because he was very much a supporter and architect of Edward Heath's social policy being the Minister for Social Security and was responsible for initiating Thatcherite politics. Although the Heath government received little credit for its social security policy Keith Joseph was extremely active pursuing the principles of 'One Nation' policy. His aim was to locate and then assist those members of the community who had not benefitted from the tremendous increase in material wealth that had taken place since the 1950s. This was illustrated by three provisions.

The first was a special pension to people over 80, many of whom had retired before the implementation of the National Insurance Scheme and thus were ineligible for State benefit. The second was provision of pensions for widows between the ages of 40 and 50. (Perhaps in view of the increasing number of women working in any event, that was an over-generous provision.) Third was an attendance allowance provided for the seriously disabled and frail elderly people who needed a great deal of attention both day and by night, later extended to all those needing attention by day or by night. Five years later nearly a quarter of a million people benefitted from these measures.

The Labour party likes to pride itself as being the party more likely to be prepared to assist those who were worse off but the Heath government had a proud record in this connection. This policy was enthusiastically supported by the Young Conservative leadership who developed a real appreciation of the plight of the less well off in society. Indeed, Clive Landa said the Young Conservatives thought the Heath government should do more for the inner cities.[5] It is my belief that the YC leadership were more in tune with reality than many senior party workers of safe Conservative seats who have little appreciation of the problems of inner cities in areas with a high ethnic minority population and although they give lip service to the need for development and modernisation often oppose it when it is on their own doorstep. This social conscience of YC leaders continued throughout the 1970s and most of the 1980s as is shown by their attitude to race, and by the policy of the NAC to hold some meetings in deprived areas such as Gateshead and Liverpool and coach tours of these areas were made.[6]

Every administration since the war thought it had the remedy for arresting Britain's economic decline, which had commenced during the late Victorian era. Labour administrations concentrated on public sector investment to achieve its aims. The Conservative party always envisaged a freer economy but had only marginally reduced the huge involvement of the State in the economy. Government had initially intervened in the economy on a massive scale to ensure that all resources should be directed towards supporting the prosecution of the Second World War and such controls were enthusiastically extended, initially, by the policies of the Attlee government.

The result of both policies had been a stop-start process of expanding the economy in order to arrest the decline and then reversing its policy with the imposition of credit squeezes to prevent inflation and assist balance of payment difficulties. Keith Joseph concluded that in order for British economic ills to be remedied a freer economy was needed than that which the two previous periods of post-war Conservative governments had envisaged. Keith Joseph realised that he did not have the charisma and/or the support of the Party to become its leader. He saw Margaret Thatcher as a person who was likely to carry out his policies although she had been a loyal member of Heath's cabinet as Minister of Education.

The next question was whether the Young Conservatives could survive much longer as a credible youth movement when its membership had been in continuous decline for twenty-five years. No figures had been released of any internal calculations of the membership during the Heath government although there is reference in Jimmy Gordon's report in 1975 that the membership stood at 30,000.[7] This is not consistent with later reports which indicated that by the end of the Heath government membership was considerably lower than 30,000. It is also quite clear that the claims of both Chris Gent and Robert Hughes of a dramatic increase in membership was justified in 1975–9.[8]

The best evidence of tremendous increase in the strength of the Young Conservatives is contained in the minutes of the Wessex Area YCs. At the Annual General Meeting of April 1975 Wessex Area stated that its membership which had been in decline for many years had been reversed, some branches doubling membership and most showing increased figures.[9]

A report presented to the Wessex Area half-yearly meeting in November 1975 showed that membership had increased from 1,700 to 2,151.[10] This trend continued and in November 1978 there were 2,879 members.[11] The renewed confidence at branch level was shown by reports of both Highgate and Hornsey Central YC branches that the party was still attracting members.[12]

The increase of support among the youth was further encouraged by the increase in membership of the Federation of Conservative Students. In December 1977 Chris Gent speaking to the Winchester YCs said that membership of the Federation of Conservative Students had risen from 5,000 to 20,000 in the last three years.[13] Stan Taylor in a book on the National Front mentioned the surge in the mid-1970s of the Conservative youth movements, the Young Conservatives and the Federation of Conservative Students. The latter, in particular, had not flourished in the late 1960s and early 1970s but began to gain support from 1975 partly because of the liberal brand of Conservatism they offered, which included liberalism on race issues.[14]

In 1975 Tony Kerpel became the YC national chairman after only 2½ years in the movement. Increasingly, the candidates for high office have received their political tuition and background from the Union of Conservative Students before joining the ranks of the YCs. During his year of office the major event was the Referendum on Europe campaign.[15] No YC branches have been discovered which did not support the referendum campaign.

The YC national committee in 1975 organised a housing campaign with four main purposes which was stated to influence the development of Conservative party policy, to involve YCs in the run-up to local government elections, to create a publicity impact showing YCs' concern for this major social issue affecting young people and finally to enable YCs to contact their local MPs and councillors and pressure groups.

Between 1975 and 1976 there was to be a build up of information to identify local problems and to make contact with other organisations and local councillors involved in housing. Areas ran their own events in support. As part of this campaign Yorkshire held a course particularly aimed at Conservative councillors on homelessness among young people although, regretfully, in view of the tremendous increase since 1979 this would be far more relevant at the present time.[16]

Michael Jack became YC national chairman in 1976 and was only the second national chairman from Northern Area, Fergus Montgomery having achieved the same distinction in 1957. The highlight of his year of office was a visit to the People's Republic of China which had been arranged previously by Edward Heath and they were known to the Chinese as Heath's children.

A thoughtful act of Edward Heath was to travel to Heathrow to see the YCs depart. It is thought that this impressed the Chinese. If a person of Edward Heath's status travelled to the airport to see the delegation depart it must be an important delegation. The delegation was received at the highest level by the then Chinese Foreign Minister, Chiao Kuan Hua and Madam Li, deputy Head of State. It received coverage in Chinese daily papers although the NAC were disappointed it did not receive any coverage in British daily papers.[17]

They visited many important centres such as Peking and Shanghai, also schools, factories and communes as well as seeing the major cities' underground defences. The delegation was left in no doubt that the Chinese considered the possibility of a nuclear war between the USSR and the USA was inevitable and they supported the UK's stand on a united Europe working with the United States as a bastion against Soviet imperialism.[18]

One of the purposes of a political youth movement should be to alert its seniors to opinions of young people on various topical issues so the party can examine whether its policy towards such issues should be changed or, when it is not directly involved, to use the considerable influence that any government has to seek such change. An example of a case where it had direct influence was the Night Assembly Bill.

Another achievement during Michael Jack's year of office was a lobby which he organised to see Hector Monro, opposition spokesman on Sport and Norman Fowler, opposition spokesman on Transport. Michael Jack assembled a comprehensive lobby to draw attention to the then lack of televised motor sport. The deputation included representatives of racing car manufacturers, circuit owners and Stuart Turner and John Davenport on behalf of the rallyists. The purpose of the lobby was to make MPs more aware of the economic and technical importance of motor sport and that James Hunt's great achievement in winning the British Grand Prix was not televised. Hector Monro agreed to

take the matter up with the Director General of the BBC, saying that the sport
needed sponsorship and the income from television which other sports enjoyed.
James Hunt's successors in the sport, Nigel Mansell and Damon Hill, were to
have no lack of television coverage.[19]

Another achievement of YCs during Michael Jack's year was the publication
of nine key policy statements covering subjects such as transport, agriculture,
the Third World, defence, foreign affairs, comprehensive schools and race
relations. Much that was advocated in these reports was not particularly radical.
Perhaps the most far reaching of the policy documents was 'A credit to us all'
dealing with the greatest problem of the welfare state: the poverty trap where
it pays people not to work.

It is my opinion that the authors of the report, Stephen Parry, Julie Shaw
and Tony Jerram saw the problem but the remedy proposed relied too much
on people's honesty. It comments that all post war governments have failed to
help the very poor and shows the importance Young Conservatives gave to
this subject compared with today when the stress is on incentives, tax cuts and
the reduction of unemployment at any cost.

The report suggested a guaranteed minimum weekly wage of £22. (Equal
in 1995, on the basis of a 37 hour week, to approximately what the TUC
have requested of £4 per hour.) It did not believe that a guaranteed minimum
wage would result in loss of jobs or that the result of a guaranteed minimum
wage would result in wages falling to the minimum and that if a business was
so inefficient that it could not pay the minimum wage its downfall would be
deserved. There would be a tax credit of approximately the amount of supple-
mental benefit so if the taxpayer received less than the tax credit he would
have no liability for tax. Those not in employment would receive the credits
as of right so the unemployed could cash the coupons.[20]

However, it did not take into consideration that many people might cash
the coupons to which they were not entitled, although one check would be
that employers would be obliged to receive tax credit coupons before paying
wages.

No doubt the cashing of credits to which one was not entitled would be a
criminal offence as well as a civil offence. In practice, even if it was a criminal
offence, the Department of Social Security discovered it would not be cost
effective to prosecute in many cases of fraud and turned its attention to trying
to prevent fraud by making enquiries at likely places such as building sites
where people on benefit might be working and force them off benefit by
refusing to make them any further payments. On two later occasions YCs at
the 1982 National Conference and in a policy report in John Guthrie's
chairmanship supported an integrated tax credit system. However such a system
did not appeal to all YCs – Martyn Dearden said at the 1982 conference 'it
was a socialist resolution and any system of credits represents a transfer of wealth
from the workers to the shirkers.'[21]

Another interesting suggestion in the report was the abolition of National

Insurance contributions and it is surprising that no politician seems to be giving this matter serious thought. When Beveridge originally designed the social security system he thought that it would be self financing but now receipts from contributions form only a small part of the cost of the social security budget. The fact that the contributions are a form of taxation rather than contributions to an insurance fund is highlighted by the splitting of the National Insurance functions between the contribution and benefit agencies. If income tax was increased to take into account the loss of the employees' contributions and Corporation tax increased to take into account the loss of the employers' contribution a huge saving in costs to the government and employers would result. Investment income would also suffer the uniform rate of tax and whether any relief should be given to such income is a political policy decision.

In 1977 Chris Gent, another product of the radical Greater London Young Conservatives, was one of the few chairmen with no political ambitions.[22] He said that he did not wish to be included on the candidates list as entering Parliament did not appeal to him and he has had a very successful business career, becoming managing director of Vodophone. No doubt his tuition in the Young Conservatives still influences him. When asked for his views on the Social Chapter he said 'I cannot see anything wrong with the Social Chapter. A good employer would have no difficulty in abiding by its terms.'[23] He had started his career as a bank clerk and came to prominence at the Party Conference in 1969 when having listened to speeches advocating increased expenditure on defence stated 'how can spending more money on armaments be reconciled with the promise of tax cuts and expenditure on social services?' His speech met with a hostile reception.[24]

Just after Chris Gent assumed office an embarrassing situation arose over a member of the NAC, Demitri Argyropulo. He was the Surrey County Councillor for Ashstead but Epson Divisional Conservative Association refused to support his re-selection by his local branch Ashstead because he supported comprehensive education and the constituency association was particularly concerned about the loss of Epsom Grammar School. A petition of seventy Ashstead members attempted to have him reinstated as the official Conservative candidate. Meanwhile, Demitri Argyropulo threatened to stand as an Independent Conservative candidate although it was reported that his local YC branch did not support him.[25]

A motion was brought before the NAC deploring the action of Demitri Argyropulo standing as an independent candidate. Nevertheless, the committee rallied to his support, rejecting the motion by 4–24.[26] This was perhaps because he changed his mind at the last moment and did not stand, although he refused to give the local press his reasons but no doubt he was influenced by possible damage to his political career.

Unlike in other issues such as unemployment, Europe, race relations and crime, YCs interest in education has been generally minimal. Demitri Argyropulo being the one outstanding exception. His interest was rewarded in 1979 when he was elected chairman, while still under 30 after a postal ballot, among six candidates, of the Conservative Party Advisory committee on Education consisting of leading MPs, Conservative academics and leaders of educational authorities.[27] In 1981 in a debate at the Party Conference he proposed a motion asking for support for a resolution calling upon the Government, local educational authorities and school governors to ensure that comprehensive schools, which the vast majority of young people attended, are staffed, rehoused and organised in such a way to provide a curriculum adequate to the needs of the rapidly changing world young people face when leaving school.

The mild rebuke to his speech by Sir Keith Joseph was typical of many Conservatives with a lack of interest in comprehensive education. While congratulating Demitri Argyropulo on opening the debate vigorously and well, what he did not address himself to was the concern over the comprehensive system not only in relation to academic standards but also behaviour, discipline and work habits. However, what Sir Keith Joseph did not mention was whether selective and private schools performed better because of more adequate funding, a more intelligent intake and more supportive and affluent parents rather than the inadequacy of the schools themselves.[28]

Robert Hughes stated that one of the priorities given to the 1979 election was in promoting mock elections in schools. It was believed that the way those over 18 voted could have an effect on the result of an election.[29]

In 1981 the YCs produced a school pack. It acknowledged that many teachers are Left wing (it is probably correct to say that the more militant teachers are Left wing). This results in the leadership of the NUT being dominated by the Left wing. They also pointed out that some organisations not supposedly political, often managed to address sixth form groups without presenting alternative argument. It also drew attention to the danger of Left-wing teachers using the classroom as an opportunity to express their political views to a captive and often trusting audience.

This particularly applied to those teachers who supported CND and, therefore, allowed speakers to talk to the children about CND without the children being told of the opposing view. By dropping nuclear bombs on Japan lives may well have been saved because the military and civilian casualties could well have been greater if the Allies had had to invade Japan. Also the possession of nuclear weapons by the USA and the USSR may well have prevented a third world war occurring at any time until Gorbachev became General Secretary of the Communist Party of the Soviet Union.[30]

Whether Robert Hughes was right in his suggestion that the result of a school election might influence how people vote is questionable. Having myself stood as a candidate in a school mock election, I would have thought that most children would support the candidate whom they liked rather than support the candidate's policies. However, Robert Hughes was right to pay attention to school elections as the Young Liberals did so in both 1970 and 1979.

Nevertheless, I disagree with the assumption often made that because YCs were becoming younger and younger they were less useful. Indeed I am certain that young people are often more influenced by their peers than their elders. The many YCs who were still at school and who were receiving political education through the YCs by hearing their own Conservative MP speak, attending conferences or weekend schools must have had an influence on their fellow pupils in the Left-wing environment of many schools.

St Ignatius Loyala was an early proponent of the view that the most advantageous age to convert children to catholicism was under 7. We have seen how the pre-war Conservative party endeavoured to influence young schoolchildren by the formation of the Young Britons after Communists with the Pioneers, and the Labour party with the Socialist Sunday Schools, had tried to influence quite young children with Left wing doctrine.

The pack warned that if the classroom was being used to preach Left wing doctrine the practice should be exposed, but it should not be allowed to generate into a witch-hunt against Left wing teachers.

Perhaps the pack should have stated that the YCs should have been similarly critical if the classroom was used to preach virtues of Thatcherism. If there was difficulty in using the word Conservative perhaps a group named after a respected former Conservative politician, a Peel or Macleod group would have been more appropriate. Although it is stressed no group should attempt to be established without the consent of the Headmaster if opposition was encountered, YCs should use the service of their president, their MP or prominent local politician to exert their influence.

The 1979 election for national chairman was between Robert Hughes and Demitri Argyropulo – both very much to the left of the party which Robert Hughes won by three votes. Robert Hughes paid a special tribute to Demitri Argyropulo whom he had beaten so narrowly and who was elected vice-chairman.[31] Robert Hughes was a harsh critic of those in the Party calling for tougher measures to limit immigration and he said that the Home Secretary should be thoroughly ashamed of the suggested measures contained in a White Paper suggesting that new immigration rules should be introduced to prevent women bringing their husbands or fiancés to the UK.

If Labour had gone to the polls in the autumn of 1978 instead of spring 1979, the outcome of the election might have been different but the widespread industrial disputes of the winter of 1979 ensured a Conservative victory. The Union strikes of that winter undermined the government and were about to cause the downfall of the Labour government in 1979 as they had achieved the downfall of the Conservatives in 1974. James Callaghan in his autobiography generously acknowledges 'during the dispute the TUC had stood by helplessly, the influence of the TUC General Council washed away by a tide of industrial irresponsibility' and he and his Cabinet colleagues told the General Council there must be an agreed code of Trade Union practice to eliminate the excesses of picketing.[32]

'The Government looks like Napoleon's grand army in retreat from Moscow' was not the comment of the Tory press but of Woodrow Wyatt writing in the *Sunday Mirror*.[33] A union leader was right when he told his supporters that 'the TUC can have a Labour government with some unpalatable policies: otherwise there would be a Conservative government.' The irresponsibility of those Trade Unionists who were militant, as Callaghan had said, would ensure a Conservative victory. Robert Hughes' claim that the majority of young people voted Tory is supported by expert analysis. Accordingly, there had been a dramatic increase in the youth vote between the 1974 and 1979 elections. Robert Hughes explained that the reason for the change of policy was that the Labour government's policy towards young people had been appalling. Unemployment had more than doubled with youth unemployment increasing eightfold and the Act in 1974 extending the Rent Act meant that it was more difficult for young people to rent property.[34]

Geoffrey Pattie addressing NAC about the increase in the youth vote, following the 1979 election said

> in February 1974 the Conservative party attracted less than 20% of the first time voters. The fact that by 1979 the figure had risen to over 40% may reflect at least in part the tremendous and sustained effort made by the Party to make its presence felt among young people. For too long the parties of the Left have held the youth arena themselves. Since 1974 the Conservative party aimed at the youth organisations, the YCs and FCS to ensure that at least the Conservative cause should not go by default. The fact that this had been achieved with limited resources reflects the tremendous credit to all concerned. There has been a tendency in the past for the Conservative party to indulge in a rather dreary cycle of brilliant groundwork in opposition followed by a run down once we took on the important business of government.[35]

In spite of this rhetoric, within two years the YC budget would be reduced by 70%.[36] As in the past the rank and file were more right wing than the leaders but there was a sense of unity although, as Chris Gent said, 'we had many heated debates'.[37] The YC conferences, were favourably covered by the media including the *Sun*, the paper most read by young people although it is hoped that the broadsheets would appeal more to the intellect of YCs.[38] Also covered were many of the other YC activities. Two of the four chairmen during the Callaghan government became MPs.

At the conference presided over by Robert Hughes in February 1980, he claimed that during the late 1970s membership had increased by 50%,[39] the YCs had at last arrested the long decline that had taken place over the previous twenty-five years and then managed to increase membership significantly. The FCS had also made great strides with its branches in the universities and colleges flourishing, as in the 1940s, appeared to be a good omen for the medium-term future of the Conservative party which kept Labour from power throughout the 1980s and beyond. The Young Conservatives had become an articulate but by no means a subservient body. The optimism of the Young Conservatives as they entered the new decade was indicated by the revival of a YC national magazine called *Democrat*. The previous one, *Tomorrow*, had died five years earlier.

# Chapter 13

# Decline of the YC Movement
# 1979–1983

At the beginning of the decade the prospect for the Young Conservatives looked bright following its revival in the late 1970s.

The 1980s showed the decline in membership of the Young Conservatives and the eventual disbandment of the FCS. In 1978 the strength of the Young Conservatives was reported at 27,500 and in view of the increase of the late 1970s various persons commented that the strength in 1979 at 30,000 would appear likely to have been fairly accurate. In the early 1980s the YCs lost one-third of its strength. The annual report of Dorking YCs showed how the confidence of the late 1970s was converted into pessimism a few years later.

The 1979 report mentioned that the YC branches continued to flourish under the guidance of Simon Marshall. It referred to dedicated support in establishing a strong YC organisation within the Division. They enjoyed well attended political and social functions and had been fortified by having interesting and important speakers.[1] By 1982 it reported that despite efforts with recruitment, the YC chairman Eric Eve and his team had a year of holding on rather than growth within the YC movement. Although small in numbers branches continued regular meetings with a new programme of events. The few have been rewarded in that their efforts provided £500 for the constituency.[2]

In 1983 it was stated that it should be noted that no great improvement had been achieved in recruitment of new members. There was a general decline in YC activities in many constituencies. No satisfactory solution could be found.[3] Another more disturbing feature came to light. Whereas up to 1980 the YCs had been remarkably united, divisions were now engulfing the movement as is illustrated by the report. Even the flagship of the Young Conservatives, the Greater London Area, which provided a variety of talent during the 1960s and 1970s including Lynda Chalker, Eric Chalker, Clive Landa, Robin Squire and Chris Gent.

The Annual Report of the GLYCs in 1982 stated 'these were relatively hard times for Young Conservatives with membership levels both in London and in the country as a whole at an all-time low level.' The branch census conducted at the beginning of the year indicated that out of an estimated national membership of considerably less than 20,000 the GLYCs share was in the region of 1,000.[2] In 1984 the position had deteriorated because the report stated, 'the GLYC has suffered mixed fortunes this year.' On the gloomy side, early in the year there was in-fighting among the YCs which prevented Party work being carried out. The energies of its officers and executive members were taken up with arguments and irrelevancies. A special meeting was called and a degree of unity within the GLYC was imposed, albeit on the basis of a reluctant truce.'⁵ For thirty-five years the Young Conservatives' strength was its unity. There was a healthy respect for the different views held by different people who, nevertheless, belonged to the same party. Divided, the YCs could, like the Young Socialists and Young Liberals become an electoral liability that people started to question whether the YCs should continue—a thought that in previous generations would have been as outrageous as YCs applying to affiliate to CND. Whereas in the 1960s the national officers were very concerned at the sharp decline in membership there appeared no evidence in the 1980s that the national officers shared such worries or were concerned that a large numbers of YCs were feeling that the national officers were not behind the prime minister.

Nevertheless, although the opinion that the NAC was not behind the Prime Minister was mistaken, should not the national officers have been concerned that this was felt by a sizeable number in the constituencies?

Minutes of the NAC of the time make it clear that on most measures the national committee supported the Government's policies, though they quite rightly expressed their concern about the rising tide of unemployment and, particularly later, of the decline of our manufacturing base which may make historians of the future look back and decide that this period was not such a glorious period of economic history. The YCs' concern over this matter is indicated by the fact that in 1986 in the ballots for the selection of motions, thirty-three of the NAC supported the motion concerning manufacturing industries, only the motion concerning the independent nuclear deterrent received more votes.⁶

One of the central themes of the election campaign which the Conservative government implemented was economic measures to shift the burden of taxation from direct to indirect taxation to bring public expenditure under control and to reduce the deplorable high level of inflation. Except for a period between 1989 and 1991 the ability of the Conservatives to first reduce inflation then stabilise it at a low level would be one of the greatest achievements of the whole period of Conservative government from 1979.

On 7 July 1979 the NAC unanimously complimented the Chancellor on his courage to implement such a long overdue package of Conservative measures in the Budget and hoped that in the near future it would continue the trend towards lower direct taxation, particularly a substantial reduction in the level of capital taxes and a complete abolition of the investment income surcharge.⁷

Eventually it was proved that in spite of the savage Defence cuts, public expenditure rose under the Conservative government due to the increased social security bill caused by receipts from National Insurance contributions and taxation declining in proportion to benefits paid to an ageing population. This is the problem that far-sighted economists and politicians had foreseen and for which there is no easy answer. There is every indication that public expenditure under a Labour government, including one led by Tony Blair, would have to be at a higher level in order to implement their election promises.

On most matters the factions of left and right of the Young Conservatives of the 1980s agreed with trade union reform, privatisation and the sale of council houses. At the time many of the YC officers were sceptical of the government's anti-inflation policy which sent unemployment to record levels. Many of the national officers, such as John Guthrie, advocated at the time that the economy should be inflated in view of the soaring unemployment figures.[8] It now appears that Margaret Thatcher's opposition to it was correct in not making a U-turn as had Edward Heath in 1972 when unemployment soared.

Although Margaret Thatcher had many critics, among them prominent former YCs Terence Wray and Gerry Wade, she had at least an equal number of enthusiasts both among the young and not so young.[9] Like many other critics both inside and outside her Party, in 1984 YC Paul Sparks wrote in a YC magazine how he 'admired Margaret Thatcher's resilient strong will, her leadership ability and the way she has steered firmly to her promised course.'[10]

In 1980 Eric Pickles, the most recent national chairman to be elected an MP, succeeded Robert Hughes as chairman. Before becoming an MP he achieved considerable fame in 1989 as leader of Bradford City Council and pursued vigorous expenditure cuts in education and other services. He acknowledged that in pursuit of such policies he was influenced by the policy of Thatcherite Wandsworth Council although Conservative control of Bradford City Council only lasted one year. He said he had a quiet year in office as YC national chairman, an ill omen for a politician who needs challenges to meet and problems to be seen to be solved.[11] The 1995 drought may well assist ex-YC John Gummer as Secretary of State for the Environment in his political standing.

From a study of constituency and area minutes quoted and other minutes, by the time Eric Pickles relinquished his chairmanship the YCs were in the decline which accelerated during the chairmanship of Iain Picton who had previously been vice-chairman of the Federation of Conservative Students.

In 1979 he had been a parliamentary candidate in Rochdale standing against Cyril Smith. In his year of office there was a disastrous YC conference at Harrogate where numbers attending declined from 1,800 to 600.[12]

During Iain Picton's year of office Ian Gilmour was elected president but he was replaced in Margaret Thatcher's cabinet reshuffle in 1981. Iain Picton has said he believed that Margaret Thatcher had made a great mistake in dropping one of the most formidable intellectuals in the government, 'it was a tragic loss.' This brought a vote of no-confidence which was substantially lost by Nick Tate. The motion stated that the comments concerning Ian Gilmour were not acceptable and did not represent the views of the Young Conservatives and it was detrimental to the Young Conservatives if the chairman made comments of this kind.

Nick Tate's argument was that the press should not be given the impression that the Young Conservatives did not fully support their leader.

Iain Picton's supporters said that he had been elected by a big majority and he should be allowed to undertake the job for which he had been elected. However, it was the lack of understanding of the opposite view that made the YCs of the 1980s different and less effectual than previous generations of Young Conservatives.[13]

In the early years of her premiership Margaret Thatcher retained many of the Heathites in her cabinet in key positions. James Prior at Employment and Francis Pym in the Foreign Office, although due to her power of leadership the cabinet had pursued the policies for which she stood. Unfortunately, her use of 'wet' to describe those who wished to pursue a more moderate policy encouraged division in the Party rather then unity. If the divisions in the Conservative party during John Major's administration cause the Party to be a long time in opposition the blame should be placed on her rather than John Major. Although Edward Heath's policies were in some respects in sharp contrast to Margaret Thatcher's, many other objectives were identical. Nevertheless, he bequeathed a far more united party to his successor and, as one would expect, many Young Conservatives had differing views.

The attitude of the Young Conservatives of the 1970s and 1980s was quite remarkable. Chris Gent mentions that debates were heated but tolerant.[14] However, his remark criticising Margaret Thatcher for not offering Edward Heath a position in her cabinet did not bring forth the hostile response that Iain Picton's remark did.[15] The divisions which almost unnoticed were appearing in the Young Conservative ranks of the early 1980s would fragment the Young Conservatives in the late 1980s and the Parliamentary Party in the 1990s.

Two significant events occurred outside the control of Iain Picton, one internal the other external. The internal problem was the reduction of 70% in the YC budget. Although the NAC budget was substantially reduced the most serious consequence was the loss of the youth officers at area level. These were the officers who helped to establish branches and in particular assisted in keeping alive branches in trouble which, but for their efforts, might collapse. This was a strange action to take place within two years of Geoffrey Pattie's speech stressing the importance of Young Conservatives and the youth vote.

The external event was the decision by David Owen, Shirley Williams and Roy Jenkins to leave the Labour party and form the Social Democratic party. It was their belief that they would attract moderate opinion from both Labour and the Conservatives. The SDP made considerable impact on the Federation of Conservative Students when five of the officers, or former officers, defected to the SDP. Apart from a misleading report in *The Times* of defection by Young Conservatives no prominent YC officer defected and only one Conservative MP, Mr Brocklebank Fowler did.[16] The SDP's greatest prize would have been Sir Edward Heath. Although he was unhappy with many of the policies pursued by his successor he preferred to fight for what he considered the correct policy from within the Conservative party not from outside it. Therefore although the impact on the Young Conservatives was minimal, as it was on the Conservative party, the impact on the Labour party with people of the stature of David Owen, Roy Jenkins and Shirley Williams campaigning against them rather than for them was devastating.

From 1982 to 1986 Iain Picton served as a Lambeth councillor and from 1984 to 1987 he chaired the Tory Reform Group. He became a researcher for London Weekend Television and then a producer of the BBC programme *On the Record*.

Iain Picton died in 1990 and Harry Phibbs who, because of his right-wing views, was instrumental in having Westminster Young Conservatives closed down and was banned from the 1988 YC Conference, wrote a generous obituary in *The Times* which indicated his many talents although the policies they advocated were so different. He described Iain Picton as

> a member of an influential group of Young Conservatives to the left of the Party who kept the movement loyal to Edward Heath during the early years of the Thatcher premiership, along with his protegees: Phil Pedley, John Guthrie and Nick Robinson. He was a strong critic of racism and an enthusiastic supporter of European union.[17]

Harry Phibbs noted the respect Iain Picton obtained for his aggressive debating style which he deployed skilfully against the hard left Labour in Lambeth. His undoubted abilities were shown when he was asked by a right-wing think tank to prepare a paper on freeing the housing market.

Iain Picton was succeeded by Phil Pedley. He had written during the early years of the Thatcher leadership a letter to the *Telegraph* stating there were a great many people who would have preferred Edward Heath to have remained as leader. 'We hear a lot about the return to basic Conservative principles, I would have thought that one of the basic principles is loyalty.' It is difficult to see how one can complain about the leader not being loyal (there is no evidence that she was other than a loyal Secretary of State under the Heath government) and the reason she was elected was that she was offering a policy different to that of Edward Heath.[18]

The fact was that the contemporary YCs were aware of that letter and Greater Manchester YCs published a pamphlet strongly criticising Phil Pedley for writing the letter.[19]

In 1982 the Falklands conflict dramatically altered the political scene. In the light of what has since transpired the conflict and tragic loss of life might have been prevented if, prior to the war, the intelligence reports of the Argentinian threat had been taken more seriously. Margaret Thatcher's resolve to free the islands won her wholesale commendation far beyond the confines of Conservative supporters. Further evidence of the support of Young Conservatives for the Campaign was a resolution in September 1984, passed unanimously, that the NAC believed that the attempts of the opposition parties to criticise the sinking of the *General Belgrano* amounted only to crude political opportunism.

> We affirm our support for the manner in which the Falklands Campaign was managed by Her Majesty's Government and requests the Government to continue its vigorous defence of the *Belgrano* decision which was a necessary military act designed to save British lives.[20]

It appears that criticism of Richard Fuller's not supporting the Falklands Campaign was unjustified and I can find no evidence of any Young Conservative being other than enthusiastic about Margaret Thatcher's leadership while the campaign was progressing. The political effect of the successful execution of the Falklands Campaign was to ensure a Conservative victory at the next General Election which was called in May 1983.

An internal survey of Conservative Central Office indicated that the Conservatives maintained its share of the youth vote at 42%, almost identical to the overall Conservative share of the poll.[21] (As the opposition was equally divided compared with 1979 the Conservative share of the vote fell by 1.5% yet gained 58 more seats). The highlight of the campaign was a rally of 2,000 YCs at Wembley (Chapter 26) which brought criticism as did the Sheffield Labour Rally led by Neil Kinnock in 1992. Whereas the Labour rally was followed by failure at the polls the Conservative rally was followed by victory.

As in 1979, the Young Conservatives targeted a number of marginal constituencies. In 1983 Phil Pedley was a candidate but failed to be elected, the seat not being sufficiently marginal to give him a chance of winning. He polled 17,923 votes.

However, unlike the Liberal revival of the 1960s and 1970s there was no revival of the Young Liberals in spite of the dramatic increase of votes for the Alliance. Young Liberal officers complained about the low popularity of both partners among the young.[22]

Before the 1983 election the left of the Labour party finally succeeded in persuading the Party to adopt a programme of unilateral disarmament and withdrawal from the EEC. However, following the Labour party's most disastrous election campaign since before the First World War these policies were quickly assigned to the dustbin following the election although the policies of withdrawal from NATO and EEC had been supported by the youth of the Labour party and the young Liberals. In the campaign a Young Liberal spokesman stated that the Alliance manifesto is incompatible with the views of the Young Liberals.

> We strongly reject the defence and disarmament section. The Young Liberals would scrap Trident, Cruise and Polaris. We do not believe that continued membership of NATO is desirable as we want a United Europe which is independent of both superpowers.

He then admitted they had more in common with CND than the Alliance manifesto and stated that the disarmament section appears to have been written solely by David Owen with little or no regard for the policy and beliefs of Young Liberals but was a vote catching exercise inserted at the last moment in a fit of desperation.[23]

However, they did not consider the failure of the policy of appeasement in the 1930s that in the pre-Gorbachev era, a United States of Europe independent of the super powers was not practical as the Soviet Union would not be prepared to allow the countries of Eastern Europe to join a United Europe not dominated by the Soviet Union. David Owen being Foreign Secretary under the Callaghan government was vastly more experienced than they were and this was the view of the British electorate who cast more votes for the Alliance than in any other post-war election. Since the 1950s, the Campaign for Nuclear Disarmament found many supporters among the ranks of the Young Socialists and Young Liberals but very few among the ranks of the Young Conservatives.

At the first YC conference in 1961 Howard Aplin must have been a brave delegate, a Young Socialist observer described him as not being well received, he was the lone opposer of a motion re-affirming its belief that until agreement on multilateral disarmament is achieved possession of nuclear weapons is essential and condemns the activities of those who would deprive the country of its independent deterrent. He claimed that unilateralists were sincere in their beliefs and that some Conservatives belonged to the movement. There was only one vote against the motion.[24]

Various Labour local authorities passed resolutions declaring their area to be a Nuclear Free Zone although it is difficult to see how any useful purpose could be achieved. Southampton Young Conservatives took up the challenge because the chairman Stephen Welch wrote to the then Soviet President, Chernenko asking for an assurance that the Soviet Union would abide by the Nuclear Free Zone. Not surprisingly he never received a reply.[25]

During the 1980s the Young Conservatives, in spite of their difficulties, were able to carry on a number of effective campaigns, the most effective being a campaign for multilateral disarmament which YC records indicate gained their unanimous support. CND's lack of a cogent policy is illustrated by their opposition to both the Falklands campaign and the Gulf War although neither conflict had any connection with nuclear weapons and without force it is inconceivable that either Argentina or Iraq would have withdrawn. Argentina had plenty of time to withdraw and thus save the lives of their nationals and those of the United Kingdom once the South Atlantic Fleet set sail and once the first bombs were dropped on Iraq that country could similarly have negotiated a withdrawal. On the other hand Turkey seized Northern Cyprus by force and in the absence of armed intervention has so remained. The effect of the policy of CND, therefore, would have been to reward aggression. Further, CND opposed US missile bases on UK territory in the hope that the Soviet Union would respect our security.

In the pre-Gorbachev era nothing would have pleased the Russians more than seeing the growth of CND throughout Western Europe and such action might well have postponed the ending of the Cold War rather than hastening its demise. The USSR old guard were not like Gorbachev who, realising that the USSR were not winning the Cold War, saw little point in pursuing it.

In 1983 Dorking YCs carried out a survey which showed the support among the young for CND. Of the forty-three interviewed under 21 twelve favoured CND, thirteen between the ages of 21 and 25 and eight out of eighteen between the ages of 26 and 30. Just under half opposed Cruise missiles being based in the UK. Another question was whether they were alarmed by the USSR or the USA. The majority were alarmed by the USSR rather than the USA.[26]

In 1981 the Greater Manchester YC chairman, Steve Fitton, organised a loudspeaker/leaflet tour of four centres: Royton, Salford, Rochdale and Manchester. Manchester City and Merseyside YCs were led by chairman Jeff Green in a Landrover, the cavalcade traversed seven shopping centres, Liverpool, Wavertree, Toxteth, Wallasey, Heswall, West Kirby and Birkenhead. Phil Pedley at that time national vice-chairman, and responsible for the campaign, was a target for attack in CND's *Sanity* magazine, the *Morning Star* and the *New Statesman*.[27]

Yorkshire YCs in 1982 organised a dramatic counter demonstration using a light aircraft in opposition to a CND rally, while Harrogate YCs took on CND youth in a debate calling for unilateral disarmament which was defeated.[28] In 1984 Western Area YCs, upon hearing that CND were planning to march on RAF Locking, decided to mount their own counter protest. When the marchers arrived Western Area Young Conservatives were there in strength to greet them with anti-CND placards. These activities helped to remind young people that many regarded the policies of CND as weak and irrelevant and an expense to the community in such activities as picketing Greenham Common Airbase.[29]

Another activity was the British Youth Council. In the 1970s, David Hunt succeeded in becoming chairman of the British Youth Council. In the early 1980s the YCs had considerable influence on this body and they enjoyed a cordial relationship. The BYC was invited to send a representative to the YC Conference of 1981 and the YCs co-operated with the BYC on a seminar on the ill-fated Youth and Community Bill. This was an important part of their work, influencing the young leaders of non-political bodies who, in later years, might become leaders in their own right.

For two years the presidency was held by a Conservative MP. In 1981 there was a very successful election when Mark Wooding defeated a left-wing candidate for the post of vice-chairman. The chairman was non-political as he was from the Scouts. The treasurer was a Conservative and there were three candidates from the far left who were defeated.[30] In January 1984 after a number of motions unpopular with the YCs such as a policy criticising council house sales, promotion of information on homosexuality, policy against the Church, private and grammar school education, policy critical of US involvement with the shooting down of a Korean Airline plane, both the FCS and YCs withdrew from the British Youth Council.[31]

It is debatable whether this was a wise course as by withdrawing they were less likely to have any influence on the non-political young leaders such as Young Farmers and Scouts. Another event during Phil Pedley's busy two-years' chairmanship was on 22 August 1982 when there was a demonstration on the twenty-first anniversary of the building of the Berlin Wall and the fourteenth anniversary of the invasion of Czechoslovakia. John Guthrie said the march was intended as a symbolic gesture to show our opposition to the denial of basic freedom.[32]

The report of the possible infiltration of the YCs by the National Front (discussed in chapter 14) brought the Young Conservatives more notoriety than any other event in the whole history of the movement.

Yardley Young Conservatives, 1949 (see Ch.5)

YC National Rally, Birmingham, 14th June 1952, The Hon Mrs J Geddes, speaking during the mock parliament. Featured in the photograph are Philip Hocking, (Chairman on Midland YCs), (See Ch.28) who subsequently became an MP, and Clyde Hewitt (see Ch.27), who was subsequently elected Chairman of National Executive.

Anthony Eden addressing the YC Rally at the Royal Festival Hall, 17th November 1956 Featured in the photograph are Geoffrey Finsberg, (YC National Chairman 1954/57), Peter Walker (YC National Chairman 1958/60), who later became a government minister, Andrew Bowden, (YC National Chairman 1960/61), Marcus Fox, now (Chairman of 1992 Committee), and Barnie Hayhoe, an MP for 18 years (see Ch.26)

Edward Heath cutting the cake celebrating the 21st birthday of the YCs in 1966. Assisting him and to his left is Elizabeth Steel (YC National Vice-Chairman), to her right is Stephen Norris (YC National Vice-Chairman). To the right of Edward Heath is Alan Haselhurst (National Chairman 1964/66), to his right is Jimmy Ferguson (YC National Vice-Chairman).

YC visit to China.
Left to right, Tony Kerpel (National Chairman 1975/76), Richard Simmonds, (Subsequently MEP), Chinese General and Demitri Argyropulo (see Ch.12)

# IMPACT

## Special Conference Edition - Blackpool 1977

# WANTED!!..

## Tuesday

**JAMES CALLAGHAN** alias
"Jim 'll fix it", is wanted for questioning
by the British Electorate in connection with
a series of offences committed in the country
over a period of four years.

## POSES AS: (MOSES!)

British Prime Minister and known
to shelter from the Electorate
with the Liberals when on the
run.

## SUSPECTED OF:

Wilful damage to the economy
by taking and driving away
incentives.

Indecent exposure of the nation's
defences by disarming public opinion.

**Catch me if you can. Maggie!**

Occasioning grievous bodily harm to education standards with the offensive weapon of
the Comprehensive system.

**BAILED** to appear before the British Electorate for judgement in the summer of '77
but failed to surrender to public opinion.

**LAST SEEN** heading towards another election victory and members of the Conservative
Party are warned that this man is armed with phoney but plausible policies..........
............could be dangerous.......do not tackle unless well prepared.............

# MARY WHITEHOUSE talks today!!

## MORALS, FREEDOM & SOCIETY TODAY.... details inside....

# The Magazine of the
# North Western Area Young Conservatives

Party Conference YC Daily News-sheet 1977.

YC National Committee meeting with Margaret Thatcher then leader of the opposition. Left to right, Roger Pratt (National Organizer), Jenny Turco, Margaret Thatcher, Chris Gent (Chairman), Stephanie Read and Demitri Argyropulo.

YC Conference in Harrowgate, 16 February 1980. Left to right, Eric Pickles. (Chairman 1980/81), Nigel Lawson, adressing the conference, (who later became Chancellor of the Exchequer), Anthea McIntyre, chairing the meeting, (National Vice-Chairman), Roger Pratt (National YC organizer) and Robert Hughes (National Chairman) (see Ch.28)

Young Conservatives attending YC National Conference at Torquay, 10 February 1990. (see Ch.28) (Photograph: Courtesy of *Herald Express*, Torquay)

YC Conference, Torquay, 10th February 1990. Margaret Thatcher adressing the Young Conservatives for the last time. (see Ch.28) (Photograph: Courtesy of *Herald Express*)

John Major adressing the YC Conference, Eastbourne, 8 February 1992. To his left Murdo Fraser (National Chairman) to the right, Chris Patten (Chairman of the Conservative Party), and Martin Potter (National Vice-Chairman) (Photograph: Courtesy of *Eastbourne Gazette*)

Young Conservative Officers (Western Region). Left to right, Graham Jackson (Salisbury), Dinah White-Adams (Weston Super-Mare), Daniel Smy (Chairman of West Dorset YCs) and Ben Yearsley (Weston Super-Mare)

Democratic Youth Community of Europe, June 1993. Andrew Rosindell (YC Chairman 1993/4), with Lady Thatcher, following a reception for representatives. (See Ch. 30)

# Chapter 14

# The National Front

A new problem affecting the Young Conservatives in the early 1980s, was the National Front which had made considerable gains between late 1972 and mid 1974, peaking in May 1973 when Murdoch Webster saved the NF's deposit in the West Bromwich by-election. Support for NF candidates in the 1979 General Election declined sharply.

It appeared that either as a result of concerted effort or individual action, because the breakthrough into British politics which the National Front had anticipated had not materialised, the Conservative party and particularly the YCs became a refuge for people who wished to leave the NF, or saw more opportunity to advance their views in the Conservative party.

From my own study I have no doubt that the NF aimed at infiltrating the YC movement. Certainly, the YCs of the late 1970s did not provide the sympathetic forum for racist ideas.

The first report I found of a meeting inviting an NF speaker was in 1973 by Sheen YCs. The tone of questions put to the NF candidate indicated that although the YCs were interested to hear the NF candidate they were largely unconvinced.[1]

Dorking YCs were more hostile. In 1976 when a NF spokesman addressed Dorking YCs he was met with jeers and laughter when he suggested repatriating all non-whites who had come to Britain. YC spokesman Donald Kerr said he did not think the National Front made any converts.[2]

In a book written by a member of Ella Young Conservatives association with suggestions for branch meetings a NF speaker was among the suggestions.[3] I believe a small number of YCs of the early 1980s felt that the authorities were giving unjustified support to the ethnic minorities as opposed to the indigenous population. John Phillips, the chairman of Eastern Area, proposed that the £750m spent on foreign policy could be spent on repatriation of Britain's black population.[4] A magazine called *Dreadnought* produced by Uxbridge Young Conservatives very much bore the mark of National Front literature.[5] A number of NF members were found in Young Conservative branches but it appeared that almost invariably they were promptly expelled.

A report in the *Plymouth Herald* reported that 'one Mark Spong (28) joined the Plymouth Young Conservatives in November despite having stood as a National Front candidate at a recent by-election. He admitted he was a member of the National Front when questioned and was subsequently expelled.'[6]

A member of Coventry South-West Young Conservatives was discovered to have been a student organiser of the NF. A meeting was called to expel him but he handed in his resignation. A West London YC was expelled when his NF membership card fell from the glove compartment of his car as he drove a YC home. A Young Conservative was expelled in Preston when it was discovered that he was a former election agent for the NF.[7]

Further concern of the activities of the National Front is shown by NF members joining a march leading to a YC rally organised by Greater London YCs in support of the Falklands Task Force. They also commenced selling their publication *Bulldog*. Another extreme right wing organisation also distributed literature with the intention that this be handed out to the general public. The chairman of Yorkshire YCs felt so strongly about it he withdrew the Yorkshire contingent from the march and seized the literature. Following his complaint the Police removed the NF members from the march. Some were seen to be wearing both NF and YC badges.[8]

Nevertheless, it is a mistake to exaggerate the importance of infiltration of the Conservative party by the National Front. It appears *Searchlight* unwittingly published an apparently forged letter written by Richard Franklin stating

> those of us who have chosen to work quietly through the Conservative Party are not altering one iota our basic ideology. Far from it! The new strategy merely represents a change of style. Compare the Tory Party of today with say the Tory Party of Edward Heath. The change is nothing short of dramatic. The Party and its supporters are now saying and doing things that would have been considered unthinkable a few years ago. Even the nature of the Right of the Conservative Party is moving from laissez faire liberalism to nationalism. Of course they have a long way to go but the situation is looking good. A large number of former nationalists are now in the Conservative Party Associations throughout the country. Big city conurbations blighted by immigration and crime are fruitful territory but even more rural areas like Norfolk are proving surprisingly promising.[9]

Any material indicating that the National Front's infiltration of the Conservative party needs to be considered as to its genuineness. Whereas, it may be considered *Searchlight* had a left-wing bias, the same cannot be said of the Board of Deputies of British Jews. The Conservative party should have been particularly worried that the Board of Deputies were sufficiently concerned about the possible infiltration of the Conservative party by the National Front that they opened a special file on the matter.

The NAC was influenced by at least one complaint from a Jewish organisation that the National Front might be endeavouring to infiltrate the Young Conservatives and resolved to set up a committee of enquiry on 28 September 1982 under the chairmanship of Demitri Argyropulo.[10] It was decided, however, to delay finalising the report until after the 1983 General Election. Unfortunately, this document was leaked at the 1983 Party Conference; the source of the leak was never discovered.

Phil Pedley expressed his annoyance concerning the leak before the National

Committee. Although the report was approved by the NAC on 28 January 1984 with only one dissenter the full report has never been published, only a summary.[11] It confirmed there had been sporadic instances of infiltration in YC branches by members or ex-members of the National Front or the British National movement and it stated that too many MPs, instead of using their energy in generating worthwhile debates on harmonious race relations, used race and immigration in an emotive manner.

Meanwhile in the election campaign in 1983 it was discovered that Thomas Finnigan was standing as a Conservative candidate for Stockton South, whereas he had previously stood as a National Front candidate for Birmingham in 1974 and had not disclosed this in his application to be included on the prospective candidates' list. Having seen the nature of the applications to obtain entry on the list there can be little doubt that he misled the selection committee. It is a long tradition that a small minority of MPs change sides but they certainly do not try to suppress knowledge of their former allegiance.

As a result of this report and the débâcle over Thomas Finnigan the procedure for selecting Parliamentary candidates was tightened and in particular candidates were asked to disclose whether they had previously been members of any other party. *Panorama* put on a programme in January 1984 investigating to what extent far-right groups which had connections with, and were infiltrating, the Conservative party also had connections with the National Front. Phil Pedley took part in the programme.

Phil Pedley strongly defends his participation in the programme. The BBC had said that if he did not participate, the reporter would endeavour to obtain the information from other NAC members and he felt, as Chairman, it was in the interest of the Party and the YCs that if anybody was to appear on the programme it should be him. His participation caused much consternation among YCs. Various MPs sued for libel as a result of the BBC *Panorama* programme and most recovered damages from the BBC. Although Phil Pedley was initially sued the proceedings were withdrawn and he recovered his costs.

I am sure that Mark Worrall is right when he said that the NF were not significantly skilled to obtain the election of any of their members to any high office in the YCs.[12]

However, by the mid 1980s the National Front realised their attempt to seriously infiltrate the Young Conservatives, mainly due to the vigilance of the YCs themselves, had failed and Tim Mitchell who became Young Conservative organiser in 1988 was of the opinion that the activities of the National Front were no longer a threat to the Young Conservatives.[13]

The 1984 YC Conference took place shortly after the *Panorama* programme. This conference is considered in some detail because in my view it showed a remarkable change. For the next few years YCs became preoccupied in fighting among themselves rather than with their opponents.

Shortly after the conference opened Portsmouth YC Mike Smith challenged

Phil Pedley concerning the programme. Describing the scene, Anne Turner, reporter of the *Portsmouth Evening News* states that Mike Smith said that he could not refer to the legal aspects at the conference but in his fifteen years with YCs nothing had been more of a threat to the movement than Phil Pedley's action. Two MPs started libel proceedings against Mr Pedley and five more took action against the BBC. His remarks drew applause and shouts of support from the floor. Phil Pedley ordered him to leave the hall. Mike Smith said he left quietly of his own accord. Anne Turner continues her report that after a short time he was allowed to return for the remainder of the conference although this was denied by Phil Pedley.

Having spoken to Phil Pedley and Mike Smith they disagree on the amount of support Mike Smith received.

Mike Smith admitted that Phil Pedley as chairman had a right to order him to leave but said, 'After 14 years of Conservative party conferences I knew better than to argue with the chairman.'

Phil Pedley argued that Mike Smith at 31 was too old to be a YC. Mike Smith said, 'The upper age limit for a long time has been 35. I find it inconceivable that the YC national chairman should be unaware of the fact.'

It is correct that subject to the rules of the Constituency association one could be a YC up to the age of 35 although one could not hold office above 30 (other than that of president or vice-president). Mike Smith was stated to be vice-president. However a President or Vice-President would not normally atend a YC conference as a delegate unless he was of YC age even if he was entitled to do so.

Phil Pedley denies he received any money for appearing on *Panorama*. This was confirmed by the *Portsmouth Evening News*'s short report on 11 February 1984. It is unfortunate, therefore, that the rather fuller report two days later failed to mention that fact.[14]

In an equally misleading report by the South Eastern area on the Conference it stated the first embarrassment for the national officers was when somebody stood on the rostrum and asked Phil Pedley how much he had been paid for his controversial appearance on the programme, which obviously indicated the writer's sympathy lay with Mike Smith. Like the *Portsmouth Evening News* the article wrongly failed to inform its readers that Phil Pedley had denied receiving any payment. However, this report was correct in stating that although one of the debates was on video nasties it was not video nasties but the BBC's video nasty *Panorama* that preoccupied the conference.[15] The *Sunday Times* reporter was of the same opinion.[16]

John Selwyn Gummer stated at the conference there had been no significant infiltration of the Young Conservatives and launched an attack on guilt by association. Surely any infiltration of the YCs should not be taken lightly and it is naive to think that unless there is an obvious explanation for such association the public and press do tend to find guilt by association and, therefore, an MP would be most unwise to participate in any organisation with even the slightest link with the National Front or other extreme right-wing groups.[17]

The ill feeling against Phil Pedley prevailed long after the end of the conference from a number of YCs as well as a section of the main party. It is unfair to blame Phil Pedley for the infiltration report in any way as the commissioning and findings were clearly the committee's decision passed with only one member voting against it.

I believe the real victor of the conference was neither Phil Pedley nor Mike Smith but the left wingers who would take delight in the continued decline of the YCs throughout the 1980s.

When I asked Mike Smith whether he was concerned about the unity of the Young Conservatives he said surprsingly that on this particular matter unity did not concern him.[18] The Conservative party's strength for the past 100 years has been its ability, unlike the record of its opponents, to close ranks behind its leader in times of crisis such as during the Munich crisis in 1938, Suez in 1956 and Profumo in 1963. This sense of unity which deserted the YCs in the 1980s deserted the parliamentary party in the 1992 Parliament. However, due to the courageous action of John Major in risking defeat by offering himself for election as a leader this sense of unity may yet return to the parliamentary party which, even if the Conservatives are defeated at the next election, the Party will put up a credible performance as it did in 1964. Phil Pedley supports my view concerning the importance of unity in the Conservative party.[19]

However, the YCs were to forfeit one of their greatest assets. Whereas the press had often trivialised its opponents the Young Socialists and the Young Liberals the YCs had always enjoyed a remarkably good press. Although the YCs were very dissatisfied with the low attendance at the 1982 YC conference at Harrogate the reports were remarkably good with such headlines as 'Nott attacks CND'[20] and 'Race job for Minister defended by Heseltine'.[21] The national press now concentrated on YCs' weaknesses rather than its strength.

# Chapter 15

# YCs in Conflict
# 1984 to 1991

John Guthrie was elected chairman in 1984. He should receive praise that although he fully supported most of the policies advocated by his predecessor Phil Pedley and his successor Richard Fuller he managed to steer clear of any action that would divide rather than unite the Young Conservatives.

The highlight of his year of office was a successful YC conference at Bournemouth when, for the third year in succession, there was an attendance in excess of 2,000. (A figure never exceeded at any YC conference except at the rallies in the 1940s, 1950s and 1960s at the Royal Albert Hall and the Royal Festival Hall.) It was addressed by Margaret Thatcher and was the first conference following the IRA bombing at the Brighton Conference.

Controversy arose over the setting up of a trust fund in the hope that YCs would gain financial independence of the Party from willing donors. At the NAC meeting of December 1984 James Goodsman, assistant director of the Community affairs office said it was regretted that the NAC had decided to go ahead with the trust without further discussion with the Party and offered YC officers urgent discussion about YC funding. Having reduced their funding by 70% it was surprising that the Party, unless its motive was to control the YCs through its budget, did not applaud rather than deplore the desire of the YCs to be more financially independent. By 43 votes to nil the trust fund was set up in opposition to the establishment and had moderate success until it was wound up in 1993.[1] It assisted the YCs to purchase a computer and also helped in the critical campaign in 1987.

During the 1980s members of the Federation of Conservative Students started to advocate libertarianism which they regarded as the development of Thatcherism although there is no evidence that Margaret Thatcher ever envisaged such policies. Libertarianism advocated the abolition of control of both hard and soft drugs, called for the decriminalisation of prostitution and drastic reduction in the State welfare benefits, the main reason for the disbandment of the Federation of Conservative Students (Chapter 16).

John Guthrie writing in 1984 on libertarianism said,

> The Conservative Party has never, does not and must never advocate the dangerous and degenerate views of the loony libertarian minority. We will never become a party that believes in the survival of the most

aggressive, nor will we lose sight of the over-riding importance we attach to public morals, the family and the rule of law.[2]

Luckily although some individual Young Conservatives supported such policies their leaders unlike the leaders of the Federation of Conservative Students who supported such libertarian views never supported these policies.

Richard Fuller was the next chairman to be elected and although I have not had the opportunity of meeting Mr Fuller it appears he was not a wise choice. When he relinquished office in 1987 the YCs were a more divided movement than at any time in its existence. Many YCs felt he was failing to support the Prime Minister. He, like every other YC officer of the decade was enthusiastic about some aspects at least of Margaret Thatcher's leadership. In September 1985 speaking to the NAC he referred to her as being 'a wonderful ambassador while in Washington'.[3]

Politics is a public relations exercise and unless a politician can engender the confidence of the members of his/her party that he is pursuing the right policy he is likely to become a political liability rather than an asset. Richard Fuller's remark, to which not surprisingly objection was taken, was his description of the party chairman, Norman Tebbit, as a political mugger, a running boy for one particular faction and then strangely he said that the Party chairman should be 'above the battle'. The use of the word 'battle', except in connection with an opponent party, is a strange choice of word to use in a speech as important as that made upon one's election as chairman.[4] Surely all the Party chairman's energies should be directed at doing battle with his opponents not with factions in his own party. However events proved that Margaret Thatcher was right and Richard Fuller was wrong. Under Norman Tebbit's leadership a heroic victory was achieved.

Further evidence of the hostility of some Young Conservatives is shown by the report of the East Midlands Area Young Conservatives that the national chairman had even said on a number of occasions that he believed that supporters of Mrs Thatcher do not have a right to be in the Party![5]

It is clear that those who felt the YC officers were not supporting the Prime Minister were not united in their aims. There were those like Gary Mond who stood against Richard Fuller for the chairmanship in 1986, who accepted the fact that due to the change of social conditions the Young Conservatives would be a small group of dedicated politicians and the movement should be a nursery for those who would seek office in the Party in Parliament or local government.[6] There were also those who felt, like Andrew Tinney and Adrian McLellan, that YCs should have a wider appeal and it was necessary to have an attractive social programme. In Surrey in the 1980s there is little doubt that Andrew Tinney and Adrian McLellan were right.[7]

Nick Robinson became national chairman in March 1987 and in his own words his 'was a quiet year, apart from the general election'. The 1987 General Election was to be Margaret Thatcher's third, greatest and final election victory. (The next national election was to be the European election in 1989 which was to end in disaster for her.) Unlike 1979 when the unions ensured a Conservative success and 1983 when an ultra-left policy assured the Conservatives of victory, Neil Kinnock was a far more formidable opponent in 1987. The Cabinet had been rocked by the successive resignations of Leon Brittan and Michael Heseltine in 1986.

After eight years of Margaret Thatcher's premiership many young voters could not appreciate the disasters of the Callaghan government, the fact that the drop in the Conservative vote was limited to 0.1% was a magnificent achievement. In May 1986 quite rightly Richard Fuller drew attention to the decrease in the youth vote. An internal survey organised by Conservative Central Office showed that between 1983 and October 1986 Conservative support among the 18 to 24 age group fell in respect of men by 13.4%, and women, who were slightly more conservative, by a reduction of only 12.4%.[8]

However, this survey showed how unreliable mid-term Gallup polls are in forecasting the result of a forthcoming general election: 38% were stated to support Labour yet in the general election eight months later Labour's support was a mere 30.6%. Of the twenty-four seats targeted by YCs, six were lost, Oxford East, Bradford North, Nottingham North, Newport West, Manchester Withington, and Newcastle Central. Most of these were in the large cities where often there is a weaker Conservative Association and the YCs should be given considerable credit for taking on these seats. They considered that they had only been moderately successful and where little YC organisation existed locally, mutual aid was minimal. Each seat received 1,000 copies of the YCs' pamphlet, financed by the trust fund, prepared specially for the election.[9]

In the course of Nick Robinson's year Edward Heath was appointed Life Patron of the Young Conservatives in place of Harold Macmillan who had died the previous year.

Controversy was caused by the banning of the right-wingers, including Harry Phibbs, at the 1988 YC Conference. The divisions at the top were already being reflected at grass-roots level as is shown in a contemporary report by a Surrey YC, Alan Parncutt. He said he attended the 1987 Conference but this time he came away with completely different memories and a completely changed view of YC Conferences.

This year the level of campaigning reached an unexpected high, with both candidates for chairman putting on a display of self-promotion in such a way as to provoke clashes between supporters of opposing sides outside the conference. Inside the Conference Centre things were little better with the Conference Ball ruined midway with rival bands of supporters waving banners, resembling football fans on the rampage. While good natured debates and discussions strengthens the Party the political enmity between the two candidates did nothing for the Conservative party, indeed when it should be shown to the country that we care about the issues of today, what occurred only served to show the general public what a bunch of fanatical opinionated promotion seekers only worthy of derision there were within the Conservative Party.[10]

Further evidence that the in-fighting at the top was seriously affecting others is shown by the decision of the Plymouth YCs which felt so strongly that they released a Press report in which they criticised the national officers for such in-fighting.[11]

There was a bitter contest in 1988 between Martin Woodroofe and Andrew Tinney which Martin Woodroofe the left-wing candidate won with 270 votes, Andrew Tinney receiving 208. Andrew Tinney felt the election had not been fair because a number of constituencies had cast invalid votes, mainly because there were people who had voted purporting to be a constituency chairman when they did not represent a valid branch. Accordingly, Central Office had to tighten the rules. First it was decided that only constituencies containing a membership of at least ten members could vote. Secondly Central Office asked for proof by production of programmes, minutes, etc. that there was a valid branch in existence.

Martin Woodroofe told me that they wished to work with the moderate right but unless they were to allow the right to share the office of chairman and vice-chairman the right would be determined to gain control, which was what eventually happened.[12]

Another sour election was held in 1989 between Martin Woodroofe and Andrew Tinney and on this occasion Andrew Tinney was successful. Allegations were made in the campaign that the phone used by Martin Woodroofe in his hotel bedroom prior to the election had been bugged. Andrew Tinney won with 192 votes to 190.[13] There was a marked drop in the electoral college of 384 against 478 in the previous poll, and 355 in the following year. Either there was a rapid decline or the phantom branches were located and not allowed to participate in the vote. In spite of the bitterness, Andrew Tinney paid a generous compliment to his predecessor, Martin Woodroofe, although Nick Robinson said it needed more than a rhetoric commitment to unity: it had to be demonstrated for the good of the movement. Martin Woodroofe's remark that his attempt to bring together all elements in the YC movement, which was not appreciated, was not necessarily correct. Politicians have to face the disappointment of defeat as well as the elation of victory. The two most outstanding Conservative politicians of the twentieth century, Winston Churchill and Margaret Thatcher, had to accept defeat. Churchill at the hands of the electorate, Margaret Thatcher at the hands of the Conservative MPs.

Unity was not helped by the appointment of Tim Mitchell as organising secretary in 1988, Mark Worrall having resigned. Tim Mitchell had previously sat on the National Advisory Council and assisted Martin Woodroofe in his previous campaign. In view of the divisions among YCs great sensitivity was needed with the selection of the organising secretary and the appointment of Tim Mitchell was likely to increase the feuding rather than reduce it, although in other circumstances it could have been an excellent choice.[14]

During his first year, Andrew Tinney worked full time for the movement although even this brought criticism that he was being funded from outside the Party. This was a strange criticism because if he was prepared to devote his whole time to the Party it was obvious in the absence of having private means he needed to receive financial support from outside the Party. One of his achievements was a most professional booklet (as one would expect from an accountant) explaining how to start a branch, how to put together a branch programme, how to organise a recruitment campaign with a section on accounts, and advice on speaking, including how to deal with hecklers.[15]

Another success was the organisation of a national lottery as a means of funding YC activities which was launched at the Torquay YC Conference in 1990 and raised £25,000.[16] He was re-elected in 1990 following another bitter election campaign between himself and his vice-chairman, Laurence Harris, who said that Andrew Tinny had had a disastrous year. However, this was not the opinion of the NAC as when Andrew Tinney was re-elected his majority increased from 2 to 103[17] and although in his first year he felt able to claim that the decline in the movement had been arrested, it does not appear this was so as active branches went down from 266 to 189.[18]

Andrew Tinney was enthusiastic about Margaret Thatcher's policies and said meetings with her were very resourceful and there was a free exchange of ideas but she was intolerant of anybody who came along with half-baked ideas. He shared Margaret Thatcher's reservations concerning the political union of Europe. Little did Andrew Tinney know when he was re-elected in 1990 that he would survive Margaret Thatcher. She was to address the Young Conservative Conference for the last time in 1990 before being succeeded by John Major. Towards the end of Andrew Tinney's two years as chairman Margaret Thatcher resigned as Prime Minister and as leader.

During the previous year the NAC supported a motion (33 in favour with only 5 against) which regarded the action of Sir Anthony Meyer in standing for the leadership against Margaret Thatcher in 1989 as vindictive and it is quite clear that most YCs believed that Margaret Thatcher should remain as Prime Minister.[19] As on many other occasions the views of the Young Conservatives were surprisingly similar to the senior party. Such a desire for change came as usual from the Conservative MPs. Notwithstanding YCs' disappointment at the forced resignation of Margaret Thatcher, they showed their loyalty to John Major with a motion by the NAC noting the change by regretting the resignation of Margaret Thatcher as Prime Minister and congratulating John Major on his appointment.[20]

The NAC gave its unanimous support to the successful campaign in the Gulf to restore independence to Kuwait as it had done with the two other armed conflicts authorised by post-war Conservative governments, Suez and the Falklands.

Andrew Tinney bore unjustified criticism throughout his two years' office. Upon the election of Andrew Tinney's successor, Murdo Fraser, James Blatch, a member of the NAC said that Andrew Tinney had used his two years to promote his personal success which appears an unfair criticism because Andrew Tinney appeared to have had no great desire to become a parliamentary candidate.[21] To think that people do not seek political office to promote their personal success shows a lack of realism.

Many who seek unpaid positions in political parties do so in the hope that by carrying out their duties well they should be praised not vilified and at least one YC chairman was honest enough to admit that his ambition was to become an MP and saw one of the best ways to achieve his ambition was by progressing through the Young Conservatives to becomes its national chairman and I respect him for his honesty. Do not most politicians achieve their ambitions by carrying out their duties as officers in the Party competently as a springboard to nomination as a parliamentary candidate and therefore both the Party and he/she are the benefactors.

At the 1992 Conference Martin Minns YC Organiser said 'we are trying to attract more talent with more professional people. If we can persuade them to join they can argue the Tory case in business over the bar.' It was the failure in the 1980s of the Young Conservatives to persuade the captains of industry to forsake the squash courts for Young Conservative activities as previous generations of YCs, such as Peter Walker in 1950 and Chris Gent in 1970, that is partly responsible for the YC decline. The more varied the talent the stronger would be the movement.[22]

The 1980s compared to the previous decades was an unhappy period for the Young Conservatives losing about 80% of their strength. Andrew Tinney had considerable talent and carried out his duties with great energy. However, during his two years chairmanship the Conservative party in the country was bedeviled by the ill-fated Poll Tax. (It might have succeeded if, initially, it had not been set at such a high level and the government gave greater support to local authorities to cushion the effect of its imposition as eventually it did, but it must have been a great disappointment that Andrew Tinney's efforts did not lead to any significant revival.)

I agree with Richard Cuming, that Andrew Tinney was the most talented of those who were critical of the YC leadership for not giving sufficient support to the Prime Minister.[23] I am sure that Eastbourne YCs were right when, in giving their support to Andrew Tinney, they rejected any suggestion that he was an extremist. Those who endeavoured to portray him as such did a great disservice both to the YC movement and the Party generally.

*Chapter 16*

# The Constitution of the Young Conservatives NAC, Area Committees and Conservative Central Office

The Council of the Central Committee of the Conservative party continued to meet throughout the war years notwithstanding the political truce. A post-war problems committee was established in 1941. The Palmer Committee was initiated on 20 May 1943 to make recommendations concerning the Party's youth movement after the war. The report was considered by the National Union on 16 March 1944 and approved subject to one exception. The proposal that one of the vice-chairmen of the Party be a Young Conservative was deleted. The committee having decided, after taking evidence from witnesses who held key positions in the constituencies, the Party organisation and the Imperial League, to recommend to the National Union that there would be a youth section of the main organisation which would be completely integrated into the National Union.[1]

The Palmer report stated that there were twelve freedoms upon which the YC movement would be founded. The politicians of both parties in 1943 thought they had found the cure for unemployment during the period of full employment in the 1940s and 1950s. Lord Woolton was of the same opinion. How wrong they were! (Chapter 20).

The freedoms:

1. Freedom of belief and expression

2. Freedom to work without fear of unemployment

3. Freedom to live adequately housed

4. Freedom from worry about sickness

5. Freedom from industrial and international strife

6. Freedom to trade without unnecessary State control

7. Freedom for improved international exchange of commodities

8. Freedom of opportunity for better education

9. Freedom from fear of an insecure and poverty stricken old age

10. Freedom from racial intolerance

11. Freedom of the air and sea

12. Freedom of opportunity for healthy recreation

As a YC branch is part of a constituency the rules must be consulted as to the power the constituency has to establish and dissolve a YC branch. The model rules issued by the National Union of Conservative Associations provide that no branch could be established without the support of the Executive Council of the constituency. I have not found any minutes formally authorising the establishment of a YC branch. YC branches were normally established on an *ad hoc* basis when sufficient young people in an area decided they wished to establish a branch, sometimes under the active encouragement of the MP or parliamentary candidate, agent or senior members of the association.[2]

Similarly, the model rules provide for the dissolving of a branch by the Executive Council of the Association. Neither the Young Conservative National Executive Council nor Central Office have any power to close a branch. There are many references to the fact that the autonomy of a Conservative Constituency Association is jealously guarded. Surprisingly, the activities of the Uxbridge YCs in publishing a magazine of racist nature (chapter 14) apparently never led to pressure on the Uxbridge association to close the branch.

The only instance found of a senior association closing down its branch due to its behaviour rather than lack of support was Westminster in 1984. Because of its libertarian or too right wing policies[3] the same reason for the Central Council at national level, dissolving the FCS in 1986 although this was also caused by the loutish behaviour and damage at Loughborough College where their conference was held.[4]

Harry Phibbs, Westminster's YC Chairman when it was closed down maintains that many of the policies for which he was once criticised have been accepted by the Party such as the privatisation of the coal mines and also road pricing.

Significantly Harry Phibbs proposed a motion before the NAC which was lost by 7 votes to 27 proposing the ending of the State monopoly in the coal mines by giving local coal miners the opportunity to own their own pits.[5]

At the NEC meeting on 25 November 1964 it was reported that Young Socialist branches at Tottenham, Wombwell, Wath-on-Dearn and Leeds North-east, North-west and South, Farnworth, Salford West, Glasgow, Drumchapel and Toker Acton and the Surrey Federation were closed down.[6]

Between the constituency and national bodies is an Area committee consisting of representatives of all constituencies in the area as with the senior association. An Area office is staffed with a chief agent, an employee of Central Office rather than one appointed by the constituency. The Area YC committee organises various events for YCs with the help of the Area office. A popular activity was weekend schools to which ministers and MPs could be attracted in healthy numbers. In 1965 Clacton held a school which was attended by 1,000 people, a greater attendance than the recent national conferences.[7]

Under the inspired leadership of Riaz Mansha a revival of Young Conservatives in Yorkshire occurred: with a membership of 800 (1993) it was only 100 less than it was in 1973. At a Weekend School in 1992 attended by 170, Riaz Mansha arranged sponsorship so it was free to participants. At Yorkshire YCs 1993 Weekend School seven MPs attended: Keith Hampson, Giles Shaw, David Curry, Timothy Kirkhope, Spencer Batiste, Elizabeth Peacock and Tim Devlin, which must be a record for a weekend school in the heyday of the Young Conservatives.[8]

Another task of Area committees was to run weekend schools for leaders and they were very effective. These were sometimes held at Swinton College which was established in 1948 as a result of a gift and regretfully closed in 1976 as a result of economy.

North-west area organised a barbecue with an attendance of approximately 750 YCs and they cultivated friends, as the kitchen of Ferranti was used to keep the food hot. Security was provided 'by one security guard, one Alsatian dog and two doormen from the Corps of Commissionaires.'[9]

Another activity of Area was to stimulate reports and local political campaigns. Western Area faced a very angry response from local hoteliers when they brought out a report which criticised the standard of service, with too many untrained staff not properly supervised. Meals were often unimaginative, with little thought given to variety, bathrooms and toilets were often insufficient in number and badly sited. Facilities for children, should have included a baby-sitting service. One practical suggestion was the provision of a phrase book at the hotel reception area for foreign visitors. Many hoteliers regarded the report as impertinent and some even complained to their MP but, since the 1960s there has been a tremendous improvement in hotel facilities, with basic accommodation providing *en suite* facilities, TV in bedrooms and tea making facilities.[10]

Although one of the advantages, both for MPs and for Young Conservatives, was the opportunity for informal contact through the numerous area functions attended by MPs but from about 1970 the liaison between MPs and the YCs became more organised with meetings called for discussions of policy between MPs and YC officers in the area. The Yorkshire Area minutes indicate such a meeting with two MPs, Roger Banks and John Osborn, to discuss educational policy on 27 August 1975.[11] In some areas, such as South East, there was also a county structure. In September 1978 Kent held a fund raising ball in Bearstead and a weekend school in November for 200 at which two MPs, John Stanley and Nicholas Fairbairn, spoke and there was a question and answer session with three prospective parliamentary candidates. Motions passed concerned: free enterprise, direct elections to the European Parliament and better representation on Scottish and Welsh issues, but one proposed on the re-introduction of National Service was defeated. The social programme included a Saturday night ball and Sunday morning disco. The event was organised at a cost of less than £10 per head.[12]

In the big cities, i.e. Leeds and Birmingham, there was an autonomous Conservative central organisation. It was particularly concerned with local government elections and was not under the control of Central Office. The YCs had an organisation based on the same area and organised social and political events for the YCs in the city. In 1949 the Birmingham YCs organised a mock Lord Mayor's Banquet for 150 guests. Edward Boyle, then a parliamentary candidate who was to achieve high office, was leader of the opposition.[13]

The most important power vested in YCs is their representation on the three executive committees of the National Union. The rules revised in 1994 provides: The YC national chairman should also sit on the General Purposes Committee of the Party.

The divisional chairman should be ex-officio vice-chairman of the Senior Association together with the CPC and Woman's Constituency committee which indicates the importance of the YCs in the Party structure.

On the Central Council, which normally meets annually, the chairman has a seat because of his representation on the Executive. The Area YC chairman and the chairman of each constituency association registered at Central Office as well as the chairman of Scottish YCs and each chairman of a Scottish YC Conservative Association also have seats. The national chairman and two vice-chairmen sit on the Executive Committee.[14] For a discussion on the powers of each of these committees and indeed what, if any, influence they have on the Party, a recent study by Anthony Seldon and Stuart Ball 'Conservative Century' will provide enlightenment.[15]

At constituency level YCs should have one-third representation on all the main committees of the Party and the vice-chairman of the Association should be the YC divisional chairman. This is not provided for in the 1993 Model Rules although, under the Recommended Code of Practice, it provides that the YC numbers are maintained.

The YC divisional chairman shall be a member of the General Purposes Committee of the Association and sit on the Executive. The YCs are also entitled to elect one representative from each ward or polling district/branch as well as a representative to perhaps the most important committee of the Association, the Candidates Committee.

At national level there is a National Advisory Committee, the members are the national officers and appointees of the various Area organisations. In 1956 its functions were defined as:

a) to co-ordinate the activities of the Young Conservative organisation.

b) to consider reports and communications from the Young Conservative

Executive committee and to act in an advisory capacity to the Executive Council of the main union.

c) to be responsible for organising national rallies and meetings which the Committee might hold with the consent of the National union.[16]

The NAC initially limited its activity to organisation rather than policy. However a change occurred in September 1950 when the NAC passed unanimously its first resolution concerning policy calling for closer co-operation with the Commonwealth.[17] Resolutions also came to be passed to the NAC having been initiated by Area committees as one was from both London and City of Nottingham in 1954 disapproving of a large rise in MPs' pay. The NAC rejected this resolution.[18]

The first occasion when there was a vote recorded was on a motion that Empire Day should be a school holiday and should be recognised by YC branches holding suitable events on or near Empire Day (24 May). Thirty were in favour with three against indicating that some saw Empire Day as an anachronism and they were right as Empire Day fell into disregard.[19]

Thereafter the NAC started to pass resolutions regularly either proposed by a member of the committee or passed on to them by the Area committees.

Central Office's most effective control over the national committee was that all expenditure had to be provided by Central Office which decided the fate of various national YC magazines and the cancellation of a holiday week to celebrate the tenth anniversary of the Young Conservatives. It was stated, financial responsibility of the function rested with Central Office and they had made the decision after consultation with the Director General.

At least one Area, Yorkshire, had no qualms about passing a resolution deploring the cancellation of the Scarborough week. The NAC Committee minutes indicate that some members of the NAC criticised this, Stanley Rostron saying Central Office had taken the line of least resistance. When it was suggested that the committee could not approve or disapprove of the decision Cllr Turner dissented saying the committee was entitled to approve or disapprove of the decision. As the NAC committee was an advisory committee it seems that it was perfectly entitled to criticise the decision even if the executive power to act did not lie with that committee. However the majority supported the Central Office decision to cancel the Scarborough week.[20]

A critical resolution of the Conservative party passed in 1958 was that the NAC is concerned that at the Party Conference this year many debates were of short duration and that a proper expression of the Party feelings was impossible and that many subjects of importance were not debated at all. In view of this the Conservative Party Conference should not be allowed to degenerate into being nothing more than a platform for government ministers. This committee urges NAC to consider extending the conference from two and a half to four and a half days.[21] Although Tony Durant (the National YC Organiser 1962–1967) was of the opinion that the Party took little notice of the resolutions this was not the opinion of Hugh Holland who thought that the ministers and shadow ministers did take into account the views expressed by the NAC.[22] The position of Central Office to the NAC was never legally defined as was Central Office's relationship with the rest of the Party but in a taxation case it was held to be the personal office of the leader.

The most critical resolution was passed in 1965:

> That this Committee feels obliged to express a growing lack of confidence in the Conservative party leadership caused by a general overall complacency, incompetence in attack in the constituencies, indicated by the lack of interest shown by leading members of the Party in undertaking speaking engagements and a lamentable failure to provide sufficient drive and vigour from Central Office in putting our case to the country.[23]

However the NAC came in for criticism as being ineffectual when in 1961 Yorkshire Area passed and forwarded to the NAC the following motion:

> That this Committee regrets the present inability of the National Advisory Committee to effectually project the feeling of Young Conservatives into Central Office and to the Party Leaders and suggests that it would achieve its purpose of 'advising' rather than the present system of 'approving' decisions already taken by meeting more frequently or by longer sessions and that more could be achieved in this direction if the NAC devoted more time to organisational problems rather than trying to influence Government policy which Young Conservatives can do by other machinery within the Party.[24]

There was one marked difference between the Young Conservatives and the Young Liberals and Socialists. The Young Socialists and Young Liberals were motivated by what they considered to be right irrespective of the wishes of the electorate. Both appear to have had enthusiasm for CND. Indeed in the 1983 General Election the Young Liberals were disappointed it was not part of the Alliance policy whereas it was party of Labour party policy at that election. However there is no evidence that the vast majority of the electorate had any enthusiasm for CND as the Alliance made its best showing and the Labour party suffered its worst reverse in the past fifty years. No doubt electoral considerations were the reason why the NAC at the time of the Profumo crisis, although they sent a message of support to the Prime Minister, decided not to notify the press.[25]

Another question to be considered is how far Central Office influenced or interfered with the decisions of the NAC. Any such interference was far more subtle than that of its Labour opponents. It seems that until the 1950s the members of the National Committee were reluctant to criticise the hierarchy but then the resolutions became far more critical. It is interesting to note that the two members of the NAC to support the party line in cancelling the

Scarborough week were Charles Longbottom and Barney Hayhoe who both became MPs.

Eric Chalker was of the positive opinion that no one became national chairman without the co-operation of Central Office. Terence Wray disagreed and said that Tony Garner his YC organiser did not interfere. However the NAC had no legal power over any YC branches as they were under the control of the constituency association.[26]

It is the constituency association who has the power to close a branch or ban it from acting in a particular way. In 1961 it was the local agent who took it upon himself to ban a magazine advocating the Campaign for Nuclear Disarmament issued by Gravesend YCs. If the YC branch wished to dispute such decision it would have to challenge it before the Constituency Executive Council. The NAC had no power to intervene.[27]

The members of the NAC each year elected a national chairman. In 1946 the first chairman, Anthony Nutting, was elected. This arrangement continued for twenty-nine years until 1975 when the franchise was widened to include all constituency chairmen. Clive Landa who was chairman at the time of the rule change showed his enthusiasm for proportional representation by adopting the transferable vote system for these elections. This PR system remained until reversed during Andrew Tinney's chairmanship.

Although Anthony Nutting was the only person to occupy the chair while an MP, it became a much sought after office and a stepping stone to becoming a parliamentary candidate and thereafter an MP. Between 1945 and 1981 sixteen out of twenty-three national chairmen became MPs. Eric Pickles was the last National Chairman to be an MP, two held high ministerial office. However, since 1981 none have become MPs.

Being national chairman is an arduous position as one is expected, and virtually all do, to travel the length and breadth of the country to carry out speaking engagements and other functions besides involvement in the NAC, the Party conference, YC National conference, National Union meetings, meetings with ministers, considering the YC attitude to the numerous political issues that arise from time to time and attending numerous functions around the country. The national chairman is also an ex-officio member of all the important committees of the party such as the policy and candidates committee.

It is easier for the chairman if he lives in London, like Peter Walker, who had his own company with secretarial assistance but very difficult for someone like Fergus Montgomery, a schoolmaster in Newcastle. His file at the Bodleian Library shows how he taught in Newcastle until 4 p.m. on Friday and then caught the train to London at 4.30 p.m. returning on the sleeper on Sunday night.[28] One important function was to attend leadership courses in order to train the next generation of YC officers. Mark Worrall, national organiser 1981–1988, states that in his opinion to be taught by your peers was one of the most valuable aspects of Young Conservatives.[29] During the time Anthony Eden was involved actively in the Young Conservatives he used to invite the chairman to his home and after Fergus Montgomery won in the 1959 election he sent him a telegram to which Fergus Montgomery replied:

> Thank you for your telegram after I managed to scrape home in Newcastle East. Your kindness is much appreciated. I still cannot believe I made it. Blenkinsop, the defeated Labour MP, was very deeply dug in and had a large personal vote. He had a team of workers from the safe seats so he could not claim he was handicapped in that respect. He had more workers and cars than the supposedly rich Tories. However I have got my chance now so it is up to me to work like a fiend to try to ensure that I am elected without the necessity of two recounts.[30]

Andrew Bowden recalls on his visit to Anthony Eden being told of his bitterness at the failure of Hugh Gaitskell to support him over Suez.[31]

Under Edward Heath the national chairman was given an enhanced status. In view of his policy that if a YC national chairman needed information from ministers he should have it. On one occasion when David Hunt had a query about an employment case and Maurice Macmillan said he was too busy, David Hunt referred the matter to Edward Heath's office and within half an hour Maurice Macmillan had rung David Hunt back.[32]

Formal meetings between the national officers and in some cases also with the Area chairmen continued through the premiership of Margaret Thatcher and in spite of the dwindling numbers annual meetings still take place with John Major.

Richard Cuming recalls a meeting with Margaret Thatcher. It was scheduled for 7.45 p.m. for forty-five minutes and although she arrived about an hour late, and her secretary suggested that it should be cancelled, she insisted on fulfilling her engagement. It was agreed that each YC present should be able to ask her one question and although the meeting had taken longer than agreed she noticed that Richard Cuming had not asked a question and insisted upon the meeting continuing, indicating her attention to detail and a very human side, despite often being portrayed as a stern character.[33]

For many years elections were conducted in a courteous manner. Eric Chalker was the first candidate to openly campaign when he stood against Hugh Holland and he visited each voter. Nevertheless, unlike the situation in the 1980s, although Eric Chalker must have been disappointed at losing, feeling that it was difficult to succeed unless one had the support of Central Office, he loyally served the victor, Hugh Holland.

One of the advantages of widening the franchise in 1975 was that it encouraged aspiring candidates to travel the country to become acquainted with the members of the various local branches. Although Demitri Argyropulo was an unsuccessful candidate against Robert Hughes in 1979 he said he travelled the country virtually non-stop, except for Christmas and, unless one did so, it would be unlikely that the candidate would obtain sufficient votes to be elected.[34]

Candidates for chairman and vice-chairman started to issue printed manifestos, one of the more healthy changes of the 1980s, as it was good that the electors should know their views on current policy and their plans for the YC movement.

During the 1980s (chapter 15) the elections became more acrimonious as the left and right factions opposed each other. Unofficial literature appeared on some occasions, directed against candidates whom one did not wish to be elected, as in the case of Richard Fuller's re-election campaign in 1986, an unofficial pamphlet was circulated by his opponent stating that Richard Fuller did not support the Falklands Campaign or Margaret Thatcher or Norman Tebbitt and, not only was he national chairman, he was standing for re-election. It appears that these allegations are mostly untrue. Richard Fuller supported the Falklands expedition, although he was critical of some of the jingoistic behaviour following the victory. Litigation even arose from these bitter election campaigns. Harry Phibbs in 1988 unsuccessfully litigated against Central Office, which had rejected his candidature for chairman (Chapter 15).[35]

# Chapter 17

# The YC Branch over Fifty Years

The diverse activities for the 15 to 30-year-old group during the immediate post-war scene in YC branches played an important part in the social life of many towns, combined with an introduction to politics to many young people. The movement's purpose was quite different to that of university Conservative associations where students obviously joined for the politics or the Bow Group, with whom it never should have been a rival.

The Bow Group's objective was to suggest to the Party interesting and progressive policies and by such policy attract recruits to the Party. The premier purpose of YCs was to influence young people to reject the policies of the Left to which they have always been attracted. Abram and Little in their critical article on the Young Conservatives in 1965 stated that, 'many joined but they politicise the few' implying that the movement's political purpose was negligible.[1] At the same time even those who were not interested in politics often assisted in election work and raised finance for the Party.

Over the last fifty years there are many tributes to the importance of YCs by their senior associations. Some are stereotyped and the annual reports repeat what was said in the previous report but many are from the heart. My favourite is one in Preston North's annual report for 1972 'We can take pride in knowing that during the year the young people have had to withstand intense propaganda from the Left . . . Our young people have championed the great Tory tradition.'[2]

However talented the National YC officers were, the strength of the movement lay in the number of large and active branches. The list of activities carried on by the branches was so diverse that one can only mention a few but it is hoped the rest of the chapter will remind those of my readers who were YCs of the diversity of activity carried out in the branches and to those who were not YCs give some indication of these activities.

## RECRUITING

Recruitment has always been at the core of the YC movement; by its nature the turnover of membership, as with all youth movements, is high. A survey of 473 YCs shows that the average time spent in the YCs by males was 3.09 years whereas by females it was 2.6 years.[3] There is no explanation why the YCs were able to retain men longer than women. There is a note of Pembroke YCs' successful recruiting campaign in 1948. 'Nightly public meetings were held at Narbeth, Newchapel, Newport, Milford Haven and Neylands. Village halls were packed to capacity and 2,000 attended the meetings.'[4]

South Kensington in the same year carried out a recruiting campaign in the neighbouring socialist constituency of North Kensington. The annual report stated that just before Christmas on an ordinary night they had thirty canvassers out in a Labour held seat and 300 new members were recruited.[5]

The same year Wickfield YCs used a pony and trap to assist them in raising their membership from twenty-two to eighty.[6]

In 1949 North Somerset YCs held a recruiting campaign at which their candidate, Ted Leather, who subsequently became an MP was, according to *Advance*, 'a tireless worker'. More than 120 new members were enrolled.[7]

The best results I could find, both in 1947, were the Pudsey and Otley Young Conservatives which recruited 400 members in one week and a 21-year-old Norman Ashton recruited 116 members for Mobberley.[8] To achieve such figures must have needed both belief and energy. Both these records of the 1940s were considerably better than any individual or branch could achieve in the one really successful recruiting drive after 1951 when in 1956 over 27,000 new members were recruited.

The greatest achievements by any in that campaign was by the four members who each recruited fifty new members and the eleven branches which recruited more than 200 (Chapter 6). A massive membership drive in 1967, Action 67, probably produced fewer than 8,000 members (Chapter 9). Recruiting drives continued on a smaller scale but to less spectacular effect throughout the 1970s and 1980s.

## ELECTION WORK

Assistance given in elections was the most important function of a YC branch. All political parties recruit workers from stronger constituencies to assist their marginal constituencies and from the outset YC branches have given similar assistance. Those national chairmen and organisers of later years who felt the YCs mutual aid programme was the idea of their own generation were wrong. Young Conservatives made very considerable contributions to the election campaigns of which they can be proud.

An early reference to mutual aid was the Normanton by-election which took place in the winter of 1946–7. *Advance* reports that in the middle of blizzards YCs from surrounding branches in Leeds, Barkston Ash, Pontefract and Wakefield assisted in the Normanton by-election.[9] In the same winter Barnard Castle YCs' publicity squad worked through one of the worst blizzards ever experienced in order that the district might be fly posted for the adoption meeting of their candidate.[10]

In February 1949 in Hammersmith, the national chairman, John Hay, led a procession of 1,500 YCs down Hammersmith Road to the Broadway – solidly Labour areas – in support of the candidate, Young Conservative Anthony Fell, chanting: 'One, two, three, four, who are we for; two, four, six, eight Fell is our candidate'.

The candidate and his wife followed the procession in an open lorry and addressed a meeting at the end of the procession.[11] Despite the seat being retained by Labour there was a 5.26% swing against the Government. The fact that the swing was not larger was considered a triumph for the Government.

Help was given by the YCs in the 1950 General Election. Between the beginning of the year and 23 February 1950, East Surrey & Dorking YCs put in 1,000 evenings helping in the neighbouring constituency of West Croydon. This contributed to the seat being won by the Conservatives.[12] For five weeks 250–300 Dorking YCs went to Merton and Morden each week to help Captain Ryder, VC, RN, score his great victory.[13]

Many of the YCs from Bromley who helped successfully to obtain the election of a new candidate, Edward Heath, with a majority of only 131, could not have realised that they might be assisting with the launching of a future prime minister. Another Conservative candidate to become a prime minister, Margaret Roberts, was less successful in Dartford. She had to wait another eight years, meanwhile having married Dennis Thatcher, to be elected MP for Finchley in 1959.

In a message to Birmingham Young Conservatives after the 1950 General Election, Lord Mancroft, stated that candidates and agents had paid glowing tributes to the YCs' work in the election. In particular, praise was given to YC James Driscoll and his agent Richard Flemington. Together they swept into West Rhonda where there was a Conservative candidate for the first time since 1929. They set up their headquarters in the local Conservative club and although Labour obtained their expected massive majority James Driscoll beat the Welsh Nationalist candidate.[14]

In the 1951 General Election Cannock Young Conservatives went to a meeting of Jennie Lee (the sitting MP and wife of Aneurin Bevan) heckling and asking questions. In Wednesbury the YCs met the candidate each evening at 6 p.m. and toured with him distributing literature while he held open air meetings. Wordsley Young Conservatives had sole charge of one polling station, the entire area was canvassed by YCs, thirty-seven members helping. In the Stratford on Avon Division there were seventeen branches and the majority of the canvassing was undertaken by YCs. Sheila Vereker, Divisional YC chairman, spoke at a crowded eve of poll meeting at Stratford and John Profumo's campaign ended with him being driven through the town on a tractor driven by a YC.[15]

The 1952 annual report of Hornsey YCs indicated that 20% of the membership (100) assisted in the 1951 election and were solely responsible for the poster campaign and in addition took on the task of monitoring the opposition meetings and all the loudspeaker campaigns throughout the constituency. Much good work was carried out by the Young Conservatives delivering literature, canvassing and knocking up on polling day.[16]

In 1952 there was a critical by-election at Wycombe where the Conservatives were defending a seat gained only in 1951. *Advance* reports:[17]

The YCs were given a separate room from which to organise their campaign. At about 7 p.m. between 40 and 60 YCs reported and proceeded to canvass until 9.30 p.m. Those who did not canvass acted as guides to volunteers coming from London and Wessex. The YCs also provided shorthand writers to monitor opposition meetings. During the weekend before polling day the YCs helped with an entire house-to-house distribution of the candidate's final broadsheet and on polling day assisted as knockers up and tellers.

An independent study of a Bristol marginal constituency in 1955 indicated that in the weakest ward, Hillfield, canvassing was undertaken by the Young Conservatives.[18]

In 1959 David Butler described the Young Conservatives 'as one of the most valuable elements in the electoral army'. I was one of the substantial contingent of about 200 South Kensington YCs who were knocking up electors on election night 1959.[19]

David Butler, dealing with the Swansea Constituency in 1964, said the YCs predominated in the numbers of canvassers and stewards although they had been less conspicuous than 'in 1959, when Rees' youth and bachelor status inspired eager feminine assistants'.[20] In Leeds West, in 1964, Dr Butler describes 'the Conservatives were able to draw on the services of the Young Conservatives'. Labour had little to match this youth effort. Its chief preoccupation with youth in the City had recently been to keep the Trotskyists outs. Leeds West was the only city constituency where the Young Socialists did any canvassing.[21]

Dr Butler reported that in the 1966 election Young Conservatives from all over the South East descended on Brighton hoping to obtain the election of their former national chairman, Andrew Bowden which, on paper, should have been an easy task as the previous Labour majority was only 7. However, the question always arises as to how far party workers influence an election. Although the election was lost there was a swing against the Conservatives of only 0.08% whereas the national swing against the Conservatives was 3.5%.[22]

In the 1970 election the annual report of Hornsey YCs commends the full part played by all their 'YCs from all the branches working every night late into the night and all day Saturday and Sunday'.[23]

In the Crosby by-election eleven years later at which Shirley Williams won the seat for the newly formed Social Democrats it was reported that the YCs formed the majority of party workers, thirty-six YC branches assisted in the campaign.[24]

The YCs' assistance in local elections has been just as significant.

In Birmingham in 1953 a poll was taken of YCs' assistance in the municipal election where 246 parties of YCs, totalling 612 took part. Fifty-two polling districts were completely canvassed by YCs. In 149 districts election literature was entirely delivered by YCs and all the clerical work was undertaken by YCs in fifty-seven polling districts: 393 YCs worked on polling day.[25]

The annual report of Preston South constituency in 1969 stated, 'We have been most pleased at the way the Young Conservatives have helped in the election campaigns. Night after night they were available for the purpose of delivering literature and canvassing the electorate.'[26]

In Exeter in 1969 the chairman of Whipton Ward stated it was entirely due to the efforts of YCs that the Conservatives won the seat.[27]

The 1971 Hornsey annual report states, 'it was a source of great amusement to see the faces and of some pride to see the reactions of the party workers who were not YCs to the great number of streets we could clear in a night.'[28]

A report of Exeter YCs in 1988 referred to the vast amount of work that the YCs were able to put into the campaign, assisting in five wards despite the branch being only recently re-formed.

In spite of all the troubles of the YCs in the late 1980s there is nothing to suggest that it affected their effort at election time. Exeter YCs travelled from Exeter to Monmouth to give help in the by-election. When John Major called the election held in April 1992, Exeter YCs reported that they had three members helping each evening during the campaign.[29]

## CANDIDATES FOR LOCAL ELECTIONS

One of the YCs' most important tasks was to provide local government candidates both in fighting hopeless seats and providing young councillors.

In April 1947 four YCs from one Consett branch stood as candidates in the local elections.[30]

In 1949 *Advance* reported that H E Buckle won a seat from a Socialist when only 23.[31]

In 1961 seven of the local Government candidates for Leeds were Young Conservatives.[32]

The 1977 annual report of Southampton Conservatives stated that the Executive committee has asked that tribute be paid to the chairman of Test YCs, Cllr Mark Rees, upon relinquishing his three years in office as at least half a dozen senior Young Conservatives have been launched into political careers on the City Council and the Hampshire County Council.[33]

## POLITICAL ACTIVITY

The political work of the early YCs was widespread, contrary to the popular belief.

Weekly outdoor political meetings were held by some city and country YC branches. South Kensington YCs with a team of thirteen of their own members held weekly meetings outside Earls Court station.[34] The City of London YCs held open air lunchtime meetings behind the Mansion House[35] and *Advance* describes how the reputation of Somerset Conservative speakers in 1948 was fast spreading.[36] The fact that young people were sufficiently confident to expound Conservative policy in public must have had an effect on young people of their own generation.

Some of the indoor political meetings were quite ambitious.

In 1949 Dewsbury YCs held a public enquiry into the question of whether the Labour government was still the people's choice. Their verdict that the Labour party was no longer the people's choice appears to have been erroneous as the Labour vote exceeded the Conservative vote in both the 1950 and 1951 elections.[37] Chippenham Young Conservatives held a successful evening school on agriculture in January 1949 with lectures on 'Agriculture Today' by Colonel Littlewood, county secretary of the NFU and Charles Hardwick a YC farmer. The meeting was concluded with an open forum with many questions asked and an interesting discussion on hill farming.[38]

The East Surrey YC branch was certainly not docile. From the *Daily Herald* of February 1950:

> Led by John Hare, a YC member and Purley councillor, a party of 30 YCs denounced their MP, Michael Astor, at his adoption meeting. Mr Hare said 'It is with a great feeling of responsibility towards not only the Conservative Party but to the country, that I oppose Mr Astor's adoption.
>
> 'I represent hundreds of people in the East Surrey Division who have not been given a chance to express their opinion. Up to July Mr Astor's record of divisions in the House of Commons was only 41%. Both the Liberal and Labour candidates in this division are looking on this bad record as a main plank in their election policy.'

Mr Hare accused the Conservative Executive of not notifying members when they considered Mr Astor's nomination.[39]

Although by 1953, nationally, numbers were on the decline there were many branches as active as ever. The 1953 Skegness AGM was attended by 350 people out of a total of 450 to hear a talk by Peter Bailey the Area Young Conservative Chairman.[40]

In 1953 Lincoln Young Conservatives held a series of four lectures with the Conservative Trade unionists. This should have pleased the NAC who complained there was difficulty in persuading Young Conservatives to become Trade Unionists and Trade Unionists, Young Conservatives.[41]

During the 1950s not all YCs were complacent. South Kensington YCs sent out a survey form to 400 members and received only fifty replies. It concluded that 'the greater number of the members treated the YCs as little more than a social club or matrimonial agency and such members can be written off as useless except in so far as their annual subscription helps to increase branch funds.' The survey calculated that 83% of members joined for purely social reasons. The compiler of the report should not have been as depressed about the report as he indicated.[42] The advantages of the non-active 83% being members was that they provided funds, some work at elections, and they would be less likely to become involved in one issue campaigns of Friends of the Earth or CND.

Political work was not always conventional. Twickenham YCs' chairman Christian Muteau happened to be passing at a time when Jack Dash one of the most militant Trade Union leaders was telling an open air crowd at Tower Hill of his wretched position as an oppressed proletarian. Christian Muteau was able to tell the crowd that the night before he had seen Jack Dash dining in Mandy's an exclusive and expensive city restaurant. The meeting promptly concluded.[43]

Branches took an interest in local as well as national issues. Winchester YCs in 1976 invited two speakers with opposing views concerning the future of the notorious Winchester bypass, Cllr Pumfrett arguing the need for a motorway. Mr Pare of the Joint Action Group strangely argued that in spite of motorways to the south and north of Winchester it was perfectly acceptable to have a stretch of non-motorway around Winchester.[44]

Normally the YC branch was the only part of the constituency to meet weekly and, therefore, the political content of the YC programme exceeded in quantity other sections of the constituency. Obviously branches in central London, like South Kensington, have a tremendous advantage in being able to attract MPs as speakers. A remarkable feature is the similarities in the programmes of Devizes YCs in 1948[45] and Woking YCs in 1992.[46]

The decline of South Kensington's membership from 1,000 in 1959 to under 100 in 1986 reflects the reduction in the number of meetings from nine to four in each month. Unlike the meetings held by Woking YCs they seem to have become of a more serious nature.

The table below shows the variety of activities carried on at a cross-section of YC branches.

| | Meetings | Election-eering | Political | General Interest | Social | Dancing |
|---|---|---|---|---|---|---|
| Devizes 1948 | 8 | | 4 | 2 | | 1 |
| Southampton Test Bassett & Portswood 1961[47] | 4 | | 1 | 1 | 2 | |
| Southampton Test one branch only 1979 | 6 | | 2 | | 4 | |
| Woking 1992 | 9 | 1 | 3 | 1 | 3 | 1 |

A meeting of the Devizes YCs in 1948 defies classification. Five speakers were advertised to be speaking on such diverse subjects as: Housing, The Work of Young Conservatives, How YCs can help during an Election and Aerial Gunnery! Other general interest meetings held by Devizes YCs included speakers on Italy Today and Atomic Energy.

In the years mentioned, Devizes YCs danced in the Town Hall, while Woking held a disco at Downside School.

Meetings at South Kensington over a period of 27 years were as follows:[48]

|      | Meetings | Election-eering | Political | MP Speakers | General Interest | Social | Dancing |
|------|----------|-----------------|-----------|-------------|------------------|--------|---------|
| 1959 | 9        |                 | 6         | 1           | 1                | 1      |         |
| 1968 | 9        |                 | 3         | 3           |                  | 1      | 1       |
| 1973 | 8        | 2               | 2         | 1           | 1                | 2      |         |
| 1986 | 5        |                 | 3         | 2           |                  |        |         |

YC Area and National Officers were sometimes critical of the fact that there was too little of political content in the programmes. In 1966 Wendy Gordon in an Area Report of Surrey YCs complained of the lack of political events in branch and divisional programmes.[49]

Andrew Bowden, National Chairman 1960–61, feels it is as much a mistake for a YC branch to have too much politics as it is to have too little and the right proportion to be aimed at is: one-third political, one-third general and one-third social.[50]

Hopefully he would have approved of the Macclesfield programme of 1981 as reported in the *Macclesfield Advertiser*:

consisting of a wide variety of both social and political events for young people between 15 and 30. The list of activities include, a repeat of the highly successful disco at Silkland Suite in September, ice-skating and a visit to a local TV studio. In contrast a strong political flavour was being maintained in this year of County Council elections. Locally Mr Nicholas Winterton has agreed to speak to his young electors. Equipped with this programme and a keen membership Macclesfield will be able to maintain its reputation as the fastest growing branch in the North West. Also planned is a debate with CND and a number of speakers. Those with a taste for travel will be provided with trips to the European Parliament, to Eastbourne to hear the Prime Minister and other Members of the cabinet, and to the House of Commons.[51]

However, it brought censure from the then agent for including a debate with CND without his consent.[52]

Normally YCs have been discouraged from participating in debates with opposition parties as it was felt that one should not allow a YC platform to be used to advantage by other parties. There was no doubt that the membership wished to have contact with the opposition and in *Advance* there are frequent references to it. In *Challenge* there are details of a debate between the Brighton & Hove YCs and the Young Communists at which John Hay, then described as a Brighton solicitor and who subsequently became the national chairman and an MP, took part.[53]

Oddly enough this is one of the few cases where YCs taking part in debates with opposition parties was not successful.

*Advance* refers to debates with the opposition parties in the 1940s, Swansea YCs debated with Llanelli Young Communists in 1948 'That this house is of the opinion that we need the return of a Conservative government'. The motion was carried by 67 votes to 48 votes.[54] Northwich YCs debated nationalisation with the local Labour League of Youth and won by a 2 to 1 majority,[55] while Coventry YCs, successful in a debate in 1950 with the Labour League of Youth, won by 119 votes to 49.[56]

The Birmingham YCs held an annual debate with the Labour League of Youth and neither the Birmingham Conservative Association nor Central Office discouraged them.[57] The minutes of a meeting held on 8 May 1954 of Trowbridge YCs reveals that several 'Any Questions' sessions were held between the Trowbridge YCs and the Labour League of Youth and it was reported that they were very successful.[58]

In the early 1950s it became popular with several branches to invite the Soviet Ambassador to speak to them and this caused such alarm at Central Office that a special meeting was convened. Lord Woolton said that Agents should be warned to discourage such invitations to the Soviet Embassy as soon as they heard of them and when it was impossible to prevent such talks the Young Conservatives must be told that they must have an anti-Communist speaker to put the other view.

Mr Ridgwell the YC youth organiser, undertook that this would be done and suggested that speakers from the Economic League might be willing to undertake these talks.[59] From this it would appear that Lord Woolton lacked confidence in the Young Conservatives' good sense.

In 1963 there is reference, at an Area meeting, to a debate between Dewsbury YCs and the local Young Socialists and it was minuted that such events are not always the best publicity for YCs although it was agreed that two of the Area officers would attend to monitor the situation but not speak.[60]

The Ilford *Leader* 1961, refers to an 'Any Questions' panel which was held in conjunction with the Young Socialists, Young Liberals and Young Communists. 'The Young Socialists hosted the meeting and provided the chairman who was both impartial and smiling but the YCs provided 75% of the audience.'[61]

At Highgate the Central Branch YCs held a good meeting in February 1961 when a debate was held with the Young Socialists, Young Liberals and Young Communists and an Independent. There was an attendance of about 65 including 28 YCs.[62]

A report to the Greater London Area committee under the chairmanship of Eric Chalker whose contribution to increasing the political influence has already been noted, stated that politics should be controversial and attempts should be made to encourage speakers with controversial views including, in the right circumstances, members of other parties.[63] Alan Haselhurst, the national chairman 1964–1966 claimed that the political side of the YCs had never been presented in a sufficiently attractive way and he suggested the remedy was for the movement to shake itself out of the orthodox Party line influence which had dominated it for so long. The process of debate needed to be more cut and thrust: speakers from other parties ought to be invited; the professionalism of other activities which were in competition with YCs either had to be matched, bettered or improved upon.[64]

A book published by a YC in the North East in 1977 gave suggestions for YC branch programmes including debates with other political parties, the National Front, Communists and Young Liberals.[65] It is assumed that if the author of the book saw no objection to speakers from the National Front he would have no objections to speakers from the Labour Party.

The fact that the attitudes of the national officers at least were changing compared with the situation in Dewsbury in 1961 was that Southend YCs' debate with the Young Liberals had not only the support of the National Chairman John Guthrie but he actually spoke in the debate. A motion supporting the Government's Nuclear Defence policy was passed by a 6 to 1 majority.[66]

Youth parliaments were organised where the various parties held a series of debates on the lines of the House of Commons and they appear to have met with less objection than where branches themselves organised debates with the opposition. It is difficult to see why there should be less objection to youth parliaments.

At Luton the youth parliament apparently met under the chairmanship of the local Labour MP at which young members of the three political parties were represented. The Conservative motion condemning nationalisation was carried by 39 votes to 38. Accordingly, the Conservatives formed the Government for the next encounter and a motion which deplored the present Government policy of disintegrating the Empire was carried by 80 votes to 10.[67] No explanation is given why Luton's youth were more critical of the Government's colonial policy than of its policy on nationalisation.

The *Ealing Chronicle* was published by Ealing South YCs for about twenty-six years from 1945 to 1971. This magazine was produced for the longest period and of a consistently high standard and, therefore, most often quoted in this book. Many YCs must have put tremendous effort into the production of their branch magazines. A number of magazines, in most cases incomplete sets, are at the British Library.

Among interesting articles in the *Chronicle* in the 1940s was one supporting the nationalisation of water on the basis that it would be much easier for a National Water organisation to increase the water supply to London and also to rural areas.[68] Particularly after about 1960 a number of the magazines included editorial comments similar to the leader column in newspapers.

Some magazines, such as Hammersmith's in 1964, printed articles on controversial matters. One month there was an article sympathetic to Apartheid, and a highly critical article the following month (chapter 26). However, the most interesting article was one published in Southend YC magazine by David Atkinson predicting the downfall of Russian Communism (appendix 3).

## INTER-BRANCH ACTIVITY

One of the strengths of the YCs' early history was the comradeship between branches. When a party of Northern YCs visited London for the 1951 Conference & Rally (twenty-six of the thirty-four constituencies being represented in this Labour dominated area) the London Area provided hospitality and invitations were extended from Victoria Lunch Hour YCs, South Kensington YCs and Fulham YCs.[69]

There were many joint meetings with neighbouring branches over a whole range of activities, both serious and not so serious and awards were made to branches for excelling in the various aspects of their activities.

Shrewsbury won the inter branch speaking competition in 1951 and 1952 with different teams.[70]

It became the tradition of the Southampton YCs to hold a pancake race at one minute past midnight on the morning of Shrove Tuesday, across Northam Bridge, the bridge over the river Itchen. A four-person team had to run across Northam Bridge as fast as possible tossing pancakes. In 1963 it was reported that, 'the race took place at two minutes after midnight. Test YCs organised the race and Bassett and Portswood Branch came first, Itchen second and Totton third, the proceeds went to the Mayor's charity fund.'[71]

In 1976 East Hants Young Conservatives who could still boast of five branches in the Division held a speaking competition. The winner was Bob Davey, chairman of Petersfield YCs who spoke on politics and the role of the politicians. The losers spoke on railways, Greek mythology, cricket, race relations and alcoholism.[72]

## CHARITABLE WORK

Branches not only raised money for themselves and the Conservative party but many undertook charitable work. In 1948 the Ealing South Young Conservatives gave a party for fifty motherless children from a children's home. In November 1948 Chislehurst & District Young Conservatives were busy organising dances, whist drives and carol singing in an endeavour to raise £150. Their object was to give a Christmas treat to 250 children at an LCC School. Seats were booked at the London Casino and arrangements made to take the children to tea at a London restaurant. A Labour councillor decided that the YCs were not fit and proper persons to give the children a treat and instructed the educational officer to reject the offer. Undeterred by such rejection 250 other children nominated by the British Legion were taken on the trip on Christmas Eve.[73]

The best financial contribution to charity I discovered is that of Romford YCs in 1967 who raised £2,000 (now approximately £18,500) for charity.[74]

The differences between Young Conservatives and Young Labour party socialists might not be as great as the politicians portray in the same way Labour and Conservative MPs exaggerate their differences. While Gosforth YCs organised a sponsored walk for Oxfam in 1967,[75] Dewsbury Young Socialists in 1966 visited fourteen clubs and pubs and collected £17.50 (now approximately £168), similarly for Oxfam.[76] Indeed in 1968, YCs, Young Liberals and Young Socialists co-operated in a World Poverty Campaign to educate public opinion in the dire necessity for overseas aid and development. A note mentioned that this was criticised from within the Party.[77]

## FUNDRAISING

The contribution made by the YCs of the 1940s and 1950s to the finances of the Party was considerable. The money raised was paid to the Constituency Associations and total figure raised by the YC movement was never recorded. However, in the absence of state funding political parties need money and when assessing the contribution of the YCs most commentators fail to give due acknowledgement for the funds raised by them.

I believe that the financial affairs of the YCs were undertaken in a very amateurish manner by Central Office. If a sense of competitive spirit had been introduced between branches even more money could have been raised. In the Macleod Report of 1965 the average branch was estimated to contribute £20 annually, which is now approximately £200, although it was revealed in the Report that there were outstanding exceptions.[78] The amount contributed by apparently similar branches varied tremendously.

Lord Woolton warned branches that they should raise money by subscriptions not by raffles and sweepstakes which might be illegal. However, most Conservative organisations have always found raffles and social events a much more painless way of raising money for the Party than subscriptions and early Young Conservatives were no exception.[79]

In 1948 Whitehaven raised £197 now approximately £3,650, at a time when taxation was at 9s. 6d. in the £1 and young people had not the benefit of the great increase in material wealth that occurred from the 1950s.[80] In four years Twickenham raised for their senior association £1,000 (now £14,920)[81] and Southgate and Woodford 1956/57 each £500 (now £6,305).[82]

The warning that membership of the YCs was on the decline as early as 1963 came from Barkston Ash where, in 1962, they raised £575 (now £6,800). In 1963 they raised only £100 (now £1,060) although most YC branches even of the 1970s would have been perfectly satisfied with this.[83]

Torbay YCs made £1,565 from two barbecues in 1964/1965 (now £16,000) and were able to contribute £450 to the senior Association (now £4,662).[84] However by the late 1960s as the branches declined in size contributions declined likewise.

## SOCIAL AND SPORTING EVENTS

Social events intermingled with political meetings were always the essence of the early YC movement. Dancing remains a popular pastime among young people although the quickstep has given way to 'bopping' and the dance to the disco.

The ability of the YCs to organise large social events during the 1940s did much to assist its rapid rise.

Among outside events in 1949 Yeovil Division held an agricultural show[85] and Minehead YCs held a swimming gala which attracted 1,000 people.[86] Northwood Young Conservatives ran the biggest event ever organised by the Uxbridge Conservative Association. The programme consisted of a horse show for which there were 250 entries and a dog show with 190 entries.[87]

A number of Young Conservative clubs sprang up. The Plaistow YC club was opened in 1948. The club was open to all subscribing YCs on paying the admission charge of sixpence. The amenities included a billiards and darts saloon, reading room, dance hall, table tennis, cinema facilites and a permanent cafe/bar. A later report indicated that it was proving most successful.[88]

One problem in this era of restriction was that in order to serve food at an event one needed a food licence. City YCs tried to evade the regulations by having the YCs bring their own sandwiches and coffee and then give them away free. Expenses were covered by a collection but such conduct was hazardous as there could have been trouble with the Civil Servants whose job it was to enforce the regulations.[89]

YCs participating in social events faced other perils as will be seen from the minutes of the South Kensington YCs. The drama group received a vote of censure because the group made a loss of £36 11s. 10d. They were ordered to pay one half of the loss themselves and received no other financial assistance until the sum was repaid![90]

Although by the 1950s, nationally, membership was on the decline, many branches were as active as ever.

The South Kensington YCs in 1959 held a ball 'from 8 p.m. to 2 a.m., dancing to Paul Savill and his orchestra, buffet served at the table, cabaret – Noel Harrison and his guitar'. Interestingly, the programme attracted considerable advertising.[91]

Eight years later when numbers were less, in a highly marginal constituency, of Preston the Fulford YCs gave a ball, booking the Top Rank Ballroom at £190 and were able to sell 1,300 tickets, the maximum with 500 turned away. A raffle was held with the prize of an Adriatic holiday for two, so in order to comply with the Gaming regulations the YCs had to sell 6,400 tickets which they did and ended the evening with a profit of £433.[92]

However, it was not all praise. David Atkinson writing in 1965 referred to the 'shoddy organisation of many social events.'[93] In 1968 a resolution of the NAC was passed calling attention to the declining standard of social events.[94]

Foreign travel in the austere 1940s was very rare but nine Young Conservatives from Nuneaton spent Whitsun in Paris in 1949 with their prospective parliamentary candidate Gordon Spencer.[95] Twenty-seven YCs in a bus driven by the chairman of Rushcliffe Notts, Harry Barton, enjoyed fourteen days driving through France and a week at Lucerne. Twice crossing the Brenner Pass, visiting the awe inspiring Thummel Bach Falls, Zurich, Berne, Basel and Paris. While in Switzerland they met a branch of their Swiss counterparts who made them very welcome.[96]

Many branches held sporting events involving Young Conservatives. Sale YCs had a football team that played in the Altrincham League.[97] Cardiff had a rugby team[98] and Abergavenny a hockey team.[99]

Devizes YCs was a branch not to neglect sport, although they had mixed fortunes. At football their defence was their undoing – they lost two games to Morses of Swindon 3–1 and 4–1 and Stable Lads achieved the double, 4–2 and 5–2. They were just as disastrous shooting, coming bottom of the local league but they were certainly better at tennis, playing three games and winning two. Their record at cricket was – played 6 won 2, drawn 2, lost 1.[100] However Colchester YCs outshone Devizes in their sport, mixed hockey. By 1959 they had a second team and in 1961 a third team and three times they won the Exiles Mixed Hockey Tournament, the largest in England.[101]

Hornsey YC cricketers found that opponents did not wish to mix politics with sport so there was a request for disaffiliation which the YC committee granted.[102]

The Otley Young Conservatives held a rowing regatta in 1952 when fifty YCs participated.[103] Some branches were even more adventurous. Adel, a Yorkshire branch, arranged for the Leeds Pennine club to take thirty of their members pot-holing.[104]

Climbing was an activity carried out by Solihull YCs during the spring holiday of 1967 when they successfully climbed Ben Nevis, Scafell and Snowdon.[105]

Equally ambitious in July 1969 Winchester YCs took to the air when twenty of their members visited a gliding centre near Alton.[106] Car rallies were one attraction well to the fore with YCs at a time when few young people had cars. A car rally was organised in Birmingham in 1953 which was won by Wendy Brown who put all the males to shame. The route was from Birmingham to Moreton-in-the-Marsh and returned to Birmingham by Broadway, Castlemorton, Worcester and Bromsgrove.[107] In 1959 South Kensington YCs ran an all-night car rally over a fifty mile circuit.

Although those who were no friends of the YCs might regard such activity as frivolous I believe the promoters of car rallies who correctly stated at the time the advantages of holding a rally. The advantages were to attract interest in the YCs and those interested in the movement. The organiser claimed that no less an important object of the rally was to foster safer and more competent driving among those taking part.[108]

The stronger branches were, as *The Times* commented in 1964, able to provide a complete social life which lasted well into the 1960s but as numbers dwindled the great variety of activities ceased in the early 1970s.

Chelsea YCs held weekly meetings in 1968. For the more serious members there were discussion evenings and speaking classes both meeting fortnightly. For the sportsman there was fencing and, for the drinkers, YCs were invited to the Beehive after the weekly meeting and to the King's Head and Eight Bells on Sundays.[109]

At neighbouring South Kensington there were twice weekly meetings and tennis every Sunday afternoon, in summer. For the serious, a policy group, and the drinkers were catered for at the Builders' Arms, where it was suggested they met every Sunday between noon and 2 p.m.[110]

Although there has been constant criticism of YCs for being too social, traditionally Conservative Associations attract helpers and money with a social programme. Who would be a better judge than the Labour NEC? On 23 February 1955 they acknowledged the Labour League of Youth had been a failure but the Conservatives had maintained a successful youth organisation. Although the Conservative party in the opinion of the NEC encouraged YC social activity, YCs have proved valuable at election time.[111]

The general picture of Young Socialists is of serious young people not interested in social activity. Although the minutes of Epsom Labour party records on 2 September 1965 that only social meetings were held it was not in vain. Seven months later acknowledgement is made that the Epsom Young Socialists had made a truly magnificent effort in the election campaign.[112]

# Chapter 18

# Women in the Young Conservatives

One of the strange features of the Conservative party is that the women who carry out so much voluntary work for the Party, arranging social events and fund-raising, manning committee rooms and telling at elections are prepared to play a subordinate role to their male counterparts. From a very early stage women joined Young Conservative branches in the same or greater numbers as men. A report on a debate of the City of London YC Forum on the Industrial Charter stated there were 275 people present and although there were many smartly dressed women, none of them spoke.[1] However, at the first YC conference in Filey in 1949 there appeared no shortage of women speakers.

Nevertheless, the Conservative party has rarely been to the forefront of the campaign for women to have equal rights. In the 1945 election there were only five women Conservative candidates. Over the whole fifty years since the Young Conservatives' foundation there has been only one woman national chairman, Frances Vale. Both the Labour and Liberal Youth movements have had more women chairmen. The radical Young Liberals had no women chairmen between 1958 and 1973.[2]

In some years, such as 1971 and 1993, all four vice-chairmen were men; 1971 is significant because at that time Greater London Young Conservatives were dominated by the radicals such as Clive Landa who had produced 'Set the Party Free'. Although in 1969 Lynda Chalker was elected the first woman chairman of the Greater London YCs, in 1971 the GLYC senior positions were held by men. From enquiries made of former national chairmen none were able to give a convincing reply to the dearth of females in high office. The general view was that the best person won the election and it just happened to be a man!

A number of very talented women have passed through the ranks of Young Conservatives. In the mid-1960s Elizabeth Steele (now a judge) opposed Alan Haselhurst (now an MP) for the office of chairman and was defeated as was Stephanie Read when she stood against Chris Gent in 1979. The achievement of Frances Vale in the even more male oriented society of the 1940s becoming chairman was a remarkable feat. In 1947 she spoke at the Party Conference at Blackpool and made a special plea for the Young Conservative women. She said:

> It is known when the list of candidates is sent down to the constituencies and if a woman's name appears on the list, her name is often struck off

because she is not considered suitable for a particular constituency. I would ask you to specially consider the Young Conservative women and do all you can. This is a resolution on which you can act. Go back to your constituencies and give a chance to Young Conservatives, particularly the Young Conservative women.[3]

Unfortunately, as in the 1992 Parliament, there are only twenty Conservative women MPs, one half the number of women Labour MPs. The reason, apparently, that talented women are reluctant to offer themselves as candidates is selection committees are biased in favour of men.

The YCs have a poor record in providing women MPs. Lynda Chalker was the only prominent YC who subsequently became an MP and indeed as Minister for Overseas Development became an outstanding member of the Conservative government. It seems reasonable to assume the reason why there were so few women Young Conservatives in high office is the same as why there are few Conservative women who become MPs.

A survey carried out in 1964 by Yorkshire YCs showed that the movement attracted too few women graduates. This might have been different if more had been done to promote women. By far the largest category, at 83, were secretaries, 47 students, 5 industrial workers, 5 housewives and just 12 were professional women and 3 executives. Further evidence that men were in power in the branches showed that out of 22 constituencies 16 had male chairmen and only 6 female. There were 18 male treasurers and 4 female treasurers but 19 women branch secretaries and only 3 men.[4]

Although the employment of women made a vast contribution to the Second World War effort it was many years after the end of the war before women's pay compared favourably with that of men. In spite of the attention the wartime cabinet gave to social legislation, such as the commissioning of the Beveridge Report on social security, they gave no attention to the question of equal pay. On the contrary, the only time during the war that the Government lost a vote in the House of Commons was on a motion that women teachers should receive equal pay with their male colleagues. Churchill was so furious that he put down a vote of confidence the next day so that the decision would be reversed. Such was the standing in the House of Commons of Rab Butler that his progressive reforms culminated in the Education Act of 1944. The Labour opposition made it clear that they did not wish to risk Rab Butler's position and therefore withdrew their opposition.[5]

In spite of the zeal of the Attlee government for reform, no progress was made during that government concerning equal pay. Both the Labour Party and Labour League of Youth believed that there should only be equal pay when the country could afford it. The Young Communists at that time campaigned both for equal pay and votes at 18.[6] These campaigns at the time were considered freakish but the voting age was reduced to 18 in 1969. It was the Churchill government from 1951 to 1955 which introduced equal pay for Civil Servants.[7] By 1975, although more difficult to implement, legislation was introduced to ensure that women's pay was equal to men's. In 1949 Stratford upon Avon YCs were reported as having a well attended and very lively debate on the question of equal pay. However as all the women voted against, it was easily defeated.[8] The same fate befell a similar motion in the City of London YC Forum.[9] As late as 1952, in what would now be considered to be an archaic opinion, a Mr Coley wrote in an article in *Right*:

> In calculating wages due to a worker the employer should take into account the worker's responsibilities.
>
> In practice this would mean that a married man with children of school age should receive more than a single man with no dependents doing the same job and the married woman whose husband received such additional pay and who still chose to go out to work would receive substantially less. Such a system would obviously tend to keep married women at home and so remedy a widely acknowledged defect in our society which is due in many cases to our present system of wage payment. It is in the interest of the State that happy and child blessed marriages should be the rule among its citizens and this system would help to make that more possible than it is today
>
> Equality of pay would tend to encourage the married women to go out to work and therefore perpetuate the state of affairs responsible in the eyes of many for the break-up of family life and juvenile delinquency.[10]

The equal pay lobby did have some allies in the Conservative ranks. In a debate in the City of London Forum, Michael Burgess, who was stated to be studying for the bar, said that the idea of women not receiving equal pay to men was unadulterated nonsense,[11] as was a remark in the *Independent* of 8 February 1993 when it referred to the Young Conservatives 'as more of a dating agency than being politically active.'[12]

The first mention of the Young Conservatives being the best matrimonial agency was on 6 January 1948 in a letter to *Advance* written by a Dorothy Lomas who, withholding her address said: 'I was disgusted the other day when I invited a young male acquaintance to join the Young Conservatives. His reply was "It is not for me it is only a glorified matrimonial club. At least that's all the girls join for in the hope of hooking a husband."' She goes on, 'Needless to say I gave him a crushing answer but I wonder if this ridiculous suggestion is deterring other young people from joining our ranks.'[13]

Why the *Independent* is wrong is because there have been many marriages among YCs, or because YCs enjoyed themselves, this affected the movement's political effectiveness.

In a mainly heterosexual society the Young Conservatives provided a place where young people met as in other institutions, such as university and sports clubs, and where many met their future partner and married. It was good for democracy because some young people who joined became interested in politics who, but for the Young Conservatives, would not have done so. At this time fewer girls left home when they left school to participate in higher education. Protective parents often thought that Young Conservative functions were a suitable venue for their daughters, whereas they questioned other forms of social activity.[14]

If the Labour Party had thought the Young Conservatives were nothing but a dating agency no doubt it would not have wished to model its Young Socialist movement on it (Chapter 3).

The YCs provided the Conservative Party with fund raisers and manpower for elections. Abrams and Little in their article 'The Young Activist in Politics in 1965' state 'The officers of the Young Conservatives aim to politicise their recruits and with a minority they succeed. Most members do canvassing and constituency chores'. One would have thought Abrams and Little, who accurately identified the two-fold strength of the movement first to convert a limited number to take an active interest in politics which before joining the YCs they did not have and, second, to obtain much needed help from the remainder, would have found this praiseworthy. Instead, strangely, the article then proceeds to gives scant reward to the Young Conservatives.[15]

During the time I was a YC from 1951 to 1964 I agree with what was said in *The Times* which saw the strength of a YC branch, stating that it provided a complete social life for a young person. 'Apart from the weekly meetings, usually some neighbouring branch is putting on a dance on Saturday. One branch meets for coffee in the High Street on Saturday and takes them off to a cinema in the evenings. As to political work when the branch sets out to canvass before an election it is a group activity. One of the members says that "we will winkle them out whether they are keen or not" and after canvassing we would meet at the pub to make it a pleasant evening.' The same reporter commented that fewer girls went to Young Socialists meetings.[16]

Another activity which sprung up in the 1940s was the Miss YC contest. There appears to be no record of exactly when it started but the contests continued until 1973 when, given a lead by the Greater London YCs in a changing more feminist climate, it ceased.

Also during this time the Labour League of Youth held similar contests. In 1949 they held a holiday week at Filey, like the Young Conservatives. A report states that 'one B Boothroyd, clerk, [now Speaker of the House of Commons] won second prize.'[17] The Labour League of Youth and its successor apparently saw nothing ideologically wrong with such activities. In 1963, 16-year-old Kay Strickland said to be an enthusiastic member of the Young Socialists and treasurer of the ward, was chosen from nine other contestants to be elected Miss Gravesend 1963, the judges included the Tory mayor and mayoress and also the Tory MP for Gravesend.[18]

Until at least the mid-1960s both the Young Socialists and Young Liberals saw nothing evil in beauty competitions. At the rally of Young Socialists in June 1965 Pat Sheppard of Norwich was crowned Young Socialist 1965[19] while Lynn Kelson the secretary of Petersfield Young Liberals was crowned Miss

Liberal for 1966 which indicates that whatever their political views young people enjoy the same pastimes.[20] Mark sheets at the Bodleian Library indicated that the judges decided upon the winner from the following categories: charm, personality, beauty, poise and dress-sense.[21]

As late as 1967 the Miss YC competition appears to have been booming. When Jeanette Brinkworth of Warminster was chosen Miss Wessex YC in 1967 there were sixty-five other contestants for the title.[22] She went on to become Miss YC 1967. In 1968 the winner was a 17-year-old member of Gosforth YCs, Karen Murphy. On women's rights Karen Murphy stated that fifty years of electoral equality had not put women level with men, possibly because women find it difficult to be rational amongst administrative complexity: 'anyway,' she said, 'I would rather be ruled by a strong man than a stubborn and misguided woman!' She hoped her success would help a personalised recruiting campaign in her constituency.

Greater London who only three years earlier in an advertisement for their ball recommended those attending the YC ball 'to stampede Miss YC'[23] began to boycott the competition on the grounds that the competition was a farce and 1972 was to be the final year of the competition by which time Eastern and West Midland areas had joined Greater London in boycotting the competition.

Zig Layton Henry, in a contemporary article in *New Society* wrote, 'membership numbers, even in the Greater London Area, were falling,[24] which eventually was to seriously diminish the YCs' political influence, both with their own generation and with the Party.' However, there is evidence that the more serious mode did more to reduce membership rather than increase it.

An amusing article appeared in the journal of the Ealing Young Conservatives giving advice for a young woman in 1961 joining the YCs on 'Essential Economics and Advice for a Female YC'.

> Clothes: With two meetings a week, plus social events and other extraneous activities involved, the clothing bill for a female YC mounts alarmingly. What other 'club' caters for varying interests such as tennis (whites of course), swimming (new swimsuit every year), skating, boating and rambling (thick sweaters and trousers).
>
> One has also to dress appropriately for visits to theatres, cinemas, gas-works, art galleries and other places of interest. Another big clothes item are dresses suitable for the many dances we attend. Also stockings worn at dances, often laddered by male clod-hoppers or female stilettos.
>
> Drinks: It may be thought that they are nothing to do with the female YC, but don't be misled. The first point to remember is that under no circumstances should one ask for gin, whisky or sherry. One might receive it the first time but she will not be asked again. If the idea of beer is loathed, start like most others and work her way up the scale: tomato juice, Babycham, lager & lime, lager, light ale and finally bitter. Never, unless you rise to chairman, ask for a pint of bitter; several halves is much

better. Once she has become a beer drinker a female YC will find it easier
to get on and no longer will men appear to be avoiding her as they slither
out of '95' and down to the Vic. The next step is to realise that it is only
fair for a female YC to buy a round of drinks from time to time and she
should be prepared to buy her own drinks occasionally, on Saturday
mornings perhaps and contribute to the kitty when there is a dance or
ramble

Draw tickets: These will be handed out every so often with the request
that she tries to sell a few books. Despite the expense, the best tactic here,
is to buy the books yourself, thereby saving you the trouble of selling
them and also keeping your friends into the bargain![25]

When Edward Heath made a comprehensive review of the Party between 1964
and 1970 he set up a Women's Committee. Elizabeth Steele, the YC vice-
chairman sat on this committee. This report was produced and debated at the
1969 Party Conference and, unlike the debate on the Women's Charter at the
1948 Conference when Frances Vale was instrumental in obtaining its rejection,
this report was almost unanimously approved by the conference.

The committee recommended a number of changes to the law because
women were unfairly treated. The income of a married woman was treated
in many respects as that of her husband and this was remedied not by Labour
but a Conservative government, evidence that many of the major reforms since
the Second World War were to be carried out by the Conservatives. The
unfair law where the domicile of a married woman, even if separated, is that
of the husband was reformed by the Heath government in 1973. Also, on the
break up of a marriage a woman who had brought up children rather than
contribute financially would not be entitled to one half of the matrimonial
property: this was similarly altered by legislation initiated by the Heath government in 1973, together remedying the bureaucracy of the Magistrates Court
in requiring women to queue for payment of their maintenance by enabling
payments to be made by post.[26]

However, none of these were issues which were pursued by the national
committee (apart from Elizabeth Steele's contribution as a member of the
committee) or given any prominence at Party conferences by the Young
Conservatives. No leading member of the Young Conservatives took part in
the debate on the report at the Party conference so the movement, despite
such an encouraging lead by Frances Vale, failed to give the impetus to the
treatment of women as she wished; that is, equal to men, unlike the feminists
who wanted to make women, not equal, but given an advantageous position
in society.

# Chapter 19

# From Empire to Maastricht

During the nineteenth century Britain was the workshop of the world and could afford to live in splendid isolation. Although it took many years to realise, from approximately 1871 Britain was in economic decline. No government since then, I believe, can state without reservation Britain's fortunes have been reversed. Only time will tell whether there has been a fundamental improvement in the British economy after Britain has emerged from the deepest recession since the 1930s or whether the improvement in living standards of the 1980s was distorted by the once-off bonanza of North Sea oil and receipts from privatisation. If the Conservative governments of the 1980s have reversed a trend which has continued unchecked for 100 years it would be a monumental achievement.

In spite of high wages, the United States as the premier exporter in the West, and then Germany overtook the UK in the early years of the present century, despite more expensive food and higher taxes.

Joseph Chamberlain at the beginning of the century first thought it would be in the country's interest to form alliances with its continental neighbours, hence the Entente Cordiale of 1904.

At the end of the Second World War Britain had tremendous moral authority in Western Europe, alone having resisted the tyranny of Nazism, now was the time for leadership. Although the Labour party showed little interest in becoming involved with the fate of Europe the Conservatives were equally to blame because, having criticised the Labour Party for the lack of a concrete policy towards Europe, they failed to seize the opportunity to display leadership when they had the chance after their election victory in 1951. Following the Second World War, Churchill was enthusiastic at the concept of a united Europe and this led to the formation of the Council of Europe at Strasbourg in 1949. Anthony Eden was not so attracted to this idea. He saw Britain as a sovereign nation with huge colonial responsibilities and our national destiny did not lie in Europe. Britain should certainly support and encourage Western Europe in its military strength but she should never become involved in any super-national entity. His prejudice concerning Europe was shared by Bevin.[1]

However, when Churchill became Prime Minister he no longer regarded European unity as a live issue. If Churchill had continued to be as enthusiastic about Europe in government as he was in opposition he could have paved the way for this country to have been one of the original signatories to the Treaty of Rome signed in 1958 and the treaty then formed could have taken into account Britain's needs. Many of the later problems in connection with the EEC, the principal one being the Common Agriculture Policy, might never have arisen.

Our influence in Europe in the post-war period is shown by the other European countries agreeing that a united Europe would not affect our right to receive and give preference to members of the Empire. (A system where lower tariffs were imposed in trading between countries in the Empire than with others.) Nevertheless, what was needed from the Young Conservatives, as with their seniors, was practical politics not sentiment. It was left to the Western European nations to determine the shape and power of European institutions. The Young Conservatives displayed a negative attitude. This contrasted sharply with the YC attitude over entry into the EEC after 1960 when the YCs of that generation advocated constructive proposals such as direct elections to the European Parliment.

Not only did the Attlee Government have pressing internal problems caused by the expense and need for reconstruction following the war but there was a massive movement for Colonial self-government. The Attlee government quickly negotiated independence for India, dividing the country between Moslem Pakistan and India.

Churchill was critical of the way that the Attlee government had granted independence to India. Eden took a more pragmatic approach. Once the Attlee government had determined to give India independence there was nothing the Conservative opposition could do to prevent it. To continue to oppose it would have been most unwise as it would have jeopardized our future relationship with India and Pakistan. Clearly Eden was right and Churchill wrong.

Nevertheless, in a pamphlet setting out Conservative party policy in 1949 the Party committed itself to 'giving self-government to those colonies which were economically sound and whose social services were reasonably efficient provided power could be transferred to the people as a whole and not to a small unrepresentative political, racial or religious oligarchy.'[2]

It is difficult to understand what other policy the Attlee government could have adopted bearing in mind the massive independence movement in India and that those who were vocal in the Young Conservatives, like their seniors, were very critical of the way 'we had given India away'.

Certainly the idea of Empire was enthusiastically supported by the Young Conservatives of the 1940s and continued well into the 1950s. There is evidence that there was a significant number of Young Conservatives, who appear to have been the least vocal, who took a more realistic view that the Empire, as it had previously existed, was a concept of the past. A motion debated by South Kensington YCs in 1947 'That this house views with concern the widespread sympathy for and, often, co-operation with, nationalists in the East and urges the government to re-adopt the more practical and farsighted policy of earlier Tory administrations' was carried by 70 votes to 57. Those who voted against the motion had correctly gauged the situation.[3]

At the 1948 Llandudno Conference, a 29-year-old Young Conservative Ted Leather, subsequently to become an MP, lit up the meeting with the challenging query 'Are not the people of this island interested in staying alive? That is what the Empire means to us. If it lives, I stay alive.' An amendment was moved to a vague official resolution on Commonwealth relations, stating, 'that the Tory Party do all it could to stop the ratification of the GATT agreement and stop the ratification of the Havana Agreement so far as these agreements touch preference.'[4]

The Geneva pact (October 1947) which the United Kingdom ratified re-defined tariff rates. It cut preference between the Empire and the UK on some goods and abolished them on others. Under the Havana Agreement (March 1948) Empire preference might be modified or eliminated by international trade organisations. It had not yet been ratified by Britain.

The following year at the Conservative Conference at Earls Court, Anthony Nutting supported a motion which stated:

> While grudging to no other State the right to make their own tariff arrangements this Conference insists that the British Commonwealth and Empire must have full freedom to exercise the same right and maintains that the future safety and prosperity of the Commonwealth depends upon a policy of Empire development under a system of mutual preference in its widest sense covering industry and agriculture, finance, shipping and aviation.

Anthony Nutting said 'there were many Empire projects that would repay the simplest and cheapest development and make Britain less dependent on dollar countries.' This was an acute problem for the Attlee government. Anthony Nutting continued:

> There is no will in the Socialist government to develop the Empire. Until recently Stafford Cripps was adhering to his declared objective of liqui-dating the British Empire. Now it appears he is to postpone the date of liquidation until after the Americans have finished investing their money in it.[5]

So great was the applause that he had to rise to bow his acknowledgement. At the same Party conference there was a further motion 'That the Conference welcomes the creation of a Council of Europe and promises its support for all practical measures to promote closer European unity consistent with the full maintenance of the unity of the Empire.' Duncan Sandys stated that 'a Europe from which Britain stands aloof would either be dominated by Germany or Russia or a combination of the two.' To the rest of Europe this would bring back memories of a pact like the Hitler–Stalin pact of 1939 which could be to the detriment of the majority of the remaining European States. C.M. Bowditch said that, 'we cannot serve two masters. We cannot be a central point of the Empire and be part of a united Europe.' But this was a minority view.

Nevertheless, in spite of all the plaudits, the Conservative party, when it gained power in 1951, having criticised Sir Stafford Cripps, had no new ideas and continued with the same policy. Except for the minor territories the Conservative government were, therefore, left with no alternative but to allow the remainder of the Commonwealth to have complete independence, both politically and, in practice, economically.

Hong Kong never sought independence. Ghana became independent in 1957, Tanganyka in 1961 and Uganda in 1962. The only colonies that Wilson's government had to deal with when it came to power in 1964 were Rhodesia which seized independence in 1965, and Malta who gained independence in 1967.

Empire Day (24 May) appeared to have been generally, although not universally, observed by YCs well into the 1950s.[6]

Devoid of trading partners, were we to become isolated like Switzerland or were we to seek trading partners by participating in the EEC and, if so, to what extent would we be able to influence its direction?

In 1961 the delegates to the first YC Conference, following Edward Heath's summing up, approved by 565 votes to 510, a motion calling for support for an economically and politically integrated Europe.[7] The argument against membership of the Common Market was that we would be putting Europe before the Commonwealth. However both John Diefenbaker, Prime Minister of Canada and Robert Menzies of Australia in 1957 wished Britain to join the Common market for a number of reasons both political and economic. If the purchasing power of Europe was improved this would benefit Australia for whom the UK was her best market at that time. As one Australian commentator aptly stated 'My country is best known for sending a cricket team every five years and an army every twenty-five years. If you fellows had taken a bit more interest in Europe between the wars we would not have to send an army and could concentrate on cricket.'[8]

It is interesting to note the world 'politically'. At a time when the European Economic Community was in its infancy it was never envisaged that it was practical or sensible to have economic union without political union. Undoubtedly a considerable number of YCs were opposed to entry. An article in the *Ealing Chronicle* stated

> Offered for sale one Empire in bargain lots. Hon Auctioneers: Harold Macmillan under the sponsorship of President Kennedy of the USA. If this is not enough we are now entering the final steps of humiliation because by surrendering our sovereign independence we may find ourselves a member of the European Common Market.[9]

Duncan Sandys in a most reasoned speech to the Second Annual YC Conference in 1962 said 'The more we study the question the more we must come to realise that if the negotiations we are now conducting with the EEC are to fail there would be a most grave disadvantage not only to Britain but

also the Commonwealth.' Although one delegate shouted 'shame' there was
also applause for his pro-European stand.[10]

In the early 1960s the EEC lobby was gaining strength and in 1965 when
Edward Heath became leader of the Party they had a most influential convert.
Peter Walker, when he was national chairman during 1958–60, opposed Britain's
entry, but in 1966 Edward Heath convinced him that it was in Britain's best
interests to seek application to join and thereafter he became an ardent pro-
European.[11]

The Greater London YCs at their conference at Clacton in 1967 passed a
resolution by a large majority showing how much YC opinion had shifted on
Europe the motion:

> Great Britain should continue to play an active role in world affairs and
> that it is in the best interests of British people and that of the Common-
> wealth that Britain should join the European Economic Community and
> play her full part in shaping the destiny of Europe.

Duncan Sandys, the opposition spokesman on the Commonwealth and Colonies, put paid to the nostalgic hankering for our role in the Empire by saying,
'Some people argued that Britain must choose between Europe and the
Commonwealth. Nothing could be more absurd. The Commonwealth did not
offer us a protected area. Empire free trade did not appeal to any of our
Commonwealth partners.'[12] He was absolutely right. In the immediate post-war
period a free trade area might have been established if Britain had shown
leadership by offering the then Empire a generous trading package. However,
in view of GATT it might have been illegal by international law. Further, as
we relied so heavily on the USA for our raw materials and other imports, a
trading pact which excluded her would have been opposed by the USA. In
practice it might have been impossible to establish, even if the will had been
present among Commonwealth members.

The alternative was to have joined with the other six and signed the Treaty
of Rome in 1958. Perhaps, then, the pound rather than the Deutschmark
would have been the dominant European currency. Britain's economic state
might have been more powerful if we had pursued either of these courses but
we dithered until Harold Macmillan's government took the decisive step to
apply for European membership in 1961. De Gaulle vetoed it and we needed
a person with real leadership to overcome anti-European prejudice and other
obstacles to gain our entry and it was fortunate for Britain that we had this in
Edward Heath who, in his maiden speech in 1950, had argued for us to join
the Common Market, which at that time was limited to iron and steel.
Thereafter, until entry was achieved, the YCs gave Edward Heath their
maximum support.

Eric Chalker in the early 1960s said that the idea of the trading partnership
of European Countries outside the EEC called EFTA (European Free Trade
Area), of which we were a founder member in 1958, first interested him but

he then became more convinced of the merits of joining the European Community.[13]

At the 1969 Party Conference, Eric Chalker declared 'in debating Europe you are debating our future. The issue of Europe is the issue of tomorrow. We are not prepared to wait until tomorrow for action'. 'Young people,' said Mr Chalker, 'are realising one of their ideals of internationalism.' He spoke of a poll which showed that 73% of the young people interviewed felt that they had more in common with young people abroad than had the older generation. Cheers and counter cheers and cries of 'rubbish' greeted this assertion. Mr Chalker continued, 'with votes at 18, six million youngsters will be voting at the next election. Europe is a great ideal and if the Labour Party and the Liberal Party are pledged to the ideal and the Tory Party goes alone down a cul-de-sac of nationalism who are the young voters to choose.'[14]

Another Young Conservative chairman, David Atkinson, said, 'Young people are not prepared to accept the political prejudice, doubt and hesitation of older people.' He admitted that the benefits of joining the EEC would be greater for today's youth because they would live with it longer. David Atkinson considered the EEC as the central theme of his year of office, 1970–71.[15]

Andrew Bowden said, 'if I wanted to be a Euro-sceptic I believe I would have no difficulty in obtaining the backing of my Association but I believe the advantages of the European Community will not be for my generation but for the next generation.'[16]

Unfortunately, throughout the history of the world, politicians generally find it easier to promote nationalism than internationalism, but hopefully in future times Gorbachev will be considered greater than Zhirinovsky and Delors greater than Le Pen.

In 1969 the Party Conference passed a pro-European resolution by 1,452 to 475 votes and at the 1971 Conference the Young Conservatives demonstrated their enthusiasm for Europe wearing European National costumes when the Conference approved by an even larger vote of 2,474 to 424 on a motion proposed by Peter Price, a YC national vice-chairman, supporting the terms the government had negotiated for entry on 1 January 1973.

Graham Bright, a vice-chairman, writing in the YC newspaper *Tomorrow*, in September 1972, made it clear his goal was 'a federated Europe, with a common monetary system and foreign policy headed by a directly elected European Parliament.'[17] From a study of a considerable number of contemporary minutes I can find no mention of any branches being against entry. The fishermen of Brixham in Devon who violently opposed the fishing policy of the Common Market certainly did not obtain any support from Paul Hills, then chairman of Western Area YCs who hit back hard at the fishermen. He advocated entry, mentioning 'the tremendous economic success of the EEC since its formation and how the standard of living of the Six, with the exception of Italy, had now overtaken Britain's.' At the end of the meeting, Paignton YCs voted by an overwhelming majority in favour of Britain's entry.[18]

In Hornsey's minutes it states the European campaign saw a large number of Hornsey YCs active throughout London both heckling at various anti-European rallies and also supporting or speaking at other pro-European rallies and also at the GLYC rally in Trafalgar Square. In addition Hornsey YCs were the mainstay of the London European Activity Committee.[19] Britain having obtained entry into the European Community, a small band of YCs in Trafalgar Square on 1 January 1973 celebrated both the New Year and our joining the European Community.[20]

Having given every assistance to gaining entry into the EEC, the YCs were now to turn their attention to the European Parliament and direct elections of the Euro-MPs.

At their 1973 YC conference a motion that the United Kingdom should lead the way by instituting direct elections to the European Parliament was passed by an overwhelming majority. Herr Alber, a member of the German Christian Democratic Union gave a generous acknowledgement of his regard for Britain's democracy. He said 'We are stagnating in bureaucracy. The democratic experience of your country would benefit all of Europe',[21] illustrating the goodwill that Britain still enjoyed in Europe. If the advantage had been exploited then I am certain that Britain's influence on the development of the European institutions would have been so much greater. On the following day Edward Heath was evasive when asked questions on the subject and made it clear it was low on the agenda and the more important question was how the European Parliament could be made into a democratic forum.[22] Nevertheless, the YCs continued enthusiastic support for the establishment of direct elections to the European Parliament culminating in Robert Hughes' successful addendum to a lukewarm motion concerning the EEC (Chapter 29).

One of the promises in Labour's 1974 manifesto advocated a referendum on membership of the EEC which was held in 1975 and for which there was overwhelming approval by the British public. The referendum was held during Tony Kerpel's chairmanship and the YCs vigorously supported the campaign.

Dorking YCs set up a stall in the shopping centre on a Saturday shortly before the referendum. They distributed literature to passers-by. Of the 508 people who were asked 378 (84%) were in favour, 65 (13%) against and 65 did not know. From such a small sample it was amazing how accurately it predicted the final result. They discovered that half the people asked were unaware of the referendum, accordingly they organised a cavalcade through the streets of Dorking to remind people to vote.[23] The Young Conservatives and the Youth Development officer, Jimmy Gordon, assisted in organising a Youth for Europe Rally where they were joined by students, Young Socialists and Young Liberals.

Harold Macmillan felt so strongly against the wisdom of holding the referendum, although he made few political speeches in his retirement, he agreed to address the GLYC Conference in April 1975 at Hastings on the referendum. He said that the reason the Labour cabinet had called the referendum was not because they wanted the people to decide but they were unable to give Parliament and the Crown whom they served a unanimous opinion and nowhere in our history could he find a case where we had renounced unilaterally a treaty we had signed two years earlier.[24] In 1979 Harold Macmillan then aged 85 stated if the EEC was to succeed then we had to have common monetary, foreign and defence policies so that the EEC could rank with the USA and the USSR.[25]

The Conservatives were returned to power in 1979 and Margaret Thatcher felt strongly that Britain had an unfair share of the burden of the European Economic budget. After protracted negotiation, under her influence, the amount Britain contributed was considerably reduced.

Edward Heath addressed the 1984 conference and said the next election would be the first that would be fought with all main parties in favour of our EEC membership. It was no longer in or out but how Britain could best further the development of Europe. He referred to the negotiations to revise our contribution reminding his audience that it was less than 1% of our national budget and, in a veiled criticism of Margaret Thatcher's European policy, stated there is more in Europe than the budget. He feared the forthcoming European elections were being fought at the lowest common denominator of self-interested nationalism.[26]

Margaret Thatcher not only supported the Act of Parliament setting up the single European market which commenced on 1 January 1993, but her speeches made it clear that the EEC would lead to a political union although nobody knew the final shape it would take. In a message in 1981 Margaret Thatcher made it clear that she regarded the EEC as a political rather than economic union by stating 'I profoundly believe that membership of the European Economic Community is in the best interests of this country above all for political reasons. It means that there is an area of democratic stability in Europe which is vital in the interests of Europe and the larger world.'[27]

Having by her strong leadership moved the Conservative party and the government to the right, she might then have turned to Europe and tried to make the European Community less bureaucratic, but she became decidedly lukewarm about the whole concept of the European Community being other than a free trade area. Cracks which had bedeviled the Labour party for so long until Neil Kinnock took a strongly pro-European stand, now opened in the Conservative party.

At the 1984 YC Conference there was evidence that the YCs were becoming less enthusiastic for the EEC when a motion welcoming the planned enlargement of the European Union and to provide further impetus for the reorganisation of the Common Agricultural Policy was impressively defeated.[28] The opponents of the motion argued that the Common Agricultural Policy had to be put on a fairer footing before the Community was enlarged.

In 1987 a motion 'that this conference believes that Britain's future lies in Europe and urges HM Government to play its full role in the economic and social development of Europe to enable it to fulfil its potential as a major world force' was only passed by 286 votes to 270.[29]

The question of Europe together with unemployment were the two issues that divided the YCs of the 1980s as there was complete agreement on virtually all other policy.

Although Mark Macgregor and Andrew Tinney jointly wrote a letter to *The Times* criticising Michael Heseltine for saying that young people foresaw their destiny in Europe, saying that the majority of YCs and Conservative students supported Margaret Thatcher's visions of Europe. However, what they needed to consider was whether this was the view of young people generally, which they did not. According to a survey by Market and Opinion research of 18 to 34-year-olds, 67% thought we should continue our membership while only 19% disagreed and 42% were in favour of a single European currency while 36% opposed it.[30]

The 1993 YC Conference was the reverse of the 1971 conference. A pro-Maastricht speaker was shouted down when the name of Jacques Delors was mentioned, although one of his assistants was present as a guest. There was hissing at any pro-Maastricht remark and the mention of Margaret Thatcher's or Norman Tebbit's names was greeted with tremendous cheers. The YCs had gone full circle.[31]

# Chapter 20

# Unemployment

A lthough the left had prided themselves on looking after the interests of the less privileged, much social legislation has been initiated by the Conservative Party. A fitting tribute was paid by factory workers to Benjamin Disraeli, the founder of modern 'one nation' Conservatism upon his elevation to the peerage.

> Zeal and anxiety you have on all occasions manifested on behalf of factory children as well as your support of their case in the House of Commons. It is now 40 years since you have raised you voice in the Imperial chamber in support of women and children employed in textile manufacturing and during the whole of the period whether in or out of office and amidst the struggle and tribulation of political strife and official duties you have been faithful to the cause of working children for which we are for ever grateful.

One section of the underprivileged in any society is the unemployed.

Britain, in the period 1919 to 1939 was, as were most parts of the developed world, plagued with unemployment. Although the Labour party relentlessly attacked the Conservative party as causing unemployment, nevertheless in the two minority governments between the First and Second World Wars the Labour party similar to the Wilson and Callaghan administrations since, have been unable to stem the rising tide of unemployment. The 1945–51 Labour government received praise for full employment although it is a mistake to think that unemployment or full employment was uniform throughout the country. Taking the figures for 1938 and 48: In 1938 Liverpool had 22.8% in 1948 7%; Manchester 11% in 1938 and 1.7% in 1948; St Albans 2.5% in 1938 and 0.03% in 1948 and Birmingham 8.2% in 1938 and 0.08% in 1948.[1] The Conservative party, inspired by Rab Butler evolved the Industrial Charter whereby, although industry would be free, the government would intervene to make special financial arrangements for industry to carry large stocks in periods of temporary loss in demand and keep industry running by stimulating strong activity in those industries which had shown themselves more liable to fluctuation, particularly those producing for capital investment and export.[2] Anthony Nutting (the first national chairman) claimed the first generation of the post-war Young Conservatives were enthusiastic for this policy.[3]

Anthony Nutting at party conferences and elsewhere supported the policy and his support of the Industrial Charter was endorsed by his successor in the chair, John Hay. He gave a speech in support to the City of London Forum, although there was a small but vocal minority of both senior and Young Conservatives against it. An Agricultural Charter was brought out to regulate agriculture, which had a certain resemblance to the Common Agricultural Policy of the European Union.

Discussing the Llandudno conference the *Daily Express* reported

> Another foolish act came out of the Conservative Conference when the delighted delegates accepted the Agricultural Charter as a basis for farm policy. So the Agricultural Charter goes with the Industrial Charter of a year ago as the second ill-bred son of unwise parentage. They rave against Socialist control and then try to persuade the Party to vote for committees to direct farmers in husbandry and to dispossess those who do not please the bureaucrats.

However out of 4,000 only 1 voted against the adoption of the Agricultural Charter.[4]

The City of London Forum indicates that a vigorous debate took place between the supporters and opponents of the Industrial Charter. Captain Roy Faithful, an ex-army officer, said the Charter had been accepted as a statement of policy: 'on it we stand or fall. It offers no strong central guidance and no vigorous alternative to Socialism. The whole country demands an alternative party of progress and reform.'

The Industrial Charter failed to convince the general public. The Charter was defended by Captain MacDavid of the Duke of Cornwall's Light Infantry. He said,

> We should look at it as an attempt to put labour in the picture and as a plan for social progress. It is merely a guide. We should look at it as a military operation. The Charter represents the general idea in the commander's mind, there is nothing definite about it. If the Tories announced a definite programme they would in duty be bound to carry it out irrespective of the conditions at the time of coming to power. As far as nationalisation is concerned it is possible that many industries will be running smoothly by the next General Election.[5]

In the late 1940s there was a genuine fear among many that if there was a Conservative government there would be unemployment as there had been before the Second World War. They conveniently forgot that there was also massive unemployment under the pre-war minority Labour government for which they were unable to find any remedy but nevertheless blamed the Conservative party for what they considered was the failure of the Baldwin and Chamberlain governments to tackle unemployment. Many believed that if the Conservative party had won the 1950 and/or 1951 election, unemployment would return. Lord Woolton did not share that belief. In his autobiography he said 'Today no government could survive without a clear policy both for the prevention and cure of this economic disease.'[6]

After three years of Tory government in 1954 an article in Spalding YC magazine stated there were 23 million people in work a rise of 1,500,000 since 1950 and only 210,000 were unemployed (0.9%) and this included those who were in many instances just changing jobs.[7] In 1958 an article in the Petts Wood YC Journal stated that under a Labour government unemployment was 338,000 and between 1951 and 1957 under a Conservative government, it was 310,000. Keeping unemployment below 2% is better than Beveridge's aims and that if the correct policy is pursued unemployment should be less than 3%.

Robert Carr, who was then the PPS to the Minister of Labour said, 'it is the firm policy of the Government to keep unemployment at the lowest level compatible with the avoidance of inflation.'[8] However, that was the policy of the Conservative party of the 1980s but when Robert Carr said those words he would never have contemplated the situation of the 1980s, i.e. that it was necessary to have more than 2 million people unemployed to combat inflation. Within five years of that speech and until the present time, similar to the period 1919–39, unemployment has dominated the political agenda.

During the current long period of Conservative rule the Party has come to tolerate unemployment, feeling it the lesser evil to inflation and in view of the Conservatives' four election victories, many of the 90% in employment agree. Regrettably, it has become easier to control inflation and strikes with such a level of unemployment but until the late 1980s the Young Conservatives can be proud that during the period of Conservative rule they did not allow the government to forget that unemployment was an evil.

By 1962 the economy was stagnating. The Government felt that inflation was getting out of hand and although inflation was not on the scale it was in the mid-1960s the government tried to control wages by means of a pay-pause. The Conservative party rapidly started to lose support in the country as unemployment rose.

Fergus Montgomery from Newcastle, where the memory of the terrible legacy of unemployment in the 1930s was still vivid, while still a fairly new MP, abstained from voting in an economics debate because of the soaring unemployment in the North East.[9] This was prior to the Arctic winter of 1962/3 which caused a significant increase in unemployment generally. By January 1963 Harold Macmillan realising the problems of the North East appointed Lord Hailsham to draw up a plan to combat unemployment. At the YC Conference in 1963 there was considerable criticism of the high level of unemployment.

Peter Wood proposed a motion for the Government 'to redouble its efforts to rapidly reduce unemployment in North East England, Scotland and Northern Ireland. A figure of 814,632 unemployed was intolerable. In national terms it meant a huge waste of resources and in human terms it meant misery and poverty for those on the dole.' He suggested, 'a selective pay-roll tax, the provision of coal-fired power stations wherever practicable and one minister to be responsible for unemployment.'

Derek Robson of Hexham said, 'while appreciating that the Party did not believe in the positive direction of industry considered that the government should apply a policy of negative direction whereby companies who wish to expand in areas of full or over-employment should be politely told that they might expand only in selected areas where labour was plentiful.' Mr R Pounder of Belfast felt 'the Conservative Government could have done more to direct industry to Ulster.'

Elizabeth Steele of Runcorn (a future YC national vice-chairman) in successfully proposing that Merseyside should be added to the motion said, 'the dole card was becoming almost as widespread as the ration card a few years earlier.' Reginald Maudling, then Chancellor of the Exchequer replying, called for 'a determined outlook' after the breakdown of the talks in Brussels on the Common Market. 'If we can keep at the right level in relation to our competitors there is no reason why we should not achieve the National Economic Development Council's growth target, particularly in the field of export.' He said, 'where there are men and women wanting to work we will push government investment even to the point of taking substantial risks.'[10] Oddly enough Reginald Maudling did not excuse the government's record on the grounds of the hard winter of 1962/3.

The winter of 1946/7 was the only other really severe winter since the Second World War and unemployment rocketed similarly. However, the government should take some credit for the fact that during the severe winter of 1962/3 the unemployment situation was assisted because there were sufficient supplies of fuel to prevent power cuts. This contrasted sharply with the situation in 1947 when the situation was much less favourable due to power dislocation. In spite of giving the workers the nationalisation programme that the Labour government said the workers desired, there was failure to dig the coal needed to keep the power stations running.

However, no resolution on unemployment was debated at the Party Conference between 1958 (when a motion calling on the Government to take measures to eliminate pockets of unemployment was passed) and 1972 (a motion critical both of the level of unemployment and lack of an effective regional policy was defeated).[11]

The Young Conservatives were treating the matter more seriously than their elders as at their 1964 Conference when there was a further debate:

> That this Conference, whilst recognising the measures taken by HM Government designed to promote economic growth and combat unemployment urges that the machinery for Regional Planning and Development be established as an essential step towards the progress and comprehensive redevelopment of this nation's industrial areas, the maintenance of full employment and the prevention of any decline in the economic prosperity in the population of rural areas.[12]

During the Wilson government, unemployment doubled to 2.5%, still a very acceptable level if inflation is to be contained. Inflation increased to 7.3%, still a modest increase compared with the inflation of the 1970s. The Wilson government's economic policy was blown off track by the 1967 devaluation, fully exploited by its opponents, as was the devaluation by the Attlee government. However, virtually all post-war Conservative governments had allowed the value of the pound to float downwards but this seemed to cause less consternation as the international financial markets had greater confidence in the way the Conservative party had handled the economy.

The declared policy of the government of Edward Heath was twofold: to decrease government interference and to make Government more cost effective. The 1979 Conservative government declared similar economic objectives, the result of which policies, on both occasions, brought soaring unemployment; in the case of Edward Heath from approximately 600,000 to 900,000 as against 1.5m to 3.2m in the case of Margaret Thatcher's government. At a meeting of the YC National Executive in 1971 the NAC again expressed concern at the rising level of unemployment.

In reply, Robert Carr stated that the Heath government had already taken substantial steps to reflate the economy. Apart from those which applied to the country as a whole he announced a number of special measures to help the assisted areas where unemployment was particularly severe. These included £162m capital expenditure on infra-structure for work which could be substantially completed by March 1973; £46m on housing improvement; £70m over three years for an accelerated naval construction programme; £100m capital expenditure by the nationalised industries brought forward into the next two years; and £60m additional expenditure over the next two years mainly on roads and defence.

The Government had taken measures to alleviate the situation in the short term and met half the cost of schemes run by the Industrial Training Boards to provide up to 4,325 additional skilled training places for young people unable to obtain apprenticeships. They agreed to extend facilities for vocational training for young people under 18, particularly those who were unemployed. The Government were also to make available £500,000 for an experimental scheme, to be run by the National Association of Youth Clubs, of social value, particularly in the environmental and community fields.

Unlike the 1990s when the Conservative government regarded the fact that many industries were 'leaner and fitter' as a major achievement, the Conservative government of Edward Heath appealed to employers not to cut back on their recruitment that year (1971) and the CBI strongly endorsed this.[13]

David Hunt, in 1972, said: 'It is deplorable that 107,000 go direct from the classroom to the dole queue. We must not tolerate it.'[14] When he made this remark he could not have envisaged that he would be Secretary of State for Employment when unemployment would be in excess of 2,750,000 and youth unemployment so much higher than it was in 1972. *Economic Trends*, in 1993, stated: 'unemployment is greatest among the young (one in five for males and one in six for females).'

Beryl Sloan, vice-chairman of Northern Area, quoted the Conservative manifesto of the 1970 campaign: 'we are not prepared to tolerate the human waste that accompanies persistent unemployment, dereliction and decline' and advocated an immediate short-term solution, instancing clearance of derelict areas, parks, playgrounds, household repairs and redevelopment.[15] This sentiment was echoed some fifteen years later by another YC, Angela Hills, who advocated a massive injection of cash into the North East.[16]

Like the Margaret Thatcher government ten years later, ministers justified the increased unemployment by claiming it was caused by increased productivity. Addressing the 1972 YC Conference Robert Carr claimed that in the space of one year British industry reduced its labour force by 400,000 while increasing production.[17]

Ian Gilmour at the 1981 YC Conference gave a warning that unemployment would continue to rise if there was a rise in productivity unless there was also a rise in production to combat the reduction of labour caused by increased productivity. Both Edward Heath and Margaret Thatcher after advocating that the government should not help the lame ducks of industry, spent vast sums of taxpayers' money subsidising major British industrial firms that were in financial difficulties; in 1971 Rolls Royce and in 1981 British Leyland. In 1971 Edward Heath's action was not criticised although when Margaret Thatcher took similar action with British Leyland, Jim Stride said at the 1981 YC Conference 'we did not elect a Conservative government to give British Leyland £4m or to keep the national Enterprise Board in existence.'[18]

However, no doubt he would be pleased that the government's solution to the economic difficulties was to pursue a monetarist policy and not to follow Roosevelt's example when he steered the US out of the slump of 1931 by inflating the economy. Roosevelt was an unlikely candidate for the Young Communists to praise but they paid a warm tribute following his death: 'His labours in time of peace resulted in work and prosperity for his fellow citizens.' This is not the usual language of a Communist describing a capitalist's economic policy.[19]

With unemployment nearing one million Edward Heath carried out a U-turn by passing the Industry Act; this Act enabled the government to give massive help to industry and Edward Heath placed former YC national chairman, Peter Walker, in charge. In December 1972 he announced that the long-term run down of the coal industry would be reversed with an annual subsidy of £175m (its accumulated deficit of £475 million was written off) and a few weeks later he announced a modernisation plan for British Steel costing £3,000 million over ten years. Further money was poured into new buildings and the system of grants and inducements developed to encourage the movement of jobs to assisted areas. The bonus was a dramatic reduction in unemployment.

During 1973 unemployment halved, from nearly 1 million to 500,000 although the reduction was assisted by the raising of the school leaving age to 16. The great majority of YCs, like their chairman David Hunt and Clive Landa who were pressing the Government to tackle unemployment in inner cities, and the protection of the environment, fully supported this policy. As with any radical policy there were critics in the Party. Former YC, Trevor Skeet was among those who proposed an amendment, which was defeated, to require parliamentary approval for subsidies in excess of £1m. Sir Harry Legge-Bourke described the Act 'as a Socialist bill by ethic and philosophy . . . obnoxious for many reasons' and Tony Benn who would himself make use of the provisions of the Act in the Callaghan government which followed described it as 'spadework for socialism'.[20]

The effect of this policy was soaring inflation which was aggravated by the huge rise in the price of oil caused by the 1973 Middle East War. Margaret Thatcher, when unemployment soared under her premiership and there was a demand to reflate the economy, said 'the lady is not for turning!'

Heath's policy was derided by many Conservatives of the Thatcher era. At the 1982 YC Conference, John Livingstone said that the present recession was not the fault of Margaret Thatcher. There were others to blame for the problems, including Mr Callaghan, Mr Wilson and even Mr Heath. The Conference should send a message 'We are right behind you.' Many prominent YCs gave her wholehearted support at the time.[21] In retrospect Demitri Argyropulo said that he did not think Margaret Thatcher 'would have done better at a time of world inflation and the trebling of the price of oil when we had not the benefit of our own oil supplies as in 1981.'[22]

Unemployment rose from 500,000 under the Labour governments of 1974 and 1979 to 1½m. At the 1977 YC conference Margaret Thatcher told her audience if any Conservative government had achieved that level of unemployment they would be hounded out of office and would then preside over an administration that would see unemployment double to 3.2 million.[23]

The YCs picketed the Labour Conference in 1977 because of the high level of unemployment only to have their own conference in 1993 picketed, there being an even higher level of unemployment under successive Conservative governments.[24]

After 1979 the Thatcher government pursued a deflationary policy which brought unemployment to the 1930s heights of over 3.2m. Youth unemployment even in the prosperous South increased alarmingly as is shown by the figures of Hampshire Careers office at Winchester. In 1980 there were 2,582 unemployed.[25] By 1981 it had jumped to 6,921 and in 1982 to 10,020. Just as disconcerting was the reduction of job vacancies in the same area. In 1974 the Careers Office at Winchester listed 1,746 unfilled vacancies, 406 in 1980 and only 75 by 1982,[26] supporting Robert Hughes' contention that youth unemployment under the Labour Government had risen by 800%.[27]

There was to be no U-turn as had been experienced under the Heath government. With soaring unemployment the Government initially became very unpopular and this was one of the factors that caused a decline in YC membership at that time. On the other hand, it is obvious that even in these difficult times Margaret Thatcher had much grass roots support among YCs.

At the 1982 conference the YCs overwhelmingly rejected a motion proposed by Jeff Green on behalf of Wallasey YCs which noted the percieved hardness of the Government's attitude towards unemployment and called upon the Cabinet to make a more positive approach in uniting the nation. One speaker said that it was up to all Tories to change the image and let it be known that the Party recognised the human indignity and distress caused by unemployment. The fact that this was a minority view indicates that the rank and file YCs were more enthusiastic for Mrs Thatcher's policy than were their leaders. Most of the speakers, some of whom were unemployed, defended Mrs Thatcher and had no wish for her to change the hard line image.

Iain Picton at the 1981 Party Conference used his customary national chairman's right to speak to air his concern on unemployment and clearly he was right to do so. Representing a political youth movement he had to be concerned about the high level of youth unemployment.[27] Iain Picton became chairman of the Tory Reform Group. Writing in its magazine in 1984 he said,

> our debate is about how we can reduce unemployment within our free enterprise economic system, whilst keeping inflation down. Inflation is a job killer and must not be allowed to rise. The only 'traitors' now are those who cannot and will not accept that the damage that unemployment is doing to our Nation and to our people is now reaching such grievous proportions that considered action is needed – and it is needed soon.[28]

Richard Fuller, when YC national chairman in 1986, expressed similar concern at the 1985 Party Conference and called 'for something a little more courageous, something a little less drab to tackle the problem.' It appears he had an ally in Kenneth Clarke, (then Paymaster General) speaking at a fringe meeting of the same Conference who said 'It would be foolish to suggest that within the pool of unemployed there were many unwilling, idle people who would not leap at the chance of a job if they could get one.'[29]

I believe one of Margaret Thatcher's greatest economic achievements was the lessening of the North–South divide.

In spite of the huge support for the Labour Party in the North, neither the Callaghan or Wilson governments were able to narrow the gap between North and South and it was left to Margaret Thatcher's policies of the mid-1980s to reverse the trend. Many of the old and outdated industries had fallen casualty to the recession of the early 1980s and the policy of attracting foreign manu-facturers, particularly the Japanese, has led to remarkable recovery in the industrial fortunes of the north. The recent recession affected the South more than the North so that the gap between North and South is very much diminished.

In 1963 in 'Blueprint for Britain', the *laissez-faire* policy was rejected by the YC policy group. The problem of declining industries in parts of Scotland and the north of England and Wales causing a drift to the South must be discouraged by assisting industry in areas of high unemployment.[30] However the much less regulated economy of the 1980s compared with the 1960s and 1970s probably brought more benefit to the North than the South.

An internal survey of the Conservative party in 1986 showed the chief concern among young people was unemployment at 54% and education at 26%.[31] Andrew Tinney and Adrian McLellan did not show the same concern about youth unemployment that many previous chairmen had.[32]

In this post-computer age, in spite of what Lord Woolton said fifty years earlier, there appears no apparent cure for this economic disease. Both the Wilson and Callaghan governments were faced with the rising tide of unemployment. The Labour party has not claimed that if they had pursued a different policy, unemployment would have been less. The failure of Labour to include in the revised Clause 4 a commitment to full employment indicates that, in spite of Left-wing rhetoric they are not confident that they have found the remedy either to what Lord Woolton called 'this economic disease'.

## Chapter 21

# Race

I believe that successive generations of YCs in particular the efforts of David Hunt and Robert Hughes have had the greates influence in the field of race relations and the National Officers have resisted the temptation to court popularity by playing the race card.

During the late 1940s, a period of austerity, Britain was not a very attractive country for immigrants. An early reference to the racist question appeared in the *Ealing Chronicle* in which a very rosy picture of race relations in the UK was portrayed. It stated that there was no colour bar in India or New Zealand or in the British Colonies or Protectorates although there was a colour bar in South Africa and the USA. It may have been correct about India, but not so likely about the other countries. The group was satisfied that the practice of the colour bar was not British government policy. They then came to the conclusion that there must be pressure to reduce the stigma of colour and eventually to establish equality in all matters.[1]

When considering race relations those communities who have seen their areas completely transformed by immigrants deserve some sympathy, but one should not forget that it was a Conservative government of the 1950s which allowed mass immigration into this country without any thought. Therefore, when considering race relations, the Conservative party should have some humility because a more orderly influx of immigrants might have been more beneficial to both the indigenous population and the new immigrants. Oddly enough, hostility to immigrants is often greatest in areas such as Plymouth, with few immigrants, who tabled an anti-immigration motion at the 1979 Conference. Discussions with the officers of various constituencies from Ilford to Leeds indicate that YCs are more receptive to ethnic minorities than other organisations, for example those previously in charge of Yorkshire County Cricket club.

Few Young Conservatives and even fewer officers have come from the ethnic minorities. Tony Kerpel rightly stated YCs are hampered in what they can achieve by the actions of the senior party and many Conservative supporters at best seem indifferent to racist problems, and at the worst, unsympathetic. There has not been any chairman and I believe no vice-chairman of the Young Conservatives from the ethnic minorities. No doubt persons from this background have far more difficulty in making progress in either the Conservative Association or Young Conservatives and, therefore, special praise should be given to David Vansertima who, during 1983–84, was vice-chairman of Eastern Area YCs, and to Riaz Mansha who in 1993 was chairman of Yorkshire Area YCs.

Evidence that the Conservative party was oblivious to the problems of mass immigration is indicated by the remark of a Central Office deputy agent in 1955 in connection with the election that year. 'We are sure that most of the coloured folk are not interested in the election. They do not understand politics. They want to be left alone. We are convinced that a large proportion are not on the electoral register but we shall be surprised if it will make any difference to the result at Selly Oak.'[2]

The first resolution debated by the Party conference to limit immigration was in 1958 and thereafter it was never far from the political scene for the remainder of the century.[3]

The question of race again arose in the 1959 General Election when Oswald Mosley, who had supported Hitler and his Fascist party and fought as leader of a fascist party in the General Election of 1931, had tried to make a comeback, but to no avail. However, from canvassing in that election, I discovered from people on the doorsteps of Notting Hill in 1959 that there was much support for his views (not transferred into votes). He came bottom of the poll with 2,821 votes. Former YC National Chairman Andrew Bowden, the prospective candidate for North Kensington, speaking to South Kensington YCs of that election stated, 'There may be great differences of policy between the parties but I am quite sure we are all against Mosley' and said, 'if he stands again he will certainly lose his deposit as he did in 1959.'

What Andrew Bowden said did not have the unanimous approval of the YC audience. A man at the back of the hall shouted, 'you will be elected by West Indians.'

Andrew Bowden was clearly angered by this remark and said, 'there are good whites and bad whites and there are good and bad blacks. If I am elected MP for North Kensington their votes are as good as those of anybody else.'[4]

In 1961 immigration was restricted and there continued to be major Acts passed to regulate the flow of immigrants. Although there have been isolated incidents where race has played a significant part in the results, such as Smethwick in 1964 where the Conservative candidate won a parliamentary seat against the national trend, and more recently in the council elections when, surprisingly, a Liberal Democrat candidate used race to bolster his election chances.

In 1968 Enoch Powell made his infamous speech warning, as he saw it, of the danger to society of the immigrant population. Support for the views of Enoch Powell in the late 1960s and early 1970s was considerable including sections of the public not normally supportive of the Conservative party, such as meat porters who marched from Smithfield to the House of Commons to demonstrate their support of Enoch Powell. Conservative supporters, or former Conservatives, echoed on the doorstep their support for the views of Enoch Powell in 1970, when I was canvassing on my own behalf in a local govern-ment election to become a Conservative councillor. It is to the credit of many people in responsible positions in all parties including leaders of the Young

Conservatives that race had never been allowed to become a major issue in any general election.

The National Young Conservative officers of the late 1960s and early 1970s opposed Mr Powell's views that the restrictions on immigration should be even more strict than they were and encouragement should be given to repatriation of such persons.

At the 1969 YC Conference a motion demanding an end to all immigration into the UK and incentives to immigrants to return was defeated by a comfortable majority. John Munton from Brighton suggested that Enoch Powell should be minister of repatriation but the vote indicated that Vernon Ward from St Albans was more in tune with the majority when he said that the way to solve the problem was through education, and as time went on the ethnic minorities would be accepted as ordinary citizens.[5]

In 1972 an ugly situation arose when the Heath government decided to admit the Ugandan Asians expelled by Amin and this brought forth a critical motion by Enoch Powell at the 1972 Conservative Party Conference. David Hunt, then National YC chairman, led the attack on Mr Powell (Chapter 29).

Enoch Powell left the Conservative party in 1974 but he still held fascination for some YC branches which wished to hear him speak, such as Banstead YCs in 1979. At least two Young Conservative chairmen felt strongly that he should not be invited. Robert Hughes described Banstead's invitation as 'offensive and immoral'[6] and in 1981 Iain Picton wrote to branches advising that Enoch Powell should not be invited as he was using YC branches to advertise his own views on race.[7]

Following the defeat of the Conservatives in February 1974, the Labour Home Secretary, Roy Jenkins, announced an amnesty for illegal immigrants and the Greater London Young Conservatives urged Mr Heath to openly support such amnesty. Chris Gent, then the chairman of the GLYCs, eventually to become national chairman, said that the benefit arising from the amnesty would eventually become negated if the Tory politicians tried to seek cheap electoral advantage by stirring public opinion.[8]

At the 1977 YC Conference, Margaret Thatcher followed the custom of Edward Heath by having question and answer sessions at the National Conference only to discontinue them when she became Prime Minister. Timothy Sawdon (22) a prospective parliamentary candidate for Coventry South East, said 'many of us in the inner city areas are finding that members of the immigrant community are willing to join and help the Party in our efforts but we find difficulty when we are not allowed to take them into Conservative Clubs. What will you do as leader of the Party to ensure that this disgraceful discrimination is ended.'

Margaret Thatcher, who had been given a standing ovation when she arrived replied 'We have a large number of the immigrant community working with us in many constituencies where they are among the most active and valued members. I think the best way in these matters is to have a quiet word with those who are running the Conservative Clubs.'

This prompted groans from the audience and Margaret Thatcher said:

Look what you are trying to do? I think we are trying to get rid of discrimination wherever it occurs and the method which I want is the one most likely to achieve that. So we can have a quiet word, but at the same time make our views very well known publicly. To me there is only one way to judge a person, whatever his background, whatever his colour, whatever his religion and that is what the person is and not by race or creed. That is what I believe and what I will try to tell everybody and that is what I myself try to achieve.

That declaration was widely applauded.

After this conference, Timothy Sawdon said that many Conservative Clubs had only tenuous connections with the Party. 'The party needs greater leadership on this issue. If you do not have backing from the top, whispering in ears is not likely to help.'

Lord Thorneycroft, the Party chairman, said he supported Mrs Thatcher,

whatever may be the problems about the flow of immigration, the attitude of the Party to those immigrants who are here is to treat them as friends and colleagues in the organisation. We are going to considerable lengths to widen the frontiers of the Conservative Party and not only among immigrants. The Party has to recognise the law on the subject of clubs. You can refuse to accept a member but not on the grounds of race or colour, that is against the law.

At the same Conference, Mr Whitelaw rejected the idea of compulsory repatriation. The degrading and disgraceful proposition would clearly be a recipe for racial violence and an open invitation to drive people from their homes.[9] As Michael Heseltine told the YCs at their 1982 Conference in any event

we have a significant minority of black population to whom this Country is and will be their only home. Accordingly the idea of repatriation was a red herring the issue is how in a short space of time the black population can be made to believe that the opportunities are real and open for every adult.[10]

This echoed the words of Peter Walker when he addressed the YC Conference nine years earlier stating it was not sufficient for blacks to have improved education but we must create an environment where blacks can obtain employment equally with whites.[11]

In 1978, as a result of the joint co-operation between the Young Conservatives and Conservative Students, a successful initiative was made to affiliate the National Union of Conservative Associations to 'Joint Action against Racialism'.[12] In 1978 a key report was brought out by the National Advisory committee by Chris Gent who advocated tight control for new entrants but

stressed the importance of good race relations with a proper line of communication between leaders of the immigrant communities and the leaders of their
countries of origin, but it was not a particularly radical document and anybody
with common sense would wish to pursue many of the suggestions.[13]

The YC officers' opposition to a racist motion at the 1979 Conference
brought them much credit. This good work was continued by Tony Hall,
National vice-chairman 1983 and 1984 who led a YC campaign in 1983 for
improved race relations. A race relations pack was issued and five one-day
courses were arranged. Writing in *Tomorrow* he said 'Young Conservatives must
take a lead in their constituencies, involving the ethnic minorities in our Party
and campaigning for equal opportunities at a local level.'[14]

In more recent times it is much to the credit of the Labour party that its
policy towards the ethnic minorities resulted in some able politicians becoming
MPs. Nevertheless, during the 1960s public ownership and trade union power
and taxation of the so-called rich had a higher priority on the Labour party
agenda than the plight of the ethnic minorities who, when they came here in
many cases, were exploited in employment, lived in appalling housing conditions and were prejudiced against in the allocation of council accommodation,
as well as receiving discrimination from the Police.

Statistics show that black people, including professional black people, such
as barristers, are more likely to be stopped and searched than white people
from similar backgrounds. However, at the 1992 General Election the realistic
prospect of the election of a black Conservative MP was dashed when in
Cheltenham where the Conservative John Taylor had every prospect of winning
he lost to a Liberal Democrat. This may not necessarily have been due to race
as in a similar seat, Bath, Chris Patten lost to a Liberal Democrat. A black
Conservative candidate might have better prospered in a constituency more
cosmopolitan than Cheltenham but his prospects were much reduced by public
opposition from a section of the Cheltenham Conservative Association. However, the right wing takeover of the Young Conservatives in 1989 was not
accompanied by any change of YC policy concerning race which is indicated
by a motion of the NAC which notes, 'the racist comments made about the
PPC for Cheltenham the NAC strongly feels that such racist remarks have no
place in the Conservative party.'[15]

*Chapter 22*

# Crime

A s in most Western countries the UK crime rate has steadily increased since 1945. It is a mistake, however, to imagine that lawlessness is the preserve of the present generation. One fact that has encouraged the crime wave is mobility.

In previous generations the majority of people lived their whole lives in the same area so it was easier to detect criminals. One of the less desirable facets of motorways is the increase in burglaries in the adjoining areas and it is difficult to accept the argument of many Conservatives that the increasing gap between, say, the 10% poorest section and the rest of the community is not a contributing factor. The argument that many poor people are law abiding is correct, yet unemployed teenagers are more inclined to commit crimes than those in work and in the 1940s and 1950s unemployed teenagers were a rare phenomenon.

John Major's desire to return to the values of the 1950s was a strange analogy as the most striking difference between the late 1940s and 1950s compared with any other time since 1914 was that this was a time of full employment among the young and Labour acknowledged that between 1951 and 1955 young people were fully employed and better off than previously. Equally absurd are those left wingers who argue if you found the solution to unemployment you would solve the problem of crime. The difficult question to answer is the extent to which increased crime is linked with increased unemployment.

In days of full employment in 1948 a report in *The Times* states 'three policemen and two park attendants were attacked and in three separate incidents outbreaks of violence occurred at Wood Green, Muswell Hill and Alexandra Palace and the police were still searching yesterday for a gang of youths who attacked PC Leighton in High Road, Wood Green. He was treated in hospital for injuries and afterwards placed on the sicklist.'[1]

In 1958, rival motorised gangs from Dagenham and Canning Town invaded a quiet dance on a council estate in Barking. The Dagenham boys went around the floor asking every boy where he came from. One, Alan Johnson, who came from Canning Town but knew nothing of the feud, said 'Canning Town' whereupon he was hit in the face and stabbed in the stomach and killed.[2]

Those who advocated the reintroduction of corporal punishment on the grounds that young people were better behaved when corporal punishment was freely used in school should take note of what happened in the Schools Strike in 1911. A major grievance of the striking schoolboys was the frequent use of corporal punishment in schools.

In spite of limited communications between different parts of the country and when the news medium was confined to newspapers, the strike grew rapidly throughout the country.

A report in *The Times* stated that

> in West Hartlepool about 100 boys at a Council school came out. The storeroom at the back of a hotel was looted and bottles of stout and whisky along with cigars were removed by the strikers, some of whom were arrested and will be charged this morning. Three boys were placed on probation and a fourth was discharged. Whilst marching through the streets the boys stopped an errand boy who was delivering some apples to a house and helped themselves freely to the fruit. The boys were also stated to have thrown stones at the windows of houses occupied by teachers.[3]
>
> At Islington just as scholars were going to school about ten strikers appeared on the scene armed with sticks, stones, bits of iron and similar weapons. They threw stones at the school windows and the policemen guarding the school had difficulty in quelling the disturbance.[4]

There is much evidence to support those who argue that the fear of detection of crime is greater than the nature of the penalty imposed. Studies of whether capital punishment is a deterrent to murder being inconclusive raises the question whether greater resources should not be made available to the Police in the fight against crime although it is equally important that expenditure is effectively used. Young Conservatives have generally supported harsher sentencing, as have their seniors, rather than other remedies. Since the war, at the Party Conferences there were eighteen motions on law and order between 1956 and 1981.

The major reform of the 1945 to 1951 Attlee government appertaining to penal reform was the abolition of the right of the Courts in cases of serious crime to award corporal punishment. In many ways the Attlee government was much more conservative than their opponents. It led one to believe because they retained corporal punishment in respect of certain offences committed by prisoners they retained capital punishment. It used to be obligatory for a judge to pass the death penalty for murder however extenuating the circumstances.

In 1979 Mr Whitelaw, at the Party Conference in post-election euphoria stated, 'we are the party of law and order' yet crime after seventeen years of Conservative government has shown at least as great an increase as in previous periods.[5]

In view of the miscarriages of justice recently coming to light it is surprising how the call for a limited reimposition of capital punishment always seems to excite Tory audiences although there is plenty of evidence that the leaders, particularly Home Secretaries such as Rab Butler and Douglas Hurd, were far more moderate than the rank and file and even the rest of the Cabinet. Whereas the National Advisory Committee were not enthusiastic for the return of capital punishment during the 1960s and 1970s, the rank and file of YCs supported its reimposition and, therefore, the rank and file appear no different from the senior party. Perhaps it is surprising that capital punishment still appears to have so much support from the Conservative Party.

As expected, Ealing YCs' political maturity was indicated by a serious discussion of the subject in 1948 before the abolition of capital punishment was part of the political agenda. Following a branch discussion, they decided that a trial period in the abolition of the death penalty should be postponed for the time being. The death penalty should be retained for murder and certain treasonable offenses. Opinion was divided on the method of inflicting the death penalty. Some thought the prisoner should choose the method of his execution, others that no choice should be allowed.[6] Those enthusiastic for the retention of capital punishment until it was abolished except for treason in 1965, thereafter advocated its return.

In many cases the same people clamoured for the reimposition of corporal punishment, often ignorant of the fact that before its abolition in 1948 it was rarely imposed. This was an argument Erica Spinney, YC Wessex Area chairman, used in a speech made at the 1961 Party Conference opposing a motion advocating the imposition of corporal punishment not only for offences of violence for which corporal punishment could be imposed before 1948, but also included offenses where the Courts have been unable to order corporal punishment since 1861. She rightly said: 'There are too many people calling for corporal punishment who do not realise what a retrograde step it would be. It is not putting back the clock 12 years but virtually 100 years.'[7] In 1963 the policy report (Chapter 8) Law Liberty & Licence the policy group acknowledged that although there was some public support for the reintroduction of corporal punishment the argument is academic as no Home Secretary will reintroduce it. Andrew Tinney came to the same conclusion as he pointed out, although he was in favour of the reimposition of capital punishment, the reintroduction of judicial corporal punishment would almost certainly be in breach of the European Declaration of Human Rights.[8]

Although the policy document 'Society and the Individual' acknowledges the most potent argument against capital punishment namely, if you execute the wrong person you cannot make recompense, it nevertheless thought capital punishment was justifiable for the murder of Policemen and Prison officers.[9]

At the 1963 Conference there was a motion proposed by Anne Pritchard of South Kensington that hanging, which she described as barbaric and cruel, should be abolished but this was rejected by a large majority.[10] This supports the view that the rank and file of the Young Conservatives, as in the main Party, on capital punishment differed from their leaders. In 1966 by 25 votes to 6 and in 1969 by 23 votes to 14 the NAC favoured the abolition of capital punishment.[11] A survey of 4,000 YCs showed that only 23% agreed that the death penalty should not be brought back under any circumstances. Hugh

Holland admitted that the National Committee's views differed from the members.[12]

An article appearing in 1969 in the *Ealing Chronicle* suggested that flogging was justifiable if it prevented the beating up of defenceless persons, particularly old people.

> Twelve strokes would not hurt them for beating up old women. Liberals who whimpered wailed and whined when the thugs were flogged, were showing misguided sympathy. Those sort of liberal perverts did not have much sympathy for the innocent victims but plenty for the criminal.
>
> The Channel Islands and the Isle of Man have corporal punishment and have not changed the law. Flogging should be justifiable for demonstrators who savagely beat up policemen, for armed robbers and rapists. Sterilisation for rapists should be instituted as a deterrent.

It is not surprising, therefore, that Mike Stevens the writer of the article was also in favour of capital punishment.[13]

One prominent YC emphasised the importance of detection in the fight against crime rather than punishment. At the 1969 Party Conference, speaking against capital punishment, Lynda Chalker said, 'As a young person I cannot support the restoration of capital punishment for murder in this country. We have fought enough wars and enough people have been killed. Capital punishment is a moral issue not a political one.' She said she believed young people would not think it morally right to support the cause even when people have been killed. 'Send them to prison and make them work hard.'

She also advocated proper jobs being performed in prison for a fair wage, the money to be used to support the State. She also supported better rehabilitation for those prisoners who, having served their sentence in prison, are determined to set themselves on the right course. She proposed strengthening the police force and also drew attention to the lack of adequate pensions for the police officers.[14]

Lynda Chalker again spoke at the 1970 Conference, criticising the fact that there was no central computer which could transmit past criminal records to other police forces and also suggested lay advisers being recruited to assist the Police. In Germany and France there have been many scientific advances to assist the police. She also praised some young police officers who, concerned about the upbringing of some lads with nothing to do in the evenings, out of their own pockets and in their own time had set up clubs and activities. She stressed the importance of public confidence in the police and said that laws were too complicated and should be simplified.[15]

Clive Landa, her future husband, again said 'the hangers and floggers would not receive any support from me. No party in the country would reintroduce any such form of punishment so why waste our time this morning considering this.' Of course, he was proved to be right in spite of the alarming increase in crime.[16] YC chairman Andrew Rosindell at the Party Conference in 1993 advocated the reintroduction of corporal punishment to rapturous cheers.[17]

In 1970 a resolution deploring the increase in crimes of violence and urging the Conservative opposition to conduct a reappraisal to deal with crime and criminals with a view to creating a greater deterrent was passed by a large majority.[18]

The conference in 1973 on a rare occasion considered the problem of law and order in a wider context than imposing harsher sentences. A motion expressing concern at the time young people spent in custody pending trial was defeated by 243 votes to 214. G. Ashworth (Derbyshire) complained that the average time spent by young people in custody pending trial was fourteen weeks while G. Wilson complained that often the Courts acted on little or no information. The fact that the motion was defeated tends to support the theory that the minds of the majority were preoccupied with the notion that the only way to tackle crime was with harsher deterrents.[19]

The 1974 YC Conference passed a resolution by a narrow majority advocating corporal punishment for crimes of violence.[20] In 1976 a motion to reintroduce capital punishment as a deterrent to terrorism was carried by a substantial majority[21] and in 1978 a motion to reintroduce capital punishment was similarly carried by a large majority. At this conference, in a question and answer session, Margaret Thatcher made it clear that she supported its reintroduction for specific crimes.[22] In view of the 1976 decision, it seems that those attending were not influenced by her views. However, she continued to maintain her support during her long premiership, but on each free vote in the Commons the reimposition of capital punishment was rejected.

At the 1985 YC Conference a motion for the return of capital punishment was overwhelmingly passed. The argument of Tim Alban, that if the death penalty was reimposed there would be less convictions by juries and there would be revenge killings by terrorists who would be prepared to be martyrs, did not impress the Conference. Neither did his warning that if it is found out afterwards that a convicted murderer was innocent he cannot be brought back to life.

The proposer of the motion, Sean Woodward (Fareham), said, 'Why should cold blooded murderers be kept alive when money could be used to keep alive a child with leukaemia.' Cllr Hayward said MPs should never forget the tremendous grass roots pressure for the return of capital punishment.[23] I wonder, however, whether in view of the numerous miscarriages of justice, he would have now changed his mind. Andrew Tinney still supports capital punishment although he accepts strict safeguards would have to be devised to prevent miscarriages of justice.[24] The question is, how to guard against the occasional corrupt police officer who misleads both judge and jury?

A major and growing cause of crime has been the increase in the use of drugs. Whereas the solution is highly controversial there can be no question of the increase in trafficking and the use of drugs throughout all classes of society.

Edward Heath was asked in 1967 at the YC Conference in his question and
answer session what could be done about it. He said it was a terrible problem
and the Wilson government were not taking effective measures.[25] However, it
does not seem to have been a party political matter and I have no evidence
that the Conservatives any more than Labour has been able to stem the rising
problem of drugs.

John Selwyn Gummer stated at the Party Conference in 1967: 'When at
Cambridge University six years ago I hardly remember one person taking drugs,
but my brother who had just left Cambridge knows hardly one person who
had not themselves been present when there were those who took drugs or
had themselves taken drugs.' An overwhelming majority supported the resolution which strongly rejected any move towards a more permissive society.
Later thirteen Conservative Students issued a statement stating why they voted
against the resolution. The students stated that the resolution said nothing
positive on the problems, particularly about hard drugs and drug peddling, but
the statement added: We are all opposed to taking addictive drugs and call for
stiffer penalties against drug peddling.'[26]

In 1969 the Young Conservatives carried out a major survey on drugs.
Unfortunately, they were unable to ask the YCs whether they had participated
in the use of drugs as such answers could have been used in support of a
criminal prosecution against any YC who admitted he took drugs. It revealed
that 43% of the YCs knew someone who had taken drugs. When that figure
was analysed 58.5% of males under 21 knew someone who took drugs compared
with only 40% over 21 and 42% of females under 21 compared with only 35%
over 21, indicating that it was then, as now, a growing problem. The second
question was, has anybody asked you to take drugs? 17% stated they had been
asked, but the answers indicated a growing problem because of 17% who had
been asked to take drugs 31% of males under 21 answered in the affirmative
compared with only 16.5% over 21 and 17.5% of females under 21 as against
11% over 21. Forty-four per cent though that penalties should be left as they
are; 32% thought they should be increased, 10% though they should be reduced,
while 13% thought the taking of soft drugs should be decriminalised.[27]

Certainly, that was the view of the YC Conference in 1984, which rejected
by a large majority any attempt to legalise soft drugs. In 1984 Martin Boxall's
remarks that if the Conservative party was the party of freedom then the
Government should not reject the freedom for individual use but the view of
Adam Pritchard of Coventry South West YCs was the majority view that the
habitual use of cannabis leads to persons experimenting with hard drugs.[28] That
view was shared by their officers as the NAC voted by 53 votes to 1 against
the decriminalisation of heroin.[29]

## Chapter 23

# Environment

Throughout this century the developed nations have been generally slow in realising the harm caused to the environment by CFCs and petrol emission. During John Watson's chairmanship in 1971–2 the environment came on to the agenda. His interest in the environment was shown when he proposed a motion at the Party Conference to call upon HM Government to aid practical schemes of population limitation and he drew attention to the fact that he believed by the year 2000 the UK population would increase by 15 million to 70 million which would create pressure on the countryside, the transport system, the cleanliness of the environment and our means of waste disposal.

He criticised the Government for having no policy when it should have one. He stated that he was pleased that the Government has set up a panel of experts to advise on population increase and hoped the committee would have the power to consider what financial measures were needed and that something could be done to increase public awareness of the need to limit family size.

As events have transpired the birth rate has fallen, mainly because more women have careers and, therefore, postpone having children to far beyond the age that their parents did. As far as overseas aid was concerned he argued for aid to be channelled into practical schemes of birth control, the developing industries and into agricultural development rather than into more prestigious technological schemes.'[1]

During John Watson's chairmanship the Young Conservative movement initiated a CURE campaign to improve the environment and many Young Conservative branches participated.[2] The YCs made a very useful contribution to the protection of the environment. An article in an Ealing YC magazine of December 1971 referred to its own River Brent by drawing attention to the fact that it was not under the control of any river authority and pollution was prevalent throughout its whole reach.[3]

Unlike many amenity protection groups, such as Friends of the Earth, the YCs did not regard the inventions of the twentieth century like the motor car as an evil but recognised the necessity to control pollution to ensure that we have a more pleasant environment in which we live and which will be protected for future generations. Rodney Gent, former GLYC chairman said, 'Pollution control costs money and it would be unrealistic to expect problems to be cured instantly.' In order to remove the unfair competition advantage of irresponsible firms over those who adopted a more responsible approach to pollution, he urged the statutory imposition of a requirement to build the cost of pollution control into the cost of the product, thus ending the era of the cheap item, the production of which was environmentally detrimental.[4]

YCs in Frome were very active in the control of rubbish. Taking photographs of pirate dumps of unsightly rubbish in the town, they made their protest to the local council. This was accompanied by an extensive report of the YCs' action published in a local newspaper. The report was well received and the YCs were commended by the council chairman during a debate in the council chamber.[5]

Another initiative carried out by YC branches was a campaign by Mitcham YCs to clear a pond which had been allowed to accumulate rubbish and restore it as an amenity for young children. Having obtained publicity in the local press they obtained an assurance from the Labour council that the situation would be remedied.[6] Lincoln YCs used a carnival mounting a float to draw attention to the failure to remove broken barges and rubbish from Brayford Pool. The rubbish removed from the pool formed part of the float.[7]

Meanwhile Barry YCs persuaded their local paper to co-operate with them by printing a photograph called 'Disgrace of the week'.[8] Among other useful activities carried out by YCs, Hornsey YC Branch carried out a study of the old railway line between Drayton Park, through Finsbury Park, Crouch End, Muswell Hill and Highgate to see whether it could be revitalised as public transport.[9]

Regretfully since the early 1970s, the YCs have made no significant contribution to the protection of the environment. Many young people feel strongly that more should be done and if the YCs had shown the same interest in the protection of the environment as they had in the Maastricht treaty, capital punishment and Sunday trading they may well have gained youthful support for the benefit of the movement and the Conservative Party generally. As has often happened, they have followed the senior party who similarly placed environmental issues fairly low down the political agenda.

# Chapter 24

# Northern Ireland

The YC attitude to the Irish problem has varied considerably over the last fifty years. In 1950 *Advance* published an article by E. J. Alexander, Chairman of Northern Ireland Young Unionists, saying of Eire politicians.

> we must always be ready to meet them by contradicting the lies and propaganda with statements containing the cold sober truth. Eire politicians make the mistake Dr Goebbels made during the war. He and his hireling 'Lord Haw-Haw' broadcast the most extravagant lies and repeated them time and time again in the hope that with the constant repetition and reiteration that there must be some truth in what they say but we all know that the broadcasts became a standing joke until at last people wearied of listening.[1]

In 1948 the Party Conference passed a pro-Unionist motion on Northern Ireland acknowledging it as a loyal province of the United Kingdom, a vital outpost of the British Isles in peace and war. A producer of food and dollars in peace. A strategic bridgehead and lifeline to America in war. 'This Conference deplores recent propaganda here and in America which seeks, against the declared will of the Ulster people, to separate her from the rest of the United Kingdom and Empire contrary to the best interests of the people of Great Britain.'[2]

It was the failure to convince Irish Americans that the IRA was a terrorist, not a patriotic, organisation and by providing the organisation with considerable funds made the task of defeating the militant republican movement a difficult problem to which the British politicians and the Young Conservatives had no answer.

Between 1950 and 1968 there was a period of fairly quiet relationship between Ireland's Protestants and Catholics both north and south of the border. Sean Lemass, Prime Minister of the Republic regarded the economic prosperity of Eire as a more important goal than a united Ireland. Terence O'Neill, Prime Minister of Northern Ireland tried to initiate a policy of reconciliation, but this policy brought criticism from Ian Paisley and a loss of support which resulted in Terence O'Neill's resignation in 1969. If British politicians had taken advantage of this quiet time in the stormy history of Irish politics then, perhaps, a period of violence lasting more than twenty-five years would have been averted. No conference resolution was debated at Party conferences between 1948 and 1969 concerning Northern Ireland.

In 1969 Hugh Holland, national chairman and Eric Chalker paid a visit to Northern Ireland and other visits were made by leading YCs afterwards. They discovered real discrimination by local authorities against the Catholics and saw the impracticability of remedying these grievances through the normal political process because of the inbuilt and maintained permanence of the political balance in local councils. They also drew attention to the apparent inability of the Unionists to accept Catholic candidates and therefore broaden its base.

They noted the fears of Protestant Unionists that, as the Catholic population was increasing much faster than the Protestant they would form the majority in Northern Ireland as they are at the moment in the schools and would eventually take Ulster into a united Ireland cut off from the rest of Britain. The Roman Catholic Church would then play a significant part in the government affairs as they do today. Also they were concerned about the Orange Order's influence on Ulster politics which seemed to be sufficiently bigoted to expel senior members of the Unionist party because they had attended Catholic functions.[3] Hugh Holland's interest in Northern Ireland's problems was rewarded by his selection to propose a motion at the 1969 Party Conference in the following terms:

> That the constitution of the United Kingdom as regards Northern Ireland should not be changed without the consent of the Northern Ireland parliament but expresses the view that all discrimination on the grounds of religion, class, race, colour or political opinion is indefensible and is convinced that the true solution of the Ulster problem depends on the ability of the two communities to live side by side.[4]

Following Terence O'Neill's resignation, an increase in violence deafened the streets of Belfast and Londonderry and led to 8,000 British Army troops being sent to keep the peace. Stormont accepted the demands of civil rights organisations in spite of opposition from within the Unionist party and polarisation of extreme opinion led to the election of Bernadette Devlin to Westminster and Ian Paisley to Stormont.

Therefore questions began to be asked in the Conservative party as to the wisdom of links between the Conservative party and the Ulster Unionist party. A further YC delegation consisting of David Atkinson, Gerry Wade and Lynda Chalker returned to Ulster in August 1970. They interviewed an impressive list of leaders in Ulster including the Ulster Prime Minister – James Chichester Clark and the Roman Catholic Primate of all Ireland Cardinal Conway. In their report they said they received so many contradictory attitudes in a short time and over and over again they were told that the situation was insoluble. However, problems that men create for themselves can be solved by them. Following their visit they had a meeting with the Home Secretary, Reginald Maudling.[5]

In July 1970 the Greater London Young Conservatives called on the Party immediately to sever its links with the Ulster Unionists and recommended the formation of a new Ulster government containing elements of all political persuasions.[6]

At the 1972 YC Conference there was a motion calling for progression towards Irish unity which was rejected by a substantial majority. Michael Beattie said,

> the alternative was to root out the IRA, arm the police and close the border and thus impose an iron curtain from the Atlantic Ocean to the Irish Sea. I have seen the Iron curtain; it is not a very pleasant sight. If you wish to impose that on Ireland, heaven help you. You will never have peace with the Country divided.

He suggested a legislature for all Ireland to work alongside the two present governments. Supporting the proposition, Gerry Wade said that the price of a military victory was unacceptable. The IRA must be isolated. It must be a long-term aim. Among points made by those opposing the motion, Jack Senior said that the Irish government was not a government of principle. He would not like to see it in charge of Northern Ireland. James Simpson said, in opposing the motion, that the majority of people in Northern Ireland did not want integration.[7]

As the YCs became less moderate in the late 1970s they became less sympathetic to the Catholics and more sympathetic to the Protestants. In 1976 the conference called for the end of bi-partisan policy on Northern Ireland as it was felt that it might be a hindrance to the party in advocating tougher measures being taken against the IRA.[8]

At the 1987 Conference a motion congratulating the government on its courage in entering into the Anglo-Irish Agreement was passed by 440 to 300. Tom King, the Northern Ireland Secretary, spoke while the votes were being counted. This was because a ballot had been called when, from a show of hands, it looked as if the motion might be lost. John Livingstone said that during the whole of the last year not one terrorist had been arrested crossing the border. How can you have Anglo-Irish co-operation when the Irish believe that the British Army is an army of occupation?

Tom King, who had expected the motion to be passed by a large majority, was clearly shaken by the strength of the opposition and said, 'I hope that those who voted against will feel thoroughly ashamed of themselves.' He attributed the strength of feeling against the accord to the big Unionist campaign and half truths.[9] It appears that Tom King, the YCs such as Hugh Holland, Eric Chalker and Gerry Wade were right. Either because the restraints of a democracy, unlike a totalitarian state, would prevent sufficiently tough measures being taken, or for other reasons, the IRA could not be defeated by force. Negotiations would be necessary and this would involve the Irish government. The sympathy of the YCs to the unionists rather than the nationalists continues. At the 1995 conference Fay Vernon and Dinah White Adams jumped up wearing identical red suits with the slogan 'Free Private Clegg' and received a standing ovation.[10]

# Chapter 25

# Foreign Policy

One of the issues that dominated British foreign policy for many years was South Africa. Two articles in the Hammersmith YC magazine represent a difference of opinion between those who had some sympathy for white South Africans and those who did not. Thomas Jaretski stated the arms trade must be stopped immediately. 'Money must not be placed before morals. This country must not be an accessory to the crimes that have been committed in the tragedy in South Africa. All support should be given to the United Nations in their campaign against apartheid in South Africa.'[1]

Bill Lucas did not agree with this stating that, 'the coloured South Africans were not slave people. The coloured Africans did not have political freedom but they had the highest standard of living of any coloured people in Africa. The policy of apartheid seemed to the majority of South African whites the only solution. 'It may not be strictly moral but it is practical.' He was against a boycott because we trade with East Germany, Cuba and China.[2]

A South African debate took place at the YC Conference in 1970. The motion 'deplored the Conservative party's policy of a resumption of arms sales to South Africa and asks for a repeal of that policy' was moved by Mr Nigel Smith of Reigate. He argued that a policy that was tantamount to active support for the Verwoerd government was against British interest. This brought shouts and countershouts from all over the hall. The motion was lost which showed the rank and file had far more sympathy for white South Africa than did Nigel Smith. The majority had the support of the Minister Mr Eldon Griffiths when he commented on the debate. He said that economic sanctions against South African would not work.[3] However, events have proved that Eldon Griffiths was wrong and Nigel Smith was right. Indeed the YCs were becoming more sympathetic to Nelson Mandela and the ANC as is shown by the resolution of NAC in September 1985 passed by 33 votes to 5:

> That this conference congratulates the Prime Minister, the Foreign sec-retary and Her Majesty's Government in their calls to the South African Government to enter into talks with the leaders of the black community and supports the Government's demands for the following steps from the South African Government as a precursor of such talks:
>
> The unconditional release of Nelson Mandela,
>
> An end to forcible removals.
>
> An end to detention without trial.

A commitment to some form of common citizenship.[4]

Margaret Thatcher's lukewarm support for black Africans and her reluctance to agree to the imposition of sanctions that other Commonwealth countries wished to impose is reputed to have brought her into conflict with the Queen. Her stance appears to have had an influence on some of the members of NAC as in 1986 a motion before the NAC absolutely condemning apartheid and viewing with horror the rising tension in South Africa and calling upon the South African government immediately to enter into discussions with recognised leaders of the black community and release Nelson Mandela unconditionally, was passed by only 21 votes to 20.[5]

Another foreign affairs matter that divided the YCs was Rhodesia. In the YC Conference of 1967 there was a motion that the Smith government was deluding itself in believing that the white man's position could be safeguarded by retaining the present power was defeated by 307 votes to 288 votes.[6] The voting indicated the YCs were as divided on Rhodesia as were the senior party. This is further confirmed by the vote at the 1971 YC Conference when the vote for keeping sanctions was 380 to 240 which, under the more liberal YC regime of the 1970s, indicates that the pro-sanction lobby was gaining ground.[7] However, it is my belief that Robin Squire put the matter into context in 1973 in a motion urging the Government to recognise Rhodesia as an independent state and to withdraw sanctions. He said,

> the question of Rhodesia pops up as a hardly perennial at the Party conference. It can hardly be claimed it is on the lips of the man in the street. In comparison with Rhodesia I submit that even the subject of Europe acquires the excitement of the Saturday evening football results in the minds of the electorate. I suggest that the average Conservative party member puts it well down on his or her list of priorities. That leaves us with the Monday Club and the Anglo Rhodesian Society. We can only hope that as the Monday Club moves steadily through the week, it recognises how isolated it is on this issue. There can be no doubt that the sanctions are damaging the Rhodesian economy and that is why it is the only lever we have to compel the Smith regime to think in terms of a proper multi-racial society. Those who wish to remove the lever and still believe that the majority of whites of their own volition will treat the Africans as equal can only be taking a mind-blowing drug of quite staggering proportion. Every year many of our Party ally themselves with those who speak for white supremacy and accordingly damage any realistic relationship with many African Countries. I request you not only to reject the motion for the umpteenth time but ensure when you return to your constituencies that this red herring is buried.[8]

The fate of Rhodesia and South Africa took very different paths under Margaret Thatcher's leadership. She proceeded to solve the Rhodesian problem, but it would be a considerable time before the South African problem would be resolved. In both the cases of Rhodesia and South Africa, it appears that the pro-sanctions lobby were proved to be right by subsequent events. Sanctions in both Rhodesia and South Africa proved to be tortuously slow in working but eventually did work.

Another foreign affairs matter in which the YCs played a very relevant part was Portugal. During the early 1970s a communistic dictatorship engulfed Portugal. Both the YCs and the Federation of Conservative Students campaigned for more help to be given to the centre right party of Professor Diogo Freitis do Amarel. After the fall of the Salazar dictatorship Portugal eventually, via the undemocratic regime of the Communists became a democracy and a member of the EEC. The YCs and Federation of Conservative students gave the Professor encouragement when he attended as an observer at the 1975 Conference and three years later he was officially invited to the 1978 Conference. YC chairman Tony Kerpel who visited Portugal to see the Professor should be given credit as being a driving force behind the YC initiative.[9]

A major foreign affairs problem was America's involvement in Vietnam where the US war machine was unable to score a military victory and there was a huge American loss of life. There was much left wing and pacifist protest across Europe at the US action including the Young Liberals and Young Socialists. I cannot find any record of their branches who supported the US action. I wonder whether one student protestor, Bill Clinton, came to regret his action. Little did he then know that action would be scrutinised during the 1992 Presidential election when Bill Clinton was accused by his opponents of being unpatriotic.

The Young Conservatives generally supported the US action. At the 1968 YC Conference a motion calling for the withdrawal of US forces was defeated by a large majority. In proposing the motion Robin Fletcher was right when he said 'it was a military conflict the Americans could not win'. On the other hand historians may in future regard Vietnam not as a humiliating American defeat but had not the Americans defended Vietnam and the Communists had easily over-run the country the Communists might then have tried to bring down non-Communist governments in other South East Asian countries such as Thailand.[10]

In 1975 YC chairman Tony Kerpel wrote to *The Guardian* a scathing attack on Vietnam protesters:

> The current and depressing news from Vietnam brings nothing but un-caring silence from those Labour MPs, Student organisations and anti-war protesters. 'Given their influence' he said 'does not the taking of Hue and Dinang and other cities constitute a clear act of war and continuing aggression by the North Vietnamese without a moment of concern for yesterday's marchers one is left to the conclusion rather bitterly that the anti-war demonstrators are more motivated by Anti-Americanism than for humanitarian considerations.'

When Margaret Thatcher became leader in 1975 she complained of the rapid build up of Soviet military power. At the Party conference YC chairman Tony Kerpel proposed a motion which was passed:

> that this Conference recognises with alarm the lack of resources available to the armed forces and calls for an immediate recalculation of the cost effectiveness of the services and a serious commitment to a European defence policy in the light of a rapid expansion of Warsaw Pact forces and the disturbing developments in Portugal, Greece and Turkey integral parts of the Western Defence Alliance.[11]

Perhaps surprisingly YCs would not have disputed a Young Socialist comment on the Soviet Union,

> The vast potential of even greater economic growth has been stifled by the bungling incompetence of the bureaucratic elite which has imposed itself on the workers of these countries. Their motives have first and foremost been to protect and expand their privileges which they have done through the ruthless form of totalitarian power. The workers' democracy which was established in 1917 has been brutally crushed and attempts to struggle for the same goal by the workers of Hungary in 1956 and Poland in 1970 have been put down by blood.[12]

These remarks were contained in a Young Socialist pamphlet.

During the 1980s the YCs continued to give their wholehearted support to the policy of a nuclear deterrent. With only one abstention the following resolution was passed by the NAC:

> That this committee notes in the past forty years the policy of deterrents as advanced by NATO has ensured a longer period of peace within Western Europe than any other in recent history. It further notes that the Conservative party is the only major party which is committed to the maintenance of a strong independent nuclear deterrent and therefore supports wholeheartedly its purchase of the Trident D5 system to continue the successful policy of deterrents in the next century but also asks that sufficient provision is made in future defence budgets to accommodate peaks of expenditure which this purchase will require.[13]

It has been seen that YCs' opinions on foreign policy, as in many other spheres, closely followed that of the senior party and the YC leadership was rarely in conflict with a Conservative government or shadow cabinet.

However in 1969 for the first time the YC national committee pursued a policy in opposition to that of the shadow Cabinet over the question of Nigeria and the help we were giving in quelling a rebellion by Biafra. There was disquiet as to whether what was done was moral and whether Biafra had a genuine grievance. An open letter was written to Edward Heath which was published in the press.[14]

We have come to the point where we must plead with you to change
your Party policy on the sale of arms to Nigeria. What may have been
a realistic policy at the beginning is indefensible now. The sale of arms
has not produced a quick kill only a mass-kill. We do not see the value
of competing with the USSR to supply these arms.

This open and public defiance by the YC leadership did not in any way
harm the relationship between the shadow cabinet and Ted Heath on the one
hand and YCs on the other. One is doubtful whether the party of the 1980s
would have taken such a relaxed attitude.

*Chapter 26*

# YC Rallies 1948, 1956, 1959, 1966 and 1983

The first National YC event was a rally addressed by Winston Churchill at the Royal Albert Hall in 1948. Anthony Eden in 1956 and Harold Macmillan in 1959 both addressed rallies at the Royal Festival Hall. Edward Heath, then leader of the opposition, addressed a similar rally in 1966 as part of massive recruiting drive, Action 67, (Chapter 9). The YCs did not hold another national rally for many years.

In 1983 as part of the election campaign a rally addressed by Margaret Thatcher was held at Wembley. At this rally a number of show business personalities and sportsmen and women, sympathetic to the Conservative cause, supported the Prime Minister with their presence. Considerable criticism arose from several of the comedians' jokes.

The phraseology used by Anthony Eden and Harold Macmillan on Conservative philosophy in the 1950s was remarkably similar to that used by Margaret Thatcher in the 1980s.

Winston Churchill addressed the YCs on only one occasion when he spoke to a packed Royal Albert Hall in June 1948. (The full text of this speech appears in appendix 4.) Andrew Bowden, the national chairman in 1960/61 is one of those who have told me of the tremendous atmosphere when Winston Churchill spoke and, when replying to the vote of thanks said, 'I am not a Young Conservative but an old man' a tremendous roar went up. Describing the scene at the time, *Advance* mentioned that,

> all the seats were filled and hundreds were standing in the gods, that wide gallery near the roof of the vast hall. Seven thousand Young Conservatives had travelled from all over Britain and Northern Ireland to be present on this great occasion. It must be remembered that these were the days of austerity although public transport was relatively cheap. Each of the twelve areas was represented by delegations of fifteen who walked through the Hall to take up their positions at the rear of the platform. There was community hymn singing accompanied by the great organ. Upstairs, the North Western delegates proudly carried their banners bearing a record number of 273 branches to the platform. When Mr and Mrs Churchill and Mr Eden arrived at the Royal Box and spotlights switched to illuminate the beloved figure of the great leader as he stood acknowledging the fervent cheers and giving the famous 'V' sign. By coincidence it was

Anthony Eden's birthday and, as president of the YCs, he was given a generous cheer. The concluding moments of the demonstration brought forth rousing cheers as the Scots led by the pipes made their way to the platform. Never before had the bagpipes been drowned indoors; the voices of the Young Conservatives even triumphed over the pipers' penetrating notes.[1]

John Hay relates how, as national chairman, it was his duty to greet Winston Churchill on his arrival and how his public warmth contrasted markedly with his personal behaviour. When John Hay greeted him at the Albert Hall, all the twelve area chairmen were there and John Hay had hoped to introduce each to Winston. However, after shaking hands with only two, he strode up the stairs and John Hay proceeded to sprint up the stairs in order to precede him into the hall. After the rally, which all believed to have been a great success, when John Hay saw Winston he expected him to comment on the tremendous reception that the YCs had given him, but all Winston said was 'You spoke very well'. Although John Hay, having been elected to Parliament in 1950, was a backbench MP during Winston Churchill's premiership from 1951 to 1955 John Hay never again spoke to the great man.

One of the interesting features showing the unity of the Young Conservative movement in those days was how many of the London Young Conservatives accommodated the delegates from farther afield into their own homes.

After a lapse of eight years it was decided to hold another rally on 11 November 1956 which took place at the Royal Festival Hall during the Suez crisis (Chapter 7) before 4,000 YCs in the main auditorium and the speech was relayed to another 700 in an overflow hall.

The proceedings started with community hymn singing and a parade of Area chairmen and their banners.

The entry of Sir Anthony and Lady Eden was described by Sheila Bradshaw of Petts Wood YCs, the reception they received as 'having to be heard to be believed. The cheering and clapping must have lasted over two minutes.' As the Prime Minister made his way to the platform Councillor Geoffrey Finsberg, the national Chairman read a vote of confidence from the Rally to the Prime Minister over his handling of the Suez crisis (Chapter 7). 'This brought forth renewed clapping and cheering and it was obvious that Sir Anthony was finding the Rally overwhelming in its sincerity.'

Although most of Anthony Eden's speech at the YC Conference was devoted to Suez, in dealing with Conservative philosophy he said,

we have two objectives to build a strong and vigorous economy and also a balanced society, one in which power and property are widely spread and not concentrated in the hands of the State or the few. A society in which there are opportunities for those with talents and for those who are willing to work hard and where the weak are not neglected. A society which is built on unity not on class war. We want to create a country in which enterprise and energy have full scope to create prosperity and a fair reward for so doing. As to the Labour party he said do not be fooled by the fact that the Socialist programme at any one time contained only a few proposals for extending the power of the State. Poison like that has to be given in small doses. The patient will not swallow it otherwise. When the electorate has had enough the stuff is just put back on the shelf and left there for later. Another mixture poured out for the present is equality. Surely this equality has never appealed to the young who are the most ambitious section of the community and rightly so.

Another topic at the conference was the result of the successful recruiting campaign (Chapter 6). The proceedings ended with everybody singing (referring the Sir Anthony) 'For he's a jolly good fellow' and everybody then sang the National Anthem. It is doubtful if anybody at the Rally envisaged, as Sir Anthony and Lady Eden left the hall, that this would be one of his last appearances at a public meeting as Prime Minister, and within two months his premiership would have ended.

Another rally was held in 1959 similar to the 1956 rally, which took place at the Royal Festival Hall. Harold Macmillan addressing 4,000 YCs together with 800 in an overflow meeting, said of the Labour Party:

They look across at our young and vigorous ranks. We have to survey their bleak ageing dispirited and sour countenances which seems to grow more sour with every bit of good news: whether it is in the budget or lower unemployment . . . Socialism has outworn theories and outmoded doctrines. Today the idea of removing wealth to cure poverty is out of date. The problem is not to liquidate old wealth but the create new wealth. The solution lies in our Conservative policy of opportunity – opportunity for all. Opportunity to learn, opportunity to earn, opportunity to own and that means to save.

In reply to a vote of thanks the Prime Minister said he had just received a form concerning his old age pension asking if he was fully employed and stating if he went on working he could build up his pension a little. He assured his audience that he had answered in the affirmative.

A rally to launch the massive recruiting campaign 'Action 67' took place in December 1966 at the Royal Festival Hall. It was also the occasion of the twenty-first anniversary of YCs.

The Young Conservatives tried to repeat the earlier successful rallies of the 1950s but the NAC regarded it as moderately successful.[2] young people of the 1960s were much more sophisticated. Although the *Sunday Telegraph* reporter found Edward Heath's speech relatively orthodox, in certain other respects it was a distinctly curious occasion, a cross between a US convention and a cup final.

The glossy programme of the afternoon's events was a bizarre enough document in itself. Item 1: Folk singing by Three Winds to be followed by a

parade of YC banners through the hall. Item 3 sounded like an excerpt from
a ballet programme: Entry of Shadow Ministers. Working up to the climax in
bolder print the programme announced further on: Leader's entrance and the
programme finally gasped its way to Item 8: Leader speaks.

The folk songs were pleasant enough, but the banner displays, complete
with running commentary by Geoffrey Johnson Smith, Party vice-chairman
proved a distinctly shy-making episode. One by one the banners of each area
were solemnly paraded through the Hall and were followed by two young
men and Miss YC, trailing awkwardly two yards behind. As this forlorn trio
walked their way slowly round the hall, Mr Johnson-Smith, tongue in cheek
by the look of it, read out a travelogue of almost unendable banality. Meanwhile
the Three Winds made musical noises appropriate to each area. In fairness to
the YCs, a considerable number of them seemed relieved to get away from
the showbiz and on to the meat of the rally.[3]

Most of Edward Heath's speech was in justification of his opposition to the
way the dispute with Rhodesia had been handled by Harold Wilson following
the unilateral declaration of independence by Ian Smith. It seemed that Harold
Macmillan and Margaret Thatcher were right in taking the opportunities of a
large young audience to expound Conservatism over a wide field rather than
dwell on a particular issue of the day.

One person to disagree with the speech was former national chairman,
Terence Wray who stated that because of the speech he joined the Labour
party, writing in the Young Socialist magazine *Focus*.[4] He obviously thought
that Edward Heath should support the measures that Harold Wilson had taken
following the unconstitutional declaration of independence by Ian Smith.

An event not tried before or since by the Party took place during the election
campaign on 5 June 1983. The rally took place on a day when William Hill
refused to take any further bets on the election, everybody being confident of
a Conservative victory. The Labour union leader the General Secretary of the
Association of Professional Executive and Clerical staffs, Roy Grantham had
advised his members in the south and west to vote Liberal in order to try to
keep the Conservatives out, so pessimistic was he of Labour's chances.

Margaret Thatcher spoke at the rally, supported by several comedians and
a variety of sporting personalities, Terry O'Neill the Arsenal manager, Charlie
Nicholas the Celtic and Scotland footballer, Sharon Davies, the Olympic silver
medallist, Frank Bruno, the boxer and Freddie Truman the former England
and Yorkshire fast bowler. Margaret Thatcher's speech was preceded by an
hour's entertainment compered by Bob Monkhouse. Lynsey de Paul composed
a song entitled 'Tory Tory'. Kenny Everett joked about Mr Foot's stick referring
to his disability and 'Let's bomb Russia' which brought forth much criticism.
It appeared to be a mistake that these jokes were made as it detracted from
the tremendous success of the rally.[5]

Phillip Webster of *The Times* described her audience as '2,500 wildly cheering
young people in an almost adoring display of their allegiance. The audience

was full of foot stamping, flag waving, horn blowing Young Conservatives who gave the Prime Minister an astonishing reception before during and after her speech.'

Mrs Thatcher asked her audience, could Labour have managed a rally like this? There was a chorus of 'no!' The PM continued, 'in the old days perhaps, but not now for they are the party of yesterday. Tomorrow is ours,' Mrs Thatcher said in contrast to Labour pessimism. 'Conservatives are full of hope. Where they are bitter we are determined to succeed. Where they fear for the future we rise to the challenge, excitement and adventure. your rights were won at Runnymede. We are committed to a civilized society where the poor and sick, disabled and elderly are properly cared for.' She also said that freedom depended on the will to defend it. In a reference to the Falklands War she said, 'We think that freedom is worth defending even if it is challenged 8,000 miles away.'

She went on, 'there are always powerful countries and powerful dictators who will snuff it out. Nations that deny freedom to others deny freedom to their own people. Dictators who cannot bear to be opposed. They must know beyond all doubt that we in Britain have the capacity and will to secure our way of life.' She contrasted that with Labour after years of wrangling had given in to the left wing and committed itself to the abandonment of nuclear weapons, while leaving them in the hands of our enemies. Such action would reduce Britain to serfdom. Mrs Thatcher also emphasised restriction on individual freedom which she said was contained in the Labour manifesto. She went through the manifesto.

'Men and women should be able to share the rights and responsibilities of paid employment and domestic activity so that job segregation in and out of the home is broken down.' She paused, looking round at her husband. 'They are going to see that Dennis does his share of the washing up.' Brandishing the Labour manifesto she said, 'it is a grim catalogue of a list of proposals aimed at destroying the spirit of enterprise, the chance to display and develop your talents, your ability wherever it may be and wherever you may choose to develop it. They think it is attractive to offer the young a future wholly controlled, the operation of the Socialist state.' She went on, 'under Labour nobody ventures, nobody gains, that is why the economy floundered for years.' Despite the undoubted success of the rally it was not repeated for the 1987 election.

On the same day Michael Foot was addressing a rally in Hyde Park. Although, optimistically, the Labour party was hoping for 300,000 about 10,000 to 15,000 turned up. John Young of *The Times* described the scene: 'The marchers filed in carrying banners and wearing bright coloured tee shirts but most seemed more weary and dispirited than fired with zeal for change.'[6]

The platform party was not unanimous on the purpose of the rally as one of them, Christina Pavli of Harringay, said that the march was not supposed to be in support of the Labour party but a protest against unemployment. Len

Murray the General Secretary of the TUC was wrong when he stated that 'the people were no longer prepared to bare their back to the scourge of unemployment.' When put to the test the Conservative support exceeded Labour's by 12%.

# Chapter 27

# Holiday Weeks and Early Conferences
# 1949 to 1959

It was not until 1961 that the YCs held their own orthodox annual conference. In 1948 it was resolved that the YCs would have their own annual conference but the resolution was later rescinded on the grounds that as YCs had representation on all the main committees of the Party the conference would be superfluous, the real reason being, as the report to the Central Council reveals, that it was feared if the YCs held their own conference they would not wish to attend the main Party Conferences. These fears were unfounded as when the YCs held their own conferences from 1961 YCs in great numbers were still eager to attend the main Party Conferences.

Between 1948 and 1960 four holiday weeks were held, and two one-day conferences at Central Hall, Westminster and Birmingham both of which were addressed by Anthony Eden.

The first holiday week was at Filey in 1949. Anthony Eden attended the mass meeting and a delightful photograph of him appeared in *Advance* showing him sitting outside the chalet, which he occupied like the other campers. Democracy at work!

Col. Oliver, the YC organizer whose idea it was to have a political conference at a holiday camp had a unique rapport with young people. Although, in Frances Vale's opinion, not strong on policy, he had a flair for organization. *Advance* describes how the roar of cheers greeting him, together with his assistant, Winifred Crum-Ewing, was a just reward for him. In those days there was no security problem but even bearing in mind the necessity for security, one wonders how many of today's senior ministers would be prepared to drink and eat in the bar with the Young Conservatives at their conference, although once inside one is very secure in view of the entry arrangements to the conference.

*Advance*, describing the dress of Young Conservatives attending (girls in slacks and men with sports jackets with strange patterns), reminds us how much more formally even young people then dressed prior to the advent of the wearing of sweatshirts and jeans. At the end of the week Col Oliver said when next year's conference came he did not want people coming to him saying they wished to come for two days of the conference only. He wanted everybody to come for the whole week. Even at his age he had enjoyed it. Col Oliver will always be young. Alas, there are some who have never experienced this joyous state.

Lord Woolton opened the conference by warning the delegates of a possible election in October. 'This is the year in which we must reap to the full all the patient formative work you have done.' Then, perhaps, tongue in cheek, he added, 'I know you have been slow in recruiting but you have been determined, quite rightly, that you were not out for numbers, you were out for quality. We can now say we have a corps of some 150,000 trained troops.' Later generations of YCs would have been more than happy with that membership figure. He went on to say, 'colossal tasks await you. In your age group there are 3,295,000 men and 3,256,000 women. I want Young Conservatives in every street in every constituency. You have the precious future of the country in your keeping. Be ready!'

Of the eight papers printed it the programme, four of those who introduced them Geoffrey Rippon, Reginald Maudling, Iain Macleod and Pat Hornsby Smith subsequently reached high political office. In the first discussion on Defence both Bryan Methley (Cheadle) and Henrietta Rae advocated the end of conscription for different reasons. Henrietta Rae alleged that economic recovery was being impeded as young men leaving school have no thought of industrial life because they will soon be going into the forces while Bryan Methley stated that those wishing to join the regular forces were deterred from signing on because of the large proportion of National Servicemen in the forces. Nevertheless, the Conservative party supported the policy of conscription introduced by the Labour government which was abolished in 1960.

The next paper, on agriculture, was presented by Peter Baker, the youngest candidate to win a seat in the 1950 election. There was an array of Young Conservative speakers who were farmers, Gordon Walton, a young farmer in Taunton, R. W. Elliot, chairman of Northern Area who praised the Agricultural Charter (see Chapter 20). Diana Cook complained of the shortage of feeding stuffs in this era of shortages, in some ways more severe than the war years. (How much of it was caused by Socialist bureaucracy and how much by world shortages is open to debate.) She said, 'if you give us the feed stuffs we will give you your bacon.'

The next subject, concerning Trade Unions, would be a favourite subject of Conservative conferences over the next twenty years. While several speakers concentrated on the need for the Conservative party to have more influence on Trade Unions, Roy Austin, a shop steward, pleaded for more Tory MPs who were Trade Unionists and for Tory Union candidates to be assigned seats where they have a good chance of success. George Peters spoke of the reasons for unofficial strikes. Firstly long delays in settling wage claims, secondly workers not appreciating the seriousness of the present situation; also, fear of unemployment and executives out of touch with the rank and file.

The Attlee government was preoccupied with nationalization, heavy taxation of the rich, satisfying the demands of the Unions and paid no attention to the problem of unofficial strikes which was to plague the British economy under both Labour and Conservative governments until Margaret Thatcher's reform of industrial relations in the 1980s. However, it was not all condemnation of Labour and praise for the Conservatives. Roy Austin complained that Conservative MPs spend too much time opposing nationalisation.

In presenting his paper on 'Prices products and production', Reginald Maudling's defence of the profits motive brought warm approval, as one would expect from a Conservative audience.

George Proudfoot, referring to the huge losses the nationalised industries were making said, 'No one wants to work for firms which are making losses yet we are all shareholders in firms that are not making money.'

Roger Thornton described the Town & Country Planning Act as 'the most wicked measure'. He said 'This act by means of a development charge took away from the individual any profit he might earn because he had been granted planning permission to use land in a more profitable way.'

In her paper on education, Frances Vale drew attention to the chronic overcrowding in schools. 'A reply to a Parliamentary question in 1947 revealed that there were 31,949 classes in primary schools with more than 40 children. In January 1948 the figure had risen to 32,925. In secondary schools there was an increase in the classes of more than 40 children from 3,542 to 3,840. In 1947 there were 2,081 primary school classes with over 50 children although by 1948 this had dropped to 2,025. There were 27,647 secondary school classes with classes of over 30 pupils.' She said that, 'the reduction in the size of classes was the most important single reform if the standard of education was to be raised.' She pleaded to raise what was described as the 'modern schools subsequently called Secondary Modern Schools' to the level achieved by grammar and technical schools. She drew attention to the lack of high quality teachers who were being attracted into industry instead. She concluded her paper by saying that the ultimate aim of the Party's educational policy was not to turn out robots built to obey a State machine but to ensure that children developed as individuals, able to reason and think for themselves, eager for the adventure of living and unafraid of the challenge of the future. Her paper was presented by Geoffrey Rippon, who at 24 was already an alderman. Being a school teacher, Frances Vale was unable to attend.

Iain Macleod's brilliant paper on constitutional changes was well received and there were cheers when he said 'we need not more legislation but less', and then dealt with a favourite Tory subject of left-wing bias by the BBC. Mr Macleod said amid laughter that

> although it might be true of the Third Programme [now Radio 3] with its heavy discussions, the Light Programme [somewhat akin to Radio 2] more than redressed the balance. I would sooner have the comedians on my side than the intellectuals, but every unbiased commentator would regard Mr Hughes-Rowlands' comparison [he was subsequently to become Conservative chief agent] between the growth of Hitlerism and the programme of the Attlee government as totally unfair.

The final paper was on the Empire by Pat Hornsby Smith, another who went on to have a distinguished parliamentary career. She made an unanswerable plea for the retention of Imperial preference.

Mr Belcher, who was stated to have spent two years in the Colonies, said that 'some of the people were feeling that Britain is losing interest in them.'

The greatest cheers came while a 29-year-old research worker, Jean Asquith, was speaking who was bewildered why she was receiving so much louder cheers than other Young Conservatives speakers until she realised that they were not for her but for Anthony Eden who had just entered the hall. However, the *Yorkshire Post* correspondent describes her speech as electrifying the audience by stating 'At the election we shall not be fighting for ourselves and the British way of life but for our Commonwealth and Empire. The fate of the Empire rests on the next General Election as to whether it will be whittled away or will be built up stronger than ever.' The applause had hardly died down when she said, 'We have no money to invest in the Empire let us export the labour. The Empire has the resources we have the manpower', and she then received applause almost as loud as when Anthony Eden came into the Hall.

Anthony Eden's speech dealt with both home and foreign affairs. He made the prediction that within a generation nationalisation would seem old-fashioned and people would wonder why it was ever thought that it was likely to provide the remedy for the problems of our time. His timing was slightly wrong and there was to be nearly forty years before the great privatisation of the late 1980s swept away much of the nationalisation imposed by the Attlee government. He stressed,

> the need to sell our goods abroad and maintain our standards of life. Many people seemed to be engaged in finding a division between the two partners in industry. There is really no division at all. Whether the Socialists like it or not in the next few years British industry must hold its own in the world and this means free enterprise.

He said that Britain had every reason to congratulate itself on the result of the export drive but warned that this had been helped by Marshall Aid from the USA and a seller's market.

His foreign affairs mainly dealt with the major problem of the time arising from the USSR who closed the access road and rail links to Berlin in the hope that the Allies would allow the Russians to take over the entire city. The Allies had responded by mounting a massive air-lift. Just before the Conference the blockade had been partially lifted but Anthony Eden complained that the USSR had imposed restrictions that did not exist before the blockade, whereas the Western powers, by carrying out demilitarization and introducing democracy in West Germany, had adhered to the terms of the Potsdam agreement. The same cannot be said of the Soviet Union.

The fact that Eden did not try to make political capital out of the matter by blaming the Labour party and even in home affairs was able to find good in a country run by a Socialist government indicates the great statesman he was. It was apparent from the vigorous debates that went on at Filey that speakers, for example, those on conscription, were prepared to depart from the party line.

The Labour party followed the Conservative example and had its own holiday camp rally in September 1949. It was not a happy affair. First the organisers were in conflict with the staff of the holiday camp as they endeavoured to involve staff at the camp in politics. A holiday camp spokesman said it was their policy to keep off politics. The delegates wanted to put political posters on the music stand in the ballroom and other parts of the camp which the staff had to remove as political posters were not allowed in the holiday camp. They succeeded in obtaining the suspension of the playing of the National Anthem following the nightly ball after the singing of the Red Flag had drowned the anthem during the first two nights. One member of staff complained that the staff had been interrogated on their working conditions. Another remark by the staff was that the YCs when they finished their political sessions relaxed, whereas with the Labour Youth it was politics from morning to night.

In the opening four-hour debate uproar broke out frequently. There were many boos. This was because the speakers criticised administration of the League. Demands were made that 21-year-old Bruce Millan, a trainee chartered accountant, be removed from the chair after a delegate, Mr J Hallas from Salford, had moved that a report on the League, which had been presented to the conference, be referred back as it did not adequately deal with the problems of the League but he was told he was out of order.

Applause and boos were combined when Mr Geoffrey Bucknell, Beckenham, suggested that the committee should be asked to take action against the Communist infiltration. John Franks, University Labour party, said that he wanted to see the League abolished. It was a waste of the Party's time and money. They could do very useful work in the Party without taking time off to play at holiday camps.

Gordon Richards (Wales), said that some people prided themselves on being revolutionary and red but all they have managed to produce were some red herrings. People cavilled and ranted about democracy but they themselves cannot show the first principles of democracy. Peter Rowland of Chesterfield described the meeting as a cross between a Munich beer cellar and a Glasgow Celtic match. There were eighteen other young people wanting to speak when the chairman passed to less exciting subjects.

Mrs Eirene White of the Labour Party national executive spoke on industrial democracy. She stated that salaries in the nationalised industries are often too high but it was unreasonable to expect people in state enterprises to earn less than those in private industry. The delegates, however, had first hand experience of the inefficiency of nationalised industries as the special train carrying them from London was 58 minutes late and the return train was 2½ hours late. Neither had refreshment cars and although the train stopped with sufficient time at Doncaster to enable refreshments to be obtained there was inadequate staff to deal with so many delegates. The next bombshell to hit the conference was Labour's decision to devalue the pound, announced during the conference. Gloom and depression spread through the camp as Stafford Cripps' speech came over the loudspeakers. At first there was a stunned silence. Then when the significance had sunk in came bitter and angry comments and one delegate said, 'this could lose us the next General Election.'

The Conference ended with a mass meeting addressed by Herbert Morrison with an audience of 3,000 to 4,000, considerably bigger than the 1,800 reported to have attended the YC rally. Not only did he not once use the word devaluation; he employed the alternative phrase 'change in the relative exchange rate of the dollar and pound'. It must have been hard work but he stuck it out. He skated over the próbable date of the General Election and in an indirect reference to the disturbances earlier in the week gave the Party's youth a wise warning 'let your head rule your tongue not your tongue your head.' After his speech, Mr Morrison, following Anthony Eden's example, spent a night in one of the holiday camp's chalets before he returned south to attend a private meeting in Oxford.

The Young Conservatives decided to repeat the 1949 Holiday Week with another in 1950, the 1950 General Election taking place in the meantime. The Holiday Week was not as popular as in 1949. The 1950 Conservative Annual Report gave the figures of those attending as 1,500 as against 1,800 attending in the previous year. There were many more non-YC campers attending this 1950 Filey Week, and although the YCs were outnumbered three to one by the other campers they took many of the non-political honours. A competition for the Holiday Girl of the week was won by Hazel Pinnock, a 17-year-old YC. The Young Conservatives led the singsong and almost all the items at the camp concert were provided by the YCs.

Anthony Eden took part in the social events and a picture in *Advance* shows him receiving advice from Frances Vale while playing bowls. He lunched in the camp's Windsor dining room.

Lord Woolton was in the United States and unable to attend the conference. In his absence Jim Thomas was given a tremendous reception when he told the conference that they had magnificently carried out the task that Lord Woolton had set before them. Lord Woolton had charged them to form a team with older members of every association and to beware of clannishness and snobbery and inverted snobbery. As the election progressed, Jim Thomas said, their most valuable work was done in the less spectacular job of canvassing street by street. If the Party had not achieved actual victory it had come within an ace of it. 'It's not sufficient for us to win one election,' he said, 'the future of the nation in these formative middle century years requires a series of strong and stable governments.'

A message was read from Sir Winston Churchill: 'No single fact did more for the Conservative Party than the evergrowing strength of the Young

Conservative movement. Your work and vigour in the past few years has clearly shown how safe will be the destiny of our Party and our nation in your care.'

As in the previous year a number of papers were presented on subjects including Trade unions, social services and defence. *Advance* reported that the debate on defence aroused the most interest against the background of the recently started Korean War. People held their breath not knowing whether this was the start of the Third World War. *Advance*, in the introduction to its report of the conference, contained a call to patriotism similar to calls at the start of the previous wars, in 1914 and 1939.

The reporter stated that the sensation of drifting towards war is intolerable. Every single Young Conservative could do something to show the USSR we mean to defend our homes and homeland. A spirit of service is not built alone by those who actually do the work. They need the moral support and self sacrifice of their friends. A girl who complains that her boyfriend cannot take her dancing because he is busy with the TA is hurting her boy friend as well as the country, and playing into the hands of Communism.

Criticism of the Conservative party was voiced in a debate on local government when local associations, such as Nottingham, preferred to allocate winnable seats to local business men rather than to able Young Conservatives. Elderly councillors held on to office for too long.

In a forty-five minute speech Anthony Eden devoted most time to the criticism by the Labour party of the Schuman Plan, which had just been published, for the pooling of French and German steel. Dalton had said that the Socialists could not enter co-operation with Europe unless it was on Socialist principles but Anthony Eden proceeded to adopt a pro-Commonwealth stance by saying that, 'in any conflict of friendship or interest the British Commonwealth and Empire will always come first because we know in our hearts that as the centre of the Commonwealth family we make our fullest contribution to promote our own prosperity and the peace of the World.' However, if Anthony Eden had shown the same enthusiasm for European co-operation when the Conservative party were in office Britain could well have been an original signatory to the Treaty of Rome in 1958. This country could have been spared many of the later problems, such as even obtaining entry, and also the Common Agricultural Policy (Chapter 19).

It was decided to have the YC Conference of June 1951 at Central Hall, Westminster to coincide with the Festival of Britain, a national exhibition of British achievement, and to celebrate the centenary of the Great Exhibition of 1851, adjacent to the Royal Festival Hall, which was erected for the festival. No doubt YCs who came from outside London and the Home Counties attended the conference and visited the exhibition. Although for only one day, it was a high profile conference, with debates in the morning summed up by R.A. Butler and a mass meeting addressed by Anthony Eden in the afternoon. Whereas Winston Churchill addressed the YC first national event in 1948,

Anthony Eden addressed the four succeeding national events in 1949, 1950, 1951 and 1952.

The two subjects discussed were full employment and housing. Mr Butler summing up the morning's deliberations optimistically, surprisingly for one who was a cautious politician, wrongly predicted that the Conservative party would win the next election 'not with a working but a great majority'. He then stressed that 'although our critics said that the Conservatives deliberately want unemployment, we want full employment. With rearmament developing there would be many jobs.' It is sad to think that but for rearmament perhaps the plague of unemployment would have started much earlier following the war.

In the afternoon there were 3,000 people attending the rally addressed by Anthony Eden. A tremendous ovation heralded him as he entered the hall. He began by congratulating the conference both on its success and the admirable attendance from all parts of the country and also on the excellent papers presented and then concentrated on home affairs. He said that the task was not to take over things but to encourage industry to modernise itself and sell its products. 'We must get rid of the wrong idea that it is evil to make a profit.' He then dealt with the Industrial Charter.

We have to create a spirit in industry where everybody engaged in the field feels that he has a direct interest in improving output. I welcome the increasing number of firms who publish a breakdown of their costs to show the proportion received by various partners in the enterprise. We all want high wages and low prices. Wages can be increased by higher production and efficiency and our standard of living and security of employment depends upon our exports. Russia has its own system of Communism where the State is all-powerful and the workers are helpless robots. The United States has a system of vital and competitive free enterprise well adapted to the special circumstances of the country which consumes about 95% of what it produces.

After a spontaneous demonstration to Mr Eden the meeting concluded with the singing of Land of Hope and Glory and the National Anthem.

Between the 1951 London Conference and the next YC Conference the Conservatives gained power. It was decided to have a one day conference at Birmingham Town Hall in June 1952. A mock parliament was held in the morning. Herbert Williams MP, played the speaker and YCs played government ministers and front bench opposition spokesmen. In the afternoon there were two debates. The first was on the Commonwealth and the second on housing. The *Birmingham Post* remarked, 'all the speakers were earnest and most were vigorous in the views they wished to promote and it was by no means a conference that had nothing but praise for the government. This was particularly so in the case of criticism of the continuance of the Rent Restriction Act. (This Act pegged rents at 1939 levels so one had the ridiculous situation that it could be cheaper to rent a house than a garage where rents were not controlled.)

Anthony Eden arrived to address 2,000 Young Conservatives accompanied by Mrs Churchill. On Home Affairs Anthony Eden laid great stress on the balance of payments crisis, that we were running into debt at the rate of £800,000 million a year not envisaging that when the Conservatives left office in 1964 they would bequeath to the incoming Labour government a deficit of £358 million. He claimed that by prudent financial management they had averted a crisis of the first magnitude. He then voiced an optimistic note on the unity of the Western world against the threat of Communist aggression referring to the treaty establishing NATO, and the United Nations joint action against the communist aggression in North Korea. The Soviet Union made a fatal mistake by boycotting the Security Council so allowing the resolution to be passed authorising for the first time the use of force by the UN to stop aggression.

Finally, Eden dealt with the agreement with West Germany which, to the dismay of many war veterans, provided for German rearmament as well as providing a contribution towards the financial cost of the Allied troops stationed in Germany. He said Europe was finding a new unity and he rightly predicted as one of the most remarkable political changes in Europe that the feuds between France and Germany could be laid aside, but he failed to predict the speed at which integration among the original six members of the Common Market would occur.

In 1953, after a lapse of three years, it was decided to hold a further Holiday Week at a Butlin's Holiday Camp but on this occasion at Pwllheli in North Wales rather than at Filey.

Debates took the form of a mock parliament. The *Western Mail* and *South Wales News* described it as having the authentic House of Commons atmosphere complete with Mace and Dispatch box, pipe smoking bewigged Clerk of the House, uniformed Commons Policemen and Messengers and a holiday mood with members of the House of Commons gaily attired in colourful sports shirts. Only the Speaker, the Hon. Ralph Beaumont who had been the MP for Portsmouth Central from 1931 to 1945, wigged and gowned seemed aloof from the holiday spirit. The debates were on familiar subjects, such as NATO, the Commonwealth and industrial relations.

The event was overshadowed, however, by the Coronation which had taken place the previous week. The delegates were in confident mood because Paul Williams had recently gained a seat at the Sunderland by-election, the first time since 1924 that the ruling party had gained a seat at a by-election. Paul Williams attended and addressed the conference on the debate on Party organisation. Indications that the YC movement was changing were reflected in his speech. Paul Williams said that the Young Conservatives were in danger of becoming an indoor organisation consisting of talks to branch meetings for the converted and what was needed was a revival of the initial crusading spirit.

This confirms that a principal activity of the YCs of the 1940s was open air political meetings attended by those who supported the speaker and those who opposed. Proof that the leadership was more passive than some of the rank and file is shown by the exchange between Bill van Straubenzee, the national chairman, and one of the delegates who complained that the debates should have been more controversial to which Bill van Straubenzee replied that such subjects could not be discussed in such a large gathering.

Bill van Straubenzee did not appear to have considered that one was hardly going to retain the interest of intelligent young people in the movement if the YC conferences were staged managed, a criticism often made of the senior conference. A telegram was sent to the YC President Anthony Eden who was ill in the USA, the first YC national event he had not attended.

The Home Secretary, Sir David Maxwell Fyfe, addressed the rally. His words were to be echoed by those of John Major in the 1990s, that the great need was for higher standards of ethics to combat prevalent materialism. He also stressed that equality was intellectual and biological nonsense and freedom to improve one's individual rights was praiseworthy. The disappearance of differentials between success and failure were criticisms made by Margaret Thatcher and other supporters of Thatcherism which shows that the difference in aims between prominent Conservatives of two eras was not as great as later generations claimed.

The final Holiday Week took place at Filey in 1958. There were a number of attractive sporting and social events. Thelma Hopkins the then British and European High Jump Champion who, in 1956, broke the world record with 5 feet 8½ inches, gave a demonstration. High profile was given to two boxers from Hartlepool YCs who gave a boxing display, as one of the participants, George Bowes, was a miner. This helped to advertise the YCs as attracting all sections of the community although all evidence shows it was largely becoming, but not exclusively, a middle class movement.

In a letter to his president, Anthony Eden, Peter Walker, the YC National chairman gave a very enthusiastic account of this Holiday Week.

> The speakers were all of a very high standard and it was a reflection of the keenness of the delegates that in spite of the surrounding attractions there was 100% attendance at each of the conference sessions. John Profumo was in very good form for the opening sessions and had the added advantage of being accompanied by his very good lady. On Monday evening the chief whip Edward Heath was put under greater fire than he would ever have sustained from the 1922 committee. At the end of an hour and a half he was loudly cheered for what was an outstanding performance. Pat Hornsby Smith is a great favourite of YCs and was in her usual good form. On Thursday after two days of very serious discussion the mock parliament was somewhat light hearted but provided a great deal of wit and un-parliamentary procedure. On Thursday evening a dance

was held and it was at 11.30 pm we had the great news that a YC candidate in a by-election had reduced the Labour majority by 4000 and the other election result gave us a very good start to the mass meeting on Friday. Lord Hailsham was in tremendous form. Of all the conferences I have attended I have never witnessed a higher contribution to the debate and discussions nor have I witnessed greater enthusiasm for the battle. I read your very kind message that everybody was delighted to receive and we can assure you we celebrated your birthday: 700 Young Conservatives gathered on Thursday evening and gave you a bumper toast.

However, this was to be the final Holiday Week. Only 600 attended, according to the Party's annual report, as against 900 at Pwllheli.

# Chapter 28

# YC Conferences from 1961

During the period of Conservative government 1959–1964 there were four conferences held at the Friends Meeting House, each of which attracted over 1000 delegates. Harold Macmillan addressed the conferences in 1961 and 1963, Iain Macleod addressed the conference in 1962. Between 1964 and 1979 the leader addressed every YC national conference which indicated the importance placed in the Young Conservatives. The second YC Conference received a less favourable press than the first. There was an extremely critical article in *The Times* which complained that it became an occasion not for the YCs to indoctrinate the platform but for the platform to indoctrinate the YCs. This was also the view of Simon Clark, Chairman of Kew YCs and an anti-Marketeer. Writing in *The Times* he stated, 'when several of us tried to voice critical opinions on Britains' application to join the Common Market we were foiled by the platform who ruled us out of order,so we tried shouting out "shame" on such policy. Then we were pursued by the stewards who ruled us out of order.'

The 1963 conference took place against the background of 812,000 unemployed, a gigantic figure more than double the unemployment figures of the 1950s and there was the most critical debate so far at a YC Conference on unemployment. There was press speculation about the successor to Harold Macmillan who had already been Prime Minister for six years. If applause was a guide to popularity rating then Edward Heath outpaced both Iain Macleod and Reginald Maudling. However, it is clear from the reception that greeted Harold Macmillan they did not want a successor at all, indicating that often YCs have been remarkably like their seniors, displaying more loyalty to the leader than the restless backbenchers who are worried about their prospects of re-election once a leader becomes at all unpopular.

Sir Alec Douglas Home addressed the 1964 Conference as Prime Minister and the 1965 Conference as leader of the opposition. The Young Conservatives, in the knowledge that an election could not be far away, rallied to the Government's cause in 1964. As *The Times* reporter commented, 'no radicals or revolutionaries, no wonder cabinet ministers and other senior Tories came in force.' The approval each received would have boosted the lowest morale. The female delegates were described as extremely attractive and showed no signs of wanting to squat in Trafalgar Square. There were only four beards, all neatly trimmed, rather different from the reportedly dirty jeans that greeted Margaret Thatcher when she came to a YC Conference eleven years later.

It seems that the Party managers in the 1960s were careful not to select motions advocating radical policies. One not debated was by Mr N. Falkner on behalf of Boston Young Conservatives advocating that the next Conservative government should de-nationalise the telephone service, as well as three others asking Conference to consider measures of de-nationalisation.

In view of the government's success in the privatisation of British Telecom and other industries in the 1980s, now accepted by the Labour party, such debates might have stimulated YCs to bring pressure to bear on the Party to formulate a policy of de-nationalisation much earlier. The only record of any of the results of the motions during these conferences being sufficiently close to require a ballot is, understandably, the 1961 Conference when the Common Market was debated (Chapter 19) and a debate at the 1962 Conference criticising the government for the meagre spending on roads which was lost by 448 votes to 332 votes. The YC Conference in 1967 was extended to two days and the venue was moved outside London thereafter to be held at various resorts: Brighton, Bournemouth, Eastbourne, Torquay and Southend in the South and Blackpool, Southport, Scarborough and Harrogate in the North. The attendance was initially about 2% of membership, 1,200, with a slight reduction to a 1,000 in the early 1970s and then, as the YCs prospered during the mid-1970s, numbers increased.

After a numerically disastrous conference at Harrogate in 1982 when a low of 700 attended, over 2,000 members (10% of the membership) attended in 1983 and 1985. As late as 1990 when the movement was very much on the decline, Conference registrations were still as high as 1,549. Thereafter, numbers declined, so by 1995 the attendance was reported to be as low as 250.[1]

More pleasing, initially a 1968 report stated that although only a maximum attendance of 1,200 was obtained for Edward Heath's speech the average attendance was 900. Motions also showed an increase in the late 1960s from 268 from 63 constituencies in 1968 to 418 for the 1969 conference. Nothing gives young people greater encouragement than their voice being heard by the higher echelons of the Party and in 1969 Anthony Barber the Party chairman, stayed for the whole conference to listen to the debates.

The debates were often lively with frequent heckling. Although Richard Kelly, who attended the 1976 and the 1986 conferences as a representative in order to write a book on Conservative conferences, states that in 1986 the conference seemed rowdy, vitriolic and fractious.[2] (When I attended the 1993 YC Conference that is an apt description of the debate on Europe but not of the other debates.)[3]

Another change Richard Kelly noted was that badges displayed by YCs in 1976 were either congratulatory such as 'I Love Maggie' or anti-Labour such as 'Jim won't fix it', whereas in 1986 they seemed directed at other factions within the party, such as, 'Kill all wets'. This indicates how, within ten years, the YCs had lost their sense of unity, although at the 1976 Conference mention of the Tory Reform Group met with a mixture of applause and hisses.

At Brighton in 1967, in welcoming the delegates the Mayor of Brighton said that the YCs could be proud that they were the largest youth political movement in the free world. The most contentious debate was on Rhodesia, the resolution debated that Smith was deluding himself in believing that the white man's position could be safeguarded by maintaining power. Mr D Kent of Plymouth said that transmitters installed near the border were being used solely by extremists to exhort Africans to kill whites. There were shouts of 'rubbish' and 'Good old Smithy' before the motion was defeated by 307 votes to 288.

Edward Heath commenced his popular question and answer sessions at the Conference of 1967. He did not mind what questions were put to him. Edward Heath was asked about his own image. The questioner said, 'We know you are good but the public outside do not' alluding to the problem for Edward Heath that he was a better politician and Prime Minister than he was portrayed. On this occasion Edward Heath sidetracked the question. His answer was 'You are perfectly right. We have to go around the Country and show people and that is what I intend to do.'

Enoch Powell held a fascination for YCs even before his inflammatory speech on race for which he was sacked from the shadow cabinet. Of Enoch Powell, Edward Heath rejected the suggestion that Mr Powell's statement embarrassed the leadership. He said, 'Mr Powell has a provocative way of putting things but this stimulates discussion.' After Enoch Powell left the Conservative party in 1974 Margaret Thatcher was asked to comment on rumours in 1978, that Enoch Powell might be joining the shadow cabinet. She said, 'I am not likely to have Mr Powell as he is not even a member of the Party.'

Three hours before lunching with Mr Kosygin, Edward Heath devoted a fair proportion of his speech to international affairs amid differences with the USSR at that time, mainly over Vietnam. Edward Heath had a positive approach to Anglo-Soviet affairs when he said, 'we do not believe in these great matters that blame lies entirely with one side or the other but surely this does not prevent us from seeking practical solutions', commenting that Mr Kosygin had succeeded where the USA and the United Nations had failed in settling the dispute between India and Pakistan. This made Edward Heath, as Peter Walker told the YCs at their conference in 1975, 'the most respected of all Western statesmen'. It was this spirit which enabled him to achieve a breakthrough in Sino-British relations, described in the 1970s as co-existence, which in the 1930s would have been labelled appeasement.

There was much merit in Chris Gent's remarks that Edward Heath should have eventually been offered a place in the shadow cabinet (he refused an immediate appointment). In view of his great experience of foreign affairs had Margaret Thatcher appointed him Foreign Secretary as Edward Heath had appointed Alec Douglas Home, his foresight and industry might have deterred Argentina from attacking the Falklands.

As the 1970 Conference at Llandudno would almost certainly be the last one before the General Election, credit is due that one of the motions for discussion was that 'the Conservative tax policy lacks credibility' which could well have been embarrassing for the Party in a pre-election year if it was passed but it was defeated by a majority of 3 to 1.

Much of the controversy centred on the Conservative government's commitment to end a tax that the Wilson government had imposed, the Selective Employment Tax (a tax on employers employing people in the service industries). Mr Oldridge appeared sceptical of the plan to abolish SET as the reduction in revenue caused by its abolition would have to be replaced by another tax, possibility VAT. Robert Hicks (Horsham) reminded the Conference that inflation would increase as soon as VAT was introduced.

Mr Clarke, chairman of the Federation of Conservative Students, in support of the Party line, stated that under the Conservative government from 1951 to 1964 (to be echoed by present day Conservatives) the government had reduced taxation five times.

R. Trench complaining of those who criticised the Conservative plans on taxation, stated that it was most unpleasant that YCs were purporting to cast doubts on the Party's ability to re-establish the country's economy. Anthony Barber stated that Labour had so debased the role of politics that a third of first time voters would not vote. However, he was proved wrong as the 1970 Conservative message did not appeal to the young electors as Labour received 16% more votes from first time voters than the Conservative party.

David Hunt presided at the 1973 Conference attended by 1,000 delegates at the Winter Gardens, Bournemouth. There were grumbles that the resolutions were not vital enough. A civil engineer, Mr Adrian Walsh of Bath, Somerset, was ruled out of order when he moved a vote of no confidence in YC national chairman David Hunt complaining that there was not a single controversial motion and what about two major issues facing the government not being debated by Conference – inflation and Northern Ireland. David Hunt said that, 'the emergency motion and amendments could be taken but if we had paid attention to all the speakers we could have a week long conference.'

It is by no means clear whether David Hunt was right in rejecting the motion. Presumably the reason why Northern Ireland was not debated was that it had been the subject of a debate at the 1972 Conference.

A motion criticising the Government for paying too little attention to the homeless was carried. This was very different from what was to be the Conservative attitude to the homeless in the 1990s although homelessness is now a much bigger problem. Ian Dobkin stated, 'many people can stand the pressures of life, but those who cannot deserve our help not condemnation.' Keith Joseph replying to the debate said although the local authorities have some responsibility the government was providing special help.

The 1974 Conference was the only occasion that a YC conference was held during the General Election campaign. A contemporary report describes how Robert Molyneux, the Labour mayor of Southport greeted the Prime Minister with his customary degree of honesty and humour. He made no bones about his political allegiance and indirectly made the point that people of all political parties show an overriding interest in the welfare of Britain and he finished by quoting Disraeli on the important part youth had to play in its inheritance.

Perhaps if such sentiments were more often expressed in the House of Commons the work of the House would be more constructive.

In view of the election, a two-day stay by Edward Heath was contracted into one day. Among the events to be cancelled was included Edward Heath's opening of the YMCA building. Robert Molyneux said, 'I intend to persuade the Prime Minister to open it on the Saturday as I do not want the young people to be disappointed.' He was successful in persuading Edward Heath to open the building, clearly giving his civic duties precedence over his political affiliation. Electors who were greeted by Edward Heath would be more likely to vote for his party than if he had let the YMCA down by not opening the building after he had agreed to do so.

Chairman of YCs, Clive Landa, who welcomed Edward Heath to the platform was looking cool, as they say in reports of royal occasions, in a 'Navy blue safari jacket and orange roll neck shirt.'

Edward Heath, having just called the election because of the stalemate of a prolonged miners' strike, perhaps wrongly devoted his speech almost exclusively to the strike. When he said that there would be no Union bashing he received sustained applause, very different from the heckling James Prior was to receive in 1980.

Among other sessions was a forum discussing pornography attended by Mary Whitehouse. Stephen Murphy, secretary of British Film Censors and Geoffrey Robertson, defending counsel in a number of obscenity trails, both violently disagreed with Mrs Whitehouse's assertion that pornography was connected with violence. She said that 55% of people in prison for rape and 35% for other sexual offenses in the USA had been stimulated by pornographic literature. The only matter upon which they all agreed was that some censorship was necessary.

The 1975 Conference received increased publicity because it took place after Edward Heath's withdrawal from the leadership contest having lost the first ballot to Margaret Thatcher by 130 votes to 119. Despite the distinguished speakers such as William Whitelaw, the Party chairman and Margaret Thatcher, the ghost of Edward Heath was the strongest presence there. A long funereal roll of applause greeted William Whitelaw's praise for his success in negotiations with Europe. Ironically for Mr Whitelaw, the applause lasted longer, stop watches recorded forty-five seconds, than the combined applause at the start and finish of his appearance.

Earlier, a warm reception was given to a personal message from Edward Heath, his final victory in exile was stamped out in the Conference when it was read to the delegates (Chapter 9).

Successive speakers described the new leadership election as 'a circus or farce and a hanging out of our dirty washing.' Mark Barker of Birmingham announced, 'there is a growing suspicion that we have not done the right thing after all.' He was halted in his tracks by a hoarse shout from the hall of 'bring back the magic circle.' Sylvia Kersley of Sutton and Cheam stated, 'it was for the directors rather than the shareholders to nominate the company chairman.' This was a minority sentiment. Perhaps conscious of it she dried up in acute embarrassment on the rostrum. A large majority then spoke on the abolition of the rules for choosing a leader and the right of the Party at large to elect him or her.

A final emotional scene came when the chairman's final speech was halted with acclamation for Heath's achievements. A motion from the floor was approved sending Edward Heath a message thanking him for the great services he had rendered to the nation and the inspiration he had given to the Party.

It had been arranged for William Whitelaw, who, besides being Party chairman, was also in charge of devolution matters, to take part in a question and answer session on devolution. As it was expected that William Whitelaw would take part in the second ballot for the leadership, he was stopped by Clive Landa from answering questions on the leadership. The suggestion of certain sections of the media that this adversely affected his chances of the leadership is ludicrous as the election for the leadership is restricted to MPs and only a handful of them would have been at the Conference.

However, it gave Margaret Thatcher the opportunity of making a stirring speech. In a crisp turquoise dress, Margaret Thatcher immediately became an unlikely favourite for 1,500 delegates in their jeans and jumpers, far from the public idea of be-suited and pin-striped Young Conservatives, when she spoke on a theme she used repeatedly and put very much into practice. 'It is not only permissable but praiseworthy to want to benefit your own family.' She took two standing ovations and one minute forty-one seconds of applause.

Among observers was the second secretary of the Chinese Embassy. In view of the rapport Edward Heath had struck with the Chinese leadership one YC asked him if he was happy about Mr Heath's demise? The blue-suited diplomat looked both ways, smiled seraphically, and replied 'That's your problem.' However, the Chinese diplomat could not have been unimpressed with what he saw as the following year, after receiving an official invitation, a delegation of YCs visited China.

As a general election had to take place in 1979, Roger Pratt (YC organiser) said that it had been decided that, as a pre-election YC Conference, it was important to have a high profile event, so besides an address by Margaret Thatcher, who better to address the conference than Harold Macmillan who, during the weekend celebrated his eighty-fifth birthday.[4] Perhaps for the only time when Margaret Thatcher was leader of the Conservative party and Prime Minister, her performance was eclipsed at a Conservative Party Conference.

Besides showing his obvious support for the European Economic Community, Harold Macmillan, although his background and political philosophy was so different, praised Margaret Thatcher because she had led the party during a difficult time. He mentioned that twenty years ago 'we had a good trade balance, strong pound, little unemployment and led Europe in productivity.' (He appears, however, to have overlooked the sterling crisis of 1955 as a result of which he replaced Rab Butler at the Treasury. An article in *Crossbow* in April 1965 by James Ackers who had been a Conservative candidate, shortly after the defeat of the Conservative government, indicates that between 1950 and 1960 our growth rate per worker was lower than the USA, Canada and eight countries of Western Europe, excluding Spain and Portugal.)[5] At the end of the speech he received a standing ovation which lasted several minutes. A seasoned parliamentary correspondent said it was more like a FA Cup tie with the youthful Tories stamping their feet, they gave him a 'Supermac' cartoon as a present. James Prior commenting on the speech, said it was a wonderful tribute to a great man, forgetting Harold Macmillan's last year in office.

Margaret Thatcher, following her 1979 election victory decided not to attend the 1980 Conference at Harrogate, unlike Edward Heath's attendance after his victory in 1971. This was an indication that the YCs would not receive the support in the 1980s that previous generations of YCs had received.

A spirited debate took place on the age at which persons could become elected as a councillor or MP. Although the age at which one can vote was lowered to 18 in 1970, one still could not stand for Parliament or as a local government councillor until the age of 21, an anomaly that YC chairman Hugh Holland had criticised shortly after the legislation had been implemented.[6]

Several speakers, such as Mark Richards of Scarborough, said there was no danger of a flood of gymslip MPs, a point agreed by Patrick McLoughlin. He said that the effect on Parliament would be slight as there was strong competition for seats but younger people would be standard bearers in unwinnable seats seeking an opportunity to win personal spurs. Margaret Thatcher first stood for Parliament at 24 and Gillian Pollard who had recently stood for the council at 21, said, 'there was need for young blood as many people stood for election as councillors in their sixties.' Although the motion was carried the YCs were by no means unanimous. Mr Andy Beckham said, the idea of 'children of 18 running other people's lives was unthinkable.'

Perhaps for the only time in its history the YCs booed their president and one YC shouted 'yellow' during a reply to a motion which called for immediate legislation to end secondary picketing, although he was given a standing ovation at the end of his speech. Perhaps it was in acknowledgement of James Prior's plain speaking, when he said it is no use rushing into legislation on industrial relations with high sounding measures that will not work or cannot be enforced.

These remarks were made in reply to YCs urging stronger action. Mike Normington wanted quick action. 'If there had to be the farce of a general strike let it come soon while the country still has a chance.' John Macmenemy (19) a steel worker said the government had been elected on its manifesto to promote freedom 'but I have been denied my freedom and right to work or not as I choose.'

His reception in 1980 did not deter James Prior returning to the YC Conference in the following year and, provoked by hecklers, abandoned his prepared speech and angrily defended his policy not to outlaw the closed shop. However, it is my belief that because James Prior was reasonable, he prepared the ground well for the successful Union legislation that ensured in future it was Parliament, not the Unions, who ruled the country. This legislation, unlike the legislation passed during the Heath government, is likely to survive an incoming Labour government.

The hecklers were complaining about the sacking of Miss Joanna Harris by Sandwell Council for refusing to join a trade union. Mr Prior said he believed her dismissal was scandalous but there was no way, and there never had been at the end of the day, in which you can force the employer to take back someone they do not wish to employ. He went on to make it clear that new legislation on the closed shop would be a cynical exercise and could not be enforced.

Against furious cries of 'resign', Mr Prior told the conference that anyone who loses their job is properly compensated. 'You have to understand there are some things you can do and some things you cannot do. However strongly you feel it is not the job of the Conservative government to pass legislation they cannot enforce.' In a final appeal to the YCs in what was going to be a difficult year, Mr Prior who, for the second year, has been coolly greeted was given a standing ovation. Eventually the Conservatives captured the high moral ground, the Unions having rejected the reasonable ideas of James Prior. Norman Tebbit, with the overwhelming support of the public and many Trade Unionists, was able to steer through tough legislation.

Margaret Thatcher attended the 1981 Conference at a time when the 'gang of four' had broken with the Labour party and were about to launch the Social Democratic party. Margaret Thatcher realising the threat Shirley Williams could be to the Conservative prospects took the opportunity to make a vicious personal attack on her stating that, 'slow motion socialism is socialism all the same, however genteel the guise. It would damage Britain dangerously today as it has damaged Britain in the past, just as it did when one of their number (i.e. Social Democrats) stood on the picket line.' She was alluding to the fact that Shirley Williams had stood on the picket line during the bitter Grunwick dispute as a member of Apex Union.

Eric Pickles', the YC chairman, chief memory of the Conference was Margaret Thatcher's excitement at the prospect of meeting Ronald Reagan for the first time, although neither Margaret Thatcher nor Eric Pickles anticipated the special relationship that Ronald Reagan and Margaret Thatcher would forge.[7]

The 1983 and 1985 conferences at Bournemouth were highly successful with record attendances, though Margaret Thatcher's standing in the opinion polls was quite different. In 1983 she was 13% ahead but in 1985 her rating slumped to the lowest since before the Falklands conflict.

The main thrust of her 1983 speech was a warning against unilaterism. Comparing the dangers posed by the Kremlin now, with Hitler in the 1930s she said the unilaterists would have ensured that his dream of a thousand-year empire would have been achieved. The most passionate debate was on a motion to make abortion easier which was passed by a large majority. The proposer of the motion, Gilly Greensit, said that a woman did not go into an abortion or motherhood lightly. Women should have control over their own bodies. However, Steve Smith of Spelthorne said, 'This is abortion on demand. Some people rely on abortion as a contraceptive.' A point made by the Young Liberals in successfully opposing a motion by Peter Hain (Chapter 3).

Although there was the usual crop of CND protesters outside the Conference Centre when Margaret Thatcher emerged, three Bournemouth women succeeded in thanking Margaret Thatcher for the pressure brought on the Soviet Union by the Government to secure the release from prison of Anatoly Scharansky.

At the 1985 Conference Margaret Thatcher spoke of the miners' strike, praising the working miner. She said it was the working miner who was showing true grit. Out of this strike is emerging a new generation of moderate and responsible Trade Unions

Among debates with a difference the Conference called for stricter controls on animal experiments.

However, in spite of speeches supporting a motion condemning the back door introduction of student loans, the Conference, perhaps surprisingly, narrowly rejected the motion. The majority did not agree with Mr Russell A'Court who said that the student loan system was fundamentally naive because as one-third of the population has no bank account or any form of credit, their children would not take on a loan of several thousand pounds for further education. This shows the difference between present YCs and their predecessors who, in 1969, voted overwhelmingly against the imposition of student loans.

The 1985 Conference was the high point of the 1980s conferences. Thereafter, there was a dramatic decline.

The National officers in 1986 invited Michael Heseltine, the former Defence Secretary, who had just resigned from the Cabinet because of his disagreement with the Prime Minister concerning the Westland Helicopter affair. His presence would guarantee that the conference be highly divisive and would assist those who argued the leadership of the YCs were not fully supportive of the Prime Minister. Michael Heseltine, speaking on the Sunday, mainly attacked the *laissez-faire* liberalism. The whole YC conference is well recounted by Robert Kelly in his book on 1986 Conservative Party Conferences.

Margaret Thatcher addressed the next conference in 1987 which attracted an audience of 1,700. At this time there was violent confrontation between management and Unions at Wapping upon the introduction of new technology after a newspaper office had moved there from Fleet Street. She said those engaged in peaceful picketing 'do not throw bricks and broken paving stones, nor do they wield poles or sawn-off railings': 572 police were injured in the incident.

One debate, not often discussed by YCs and never at the main Party Conference, was on AIDS which is of particular relevance to young people. The motion before the Conference 'Young people are now a high risk group, calling for the government to spend more on research and health care' was carried by a substantial majority. At the conclusion of the debate Norman Fowler said, 'The public recognises the dangers, while evidence from hospitals that sexually transmitted diseases have fallen sharply among homosexual adults and there are encouraging signs that our campaign is having an effect. We ignore AIDS at our peril. Nobody has any confidence that any vaccine or cure will be developed within the next five years.'

The 1988, 1989 and 1990 conferences were all dominated by the heated battles for the chairmanship, all of which involved Andrew Tinney.

In view of the libertarian wing of the banned Federation of Conservative Students, twenty people, including Harry Phibbs, were banned from attending the 1988 Conference. The National chairman, Nick Robinson accused Andrew Tinney of being aided by an ultra right think-tank, Free Britain, sponsored by British businessman, David Hart. One of Andrew Tinney's prospective vice-chairmen, Alan Griffiths, said the allegation to whip up hysteria was quite deliberate.

Eastbourne YCs indicated support for Andrew Tinney. They believed he was a main stream Thatcherite and not a libertarian.

I have no doubt that Eastbourne YCs were right and those who made these allegations did a grave disservice to the YC movement. However, the dispute for the chairmanship dominated the media's attention rather than the image the conference wished to convey of young people discussing sensibly the political controversies of the day.

As they were Conservatives they generally supported Government policy, such as the failure to condemn student loans at the 1985 conference. Press reports indicate that in 1988 the Party chairman, Peter Brooke, surprisingly regarded as provocative a motion criticizing a proposal to charge for regular eye and dental check-ups and persuaded the officers to draft an amendment making it a wishy-washy motion by welcoming the review of NHS finances, but urged the minister to ensure that charges did not infringe upon its commitment for high standards or ability to pay. However from the speech of Cardiff YC Edwina Carnie, the YCs wanted to debate the original motion. She said, 'charges were a deterrent to good health and the answer did not lie in penny pinching. We are talking about people's lives.'

John Moore indicated there would be changes in the Health Service which would limit free care to emergency cases and there would be a safety net for

those on low incomes but, increasingly, others would be expected to fund
their own health care. He was addressing an audience two-thirds of which
were enthusiastic Thatcherites, indicated by the fact that only about one-third
of the audience gave their National chairman, left-of-centre Nick Robinson,
a standing ovation in his closing speech. Mr Moore's speech received only
polite applause which should have been proof to the Party that, as electors,
they wanted a comprehensive free Health Service even if the government had
to increase taxation to meet the cost. The lukewarm applause which Mr Moore
received was in sharp contrast to the applause received by the Education
Secretary when he said the school is not the only place children receive
education; the primary educator is the home.

The debate on the Community Charge was not on the merits of the charge
but on a motion which, while generally supporting it, considered that it might
deter young people in particular from registering to vote. It urged that a
publicity campaign should be undertaken to explain the policy more clearly.
The press commented, 'Michael Howard was left with a message that the Party
needed to undertake a more vigorous publicity campaign' but it seems the
Conference and the press missed the real issue that the effect of the publicity
might deter people even more from registering so as to avoid paying it. Michael
Howard in justifying the charge stated, 'young people would lose out in the
short term but should remember that it was the widows and pensioners who
were subsidising the community.'

It seems that Central Office at this time successfully managed to prevent
controversial motions being debated. Clearly the Community Charge was a
controversial issue, the merits of which I believe the YCs should have debated.
If they had rejected the idea they would have been right because it was a
decisive factor in ending Margaret Thatcher's long premiership.

In view of the bitter leadership campaign, Mrs Thatcher, departing from her
practice of attending the YC conference every other year, decided not to attend
the 1989 Conference which still attracted 1,500 members. The result in two
of the motions was contrary to Government policy.

The first was when the Conference supported a motion to allow Conservatives to organise in Northern Ireland, and secondly a motion criticising the
'Guardian Angels' being employed on the London Underground was narrowly
defeated. They gave a generous ovation to Lord Whitelaw making his first
important conference speech since his retirement from politics the previous
year on the grounds of ill health.

Richard Cuming, the area chairman of Western Area, worked very hard to
bring the Conference to the South West for the only time in its history when
it came to Torquay in 1990. As with the last two conferences it was again to
be dogged by the battle for the chairmanship. Vice-chairman Laurence Harris'
public remark that 'the conference was half dead' was hardly encouraging and,
as he was the vice-chairman, one wonders if the Conference was half dead
what steps he was taking to liven it up. It appears he was not sorry if it was

half dead, as he was arguing that Andrew Tinney had had a disastrous year as chairman and ought to be replaced.

In his opening remarks, Andrew Tinney set the tone with 'We are on trial with the media.' Few who heard Margaret Thatcher's address believed that within a year they would have a new Prime Minister. The year 1989 was momentous. One after the other of the Communist dictatorships in Eastern Europe collapsed. Margaret Thatcher said, 'in Eastern Europe the Communist dogma of Marxist-Socialism is crumbling, scorned by the very men who a year or even a month ago, had posed as the creed's most ardent apostles. In the Soviet Union the rising demand for democracy and the rule of law now echoes against the walls of the Kremlin itself . . . Keeping our nuclear deterrent had never been more important,' she told the Conference which gave her a standing ovation, both before and after her speech. Of NATO she said, 'Let us not forget that strong defence, which has kept peace in Europe for 40 years. In future there may be more countries with access to nuclear weapons than the present few.'

A sad aspect of the Conference was that in view of the high security risk the police operation cost the ratepayers and Community Charge payers over £10,000. Mr John Newcombe said the Conservative party should pay for the police operation as when his club Torquay United played West Ham they had to pay £4,000 police costs.

One of the attractions was a fringe meeting by Mr Chasnikov, the Second Secretary of the USSR Embassy and the US Embassy Political Military Counsellor, Mr Jim Hard, at the Rainbow Hotel. The meeting was arranged by the Young Conservatives' Peace Through NATO Group. Mr Chasnikov said the Soviet Union did not wish to create the impression abroad that it was destabilising the security of Europe but he could not predict how the future would lie between the US and the USSR. It was difficult to predict how Europe would be in a few years' time. 'I cannot imagine what it will be like. We cannot look into the future.' He promised the West's perception of the nuclear threat would change in the coming years.

In 1991, with Margaret Thatcher gone, the Conference was held in Scarborough in snow. This did not deter the Prime Minister from travelling by road when he was informed that he could not fly because of the weather. He called at the Happy Eater at Carcroft, Doncaster, with his three bodyguards for a cooked breakfast on the five and a half hour trip from Downing Street. When he arrived late he joked, 'My Daimler does not go as fast as John Prescott's, a reference to John Prescott's recent Court appearance for speeding.

Unlike his predecessor, he stepped quietly on to the platform but was immediately given a rapturous standing ovation. When he concluded his twenty-eight minute speech he was again given a tremendous ovation.

During his speech he referred to Europe. 'We will remain an important and enthusiastic member of the EC. It is simply not enough for some people to say "I don't really like Europe but I will tolerate it." If we take that view we will never be the centre of Europe and cannot lead in the direction which we wish to go.'

On public services, forecasting his Citizens' Charter, he said, 'I will not tolerate public services which are just not good enough, council house repairs which are shoddy and slow, hospital appointments which take all day, trains that run late, buses that travel in packs.' He questioned whether the public were getting proper value for the money which had been invested in health, transport and education. 'We must make sure those services operate better for the people who use them.'

Perhaps if the MPs who elected him had enthusiastically backed him on the policies outlined in his speech instead of comparing him to his illustrious predecessor, feeling they could do better, then his premiership and the Party would be in a stronger position.

# Chapter 29

# Impact of YCs
# on Party Conferences

One of the most remarkable differences between the Conservative and Labour youth movements was, whereas the Labour youth movement was permitted, as a privilege, to send a handful of young delegates to the Party Conference, two out of seven representatives at the Conservative Party Conference were Young Conservatives. Through the years as YC branches collapsed the number of YCs attending the Party Conference dwindled but the YC impact on the Party Conference has been dramatic. During the Attlee government of 1945–1950, four conferences took place. After a period of intensive activity by the Labour government which had nationalised much of Britain's industrial wealth (Chapter 5), the first post-war conference was commenced in considerable gloom at Blackpool but, due to Lord Woolton's brilliance, ended with considerable optimism.

For many years to come it was Lord Woolton who dominated the conference by the quiet and confident way in which he always conducted himself. It was strange that Lord Woolton who had never before attended a Party conference should attend his first Party conference as the chairman. As is shown in his autobiography, he was able to instil in the Party the folly of the Labour Party's programme of wholesale nationalisation (Chapter 5).[1]

When the Party faithful attended Blackpool they wondered if the Conservative Party would ever regain its position as the dominant force in British politics and there was talk of trying to persuade the Liberals to form an anti-Socialist alliance and for the Conservative Party to change its name to Unionist, or some other name. It was considered by many that the name 'Conservative' in post-war Britain was not an asset, as many politicians both before and after have regarded it, but a liability. As in many other tasks which he performed Lord Woolton could honestly tell the Party Conference at its conclusion that the conference was the beginning of a great revival.

In the next half century the Conservatives were to rule for 33 years, all with a working majority, whereas of Labour's 17-year reign only 8 were to be with a working majority.

Harold Macmillan complained that, 'demands were made that good Socialists should be appointed to high positions. Trade unions, professions and even art and literature were permeated with Socialist dogma and we were about to be told that we had to have Socialist poetry, Socialist pictures and Socialist music.' He stressed he was not in favour of *laissez-faire* as 'the Government must

intervene in and indeed largely manage economic life.' Such words would not
have found favour in the Thatcher era. He continued, 'The question was by
what means and at what level and for what purpose: the monetary policy, the
tariff policy and the broad guidance of an appropriate balance of imports and
exports were functions of Government . . . During post-War reconstruction
the broad priorities must be settled at a Government level.'[2]

Surprisingly, at each of the first three conferences, a motion was debated
in connection with the Young Conservatives. This raises a point often
forgotten, particularly by the hierarchy in the present-day Conservative Party,
namely that the Young Conservatives' success in the first four years was
not accidental but the result of a deliberate policy where a large portion of
the Party's resources was invested in the movement to ensure, as far as
possible that it flourished in order to defeat socialism and to return the
Conservatives to power. The fact that, since 1950, Britain has been so much
dominated by the Conservative Party shows the foresight of Lord Woolton,
Anthony Eden and Jim Thomas and what they did was not misguided but
extremely sound.

At Blackpool a motion proposed by YC national chairman Anthony Nutting
was passed unanimously:

> The Conference urges the Executive Committee of each parliamentary
> division to afford full representation on its main committee and sub-
> committees to Young Conservatives and embark upon an intensive cam-
> paign of recruitment of additional Young Conservative members, to
> provide a rota of speakers of moment as a help to this end and to use
> every endeavour within their respective powers to form a Young Conser-
> vative branch in all towns and villages within each constituency, recog-
> nising that the future success of the Conservative Party in the polls depends
> more largely on the measure of youthful support than on any other single
> factor. This Party urges Party Headquarters, Area and constituency organis-
> ations to provide facilities for Young Conservatives to achieve a sound
> and comprehensive political education and encouragement be given to
> take a more active part in all branches of local government.[3]

However, a Young Conservative had a most prominent part to play at the
Conference. John Hay, who was to be the next YC chairman, described how,
on the special Conference train conveying passengers to the North a number
of the representatives attending the Conference expressed dissatisfaction at the
absence of detailed Party policy on numerous matters and felt strongly that the
Party would not regain any credibility and impact on national affairs if it did
not state its policy. This is a common criticism of a defeated party in opposition
and in spite of the impatience of the delegates the Party was probably right in
being cautious so soon after such a decisive election defeat as it suffered in
1945. John Hay proposed the Council's report be referred back because of a
lack of any clear statements of future policy. He relates how;

before the proceedings began I walked from my seat in the hall, tactically chosen on the aisle and handed to the Party secretary the notice of motion on many pages carrying all the signatures I had obtained. The Party secretary was clearly puzzled and conferred with the chairman. When the conference commenced after suitable prayers for wisdom by a local clergyman and an address of welcome from the Mayor of Blackpool the annual report of the National Executive was the first item of business on the agenda. A motion was formally moved to take note of it. The Chairman then rose, looking somewhat apprehensive and nonplussed, saying he had received a notice of motion that the report should be referred back to the committee and I was called upon to move it. With some trepidation I walked to the small rostrum below the platform and looked over what until then was the largest audience I had ever addressed. Speaking calmly and slowly I began, 'Let me say at the outset this is no idle or frivolous matter. It has been signed by representatives of every provincial Area throughout the country for several reasons. First we see no reference anywhere in the report as to what has happened to the resolution passed at the last conference and what action has been taken. Secondly eight particular resolutions sent in for discussion by this conference have not been chosen but have been tucked away in a kind of annexe at the back of the agenda. We say that this matter of Policy should have been brought forward and we think it is very wrong, at this time when the paramount cry throughout the Party is 'What is our policy? What are our aims and objectives?'

I have been told that the Leader of the Party is going to deal with this matter when he speaks on Saturday, but I feel that we, the rank and file, should have our chance to say something about policy too. This matter should be put down for debate somewhere on the Agenda and I ask that something be done even now to ensure that it will be.

There was renewed applause and cries of 'Hear, hear!' and 'well done' from all over as I resumed my seat. My motion was then seconded by Gordon Lilley.

The platform was obviously taken by surprise at this move and the vociferous support for the matter of my remarks. Accordingly the vice-Chairman of the National Executive, Sir Herbert Williams MP rose to intervene on its behalf, completely misjudging both the subject and the mood of the Conference.

He argued that 'if we are going to open the Conference with a Policy announced from "on High" what are we here for? If would be useless for us to come here if policy is going to be decided before we have our say about it. The proposer of the reference back is moving something entirely reactionary . . .' (There were loud and prolonged cries of 'No' at this point, because he had clearly not understood what the purpose of our action was) but he continued, 'The more you say "No" the more I think you have not troubled to think out the logic of the problem. Policy is not a thing you state; it grows out of circumstances. You must go bald-headed for the other side and gradually out of that will be built the policy you want.

John Hay proceeded to gain support from other speakers who disagreed with the view expressed from the platform.

As the meeting looked like getting out of hand from the platform's point of view, the platform came to a quick decision to ask Sir David Maxwell-Fyfe (Attorney General in Churchill's 'caretaker government' between the end of the Coalition and the General Election) to address the conference. He had just returned from the trials of the Nazi war leaders at Nuremburg, where he had been one of the leading members of the prosecution team, and thereby had received great kudos at the time.

Sir David had certainly grasped the point at issue and while making a more far-reaching speech on party political matters, which calmed the atmosphere and took people's minds off the 'policy' argument somewhat graciously said, 'We should be the vehicle and medium of fearless discussion. We are in the deepest sympathy with Mr Hay and I give an undertaking that these matters will be fully considered by the Executive Committee. And would we, the mover and seconder of the motion, allow the report to go forward?'

It remained only for the chairman to undertake to make an opportunity before the end of the Conference for debate on one of the policy resolutions. Regaining the rostrum, John Hay briefly withdrew the motion to refer back which received general acclamation and the Conference proceeded with its regular business. The timetable of the conference was rearranged for a debate on policy to be included. But for John Hay's action this would not have taken place.[4]

At the 1947 Brighton Conference John Hay proposed the motion on the Young Conservatives:

The Conference viewed with satisfaction but not complacency the increasing strength of the Young Conservative movement throughout the country, recognised the necessity of giving fair encouragement and incentive to all Young Conservatives and felt that the numbers and capability of this movement warrants Constituency Associations making greater use of the efficient and able Young Conservatives as municipal and parliamentary candidates and in responsible offices throughout the Party organisation.

He complained that 'too many Young Conservatives had been given hopeless seats to fight and their talents would be far better used if they were allocated winnable seats for the councils. There were 219 candidates for county and municipal elections.[5]

The principal achievement of the 1947 Conference was the adoption of the

Industrial Charter which was a U-turn on the *laissez-faire* policies of the 1930s (Chapter 20).

For the third year in succession a motion concerning Youth Conservatives was selected for debate at the Party Conference at Llandudno in 1948. It was proposed by John Hay, who had been re-elected national chairman for a second year, speaking at the Conference for the third year in succession in support of the following motion concerning the Young Conservatives:

> That this Conference acknowledges the value to the Party of the Young Conservative organisation, since as the years progress the votes of the youth of Great Britain become of increasingly vital importance in future elections for the following reasons:
>
> 1. There are in Great Britain now approximately four million persons between 14 and 20 years of age who will come on to the electoral register before 1950 or 1955, a large number of whom have no Tory traditions
>
> 2. There are nearly six million persons in Great Britain on the electoral register between 21 and 29 years of age, and only a very small proportion are either Young Conservatives or can be viewed with any certainty as supporters of the Conservative Party.
>
> 3. There are more than five million persons in Great Britain of 65 years of age or over many of whom are Tory and of whose votes many will be lost by death before 1950 or 1955.
>
> It pledges itself to extend the propagation of Conservatism among the young of Britain and urges Young Conservative branches to continue to develop their political efficiency.

This shows how important the Party considered was the success the Young Conservatives were achieving in winning the youth vote. John Hay was able to report that there were 150,000 YC members, 45,000 more members since the Brighton Conference. He went on to criticise the fact that one or two Conservative Associations had allocated their tickets for the overflow meeting to the Young Conservatives, whereas the seniors had retained all the tickets for the main hall. 'I still hear of places where Young Conservatives are used exclusively as delivery squads for literature.'

John Hay advocated more Young Conservatives for local government. He was critical of the high cost of Conservative functions which could not be afforded by Young Conservatives, also mentioning that some seniors could not afford them either. In a moving speech he said,

> The future of the movement of which we are very proud is at the cross-roads. In front of us lies a great election fight. I know that Young Conservatives are ready, willing and eager to play a decisive part in bringing our Party to power but beyond the necessity of winning the next election, beyond the necessity of building up membership of our Party lies the fundamental basis upon which the Young Conservatives have built the

need of providing better systems to serve our Party and for the future of
the country. This is our aim. We ask for help and support for our activities
from all of you that have anything to do with the Young Conservatives.
We have no desire to be complacent and I hope very much that we will
go from strength to strength and that in the next year we will be able to
bring before you an even better and more satisfactory record.

Eloquent though the speech was, such rapid rise in the numbers of Young
Conservatives would never again be achieved although their power and influence would continue for the next three decades.[6]

However, it was not only John Hay of the Young Conservatives who played
a significant role at the 1948 Conference, but also the national YC vice-chairman
and future chairman, Frances Vale.

One of the debates on the agenda was a request to Conference to approve
a Women's Charter which had been prepared by the Party. For such a charter,
prepared with the approval of the Party, to be rejected at a Conservative
Conference was extremely rare and it was Frances Vale who was instrumental
in the rejection of the charter by the Conference. Frances Vale, described as
'addressing the Conference in her vivid green dress', persuaded many attending
to vote against the charter. She said, 'It is not only men who are becoming
sentimental about women. We should not look at a policy that looks at women
alone. Let us not come to the rostrum to put the women's view but speak
from the national point of view.'[7] However, the *Evening Standard* reporter at
the Conference would not have had Frances Vale's approval. The *Evening
Standard* report said, 'Prettiest Girl at the Tory Conference at Llandudno was
Diana Fennell, brown eyed, brown haired, the vice-chairman of South Kensington YCs, she was cheered before she opened her mouth.'[8]

The final Conservative Party Conference before the General Election was
held at Earls Court in 1949, the only post-war conference to be held in London
but, unlike the previous three conferences, there was no resolution specifically
referring to the Young Conservatives. The most significant events were the
apparently conflicting motions concerning Empire & Europe referred to in
Chapter 19.

One touching moment was when Mrs Churchill joined the platform and
shook hands with Frances Vale who had just been elected chairman of the
Young Conservatives.[9] Frances Vale had fonder memories of Winston Churchill
than her predecessor John Hay. As president of Home Counties North YCs,
Mrs Churchill used to invited Frances Vale to their London home where she
met Winston. She says Winston showed an interest in any activity in which
Mrs Churchill participated, and as she took a great interest in Home Counties
YCs so did Winston.[10]

The Conservative Party Conference returned to Blackpool in 1950 in a very
different mood than when it last met in Blackpool in 1946, then in considerable
gloom following its crushing 1945 defeat.

The YCs made their debut in 1946 and by 1950 it was calculated that of the 4,000 delegates, approximately 1,500 were Young Conservatives. It was fitting that the first YC National Chairman, Anthony Nutting, had made such rapid progress that he was then chairman of the National Union. During the long period of Conservative rule in the 1950s it was many years before the YCs made the same impact as they had at the first three post-war Conferences. Gradually, with the policy of making the YC movement more political, in the early 1960s the YCs began to propose motions, as did Cllr Andrew Bowden in 1961 in support of the negotiations to join the Common Market[11] and Sydney Chapman in 1963 who proposed a motion welcoming the Beeching Report, but urging HM Government once again to stress that no railway line or station would be closed unless an alternative, adequate and efficient public transport service was available.[12]

The YCs constantly criticised the format of the Party Conference. A critical motion was passed by the NAC in 1958.[13] Eric Chalker as a leader of Greater London YCs said that they wished to wield more influence on the Party and they also wanted to attempt to have more influence on the Party Conference. In 1966 when Eric Chalker was called to speak in a European debate he made a brave remark. While thanking the chairman for calling him, he said, 'many more YCs should have spoken this week. As they had one-third of the representation, they should have one-third of the voice.' The Chairman retorted that, 'in 1962, 16 YCs had spoken, in 1963, 13 and in 1966 so far 15, so the 1962 figure was likely to be exceeded.'[14]

YCs continued to criticise the Party Conferences. When the Greater London YCs in 1969 produced 'Set the Party Free' referring to Party Conferences 'year after year there is criticism of woolly motions, boring speeches, over-long Shadow Cabinet replies, too many subjects discussed, insufficient amendments called, too many MPs and candidates speaking', and they were scathing of the submission 'of Labour bashing motions rather than controversial motions.'[15]

The NAC passed a motion in 1989 for a more genuine debate on the motions submitted, without seriously impairing the public perception of the Party.[16] Little appears to have changed in twenty years.

From the late 1960s YCs livened up the Conferences although initially at the seniors' instigation. At the 1967 Conference, six girls wearing Union Jack dresses, sold booklets *A Century of Achievement, the History of the Party over 100 years*, to boost party funds. Some of the more conservative of the delegates were shocked at the girls' outfits although Central Office stated they received no official complaint.[17]

At the 1968 Conference, Greater London YCs produced a daily newspaper, which was published either by the GLYC or the National YCs for well over the next decade, with provocative articles on the Conference and also containing undelivered speeches of those YCs wishing to speak on a motion but not being called by the chairman to speak. Page 238.

In 1969 the GLYC obtained considerable publicity as they released 'Set the Party Free' on the first day of the Conference.

After the Tory party won the 1970 election at the Party Conference the Young Conservatives openly demonstrated their support for Edward Heath, particularly over Europe. The *Ealing Chronicle* reporter in 1970 stated that following a campaign to persuade all delegates to sport 'I'm for Europe' badges, 'melodious chants of Young Conservatives were heard throughout the hall towards the end of the debate. Some delegates criticised this behaviour and compared the YCs to Young Liberals', but the *Ealing Chronicle* continues 'the difference between our behaviour and the Young Liberals was that we were backing Edward Heath and the Government's policy to the hilt.'[18]

In 1971 the YCs played an even more prominent part than in 1970. After Alec Douglas Home's speech in favour of the Common Market, six YCs representing the existing six EEC members in their national costume appeared in the hall and there was a great show of placards with the message 'Yes to entry'.[19] In view of the YCs' enthusiasm for entry it was fitting that a national YC vice-chairman, Peter Price proposing the motion received the loudest cheer when he said 'Are we now a timid people afraid to venture beyond our shore?'[20] Also in the same year during John Watson's year of office the national chairman proposed one of the motions as did his vice-chairman.[21]

John Watson's interest in protection of the environment was recognised by his proposal of the motion 'This Conference expresses its concern of the problem of population growth in Britain and the world and calls upon HM Government for a practical scheme for population limitation.'

In 1972 David Hunt proposed the amendment congratulating the government for welcoming Ugandan Asians holding British passports who had been expelled by General Amin. Earlier, Enoch Powell proposed a motion endeavouring to have the policy stopped. The *Daily Mirror* described the YC participation in the conference as 'a victory for all that is young and liberal and compassionate in the Conservative party. One young person after another pledged himself or herself to the simple moral issue. "We must keep our word. We must display humanity".'

A remarkable feature was David Hunt's reception 'The Young Tory National chairman was given a tremendous ovation in which all members of the Cabinet who were present, joined. During his speech every possible emotional appeal to loyalty was evoked. Winston Churchill and Iain Macleod were quoted reverently.' David Hunt said it was a pity that the problem of admitting the Ugandan Asians had been exaggerated and distorted. He continued:

> It is completely and utterly indefensible to grant a person a British passport and when that person is in trouble to try and pretend that it is a worthless document. How could anybody send back the refugees into the arms of General Amin, into the arms of a self-confessed racist, who the other day said Hitler was right because he had burned six million Jews.[22]

As David Hunt was speaking Young Tories in one gallery held up score cards, like those used in *Come Dancing* which awarded him marks. David Hunt's amendment was carried by 1,731 votes to 738.

David Hunt was not the only speaker to receive publicity. So, too, did Clive Landa, chairman of the Greater London YCs who had mounted a campaign 'Youth is a wasting asset'. Two YC girls were wearing tee shirts with that slogan to promote the campaign. Clive Landa encouraged them by wearing a similar tee shirt when he was unexpectedly called to the rostrum to speak. However, the *Mirror* correctly summed up the Conference: 'A remarkable feature was the enthusiastic support given to the Government by the Young Conservatives.'[23]

The Young Conservatives continued to have a high profile at the Conferences throughout the 1970s. In 1977 Robert Hughes proposed an amendment to a lukewarm European motion stating 'while enthusiastically supporting the Common Market, rejects unnecessary harmonisation proposals which smack at bureaucratic busybodyness serve to eliminate the traditional and often colourful differences among the peoples of Europe and furthering the interest of ordinary men and women.'

The amendment Robert Hughes proposed was 'that this Conference believes that the only long-term solution is to control bureaucracy by a directly elected European Parliament and therefore recognises that holding European elections for such a body in 1978 must be regarded as a major objective.' He was supported in that motion by the national chairman, Michael Jack, and the fact that two Young Conservatives were called to speak in the same debate showed that in spite of the change of leadership the YCs were still considered to have a significant part to play.[24]

An unusual commendation of the 1979 Conference was received from the *Guardian*. Simon Hoggart wrote,

> They have been hugely in evidence at Blackpool this week, where they have sold hundreds of white boaters with a pink band declaring 'We all won with Maggie . . . The YC Ball was always the best social occasion . . . In spite of all this, the Young Tories, still shedding their image as a middle-class marriage bureau, are by and large quite a force of moderation in the party. Time and again in the debates it was the Young Conservatives who with considerable courage put the left-wing case. The Tory Conference is a harder audience than its subservience to the party leaders implies, the boos are quick to come, and no one with great ambition wants to leave the rostrum to a fusillade of jeers.
>
> Yet it was the Young Conservatives that put a case for relaxed immigration control and race tolerance that few Labour or Liberal speakers would have been ashamed of.
>
> Throughout the Conference the YCs have produced a daily newspaper, sometimes boring but often sharp and witty. Their self-congratulation for offending some of the leaders can be annoying but one can forgive them

much for their mock poll of Mrs Thatcher's worst Cabinet, featuring Julian Amery as Foreign Secretary, Winston Churchill as Home Secretary and the ineffable Jill Knight as Secretary of State for Social Services. They have come a long way since the London Young Conservative, Clive Landa, was booed on the platform for daring to appear in a tee-shirt.[25]

It was the highwater mark of the Young Conservatives' impact on the Conference. From then on no longer were they encouraged by the Party to have the high-profile which, encouraged by Edward Heath during the early 1970s, they had at Party Conferences which survived the change of leadership. As the Conservatives prospered during the 1980s the YCs were no longer vital to the Party retaining power and their impact waned.

## Chapter 30

# Towards Fifty Years Without Glory

In March 1991 Murdo Fraser became the first Scottish YC National chairman and he avoided during his year of office, the in-fighting among YCs which in seven years had destroyed the YCs' good name built up over more than thirty years.

In view of the YCs' move to the right the decision to invite Edward Heath to deliver the Macmillan lecture with a pro-European message was an action which helped unite the Young Conservatives instead of dividing them.

The NAC passed the following resolution: 'in order to leave people in no doubt that they supported the Prime Minister, the NAC believes that his statesmanship in response to the abortive Soviet coup has further enhanced the standing of John Major as leader. We know exactly where we are going at the next election.' They asked that a copy of this resolution be sent to Central Office in case support for John Major from YCs is called into question.[1]

Figures in September 1991 indicated membership was:[2]

| | | | |
|---|---|---|---|
| Eastern | 384 | South Eastern | 559 |
| North West | 242 | Wessex | 573 |
| East & West Midlands | 372 | Western | 127 |
| Yorkshire | 295 | Scotland | 314 |
| Northern | 142 | Northern Ireland | 23 |
| Wales | 50 | Total | 3933 |
| London | 852 | | |

In spring 1992 the Youth Officer Martin Minns was able to report branches were again on the increase from 189 to 218. It was claimed that membership was about 8,000 although it would be disappointing if there had not been an increase in the period before a General Election.[3]

YCs should not have taken comfort in the state of the Labour and Liberal youth movements because the YCs had persistently outshone the youth movements of the other political parties. Whereas the Labour and Liberal youth movements had often assisted their parties to lose elections the YCs had been a contributing factor in ensuring that during most of the post-war period the Conservative party was in government.

The Young Socialists had for a long time been influenced by Militant at national although not necessarily at branch level. For the fourth time since the war, drastic changes were made to the Young Socialist movement despite bitter opposition from the chair of the Young Socialists. In 1988 Paula Hanford stated 'Every initiative put forward by the Young Socialists had been blocked . . . Get off our backs, leave the young people in the Party to fight the Tories.'[4]

In 1987 the upper age limit for a Young Socialist was reduced to 22 and a branch with less than ten members was not recognised.[5] The YCs had an identical requirement as a YC branch with less than ten members was not entitled to vote for its national officers. The 1988 LPYS national conference was again cancelled. The 1987 Labour annual report claimed that there were 558 Young Socialist branches, although in the conference debate on youth in 1988, NEC member, Derek Fatchett estimated the total strength was 2,500.[6]

After implementation of these reforms, a staggering 435 branches apparently did not comply with the new limits on age or numbers. The seat of one of their representatives on the Labour NEC was maintained. In the absence of a youth conference in 1988 officers were selected by a postal ballot.[7] Although a new youth conference was convened in Bournemouth in November 1989 there were no debates on policy (unlike the Young Conservatives and Young Liberals who were never prevented from holding debates on policy even if the verdict was not to the liking of their seniors).

The position was, therefore, similar to the pre-war position of the Labour youth movement. The conference programme was limited to political educa-tion, skill training and campaign workshops. These were also regarded as important by the Young Conservatives but these skills were more appropriately taught at the Summer Schools that were organised by the YCs throughout the 1980s and the purpose of the annual conference was to debate policy issues in the presence of the Minister who would reply after the debate. By 1991 policy resolutions were again allowed at the Young Socialist Conferences. The 1991 Labour party report indicated that only thirty-four constituencies had youth movements.

The next YC National chairman, Adrian McLellan, came from Woking so it joins Macclesfield, Hampstead and Brighton in being the only branches to produce two National chairmen. The highlight of his year was the magnificent election victory of John Major against all odds and YCs up and down the country worked, as their predecessors had for the past forty-two years, enthusi-astically in the election campaign.

The YCs should have had mixed feelings that the *Daily Telegraph* devoted a full page to the YCs as the worst fate for them is for the media to ignore them. In misguided criticism of the YCs election for National Chairman Roger Hardman stated that there was no ideological divide and the chief point of difference between competing camps quickly became the quality of the two prospective chairmen. The talk in the hotel bars was how best to manage the organisation in the interest of the parent Party. On that basis Robert Hardman should, as his predecessors in the media had, have praised the YCs but he seemed disappointed that he could not find more wrong with the YCs.[8] He should have made it clear that the annual bout of in-fighting (a phenomenon which occupied a short space of time following a period of forty years during which the strength of the YCs had been built on its unity).

The most significant political event of John Major's first year of office following the election was Britain being forced out of the ERM a subject upon which Adrian McLellan spoke in the European debate at the Party Conference. At the NAC Murdo Fraser successfully proposed a motion to abandon permanently the membership of the ERM and also called upon the government instantly and decisively (which the Government did) to stimulate economic growth by allowing the pound to float. Although an occasional YC magazine *Campaigner* described the motion as controversial it appears that the Exchange Rate Mechanism was of doubtful benefit if it failed to protect a currency against professional speculators.[9] Whether a common currency would exacerbate or solve such problems will be one of the greatest issues that the EU will have to consider.

In 1993 Andrew Rosindell, an Essex councillor was elected national chairman unopposed. It is more difficult to engender enthusiasm in a post-election year but the highlight of his year of office was hosting a European weekend conference of leaders of the DEMYC an organisation of centre-right political parties in June at which many of the emerging centre right wing democracies of Eastern Europe sent delegates. Two days previous to the conference a cocktail party was held which Lady Thatcher attended.

At the conference dinner, Lord Archer took the opportunity to make a most powerful speech in support of John Major and the way he had led from the front to win the 1992 election. One felt that although the speech would have been better directed at the YCs in the 1980s or the Conservative backbenchers in the 1990s the foreign members of the audience loved it.[10]

One innovation in 1994 was the decision to re-title the annual Harold Macmillan lecture, the Ian Gow lecture in recognition of the MP murdered by the IRA. The media mischievously alleged senior members of the Party were furious that Macmillan's name was dropped from the lectures. Andrew Rosindell said there was no truth in this and it is quite natural that YCs would wish to associate the lectures with a politician they knew and I have no doubt that Ian Gow was a most worthy successor.[11] The presence of Ian Gow's widow increased the sense of occasion. In view of the YCs' right-wing outlook no doubt they were delighted that Peter Lilley accepted the invitation to deliver the first Ian Gow lecture.[12]

In the early 1990s both the Conservatives and Labour were in danger of becoming geriatric parties. An analysis of Conservative party membership revealed the average age was 62.[13] A 1993 report of the Labour party indicated that there were three times as many members over the age of 66 then under 25.[14] Nevertheless, evidence indicates that whereas membership of the Conservative party, particularly among the young, is declining Labour membership among the under 25s is increasing significantly.

In 1993 in the final period of John Smith's leadership even more dramatic changes were made to the Labour youth movement in character with the retreat of the Labour party from Socialism shortly to manifest itself in the dropping of Clause 4. The name of Young Socialists changed to Young Labour. To prevent extremists penetrating the youth movement by forming small branches the whole country was divided into sixty areas, each large town having just one central branch and in country areas a number of constituencies were grouped together to form one branch.

Delegates to the Young Labour Conference have to be under the age of 23, but otherwise membership continues until 25. One cannot compare the claim of Tom Watson that Young Labour has 22,000 members (a 33% increase in two years)[15] with the strength of the YCs. The difference is that the Labour party count all young members under 25 as members of Young Labour. A member of the Conservative party under the age of 30 can only be a YC if he joins a YC branch.

Throughout the 1960s and 1970s in spite of the lack of enthusiasm for further nationalisation and the success of the Tory privatisation programme of the 1980s the Young Socialists constantly advocated further and extensive nationalisation.[16] Would the change of name lead to a change of attitude of Labour's young people? The evidence is that the claim of the Labour party youth officer Tom Watson is correct, because at the 1995 Young Labour conference 70% voted in favour of dropping Clause 4.[17]

Another initiative was a new Young Labour monthly glossy magazine *Regeneration* not unlike the YC *Impact* of the 1960s.

The rise of Young Labour could prove to be a bigger threat to the Young Liberals who have declined rapidly since the early 1970s when they helped to increase Liberal support among first time voters from 8% to 28%. Since the 1970s the Young Liberals suffered a much greater decline than the Young Conservatives. By 1981 their membership fluctuated between 700 and 1,000.[18] In 1988 they had a disastrous conference at Llandudno. It is disputed whether the maximum number attending was twenty-four or forty.[19]

In 1993 the student organisation and Young Liberals merged with a joint membership of 2,000. It has its own magazine *Free Radical*, two conferences a year and three campaigns have been organised: Youth Rights Campaign, Animal Welfare Campaign and Housing Crisis Campaign.[20]

One political youth movement that did not survive was the Young Communists which had been established in 1924, and even if the Communist party had survived the youth movement was not likely to have done so. From a peak of 6,000 members in 1967, membership declined to a mere 350 by 1983.[21]

While Labour has been making strenuous efforts to rebuild its youth movement the YCs have struggled on, with minimal resources. YCs have not been helped by the withdrawal of financial support for their annual conference and the closing of the youth department at Central Office. If Lord Woolton had been party chairman now one cannot imagine him daring to attend a Party Conference without some new initiative to attract youth to the Conservative party. For three years John Major has stayed away from YC conferences. Nevertheless, their current chairman, Paul Clarke, feels the YCs' greatest achievement in recent years has been the relaxation of the Sunday Trading laws and Licensing laws. As national chairman he still has an *ex officio* place on all the important committees of the Party including the candidates committee.[22]

I believe that if the Young Conservative movement was closed down not many YCs would join the senior party (after all, what social occasions would appeal to them) and their services particularly at election time would be lost. If ever a massive drive for young blood in the Party was needed the time was after John Major's great election victory of 1992.

Regretfully, present day YCs are only a shadow of their former selves. Will there be a revival? Although social habits have changed I am certain that if the present leaders of the Conservative party had the same enthusiasm as Lord Woolton, Anthony Eden and Sam Oliver there could be a revival which, with an ageing membership, could only be of benefit to the Conservative party.

## Appendix 1

# Reigate Division of Surrey Conservative and Unionist Association Annual Report for 1942

The Association contines to maintain the efficiency of its organisation and to develop and extend its war activities in the National interest.

Although political activities have been suspended and the Party truce strictly observed, several of our branches hold regular gatherings and others, by the monthly distribution of *The Onlooker* (the official journal of the Party), or by other means, are maintaining contact with their members.

Throughout the constituency our Branch Associations as such, and their individual officers and members are taking a large part in the war effort in their respective districts. They have achieved some splendid work of a most diverse character, and we would reiterate that the efficiency of many of the local wartime organisations can be ascribed in no small measure to the work of those who have contributed so greatly to the success of our Association.

The activities of our Member, Mr Gordon Touche, both in the House and throughout the constituency have been much appreciated. Both he and Mrs Touche have attended gatherings in many parts of the Division and the helpful and sympathetic manner in which our Member has dealt with many and varied problems about which he is consulted and his readiness to be of service to his constituents at all times, evokes many expressions of gratitude both from individuals and local bodies. In October, the Reigate Town Council, at a special meeting, unanimously decided to confer upon Mr Touche the Honorary Freedom of the Borough and at the subsequent gathering when the ceremony was carried out, warm tribute was paid to the work of our Member. This honour – the greatest which the Borough can bestow – is shared by only two other living Freeman.

Once again we are pleased to report that substantial sums have been raised, both by the Association and its branches, for War charities. As an instance, we joined in a scheme promoted by the S.E. Area Women's Advisory Committee to raise a fund for the provision of parcels for Prisoners of War through the British Red Cross and succeeded in making £157.12.8.

The Association's offices are being used as depots by our members and other voluntary workers for the distribution of wool and for the reception of comforts for the forces. Our Dorking Headquarters are being used for a similar purpose, and not only do our local Women's Branch provide a host of Workers, but it also raises money by means of whist drives, etc. to pay for all the wool used. Upwards of 4,000 knitted garments have passed through our hands since we commenced this work.

We have established our own information bureaux and have done excellent work in assisting members and others in all parts of the Division with cases of difficulty, particularly those arising from War-time legislation.

Our organisation continues to be of real service to the National Savings Movement. Groups have been formed in various parts of the consitituency and full support has been accorded Savings Committees in the matter of the systematic collections of contributions. One Group is administered from our Redhill office and there is another operating from our office at Dorking. The Dorking Women's Branch, in particular, is to be congratulated upon possessing one of the strongest groups of its kind in the country. Over 900 members are weekly subscribers and a sum of over £14,000 has already been contributed.

Practical assistance in connection with Civil Defence, Salvage, British Restaurants has been rendered by the Association to the various Local Authorities, and in many ways to the Women's Voluntary Services, the Ministry of Information, War Hospital Supply Depots, Canteens for the Forces, the British Red Cross Society, local units of the Home Guard, the Air Training Corps, the Women's Junior Air Corps and other organisations. In general, everything possible is being done at Headquarters to demonstrate that the Association is alive and active.

It is pleasing to recall that the Association's Hall at Earlswood is now occupied seven days a week. It is being used as a school for evacuated children, as a Sunday School and by local Platoons of the Home Guard for drills and lectures. For these purposes only a nominal fee is charged, but other lettings enabled the Committee to make a grant of £50 to the Association towards administration expenses and also to show a small profit on the year's working.

Once again Mr Stanley Miller has given most valuable assistance to various war-time activities, both in the office and outside, in addition to his normal duties as your Secretary. Among these may be mentioned his work as Chairman of the Villages Committee of the Dorking District War Savings 'Weeks' and as Adjutant of the Dorking Squadron Air Training Corps. During the year he was also instrumental in inaugurating a local unit of the Women's Junior Air Corps. Miss Dealing has assisted greatly in the extra office work, and our thanks are again due to them both.

In conclusion, your Committee desires to appeal to all members and subscribers to continue their efforts to maintain the efficiency of the Association to enable it to carry on its present good work and to be readiness for the time when the full influence of the Party will be brought to bear in Post-War policy in the best interests of the country.

R.W. Barclay – Chairman

# Extract from Speech of Dr O'Donovan to South Kensington YCs in 1947

Dr O'Donovan said that the proposed National Health Service had nothing to do with health. Health did not depend on doctors but on breeding and we should neither breed out hereditary weaknesses by herding together those with physical handicaps in such places as Deaf and Dumb schools, not expect children to have a chance of health if their parents suffered from confirmed disabilities. The responsibility for health depended on wise marriage and doctors would see that people had advice before marriage if only they were consulted in time. Children would then start life with good health and the promise of longevity, and this was a matter which was not touched upon in the National Health Bill.

A second contribution to good health was food, and we must be well fed on wholesome fresh food straight from the place where it was produced. London's food was too long on the way to the shops to be very good, and Dr O'Donovan despaired of people's health when he saw women queuing for such things as mangold wurzles to offer to their hungry husbands. But the doctor was not, apparently, to be consulted about the nation's food.

Cleanliness – one of the biggest trades in the country – was important to health. From babyhood onwards clothes must be washed regularly, and houses and their contents, roads and sewers must be thoroughly cleaned. If this was not per-severed in there would be an outbreak of typhus, typhoid or plague. We also needed fresh air, transport to our places of work with as little fatigue as possible, and pleasant working conditions. Good food, good sanitation and good breeding made for good health.

The Bill dealt with the failure of health, but we must not judge the intelligence of the community by the number and fullness of our hospitals. National Health Services meant more work out of the doctors on the cheap. If you gave more work to bad doctors it would put the nation's subjects in peril, but if you gave more work to good doctors they would merely die earlier than they did already. The Bill called for administrators rather than good doctors and they would only be found among Medical Officers of Health and old soldiers. The administrators would control the medicine of the future, and the first effort in this direction had been the receipt of a letter by the teaching hospitals requesting them to confine themselves to under graduate teaching. This would mean that the great London teaching hospitals would become academies of elementary medicine and post-graduate training would be done elsewhere.

Those who had passed through our Schools of Tropical Medicine had kept our troops fit in all parts of the world and had in the past improved the health of other countries where we had gone, such as Egypt and India, so that they were not fit nations capable of self-government. We must maintain the standards of our tropical medicine if we and the Empire were to survive.

Dr O'Donovan stressed the importance of the work done by Port Doctors in examining people arriving at our ports in ships from all the seas. The Port Doctors had to go out in all weathers and guard against the possibility of diseases being brought into this country from which we were not immune although we had been free of them for years because of the vigilance of our doctors. Yet financially the doctor was often no better off than the man who drove a bulldozer.

For National Health Services the Government proposed to take five shillings a week from everyone, which was in other words the imposition of an unavoidable Poll Tax. If this provided a first class service it would be worth it but if the present shortage of hospital beds and nurses continued it would be robbery. Nurses used to come from the middle classes of England and were women of spirituality trained in high standards of cleanliness and good manners. Now those classes could not provide enough recruits to nursing, yet with the demand for shorter working hours for the medical profession many more people would be needed.

The Conservative Party could best serve the needs of the nation's health services by foresight and planning. We should concentrate on medical schools and train a new army of doctors in the great cities.

The Conservative remedy was to build up the medical profession but the remedy of the Socialists was to make a machine of the profession. It was a gloomy prospect unless Conservatives took charge of Health Committees, and stood out for our rights, with the assistance of the doctors. When all doctors became officials any complaints of the medical service would be complaints against the Government. Dr O'Donovan hoped that the Young Conservatives with their strength and keenness would save his profession and said that in so doing they would be doing something to save England.

## Appendix 3

# Article by David Atkinson MP, forecasting the demise of Soviet Communism, following a visit to Moscow in 1963

When I visited Russia for the first time in 1961, I could come to few conclusions as to how the ordinary people lived, the cost and standard of their living, and how things had changed or were to change for them over the years simply because I had little to make comparison with. One could, of course, make obvious deductions but one could not be sure that they were right because I was unable to make any real contact with the people since few spoke English and those that did, did not wish to talk.

This year, however, the story was different because not only did I have what I saw two years ago for comparison, but I also conversed with several people in English from different walks of life who gave me many differing answers to my questions. Here, then, are the facts as I saw them and the conclusions I have made which I believe to be true.

There are three faces of Russia today, three different groups of people who represent the past, present and future of this vast country. The PRESENT is represented by those, and the sons of those who took park in and were brought up by the Revolution. They are generally shabbily dressed people because, having been used to the hardships of the early post-Revolutionary years, they do not adjust easily to the more luxurious way of living of today. But they have an earnest look of determination in their eyes believing that the ideals they have fought for will soon come to fruition, or they had a depressed look of disappointment with the new theories and practices now being put into effect. These people cannot change to the more moderate, pro-Western economic ideas the Government today produces and although they are a majority now, in twenty years their influence will have vanished.

The Present group must change or remain like the second group who represent the PAST. These are the old people, chiefly women because their menfolk have not survived the Stalinist repressions or the two wars, and they are a decaying minority. They were brought up under the Czar and the Church and today they remember only the better points of their early lives under the old regime which, of course, will never return. They have nothing to live for except God for they remain intensely religious, but even in this respect they are often prevented by the authorities from practising their reverence. They are poor, often beg, and usually do not work though they are kept from starving by a meagre State pension; the old women wear black shawls and coats, and pass away their lives sitting together on park benches reliving their past.

Their lot is a pathetic one for they will not accept the present and have nothing to live for in the future.

The FUTURE, the third face of Russia. Today a young minority, tomorrow the leaders of a Russia that will not be the Communist start of today but quite a different country. These are the young men and women who try to look smart in Western clothes that may well have originated from some Western tourist. Some may be Party members who, as they rise to power, will modify the Marxist theory and regime to such as extent that it would be described as a 'Socialist-Liberal, one-party system' allowing free speech, freedom of religion, less state controls and so on, picking out the best of a Capitalistic economic system to mould with the best of the Marxist one to ensure the quickest means to prosperity. And the others will provide the outside pressure on the regime to be more liberal because no state propaganda will be able to persuade them that life in the West is worse than theirs. They know that clothes, cars and TVs are cheaper, that Western life is freer and gayer and they will provide the pressure that will make it the same in Russia. Give these young people twenty years and we will see the end of the Communism of today.

With these points in mind, and walking the streets of Leningrad one can see the embryo of a new Russia emerging from the hum-drum of everyday life in the present post Stalinist regime. Gradually the shops are turning themselves from dingy pokey, ill-lit and small windowed establishments into invitingly open places with large windows containing attractive displays, and bright neon advertising lights. Goods must conform to a quality standard set by the state; all that remains is to lower prices and to supply the demand more quickly (cars, for instance, have a three year waiting list). Examples of prices of luxury goods, on a similar wage rate to ours, re: Ladies high-heeled shoes – £20, boys baseball boots – £2, plastic comb – 2/-, a Hoover – £11.10s., mens shirt – £5.10s., movie projector – £55, small TV – £100, radio – £40. However, periodic scarcity of basic commodities such as flour remain a problem as the present bread shortage illustrates (this surprises me, because less than a month ago there seemed to be ample).

Modern building design has swung away from the traditional and Stalanistic styles to our own concrete and glass monoliths. Blocks of flats in the suburbs are prefabricated and look it! Cinemas still show films with a subtle propaganda theme, but when a Western film, such as 'The Magnificent Seven' comes along every so often, then everyone goes to see it. 'Coffee Canteens' are becoming more common where one can buy quite a good 'drink' and a plate of hot doughnuts or savory buns, and ice-cream parlours are most popular, though expensive, where one can buy a form of milk shake. Records are cheap (3/9d. for an EP, 8/6d. an LP); so is public transport (3d. to 5d. for anything up to five miles – the public are trusted to put the correct money in a box because there are no longer conductors), and on the waterways are to be seen the shape of things to come in the form of extremely fast, space-ship looking hydrofoil craft which are a great experience to use.

Finally, the people themselves; in two years the looks on their faces have changed from one of a depressed attitude of putting up with things as best they could to one of hope for a progressively better life in the comparatively near future. Despite some shortages, often inaccurately reported in our own press, the Russian today has never had it so good. If he wants luxury goods such as a car, then he must make sacrifices to pay for it, but ordinary goods for basic living are not beyond his means. He is quite free to say what he likes, for Russia is no longer a police state but he is encouraged to criticise constructively within the Party machine. However, 'capitalistic business clubs' such as Rotary are forbidden because they are against the classless society; workers groups only are allowed. The one-part form of government is not an undemocratic one, even if we do not agree with its views, and it is quite possible for anyone with ability to get to the top whether he is a Communist Party member or not.

The state keeps only about 5% of the churches open (the rest are shut or museums, because, it says, it is only supplying what demand there is, which seems logical until one goes into an open church to find it packed to the doors. But because it is only the old who frequent the churches, I do not think Russia will become a religious country again for quite some time even though the practising of it will be freer and more churches will be opened.

Today, there should be great hope for the future of Russia in the West, and twenty years should see the end of Communism for her and the European satellite countries despite China.

This, in the light of what I saw, is what I fully believe.

David Atkinson 1963

## Appendix 4

# Verbatim report of an address by the Rt Hon. Winston Churchill, O.M., C.H., M.P., at the first Young Conservatives Rally at the Royal Albert Hall on Saturday 12th June 1948

Mr Eden, My Lords, ladies and gentlemen, I have seen many meetings in this famous hall, and I can truthfully attest that none which I have ever attended in the last forty or fifty years is the equal of the one I see before me now, not only in its grand array but in the sense it gives of force and will-power and conviction. I congratulate the Young Conservative movement upon its rapid growth, both in quantity and quality, of which an account has been given by your President. To have grown in the manner he described from, I believe, fifty-one branches, in 1945, to over 2,000 three years later, is indeed a triumph and a reward for those who have worked so hard. But the tide is with us and everywhere we see the youth of the British nation in the universities and throughout the land coming together spontaneously in their resolve to fight against the paralysing and stifling theories and conditions of Socialism.

I do not wonder that we have here this afternoon young trade unionists, young men from the pits of Yorkshire and South Wales, aero-engineers, school teachers, young women from the cotton mills of Lancashire, clerks, solicitors and workers of every kind by brain and hand, and above all workers in spirit. And although we have them here in the van of the great movement of Conservative revival in progress throughout the country, many of those who are here, I am told are converts from the doctrines of Socialism; many are the sons and daughters of Socialists; many represent the forces of Liberalism . . . aye and Radicalism . . . which played so great a part in the enfranchisement of our national life in the last generation.

It used to be said, ladies and gentlemen, when I was young, that the choice of youth was whether to carry the Torch, the Flag or the Lamp in their march through life. But I think now we need all three. We need the torch against tyranny in all its forms, whether it be petty, needless, internal restrictions and regulations at home, or whether it be the foul obsession or infiltration of Communist Fifth Column menace directed from abroad in all their actions, while enjoying the protection of the free laws of this country. We can all see the need for the Torch in all this; of freedom to break down the shackles of the past, break down the old obstructions to the rise of merit and the free-play of the genius of the nation . . . all these have now to be employed in defending what we have won. In this we shall have the support from every party.

I say we can all see the need for the Torch. But foremost in the Conservative faith, or Tory faith . . . and don't be ashamed of the word 'Tory'; it is one of those things which cannot be revived but which everybody understands . . . foremost in the Conservative faith, as Mr Eden has reminded us, flies the Flag of patriotism, of national honour and the maintenance of the British Empire and all it has stood for in the struggles of the past. And there is also the calm Lamp of wisdom which we shall surely need if we are to bring back prosperity to our island home and establish a lasting peace in the world after all our toils and sufferings and triumphs. We need all these three symbols of human duty if we are to regain our rightful position among the nations and do our work not only for ourself but for others, not only for our lifetime but for generations yet to come.

Ladies and gentlemen, we are met here this afternoon at a time of British decline abroad and of a growing sense of frustration at home. There is no one here who is not conscious of our fall from the glorious position we had reached at the moment of our victory three short years ago.

I will take a small instance which has just occurred to me to illustrate the foolishness with which our affairs are conducted on the world stage. You all remember the gallant part played by the cruiser 'Ajax', in the battle of the Plate River, in 1939. Flying the flag of Admiral Harewood she advanced under the overwhelming gunfire of the heavy German battleship. And now she is for sale; she is for sale, not even as old iron, but her reputation is to be sold with her to the Chilean Government, a government which has quite recently affronted our country and laid all kinds of claims to the Falkland Islands and elsewhere. She is to be sold because she is the symbol of British majesty and greatness, and perhaps a small additional premium may be paid for that. But I cannot but doubt that any increase in price that may be gained by the Admiralty will be paid for ten times over in the loss of reputation so needlessly incurred; and in the sense of humiliation which British men and women, living and playing important parts throughout South America will feel, at what looks like the auctioning of the remaining assets of poor old John Bull, with a special price upon his famous cricket victory.

There is no one, I say, who does not feel the sense of decline of our reputation abroad, and there is no one who does not resent the attempt of our rulers to bring our life at home down to the level of the Tired Tims and Weary Willies, and to deny or discourage all incentive and opportunity for men and women to give the best that is in them for themselves, for those – yes, for those! – for those they love and the land they live in. I do not at all wonder that British youth is in revolt against the morbid doctrine that nothing matters but the equal sharing of miseries, that what used to be called, the 'submerged truth' can only be rescued by bringing the other nine-tenths down to their level; against the folly that it is better that everyone should have half-rations rather than that any, by their exertions or ability, should earn a second helping.

No Army could ever be victorious if its exertions were limited by those of its weakest, slowest and least intelligent soldiers. We have to win the battle of life for ourselves and our country, and for the great causes we champion, and thus alone shall we have the strength to bring in the stragglers and the weaklings, and to establish from our strength, not from our feebleness, from our strength, those minimum standards of life and labour which our Christian civilisation demands.

Let me now apply these general themes to our practical day-to-day affairs. What is the outstanding fact in our politics at home. Your President has alluded to it; it is the complete failure of the Socialist policy of nationalising industry. It is already apparent, obvious. The experiment has cost us dear. It was made at a time when above all others we should have concentrated upon practical aims and upon increased efficiency of production and management. Some may think it was necessary that the experiment should be tried in order to convince sections of the wage earners that private enterprise and management, within the well-conceived laws of a modern state, is the only fertile form by which profitable production can be conducted. We have already seen that the experiment has failed. One great industry after another has been transferred from profit-making to loss-making, from the credit to the debit side of our national fortunes. The cost of management and the number of officials employed has laid a heavy burden on the nationalised industries and on the National Exchequer.

Already, Mr Chairman, already the working people are beginning to realise that they will receive far less instructed and flexible direction, and far less consideration from the State as a supreme all-powerful agent, than they would get by making their bargains through the proper trade union machinery with a variety of private employers. Although every effort is made by the Government in the House of Commons to conceal the facts about the nationalised industries, all this will become more obvious every day. Bureaucratic management cannot compare in efficiency with that of well-organised private firms and business.

We are told that management by officials is disinterested. This may be true. The bureaucrats and officials, however well meaning and upright suffer no penalties for wrong judgment. So long as they attend their offices punctually and do their work honestly, as they do, and behave in an upright manner towards their political chiefs and masters, they are sure of their jobs and of their pensions. I am sure they do their best, but the ordinary private trader faces impoverishment today, or even bankruptcy, if he cannot measure things rightly. That is a far sterner test, and produces keener and more accurate results. The key industries now nationalised are to be ruled by people who have no reward for being right because the credit is given to the Minister in that case, and suffer no evil consequences for being wrong because you simply send in the bill to the Exchequer. The settling of the complicated trade problems of the nation by officials and boards and committees cannot possibly enable Britain to live and maintain her population in the competition of the modern world. Nothing less than the complete discrediting and abandonment of the Socialist conceptions about industry can restore the country. The old radical campaign against exploitation, monopolies, unfair rake-offs, was a healthy and necessary corrective in the system of free enterprise. But this grotesque idea of managing vast commercial enterprises by centralised State direction can only lead us into bankruptcy and ruin. The loss I should like to point out to you is not only confined to the industries that are nationalised. It is not only a question of transferring their realised deficits to the shoulders of the taxpayer. The basic industries . . . coal, transport, gas and electricity . . . affect all other industries by which we earn our livelihood. Everywhere we see higher costs and increased prices, and this injures the competitive and productive power of every firm, every business, every private industry throughout the country. Mr Herbert Morrison told us some time ago that only twenty per cent of our industries would be nationalised during the present Parliament. Is it not throwing a hard burden on the other four-fifths that they must keep this twenty per cent? But that is not all. The other four-fifths, the only profitable part of our production, is itself hampered by the higher basic charges for our transport, fuel and light, by the innumerable regulations often imposed without any Parliamentary control, and by every form of carping and spiteful propaganda. Is it not a mad way to govern any country, but above all our island, with its crowded population, gathered here during the nineteenth century on whose size we have depended to be a great power, strong enough to save the world in the moment of peril; and yet, now when this great population is built up here, the pillars of strength upon which it grew are being pulled away one by one and leaving the country in a most perilous, precarious situation.

There is also the policy of nationalisation to remove from the profit-making sphere a fifth, and to snarl and bite and hamper and curb the other four-fifths. Insanity cannot be exemplified more exactly.

In the New Prison Reform Bill the Government have made a great humanising advance; people who commit foul murders and are found insane are no longer to be called criminal lunatics – that might hurt their feelings; they are to be called Broadmoor patients. Yes, there may be other candidates for that euphonious description than those who are the subject of current legislation.

The increasing proof of the fallacy of nationalisation has caused misgivings and division in the Socialist ranks. At the Scarborough conference we had the old spectacle of those behind crying 'Forward', and those before crying 'Back'. Dr Dalton – you have heard of him – they say he is the doctor who never cured a patient, – not even a Broadmoor patient; Dr Dalton again presented arguments for nationalisation which none but he would use. He told us, in fact, that if private firms made undue profits they would be punished by being nationalised.

I had better read you his words, which I read in the *Daily Herald*, the only Party-owned newspaper in this country, except, perhaps the *Daily Worker*. But I checked the report by the Hansard: 'If it appears that certain monopolies are ignoring the Chancellor's request, then that would be an argument for putting them in the next list of industries for Socialisation. Our programme will depend upon the conduct of private enterprise in this period.' It is a strange admission for one to make who was so recently Chancellor of the Exchequer. First he admits that the compensation paid to the shareholders has been penal and unfair in character, and secondly, that nationalisation or Socialisation, instead of being a boon, blessing and refreshment to our energies, which it was represented to be, is now becoming a method of threatening and chastising firms and businesses who don't comply with Socialist admonitions.

In effect, this leader of Left Wing Socialism cries 'Abandon making profits or we will maltreat you as we have done the basic industries'. No wonder Attlee took him back into the Government! A desperate measure, no doubt, but still carrying with the hope that some sort of muzzle could be put on him if they had him behind the scenes. It is certainly quite easy for private businesses exposed to these threats to avoid making profits in the same way as the nationalised industries have done. They have only to allow the cost of management to rise and desist from enforcing a high standard of economy in administration in order to avoid committing the offence of making profits. But, ladies and gentlemen, considering that all profits which take the form of dividends are already taxed for income and surtax, up to perhaps twelve shillings in the pound, it is easy to see how the revenue will suffer, and this no doubt will be used as an argument for increasing still further the rates of taxation, already, I see, at a point where it is crushing the life and prosperity of the whole country. We are indeed in a vicious circle. The Socialists make every error, and they make every error they commit and every misfortune they inflict upon us an argument for further controls and exactions. Every failure of Socialism is used as a reason for a larger dose. I warn you once more, and solemnly, that this small island with its large population cannot earn its livelihood under the conditions which are being increasingly enforced upon it by the Socialist Party.

The crucial test will, of course, be steel. The Government have declared their intention of nationalising this, the most efficient bread-winning export-conquering industry in Britain. This reckless act of partisanship will carry them into deep waters. They are not even agreed among themselves upon the policy.

Last year, the differences in the Cabinet over steel reached the point where resignations were threatened on either side. In the end a compromise was reached by which this ugly deed was to be put off for twelve months on the condition that the constitutional settlement, embodied 35 years ago in the Parliament Act, should be altered so as to make sure that the Steel Nationalisation Bill, if they could agree upon it, would be passed into law before the people had a chance to be consulted. This disreputable transaction, and I must describe it as such, is the sole cause of dispute between the peers and the people on the one hand and the Socialist caucus and party machine on the other. That is how the lines of battle are drawn up. In reaching this decision the socialist ministers were also no doubt glad of an excuse to hold on to their offices until the full time limit of their Parliament was up, and until they had spent all our overseas savings and squandered every asset we had at home. Party first, party second, party third; and all other rights and interests of the British people nowhere! That was and that is the Socialist slogan. In my long experience I have never seen such an exhibition of squalid party malice and intrigue or one more cynically divorced from the revival and well-being of our country. At no stage were any of these important issues looked at by Mr Attlee and his colleagues from the stand-point of what would help the country. No one seeking to revive British national industry would strike at the iron and steel trade now. No one with any sense of fair play would try to break down the constitutional settlement reached and so long respected under the Parliament Act. No one with any sense of responsibility would try at this time of all others to provoke a needless dispute between the two Houses of Parliament. However, Mr Chairman, I have often noticed in my life that people who make clever and cold-blooded calculations often find themselves upset by the unexpected turn of events. Just at the very moment when the Socialists wanted to turn public attention from mismanagement of our affairs to a deliberately worked up quarrel with the House of Lords another astonishing series of their blunders raised a new issue. The question of the abolition of capital punishment, decided by a majority of 23 unguided casual votes in the House of Commons against the advice of the responsible Minister, the Home Secretary, gave the House of Lords the opportunity of proving to the whole country how much more representative they are on this issue of public opinion than a small, callow, thoughtless majority in the House of Commons. The Home Secretary has had to recede from his policy of automatic cancellation of death sentences and still lies under the charge of the Lord Chief Justice of having acted unconstitutionally. The Socialist Government is now looking about on every side for some excuse or formula that will save their faces, and the Second Chamber has made good its claims to express the will of the people on a great sentimental and moral issue.

Now, let me return to Dr Dalton. 'We are entitled,' he said, in his last Budget speech – I am very glad it was the last one – 'We are entitled to say that the new Britain represented by the House of Commons has taken the cost of social security proudly in its stride.' Ladies and gentlemen, how Socialist ministers can go about bragging of their Social programme and of the nationalisation of industry on party grounds; how they can deride the system of free enterprise and capitalism which makes America great and wealthy, and, at the same time, eagerly seek the aid which has been so generously granted from across the Atlantic!

That is a grimace which baffles the limitations of our language to describe. But all this structure of Socialist obstinacy and unwisdom, erected for party and not national aims, must be viewed in the light of the supreme and dominating fact of our present position. The Socialist Government in London has become dependent upon the generosity of the capitalist system of the United States. We are not earning our living nor paying our way, nor do the Government hold out any prospect of our doing so in the immediate or even the near future. It is this terrible fact which glares upon us all. I had hoped, and my Right Honourable Friend with me, that the one thousand million loan, borrowed from the United States in 1945, would have been a means of tiding us over the transition from war to peace, and that it would give us that breathing space to adjust our affairs after the exhaustion of the war. But it was spent and largely squandered in two years, and we are now dependent upon further American generosity and also eating up from hand to mouth the remaining overseas investments and assets accumulated under the capitalist system of former years.

Boasting of everything they have done, Mr Attlee's cabinet – I suppose he has something to do with it – has reduced this country to a position in which it has never stood before, and which cannot continue. All their Social legislation was conceived by the National Coalition Government with a great Conservative Parliamentary majority, and all is now being paid for by a friendly but foreign country, whose economic and social system the government abhor. A little while ago we were told 'See how few are unemployed under Socialism,' but now Mr Morrison and Mr Bevin are forced to admit that but for American loans and doles there would be unemployment on the scale of millions. It is not Socialism that has prevented it. It is the aid which has been given us by capitalist America.

Any Young Conservative going about the country should expose this horrible fact and bring more to the people the manner in which they are being misled and the evil consequences which might follow if they continue to be the dupes of lies, falsehoods and absurdities. Under the old system followed by society, by which our improving civilisation has been built up, of free enterprise and with personal incentive and prizes for the victory, prizes for those who by their thrift, self denial and contrivance added exceptionally to the national wealth – under this system we were, at any rate, able to live independently.

You cannot have independence unless you pay your own way. The very word 'independence' means that you do not depend on anybody, but your own strong right arm and the sweat of your brow earn your daily bread and bring up your family and make and keep a home. That is equally true of men or states, and it must ever be our aim.

Now we are oppressed by a deadly fallacy. Socialism is the philosophy of failure and the gospel of envy. Unless we free our country while time remains from the perverse doctrines of Socialism there can be no hope of recovery. This island cannot maintain its position under a Socialist or collectivist system. The most energetic and the nimblest will emigrate, and we shall be left with a horde of safe officials brooding over a vast mass of hungry worried and disheartened human beings. Our place in the World will be lost for ever, and not only our individual self respect but our national independence will be gone.

It is just as well to face facts, whether you are young or old. But the consequences of a wrong decision bear more hardly on the young who have so many years before them. That is why they should come forward now and make politics the central purpose of their duty in life during these critical years. Leave the football pools and the greyhound races to their proper places as amusements. Concentrate your thoughts upon bringing our own country out again in its proper position in the world.

We are asked Mr Chairman often what we should do. You may be sure if we had the responsibility we should act with single regard to national interests and deal with the difficulties of our time by practical measures without regard to the special interests of any class or party, but rather as we did in the war, solely the overwhelming hope of national salvation.

I have consistently warned you and the party against the folly of trying to outbid the Socialists in an effort to win votes at any cost. It is a grave mistake for a party in opposition and without executive powers to try to furnish precise, elaborate programmes of what they would do at some unspecified future date and in circumstances which no man can yet fortell. By doing so we should only have fallen into the trap that was set for us by our political opponents.

But it is only right that we should even now give in broad outline what with our present knowledge we believe to be some of the right and necessary steps that should be taken. We should stop or drastically curtail the failure and waste of State planning and State trading.

Sir Stafford Cripps, Chancellor of the Exchequer and head of our economic affairs is a heavily burdened man with great responsibilities. The time has not yet come for us to say that he will repudiate his duties. But if we look at his past history we see how he swept away, for pure party spite, the Liverpool Cotton Exchange, which was a great aid to the cotton trade of Lancashire, and how he brushed it on one side. I suggest that if a thousand men worked night and day for a whole year they could not make up a half or a quarter of the foreign exchange that the Liverpool Cotton Exchange used to earn. We should stop this state planning which has made so many bad bargains and substitute a guidance from the State but based upon the full knowledge, freely expressed, of all the public bodies and industries concerned.

We should reduce the enormous outpouring of expenditure – three thousand millions this year – and effect substantial reduction in taxation, far more than the Government have already done as a result of our demands at the Brighton Conference. Taxation should be reduced in such a way as to stimulate the exertions of all classes.

We have proclaimed and published our Conservative Industrial Charter. I am glad to see you have all read it attentively. We are taking measures to see that it is widely circulated and that the points in it are brought forward in a clear and precise form. This Charter shows you that in Industry we must first of all eradicate the effects of years of Socialist teaching and the fact that there is an inevitable conflict between the interest of employers and employed. This can never be done by Socialists in their system, which merely makes the employer more impersonal and more remote from the worker in the mine and factory. It can only be done by enlightened management in private industry. We must encourage payment by results so that the good worker can earn more and enjoy the more he earns. We must clear the way of promotion for talent, merit and fidelity. We must provide greater facilities for education and training in industry, and finally we should encourage joint consultation and co-partnership in the widest sense between employers and employed. They must share the knowledge of their common problems and their common achievements. The authority of management must be maintained by those who have the control of the business and take the risk. Leadership is needed in industry as in every other sphere. Much that we have advocated in our Industrial Charter is already the practice of the best firms in the country. Our aim will be to bring all other firms and businesses up to the standards of the best, always within the Industrial Charter, which, in my view, can afford you Young Conservatives a fertile field from which to gather arguments which can be used in every part of this country, with a backing of thought and knowledge which cannot be overturned.

The Agricultural Charter, which will be before you in a few weeks time, and which seeks to establish the most favourable conditions under which our greatest industry and the one on which we all directly depend for our livelihood shall flourish with contentment and scientific progress.

When I was last in this hall I heard Lord Woolton, to whom our organisation owes such a debt of gratitude, state a list of the controls he would immediately remove from rationing – bread, potatoes, leather, children's shoes (and these have been removed since he spoke) – the controls which impede the private housewife. And direction of labour. All these, he said, could be swept away without harm, and, after all, he is a man who knows what he is talking about and doesn't say anything about these things without good reason, having done these difficult things himself during the war.

When I was in Scotland two years ago, the Scottish Association used a phrase which my friend Mr Eden and I have often repeated – 'A property-owning democracy'. That takes many forms. Owning one's own house and having the power to acquire one's own house by thrift and energy and careful management over the years is a very precious thing to people who like to stand on their own two feet and not be ordered hither and thither by the State Authorities.

We propose, if we have the power, to extend the principle of the purchase of houses by instalments to council houses. There are many other ways, especially in respect of savings, especially in the maintenance of an honest and staple standard of life. There are many ways in which this principle of a property-owning democracy can be established. That is another important element in our Conservative policy. And when I was in Scotland a fortnight ago I heard another phrase which I like very much – 'the Party of opportunity'. Youth is right to join the party of opportunity.

They talk about emigration. Though, of course, much can be said for populating the wide, wide lands of the British Commonwealth and Empire, I don't like a future where, the statisticians tell us, our population twenty or thirty years hence will be far older than it is now, with a far smaller proportion of men in their prime. I cannot see how we are going on if all the boldest, impatient and active of our race go off to other lands and leave us here, or leave the Old Country here, to be a vast problem of vanished life and power. 'No.' I said to the youth. 'You and others, whatever your love for the Empire and your desire for adventure may be, stay here and fight it out here for Britain.'

Recovery will not be swift or easy. Every day that our remaining resources are dissipated, every day that class and party warfare sinks more deeply into our national life, every day that the cohesion of our Empire is weakened and that our prestige sinks in the world may mean many weeks of loss in the process of recovery.

How easy to fall and how hard and slow to rise! Do not, I beg you, fail to realise the peril and gravity of the hour or the greatness of the opportunity presented to you. One thing is certain, that is, that this Parliament, elected under conditions which were altogether abnormal, is not respresentative of the will of the people or equal to solving their problems. We require a new Parliament which alone can be the foundation of a government which truly sets the long-term welfare of the people as a whole before and above any other considerations in political life. We require a new Parliament which will create a government representative of the strongest forces in the country.

Therefore, I have been calling continually for a new Parliament. Some say the longer it is delayed the better it will be for our electoral prospects; that people will have to suffer much more before they will be convinced. But I fear and I feel that we shall all be running a grievous risk of irretrievable disaster if the life of the present Government is prolonged to the normal end of Parliament.

The need of the nation is a new Parliament in which the experience of age will be refreshed by the new impulse of youth; in which the majority of the nation will be united in an inflexible resolve that our country shall remain a great Power in the world – earnest, merciful, vital, self-supporting, valiant and free.

# Introduction to Notes and Sources

There are many records of YC activity among the Conservative party archives at the Bodleian Library at Oxford but the more recent records are only open for inspection with permission of Conservative Central Office. National YC magazines have been a great help. However, there are a few copies of Advance published between 1947 and 1953 in private hands, an incomplete set at the British Library and some copies at the Bodleian Library, Rightway, 1954 to 1958 Bodleian Library Impact 1964-1968 both at British and Bodleian libraries. An extensive collection of branch magazines is at the British Library and a number of local record offices.

There is a wide range of material of the Labour party's youth movement at the Museum of Labour History. Manchester and the Party's Youth Magazines. Socialist Advance and New Advance are at the Labour Museum and British Library, Focus 1966/1957 at the London School of Economics and British Library and Socialist Youth published in the 1980s at the British Library.

The records of the Liberal party are at the London School of Economics but contain little material of Young Liberals (the more recent records are only open for inspection with permission of the Liberal Party, and much of the information has been obtained from Liberal News published since 1936 and New Outlook a more radical magazine published from 1963. The only YL magazines I have been able to locate are copies of the Liberator published in the early 1970s at the Bodleian Library, Challenge published from 1935 to 1987, strangely the longest published of all political youth magazines is a principal source of information on the Young Communist League and Young Communist material. Incomplete sets are at the Museum of Labour History and the Marx Memorial Library.

I do not believe that any books have previously been published concerning British Political youth Movements. To my knowledge there are four theses on political youth movements. One was written by John Ferris. Labour Party League of Youth 1924 to 1940 unpublished MA Thesis, University of Warwick 1977. The second was written by Dr Zig Layton Henry at Birmingham University PhD thesis and the third Mike Waite – Young People and Formal Political Activity. (A case study of Young People and the Communist Party in Britain 1920 to 1991 aspects of the history of the Young Communist League which although unpublished has been extensively used in respect of other of his works published by Pluto Press 1995). Finally an interesting thesis, Libertarianism in the Conservative Party Youth Structure 1970 to 1992' at London School of Economics is mainly devoted to the Federation of Conservative

Students a subject not covered by this book. However there is a most interesting chapter on the period covered in Chapter 16 although I do not entirely agree with Timothy Evans assessment of Andrew Tinney.

Exeter University has agreed to a accept the material in due course that has been given to me and used in connection with this book. Where NU has been used it denotes Minutes of the national Union at the Bodleian Library. GP the General purposes committee of the same committee and NAC the minutes of the National Advisory Committee of the Young Conservatives.

# End Notes and Sources

## Introduction

1 *Palmer Report*, Bodleian library
2 Lord Woolton's memoirs p.337
3 *Sunday Pictorial*, 29 May 1955
4 NAC meeting, 6 March 1965
5 Abram and Little, *British Journal of Sociology*, December 1965; *Independent*, 8 February 1993;
6 Twickenham Young Socialist's report; Daily Herald, 20 October 1959 *Challenge*, 8 October 1955
7 Milne and Mackenzie, 'Marginal Seats'; Benny Gray and Pear, 'How People vote'
8 Bruce Anderson, *John Major* p.213
9 Conversation with Gerry Wade, 1993
10 Conservations with Nicholas Scott and Michael Jack, 1993
11 Conversations with David Hunt and Sydney Chapman 1993

12 *Guardian.* 11 April 1992
13 *Tomorrow.* July 1992, October 1973
14 *Hansard.* 13 July 1987 and conversation with Robin Squire 1993
15 NU Executive meeting, 19 January 1978
16 Conversation with Eric Chalker, 1993
17 Zig Layton Henry. *Journal of Contemporary History* 1973 8/2
18 Conversation with Nicholas Scott,1993
19 Conversation with Terence Wray and see *Iain Macleod* Richard Shepherd 53
20 *Times*, 1 February 1972
21 Conversation with Roger Boaden 1993
22 NAC, 3 September 1988
23 NAC meeting, 10 December 1988
24 Conversation with Robert Cuming 1995

## Chapter 1  Politics for the Under 15

1 Socialist Sunday, school declaration
2 Socialist Sunday School Precepts
3 Manual of National Council of British Sunday School 1923
4 Mick Waite. 'Thesis on Young Communist league'
5 Pamphlet 'Baden Powell Exposed'
6 Official History of Boy Scouts, Henry Collis 1961

7 Final Report of Young Britons
8 Conversation with Rowena Harrison
9 Minutes of Ealing Grosvenor Ward Great London Record Office
10 'Young Britons Talks'. Bodleian Library, Oxford
11 Final Report of Young Britons

## Chapter 2  Junior Imperial League

1 'Junior Imperial League'. See *Impact*, Autumn 1964
2 Labour Party's Annual Report 1924 and 1925
3 Labour Party Report 1926
4 Reports of ILP. British Library

5 Labour Party Report 1929
6 Labour Party Report 1935
7 Labour Party Report 1935
8 Labour Party Report 1936 and see debate at 238

9 Annual Report 1939 and see debate at 320
10 Letter. Museum of Labour History, E Emmanuel to Morgan Phillips, 17 February, 1960
11 Zig Layton Henry. Journal of Contemporary History July 1976
12 'Early years of Young Liberals'. *New Outlook*, November 1963
13 Liberal annual reports 1912 and 1932
14 *Liberal News* 25 June 1965

## Chapter 3  Post-war Labour and Liberal Youth

1 *New Advance* February 1961
2 'Keep Left'. Wembley YS magazine
3 Report 1950. Museum of Labour History Manchester
4 *New Advance* October 1961
5 See running a branch, Young Socialist August 1947
6 Labour Monthly Youth letter November 1957
7 Letter written by Morgan Phillips to CLP January 1960. Museum of Labour History
8 Programme of West Lewisham Young Socialists, 5 March 1969
9 *'History of Chichester Labour Party'*
10 'Memorandum on their branch' 1967. Twickenham Young Socialists
11 Iain Macleod challenged the YCs to increase their membership from under 70,000 to 250,000 in the course of Wilson Government
12 Report of Twickenham Young Socialists
13 West London *Observer* 2 December 1960
14 *Kensington News* 22 September 1961. In 1964 3 members of new YS branch expelled *Kensington News* 6 November 1964
15 Labour Party report 1965 and memorandum by Streatham Young Socialists
16 Progress Windsor Young Socialists Summer 1985
17 Michael Crick. *Militant* p.59
18 London Liberal Party minutes 15 May

1947, 15 September 1947, 18 November 1948
19 Peckham Liberals minutes, 28 November 1951
20 National League minutes, 10 September 1950
21 *The Times*, 26 June 1974
22 Conference reports, 12 April 1977
23 *New Outlook*, November 1963
24 Minutes of London Liberal Association, 10 November 1953, 19 December 1959
25 Liberal Party Report 1963
26 *Hampshire Chronicle*, 3 June 1968
27 *The Times*, 23 May 1970
28 YL Conference report, 31 March 1970
29 *Hampshire Chronicle*, 7 September 1973
30 *The Times*, 17 & 28 March 1970
31 *The Times*, 27 March 1972
32 Party Conference Report, 30 September 1977
33 *Kensington Post*, 16 May 1975, see *Criticism of Young Liberals*, Ray Douglas, Liberal Party, p.286
34 Liberal News, 26 April 1977
35 Letter T.J. Austin, 28 May 1970
36 Reports of Liberal Party Conference, 26 September 1970 and see *Community Politics 1972*. British Library
37 Conversation with local resident, 1995
38 Letter, Morgan Phillips to Jean Mann 21 January 1960. Museum of Labour History
39 Twickenham Young Socialists report
40 Conversation, Clive Landa and as to size of Young Liberals see *Liberator*, December 1974 estimated average YL branch 11 members

## Chapter 4 Politics in Second World War

1 Arthur Ward: Conversation
2 Letter written by J Miller to Central Office dated 20 December 1941 and reply dated 1 January 1942
3 *Hansard*, 28 May 1935
4 *Hansard*, 17 March 1936
5 Conscription: by 7 votes to 6 Liberal party voted against conscription. *Hansard*, 1939 and see Liberal News, December 1936

6 *Ernest Bevin*, 29 July 1941. London School of Economics
7 Reigate Conservative party
8 Minutes of Merton and Mordon Labour party. London School of Economics, 18 December 1941
9 Express Leader, 5 June 1945
10 *Express*, 27 July 1945
11 Churchill: election message to Douglas Marshall

## Chapter 5 Rise of YCs 1945–51

1 Butler Memorandum. Trinity College, Cambridge
2 Liberal Memorandum on Russia. London School of Economics
3 Lord Woolton. Autobiography 1959 pp.337, 354
4 Kennington minutes. Stanley agreed to pay £100 a year if elected but he was not elected
5 Lord Woolton. Autobiography 1959 pp.337, 358
6 Conversation with Fergus Montgomery 1993 and see also Torbay Newsletter British Library as to the ex-service influence in the 1940s: February 1957
7 Letter from RA Butler to Anthony Nutting, Trinity College, Cambridge
8 Central Council minutes of 29 April 1950 indicate that membership was 160,400 on 31 December 1949 among 2,345 branches, NAC minutes 12 October 1949 indicates 164,535.

Annual report 31 July 1949 indicates 157,825. The fact that membership figures were never again given indicates membership had peaked
9 *Right*, December 1949
10 *City Press*, 16 July 1948: *Evening News*, 8 July 1948: *Mail*, 9 July 1948: *The Times*, 9 July 1948: *Evening Standard* 8 July 1948
11 *Television City Press*, 23 July 1948
12 *Searchlight*, Leeds, November 1946
13 Beryl Goldsmith. Memorandum
14 Dr Butler. 'British General Election 1970', p.98
15 NAC, 6 July 1946
16 *Birmingham Post*, 18 May 1955
17 *Hansard*, May 1939
18 *City Press*, 28 May 1948
19 Attlee Papers. Bodleian Library, Oxford
20 Attlee Papers. Bodleian Library, Oxford
21 Conservative Party Annual Report 1952

## Chapter 6 YCs to Suez

1 Conservative Central Office press release 4085 on 19 March 1953
2 Labour Party membership. Membership figures for past year published in most of their brochures
3 Yorkshire minutes, 26 September 1953
4 Membership figures for 1952. Bodleian Library

5 Wessex and Eastern Annual Reports. Bodleian Library
6 NAC Ridgewell, NAC 24 October 1953
7 NAC 21 March 1953
8 NAC 26 June 1954
9 Greater London minutes, 8 October 1966

10 Conversation with Andrew Tinney, 1993
11 West Wickham, *Young Tory*, May 1957
12 'Younger generation'. Report commissioned by Hugh Gaitskell under chairmanship of Gerald Gardiner, April 1959
13 *Daily Herald*, 9 February 1950
14 Socialist commentary
15 West Wickham YC magazine *Young Tory*, September 1955
16 Speech by Aneurin Bevan
17 *Crossbow*, January 1960
18 West Wickham, *Young Tory* February 1959
19 *Sunday Pictorial*, 29 May 1955
20 Labour Party Conference 1955 and NU minutes. Decrease in year from 366 to 237
21 *The Times*, 7 October 1954
22 Conservative party archives. Bodleian Library, Oxford
23 NAC, Lord Mancroft, 12 January 1957
24 Internal report Bodleian Library
25 YC Numbers 1957. Introduction to Macleod Report and NAC meetings, 17 March 1956
26 NAC minutes, 17 November 1956 and file at Bodleian Library
27 *Challenge*, 8 October 1955

## Chapter 7  *Suez*

1 NAC minutes, 17 November 1956
2 Pamela Pardey's recollections 1993
3 *Ealing Chronicle*, October 1956
4 Conversation with Fergus Montgomery 1993
5 Petts Wood magazine, *Daylight*, December 1956
6 Robert Rhodes James, Anthony Eden p.533
7 Letter, Trinity College, Cambridge
8 NAC, 17 November 1956
9 Hungarian deaths, see Labour Party report, 1960. Liberal Party report 1957
10 *Challenge*, December 1955
11 Conversation with Lord Finsberg, 1993
12 Anthony Nutting. 'No End of a Lesson' 122

## Chapter 8  *YCs during Harold Macmilland and Alec Douglas Home*

1 Peter Walker. Leeds *Searchlight*, February 1958
2 *Express & Echo* (Exeter), 7 March 1958
3 Ian Macleod speech to 2nd YC Conference, 25 February 1962
4 Lord Hailsham. *Sparrows Flight* p.324. NAC 24 October 1959
5 Memorandum on Recruiting Campaign. Bodleian Library, Oxford
6 Minutes. Home Counties minutes, 11 October 1947
7 *Daily Mirror*, 12 & 13 October 1979
8 *Telegraph*, 5 February 1973. *The Times*, 13 February 1978
9 Kenneth Baker. *Turbulent Years*
10 Policy Document, 'Young Idea'
11 YC Conference reports, 1969
12 *Times Higher Educational Supplement*, 15 February 1985
13 'Changing Partnership'. Bodleian Library, Oxford
14 'Memorandum of Taxation'. Bodleian Library
15 'Law, Liberty and License' Bodleian Library
16 Reconstruction of Britain. British Library
17 No copy of the *Welfare State* has been found.
18 Zig Layton Henry – Young Conservatives, Journal of Contemporary History, 8 February 1973
19 *Crossbow*, December 1961: Spring 1962
20 David Butler. 'General Election 1964', p.39
21 Deptford Dolphin Spring 1963
22 Minutes of Barkstone Ash, 28 January 1963

23 David Butler. 'General Election 1964', p.37

24 Post Orpington Memorandum. London School of Economics

25 Annual Report of Liberal party, 1962

26 Annual Report of Liberal party, 1963

27 Annual Report of London Liberal Association, 1960

28 Annual Report of London Liberal Association, 1962

29 Annual Report of London Liberal Association, 1964

30 Annual Report of Labour Party, 1960 & 1965

31 Merton and Mordon Labour Party Annual Reports. London School of Economics

32 Conversation with Nicholas Scott, 1993

33 *Impact*, Spring 1964

34 Copy letter Anthony Eden to Alec Douglas Home. Birmingham University

35 Conversation with Sydney Chapman, 1993

## Chapter 9 YCs during Wilson Government

1 Introduction to Macleod Report papers. Bodleian Library, Oxford. Many commentators overstated membership. Elections in Britain

2 Nigel Fisher. *Iain Macleod*

3 Macleod Report, Bodleian Library, Oxford

4 List of Supper Clubs. Bodleian Library, Oxford

5 Blue Link Scheme Report to NAC, 5 September 1962

6 See NAC minutes as to NAC attitude, 18 September 1965, 11 December 1965

7 Impact see article 'Diagnosis' by Alan Haselhurst, February 1965

8 NAC minutes, 23 April 1966

9 Conversation with Eric Chalker

10 Torbay minutes, 18 October 1965

11 Minutes of South Kensington YCs, 30 April 1966

12 West Wiltshire minutes, 13 January 1966

13 Torbay minutes, 16 November 1966

14 *Hampshire Chronicle*, 8 April 1967, 5 April 1969

15 NAC minutes, 22 June 1963 and 14 September 1963

16 *Impact*, Spring 1966

17 East Surrey minutes, 23 August 1966

18 Conversation with David Atkinson, 1993

19 Iain Macleod biographies by Nigel

Fisher p.272 and Richard Shepherd p.389

20 NAC minutes, 7 January 1967

21 Dr Butler. 'Election 1970' p.98

22 NAC minutes concerning progress of Action 67

23 Portsmouth minutes, 25 January 1967

24 Report to executive, 1 May 1968

25 South Kensington minutes, 3 December 1968

26 Annual reports of Liberal party 1965

27 Annual report of Liberal party 1966

28 Annual report of Liberal party 1969

29 *Daily Mirror*, 19 October 1967

30 Annual reports of Merton and Mordon Labour party

31 Annual Reports of Labour Party 1965 & 1970 and decline of Young Socialists, *The Times*, 11 May 1967

32 Young Socialists conference 1963. *The Times*, 15 April 1974

33 'Roadway'. *Journal of Road Haulage Association*, May 1968

34 Conversation with Eric Chalker

35 Policy Report 'Young Idea', 1961. After war Young Communists were only political youth organisation in favour of votes at 18. *Challenge* 7 & 28 July 1948

36 *Trend*, Summer 1966; *Yorkshire Post*, 12 February 1968

37 Address of Hugh Holland 1969 Conference. Bodleian Library

38 Nigel Fisher. *Iain Macleod*

39 *Ealing Chronicle*, March 1970

40 Message to 1975 YC conference.
Bodleian Library, Oxford

## Chapter 10  Set the Party Free

1 Iain Macleod. *Forward* 'Set the Party
Free'
2 Bill Jones, 4 March 1964
3 'Daggers Drawn' *Mirror*, 8 October 1969
4 Conference Report, 9 February 1975,
p.65
5 Conference Report, 13 October 1978
6 Kensington YCs 1985, Robin Squire
7 Clive Landa Electoral Reform 'The
Way Forward' and see Liberal News,
January 1937. Liberal Party only
favoured PR when they realised they
could not win outright

8 Conversation with Robin Squire, 1993
9 YC Conference Report, 1977
10 'Set Party Free' ch. 10
11 YC Conference report, 1975
12 Conversation with Edward Heath, 1993
13 Set Party Free, ch. 12
14 Conference Report 1968, p.73
15 Zig Layton Henry. Central Council
reorganisation of Conservative party.
*Journal of Contemporary History*, 8
February 1973
16 Conversation with Eric Chalker, 1995

## Chapter 11  The Heath Premiership

1 *Ealing Chronicle*, July 1970
2 *Hansard*, 26 June 1950
3 Dr David Butler. General Election
1974, p.314
4 AGM Welsh Conservatives, 28 July
1971
5 Law Society's Gazette 29 November
1995
6 Letter Community Industry to David
Hunt, 12 July 1993
7 *Herald Express*, 4 November 1972
8 *Western Morning News*, 26 October
1972. *Evening Herald*, 26 October 1972
and 17 February 1973
9 *Tomorrow*, 'CURE', 2 February 1972
10 *Tomorrow*, May 1973 and brochure of
1973 YC Conference
11 *Tomorrow*, May 1973
12 *Tomorrow*, July & October 1973
13 GP NU minutes, 1 December 1971
14 Youth Officers Report, 22 January 1975
15 Peter Thomas speech to YC
conference, 6 February 1971

16 Youth Department Report, 22 January
1975. Bodleian Library
17 Conversation with Jimmy Gordon, 1993
18 Youth Officers Report, 22 January 1975
19 Wales Conservative Annual Report,
1973
20 Parliamentary papers 1973, V2, 19,
1974 fell at February General Election.
Bill re-introduced 1974, 19 by Sir
Edward Brown during Labour
government 2, 19 re-introduced 1980,
166
21 *Hansard*: 2nd reading debate 1972, 742
22 Conversation with Eric Pickles, 1993
23 Yorkshire minutes, 8 August 1973 and
minutes of 23 November 1974 –
continued decline in Urban Areas
24 Annual Reports West Wiltshire
Conservative Association, 1970
25 Reports of Chippenham Young
Conservatives. Wiltshire Record Office
26 Torbay YCs minutes, 12 March 1974

## Chapter 12  YC Revival. Lib/Lab Pact

1 GP NU, 4 December 1974
2 Conversation with Chris Gent, 1993

3 *Yorkshire Post*, 9 February 1976
4 *Guardian*, 9 February 1976

5 Conversation with Chris Landa

6 NAC meeting, Toxteth, 19 September 1981

7 Youth Officers Report. 22 January 1975. Bodleian Library

8 Speech to Winchester YCs by Chris Gent. *Hampshire Chronicle*, 2 December 1977 and conversation with Robert Hughes

9 Wessex Area minutes, 5 April 1975

10 *ibid.*, 15 November 1975

11 *ibid.*, 26 November 1978; See also GPNU, 9 November 1977 reported that YCs expanded first time for a decade

12 Hornsea Annual Report, 1976/1977

13 *Hampshire Chronicle*, 2 December 1977. FCS report to NUGP, May 1975. FCS delegates to NUS conference risen from 50 to 150 out of 800.

14 Stan Taylor. *National Front*, p.139

15 NUGP, 11 June 1975, large attendance of YCs out of 3,500 who attended mainly co-operation with Young Liberals

16 Housing Campaign YC national organisation, 1975

17 People's Daily. Chinese Department, Bodleian Library, Oxford

18 Conversation with Demitri Argyropulo and Tony Kerpel, 1993

19 *Motoring News*, 29 July 1976

20 Stephen Parry, Julie Shaw and Tony Jerram. Key statement 'Credit to us All'

21 YC Conference 1982. *Yorkshire Post*, 15 February 1982

22 see article in *The Times*, 1 February 1983

23 Conversation with Chris Gent, 1993

24 Conference Report, 9 October 1969 p.14

25 Report that his local YCs did not support him is disputed by Demitri Argyropulo *Dorking Advertiser*, 1 & 22 April 1977

26 Demitri Argyropulo, NAC 7 May 1977

27 Dorking Advertiser, 5th July 1979

28 *Times Educational Supplement*, 16 October 1981

29 Conversation with Robert Hughes, 1993

30 School pack 1981 and Liberal Annual Report 1970 and Liberal News, 24 April 1979

31 NAC minutes, 10 March 1979

32 James Callaghan. 'Time for Change'

33 *Sunday Mirror*, 11 February 1979

34 NAC Robert Hughes' speech, 3 April 1979

35 Address by Geoffrey Pattie, NAC 1980

36 NAC minutes, 23 May 1981

37 Conversation with Chris Gent, 1993

38 *Sun*, 13 February 1978

39 Robert Hughes' speech, 16 February 1980

## Chapter 13 Decline of YC Movement, 1979–1983

1 Dorking Conservative Association Annual Report 1982. Surrey Records Office

2 Annual report 1982

3 Annual report 1984

4 GL Conservatives Annual Report 1982

5 GL Conservatives Annual Report 1980

6 NAC report, 12 July 1986

7 NAC minutes, 7 July 1979

8 Conversation with John Guthrie, 1993

9 Conversations Terence Wray and Gerry Wade, 1993

10 Woking AGM minutes 1984

11 Conversation with Eric Pickles, 1993

12 Phil Pedley's speech to NAC, 10 March 1984

13 NAC minutes, 12 December 1981

14 Conversation with Chris Gent

15 Daily Mail, 5 July 1978

16 *The Times*, 12 August 1981

17 *The Times*, 29 August 1991

18 *Telegraph*, 29 August 1975

19 Pamphlet issued by Gt Manchester YCs

20 NAC meeting, 22 September 1984

21 Internal survey of Conservative party

22 Liberal News, 20 April 1982

23 *Evening Dispatch*, 16 May 1983

24 YC Conference reports 1961

25 *Southern Evening Echo*, 4 August 1984
26 Surrey Records Office
27 *Tomorrow*, December 1981
28 *Tomorrow*, September & October 1982

29 *Tomorrow*, Spring 1984
30 *Tomorrow*, December 1981
31 *Tomorrow*, Spring 1984
32 *National News*, September/October 1982

## Chapter 14  The National Front

1 East Sheen *Richmond Herald*, 25 January 1973
2 Dorking Advertiser, 4 June 1976
3 Ella Young Conservatives. British Library
4 Hunts *Post*, 3 December 1981
5 Phil Pedley address to NAC, 10 July 1982
6 *Evening Herald*, 26 March 1986
7 File at Board of Deputies of British Jews
8 Letter T., Elkins to P. Pedley, 16 August 1982
9 *Searchlight*,November 1983 and letter dated 10 August 1995 from magazine stating the belief that letter was forged

10 NAC, 28 September 1982
11 NAC, 28 January 1984
12 Conversation with Mark Worrall, 1993
13 Conversation with Phil Pedley, 1993 & 1995
14 *Portsmouth Evening News*, 11 & 13 February 1984
15 Report on conference of SE Area
16 *Sunday Times*, 12 February 1984
17 Lancashire Evening News, 13 February 1984
18 Conversation with Mike Smith, 1995
19 Conversation with Phil Pedley
20 *Sunday Telegraph*, 14 February 1982
21 *Guardian*, 15 February 1982

## Chapter 15  YCs in Conflict, 1984–1991

1 NAC, 8 December 1984
2 Article *Tomorrow*, Autumn 1984 and article 'Liberty and Responsibility' *Tomorrow*. Party conference Edition. Martine Kushner also condemning libertarianism
3 NAC, 7 September 1985
4 Speech on relection as chairman
5 East Midland Report
6 Conversation with Gary Mond, 1993
7 Conversation with Nick Robinson, 1993
8 Internal survey, Central Office
9 NAC meeting, National officers report, 4 July 1987
10 Epsom and Ewell programme, April/June 1988
11 *Evening Herald*, 24 February 1988

12 Conversation with Martin Woodroofes, 1993
13 NAC, 4 March 1989
14 Correspondence with Conservative Central Office, NAC, 3 September 1988
15 SE Area Branch Handbook
16 Campaigner, Spring 1991
17 NAC, 3 March 1990
18 NAC, 2 March 1991
19 NAC, 9 December 1989
20 NAC, 8 December 1990
21 NAC, 2 March 1991
22 Conversation of Martin Minns, *Daily Telegraph*, 10 February 1992
23 Conversation with Richard Cuming

## Chapter 16  Constitution of YCs

1 Palmer Report. Bodleian Library, Oxford

2 Model Rules 1993 National Union

3 Westminster YCs Fullest report in *Guardian*, 2 February 1984.
4 Times Educational Supplement, April 1985
5 NAC, 10 December 1983 and conversation with Harry Phibbs 1993
6 Labour Party NEC minutes, 26 November 1964
7 *The Times*, 22 May 1965
8 YC Brochure
9 North West minutes, 15 May 1969
10 *Impact*, Summer 1967
11 Yorkshire minutes. Roy Galley Report, 6 November 1975
12 *Right*. County Group Report Manifesto Editorial, January 1957
13 *Birmingham Post*, 10 September 1949
14 National Union Rules
15 Anthony Seldon & Stuart Ball 'Conservative Century'
16 NAC, 12 January 1957
17 NAC, 2 September 1950
18 NAC, 26 June 1954
19 NAC, 22 October 1955
20 NAC, 25 June 1955
21 NAC, 4 January 1958 passed 39; 7 abstentions
22 Conversations with Hugh Holland Tony Durant
23 NAC, 12 December 1965
24 NAC, 25 March 1961
25 NAC, 22 June 1963
26 Conversation with Eric Chalker and Terence Wray
27 *The Times*, 16 January 1962
28 Chairman's file. Bodleian Library, Oxford
29 Conversation with Mark Worrall, 1994
30 Letter Fergus Montgomery to Anthony Eden
31 Conversation with Andrew Bowden, 1993
32 Conversation with David Hunt, 1993
33 Conversation with Richard Cuming, 1995
34 Conversation with Demitri Argyropulo, 1995
35 File at Bodleian Library

## Chapter 17 YC Branch over fifty years

1 Abram and Little British Journal of Sociology, December 1965
2 Preston North Annual Report, 1972
3 Survey of Yorkshire YCs. Bodleian Library
4 Pembroke *Advance*, August 1948 (1.9)
5 South Kensington Annual Report, 1948
6 Wickfield *Advance*, January 1949 (1.11)
7 North Somerset *Advance*, September/October 1949: 2.3
8 Pudsey *Advance*, January 1947 (1.2)
9 Normanton by-election, April/June 1947 1.3
10 Barnard Castle *Advance*, April/June 1947 (1.3)
11 Hammersmith by-election recollection of John Hay and Beryl Goldsmith *Advance* 1949 2.1
12 East Surrey *Advance*, January 1950 (2.6) & July/August 1947 (2.70)
13 Dorking *Advance*, July/August 1950 2.7
14 *Right*, No.4, 1950, No.2
15 *Right*, 1951, No.5 & No.6
16 Annual Report, 1951/1952
17 High Wycombe *Advance*, December 1952
18 Mark Bennett and A P Grey. 'How People Vote' p.19
19 Dr Butler, 'Election 1959' 121, 177
20 David Butler, Swansea, General Election 1964, 268
21 David Butler, Leeds, General Election 1964, p.285
22 David Butler, Brighton, 1966, 226
23 Hornsey Annual Report 1970
24 Crosby YC News, 1981
25 Election report of Birmingham Agent
26 Preston South Report, 1968
27 Exeter Management minutes, 16 June 1969
28 Hornsey Annual Report 1971
29 Exeter YC minutes, 18 May 1988. Exeter YC Annual Report, 1992
30 Consett *Advance*, April/June 1947 (1.3)
31 Bristol *Advance*, September/October 1949 2.3

32 Leeds *Searchlight*, 1961
33 Southampton Test Annual Report, 1977
34 South Kensington YCs Annual Report, 1948
35 City of London Mansion House. *Advance*, March 1948 (1.7)
36 *Advance*, January/February 1950 (2.6)
37 Dewsbury, *Advance*, August 1948 1.9
38 Chippenham YCs *Advance*, March/April 1949 1.12
39 East Surrey *Daily Herald*, 7 February 1950
40 Skegness *Advance*, Spring 1953
41 Lincoln *Advance*, Spring 1953
42 Attitude Survey, South Kensington, July 1956
43 Twickenham YC GLYC News sheet, 1968
44 Winchester YCs *Hampshire Chronicle*, 1 October 1976
45 Devizes *Young Tory*, December 1948/January 1949
46 Working Programme, October/December 1992, August/November 1979
47 Southampton Test, January 1961
48 South Kensington Programmes
49 Surrey minutes, 23 August 1966
50 Conversation with Andrew Bowden
51 *Macclesfield Advertiser*, 8 January 1981
52 Letter from Agent to Macclesfield YCs
53 *Challenge*, 13 July 1946
54 Swansea *Advance*, August 1948 1.9
55 Northwich *Advance*, March 1948 1.7
56 Coventry, 2.7 June & July 1950
57 *Right* December 1951 5.5
58 Trowbridge Annual Report, 1953/195
59 Conservative Central Office. Bodleian Library, Oxford
60 Dewsbury Yorkshire Area minutes, 1961
61 Ilford Leader, July 1961
62 Highgate, minutes, 1961
63 GLYC minutes, 29 June 1966
64 'Exit Alan Haselhurst'. *Impact*, Spring\Summer
65 Ella YCs Branch Programme Charlesworth. British Library
66 Chalkwell *Tomorrow*, Summer 1984
67 Luton *Advance*, March/April 1949 112

68 'Nationalisation of Water'. *Ealing Chronicle*, October 1949
69 Northern Area *Advance*, August/September 1952 3.2
70 Shrewsbury YC *Advance*, June 1952
71 'Pancake Race'. *Southern Evening Echo*, 26 February 1963
72 East Hants Speaking Competition *Hampshire Chronicle*, 8 October 1976
73 Chislehurst *Advance*, March/April 1949 (1.12)
74 Romford GLYC Newsheet, 1968
75 Gosforth *Impact*, Summer 1967
76 Dewsbury *New Advance*, February 1966
77 File at Bodleian Library, and Labour party report, 1968
78 Macleod Report
79 NAC, 25 June 1949
80 Whitehaven *Advance*, June/July 1949 (2.1)
81 Twickenham *Advance*, Spring 1953
82 Home Counties North Annual Report, 1956/1957
83 Barkstone Ash Annual minutes, 3 February 1964 and 6 April 1964
84 Torbay Annual Report, 1964/1965
85 Yeovil *Advance*, November 1948 1.10
86 Minehead *Advance*, September/October 1930 2.9
87 Northwood *Advance*, September 1947 1.4
88 Plaistow *Advance*, November 1948 1.10, January 1949 1.11
89 City Forum. Ealing YCs were more cautious they applied for a Food licence, 23 February 1949, which was refused as it was felt it was not necessary.
90 South Kensington minutes, 31 March 1948
91 YC Kensington ball, 1959
92 Preston North Annual Report, Preston & *Impact*, Summer 1967
93 *New Enterprise*, 1965
94 NAC minutes, 7 December 1968
95 Nuneaton, *Advance*, November/December 1949 (2.4)
96 Rushcliffe *Advance*, January 1951 (2.10)
97 Sale *Advance*, June & July 1951

98 Cardiff *Advance*, March/April 1949
   (1.12)
99 Abergaveny *Advance*, 1.12
100 Devizes, October/November 1949
   *Young Tory* magazine
101 *Impact*, Winter 1966
102 Hornsey minutes, 1951
103 Otley Leeds *Searchlight* 1952
104 Adel. 'Pot-holing', Searchlight August
   1947
105 Solihull *Impact*, Winter 1967/1968
106 *Hampshire Chronicle*, 12 July 1969

107 Birmingham Car Rally. *Right*,
   December 1953
108 South Kensington Car Rally, 26
   September 1959
109 Chelsea Young Liberal Programme,
   September to November 1968
110 South Kensington Programmes, 1968
111 Labour party NEC minutes, 23
   February 1955
112 Young Socialist records. Surrey Record
   Office

## Chapter 18 Women in Young Conservatives

1 Recorder, 30 August 1947
2 *The Times*, 21 April 1973
3 Frances Vale. Conference report 1947
4 Survey of Yorkshire YCs. Bodleian
   Library
5 *Hansard*, 28/29 March 1944
6 'Equal pay for women'. *Challenge*, 5
   July 1947
7 *The Times*, 14 & 22 May 1955
8 *Right*, May 1949
9 *City Press*, 25 April 1947
10 *Right*, March 1954
11 City Press, 25 April 1947
12 *Independent*, 8 February 1993
13 *Advance*, January & February 1948
14 Diana Coles, 26 August 1994, *Guardian*
15 Abram and Little *British Journal of
   Sociology*, December 1975

16 The Times, 18 September 1964
17 Newspaper article that cannot be
   identified
18 *New Advance*, September 1963
19 *New Advance*, June 1965
20 Liberal News, February 1966
21 Miss YC mark sheet. Bodleian Library
22 Minutes of Warminister YCs, 16
   February 1967
23 Advertisement for GLYC Ball
   *Tomorrow*, Last Miss YC April 1972,
   Abolition March 1973
24 Zig Layton Henry 'Young
   Conservatives'. *New Society*, 28
   October 1971
25 *Ealing Chronicle*, October 1961
26 Conference report, October 1969,
   pp.112–118

## Chapter 19 From Empire to Maastricht

1 Robert Rhodes James. *Anthony Eden*,
   p.321
2 Imperial Policy, Conservative Central
   Office, June 1949
3 *Kensington News*, 28 November 1947
4 Party Conference Report, 8 October
   1948 pp.68, 69
5 Party Conference Report, October
   1949, 54 & 55
6 'Empire Day'. *Advance*, May 1952.
   *Ealing Chronicle*, June 1961
7 YC Conference reports, 1961

8 Anthony Nutting 'Europe will not
   wait' pp.105, 106
9 *Ealing Chronicle*, May 1961
10 Verbatim speech, Duncan Sandys
11 Peter Walker 'Staying power' p.53
12 Clacton YC area Conference, 1967
13 Conversation with Eric Chalker, 1993
14 Party Conference Report 1969. pp.88,
   89
15 Conversation with David Atkinson,
   1993
16 Andrew Bowden conversation, 1993
17 *Tomorrow*, September 1972

18 *Herald Express*, 16 July 1971
19 Hornsey Annual Report, 1971
20 *The Times*, 1 January 1973
21 *Bournemouth Evening Echo*, 3 February 1973
22 Edward Heath, 1973 YC conference speech
23 *Dorking Advertiser*, 2 & 7 May 1975
24 *Hastings Observer*, 12 April 1975
25 'Harold Macmillan'. *Bournemouth Evening Echo*, 10 and 12 February 1979

26 Edward Heath, 1984 YC conference speech
27 Margaret Thatcher Group for Europe, 15 December 1981
28 1984 Conference, SE Conference Report
29 YC 1987 Conference Reports
30 *Sunday Times*, 4 November 1990 and The Times, 19 November 1990
31 Personal attendance

## Chapter 20  Unemployment

1 Figures supply by Ministry of Labour to Clement Attlee. Bodleian Library, Oxford
2 Industrial Charter CCO, May 1947
3 Conversation with Anthony Nutting 1993 and John Hay speech City Press, 9 January 1948
4 Party Conference reports, 8 October 1948
5 Debate was reported in *Daily Telegraph*, 27 August 1947. *City Press*, 29 August 1947. *Recorder*, 30 August 1947
6 Lord Woolton. Autobiography p.426
7 Spalding Young Conservative magazine, November 1954
8 Wickham YC Magazine *Young Tory*, May 1958
9 Conference Report, 1967 p.76
10 YC conference report, 17 February 1963
11 Party Conference Report, 1958 motion calling for vigorous measures to eliminate pockets of unemployment carried. Whereas in 1972 a critical motion complaining of a lack of a regional policy for dealing with unemployment defeated.
12 YC conference report 1964

13 YC reply to NAC, 4 December 1971. Bodleian Library
14 *Tomorrow*, September 1972
15 *Tomorrow*, December 1971
16 Conversation with Angela Hills, 1993
17 YC Conference Reports, 1972
18 YC Conference Reports, 1981
19 *Challenge*, 21 April 1945
20 *Hansard*, 28 July 1972
21 YC Conference Reports, 1982
22 Conversation with Demitri Argyropulo
23 Guardian, 14 February 1977
24 NUGP, 9 November 1977. YC picket Labour Party Conference. Personal attendance. Socialists picket YC Conference
25 *Hampshire Chronicle*, 30 January 1981
26 *Hampshire Chronicle*, 29 January 1982
27 Robert Hughes speech, 3 April 1977
28 Party Conference Report, 1981 and*Reformer*, Winter 1984
29 Party Conference Report, 1985
30 Policy report 'Reconstruction of Britain'. British Library
31 Internal Report of Conservative Party
32 Conversation with Andrew Tinney and Adrian McLellan, 1993

## Chapter 21  Race

1 *Ealing Chronicle*, April 1948
2 *Birmingham Post*, 23 May 1955
3 Party Conference Report, 1958 149 to 151

4 Kensington Post, 27 July 1961
5 *Bournemouth Evening Echo*, 10 February 1969
6 SE Area magazine, 1979, No.42

7 *West Indian World*, 15 November 1981
8 *Amnesty Times*, 11 April 1974
9 YC Conference Report, 1977
10 *Yorkshire Post*, 15 February 1982
11 Bournemouth Evening Echo, 3 February 1973

12 Executive Council minutes, 19 January 1978
13 Key statement 'Race without Discrimination' by Chris Gent
14 Tony Hall. *Tomorrow*, 1983 Party Conference edition
15 NAC, 8 December 1990

## Chapter 22  Crime

1 *The Times*, 12 July 1948
2 Peter Laurie. 'Teenage Revolution', p.127
3 *The Times*, 15 September 1911
4 *Herald*, 13 September 1911
5 Whitelaw speech. *The Times*, 11 October 1979. *Hampshire Chronicle*, 29 January 1982, crime rose by 14% in 1981
6 *Ealing Chronicle*, November 1949
7 Conference Report, 1961, p.67
8 Policy Report. 'Law Liberty and Licence'. Bodleian Library and conversation with Andrew Tinney
9 Policy Report 'Law Liberty and Licence'
10 YC Conference Report, 1963
11 NAC, 24 September 1966. NAC, 14 December 1969
12 *The Times*, 15 December 1969

13 *Ealing Chronicle*, November 1969
14 Party Conference Report, 1969, p.74
15 Party Conference Report, 1970, p.71
16 Conference Report, 1972, p.22
17 Party Conference Report, 1993
18 *Tomorrow*, May 1970
19 YC Conference Report, 1973
20 *West Lancashire Visitor*, 12 February 1974
21 *Yorkshire Post*, 9 February 1976
22 *Yorkshire Post*, 13 February 1978
23 *Bournemouth Evening Echo*, 11 February 1985
24 Conversation with Andrew Tinney
25 YC Conference Report, 1967
26 Conference Report, 1967. p.105
27 Drugs survey. NW Area minutes, July 1969
28 YC 1984 Conference Report
29 NAC minutes, 26 May 1974

## Chapter 23  Environment

1 Party Conference Report 1971, p.111
2 *Tomorrow*. Cure, February 1972
3 *Ealing Chronicle*, December 1971
4 Rodney Gent, *Tomorrow*, February 1972
5 Frome, *Tomorrow*, November 1972

6 Mitcham, *Tomorrow*, September 1972
7 Lincoln, *Tomorrow*, September 1972
8 Barry *Tomorrow*, April 1972
9 *Hornsey Journal*, 20 November 1970

## Chapter 24  Northern Ireland

1 Ulster *Advance*, January/February 1950
2 Party Conference Report, 1948
3 Report. Hugh Holland Eric Chalker, 1969
4 Party Conference Report, 1969 44/45
5 Report of David Atkinson, Gerry Wade and Lynda Chalker, 1970

6 *The Times*, 6 & 7 July 1970
7 YC Conference Reports, 1972
8 Conference, 1976. *Yorkshire Post*, 9 February 1976
9 YC Conference Report, 1987
10 *Daily Telegraph*, 13 February 1995

## Chapter 25 Foreign Policy

1 *Hammersmith Digest*, July 1964
2 *Hammersmith Digest*, October 1964
3 *Ealing Chronicle*, February 1971
4 NAC, 7 September 1985
5 NAC, 20 September 1986
6 YC Conference debate, 1967
7 Ealing Chronicle, March 1970
8 Party Conference, 1973 p.83
9 Conversation with Tony Kerpel

10 See articles in support of Vietnam.
  Petts Wood Daylight 1967 and Ealing
  Chronicle May 1968
11 Party Conference, 1975, 91–95
12 YS pamphlet Common market no
  Socialist United states of Europe Yes
13 NAC, 7 September 1985
14 Conversation with Roger Boaden,
  1993 and see Times, 25 November 1969

## Chapter 26 Rallies

1 *Advance* and letter from John Hay.
  Recollection of Andrew Bowden
2 NAC minutes, 7 January 1967
3 *Sunday Telegraph*, 11 December 1966

4 *Focus*, February 1967
5 Rally file at Bodleian Library, Oxford
6 Times, 6 June 1983

## Chapter 27 Holiday Weeks

The reports of the Filey Holiday
Weeks of 1949 and 1950 have been
both based on the reports in *Advance*
and *Yorkshire Post* and used by courtesy
of *Yorkshire Post*. The 1951 Rally by
the report in *Advance*: 1952 rally by

both the reports in *Advance* and in
*Birmingham Post*; 1953 Holiday Week
exclusively by the report in *Western
Mail*. The 1958 Conference written by
Peter Walker is with the Papers of
Lord Avon at Birmingham University.

## Chapter 28 Conferences from 1961

The recording of the YC Conferences
since 1967 have been greatly assisted by
the full reports in the local paper. In
Yorkshire by courtesy of the *Yorkshire
Post*, in Southport by *Southport Visitor*.
In Eastbourne by *Eastbourne Herald and
Gazette* and in Bournemouth by
*Bournemouth Evening Echo*
1 NAC, 3 March 1990. Daily Telegraph,
  13 February 1995

2 Richard Kelly. Conservative Party
  Conferences Manchester University
  Press
3 My attendance at 1993 Conference
4 Conversation with Roger Pratt, 1993
5 Crossbow, April 1965
6 *Tomorrow*, May 1970
7 Conversation with Eric Pickles, 1993

## Chapter 29 Impact of YCs

1 Lord Woolton. Autobiography
2 Party Conferences. Speech 1946
3 Party Conference, Report 1946
4 Letter from John Hay, 1993
5 Conference Report, 1947 p.43

6 Conference Report, 1948 p.141
7 Conference Report, 1948 p.113
8 *Evening Standard*, 7 October 1948
9 *Advance*, November 1949
10 Conversation with Frances Vale, 1993

11 Conference Report, 1961 46
12 Conference Report, 1963 57
13 NAC, 4 January 1958
14 Conference Report 1966, pp.116, 117
15 'Set Party Free' ch.8
16 NAC, 9 December 1989
17 Conference 1967. *Express* Photographs, 19 October of YC dress in Union Jack
18 *Ealing Chronicle*, October 1970

19 *Daily Express*, 11 October 1971. Photographs of YCs on Front page
20 Party Conference 1971 p.8
21 Party Conference report 1971, pp.111–112
22 *Daily Mirror*, 13 October 1972
23 *Daily Mirror*, 12 October 1972
24 Conference Report, 1976, 69
25 *Guardian*, 13 October 1979

## Chapter 30 *Towards Fifty Years without Glory*

1 NAC, 14 September 1991
2 YC statistics, Bodleian Library
3 *Campaigner*, Spring 1992
4 Speech of Paula Hanford, Labour Party Conference, 1988
5 Labour Party Conference Debate, 1987
6 Labour Party Annual Report, 1988
7 Labour Party Annual Report, 1988
8 *Daily Telegraph*, 10 February 1992
9 *Campaigning*, Autumn 1992
10 Personal attendance at Conference
11 Conversation with Andrew Rosindell, 1993
12 Attendance at Conference
13 Paul Whitely, Patrick Seyd and Jeremy Richardson, 'True Blues'

14 Labour Party Report, 1993
15 Letter from Labour party, 8 March 1993
16 Resolutions of Young Socialists at their Conference. British Library
17 Conversation with Tom Watson, 1995
18 National League minues, 24 October 1981. London School of Economics
19 *North Wales Weekly News*, 7 April 1988
20 Liberal Youth Officer, letter, 31 July 1995
21 Z. Layton Henry, *Journal of Contemporary History*, July 1976, Mike Waite thesis and letter from Ian Fraser 1983
22 Conversation with Paul Clarke, 1995

# Index

## YC BRANCHES

## YOUNG SOCIALIST BRANCHES

## YOUNG LIBERAL BRANCHES